Practical SharePoint 2013 Governance

Steve Goodyear

Apress®

Practical SharePoint 2013 Governance

ISBN 978-1-4302-4887-3

ISBN 978-1-4302-4888-0 (eBook)

President and Publisher: Paul Manning
Lead Editor: Jon Hassell
Developmental Editor: Douglas Pundick
Technical Reviewer: Zach Millis
Editorial Board: Steve Anglin, Mark Beckner, Ewan Buckingham, Gary Cornell, Morgan Ertel, Jonathan Gennick, Jonathan Hassell, Robert Hutchinson, Michelle Lowman, James Markham, Matthew Moodie, Jeff Olson, Jeffrey Pepper, Douglas Pundick, Ben Renow-Clarke, Dominic Shakeshaft, Gwenan Spearing, Matt Wade, Tom Welsh
Coordinating Editors: Brigid Duffy, Anamika Panchoo
Copy Editor: Linda Seifert
Compositor: SPi Global
Indexer: SPi Global
Cover Designer: Anna Ishchenko

Distributed to the book trade worldwide by Springer Science+Business Media, LLC., 233 Spring Street, 6th Floor, New York, NY 10013. Phone 1-800-SPRINGER, fax (201) 348-4505, e-mail orders-ny@springer-sbm.com, or visit www.springeronline.com.

For information on translations, please e-mail rights@apress.com, or visit www.apress.com.

Apress and friends of ED books may be purchased in bulk for academic, corporate, or promotional use. eBook versions and licenses are also available for most titles. For more information, reference our Special Bulk Sales–eBook Licensing web page at http://www.apress.com/bulk-sales.

Any source code or other supplementary materials referenced by the author in this text is available to readers at www.apress.com. For detailed information about how to locate your book's source code, go to http://www.apress.com/source-code.

To my fellow SharePoint freedom fighters, fighting a thousand battles with very little back up and not enough support. I have some of the ammo you need right here, my friends.

Contents at a Glance

Contents

About the Author

Steve Goodyear works as an independent consultant based in Vancouver, Canada, where he engages as an enterprise consultant, solution architect, and strategy advisor for large enterprise and government clients.

Recently, Steve worked for Microsoft as an Enterprise Consultant in Microsoft Consulting Services where he engaged as a SharePoint specialist with Microsoft's largest enterprise and government customers around North America to design technology solutions to solve their most challenging business problems. Before joining Microsoft, Steve also worked for Electronic Arts as a Software Engineer and Technical Lead, where he was also responsible for a global multi-farm SharePoint environment.

Steve is a Microsoft Certified Trainer and he holds several Microsoft Certified Professional (MCP) certifications, including: MCITP: SharePoint Administration, MCITP: SQL Server Administration and SQL Server Development, MCPD: ASP.NET Development, MCTS: MOSS and WSS Configuration and Development, and MCTS: TFS Configuration and Development.

You can connect with and follow more of Steve's SharePoint discussions by sending him a tweet on Twitter @SteveGoodyear or reading his occasional blog posts at http://stevegoodyear.wordpress.com.

Microsoft
CERTIFIED
Trainer

Microsoft
CERTIFIED
Professional Developer

Microsoft
CERTIFIED
IT Professional

About the Technical Reviewer

Zach Millis works as a Senior Consultant for imason inc, where he specializes in SharePoint infrastructure and long-term sustainability for imason solutions. His experience includes working for some of Canada's top SharePoint services firms and advising some of Canada's largest corporations on their SharePoint operations. Zach's latest infrastructure projects have included his consulting on SharePoint 2013 implementations on-premises and in the cloud, Office 365 deployments, and exploring Windows Azure Infrastructure as a Service platform for SharePoint 2013 websites.

Originally from Madison, Wisconsin, Zach's infrastructure skills have taken him across the United States, New Zealand, and Canada, to his new home of Toronto, Ontario. Zach holds several Microsoft Certified Professional (MCP) certifications, including: Microsoft Certified Systems Administrator; SharePoint 2010 Administrator; Enterprise Desktop Administrator on Windows 7; Enterprise Desktop Support Technician on Windows Vista and Windows 7; SharePoint 2007 and 2010 Configuration; and Windows 7 Configuration.

You can connect with Zach on LinkedIn at www.linkedin.com/in/zacharymillis, and read his blog posts on www.imason.com.

Acknowledgments

Many thanks to all my family and friends who offered their constant encouragement and ongoing support from when I first conceived of this book and throughout the writing process, and who were patient with me at times when I seemingly disappeared and let myself grow consumed with writing this book.

Thanks as well to everyone who took the time to weigh in and share some of their own perspectives on governance that you will find in the Guest Q&A sections at the end of some chapters: Maxime Bombardier, Chris Izquierdo, Annie Kalfayan, Michal Pisarek, and Stuart Macleod. Thanks for adding your great insights to the book!

A huge thanks and kudos to the dream team I worked with at Apress (in order of appearance): Jon Hassell, Brigid Duffy, Douglas Pundick, Ana Panchoo, Linda Seifert, and everyone behind the scenes who I did not get a chance to meet. Thanks to Kumar Dhaneesh and the rest of the production team at SPi. Thanks also to the technical reviewer, my good friend Zach Millis, for lending his expertise and for giving me a portrait of the reading experience for my readers. Thank you all for helping me make a quality book!

Finally, a special thanks to all my customers and clients, working with each of whom helped me formulate and refine the ideas and practices I share in this book. Without my experiences with each of you, this book would not have been possible.

Introduction

SharePoint governance is one of those topics that frequently comes up. Yet, whenever I have heard it, it was always a little ambiguous about what it actually means or what it should include. Documenting a governance "plan" was a common start, but what happens then? There seemed to be tons of resources available that dedicate their attention to governance plans and how to document one, but I found a gap when I looked beyond this and looked at how to put governance into practice.

When I was new with SharePoint administration, I felt the pain of that gap while I tried to figure out where to go next and how to apply some of these standard governance plans in practice. Later, as I moved into consulting, I felt the gaps again with my clients. Where could I point them so that they would have clear direction on what are the actions they need to take to put their governance into practice?

This book grew out of those gaps. It is a collection of my own personal practices, practices I picked up from colleagues and clients, and general practices I have collected over the years. It is a collection of e-mails I sent to advise clients, notes I have captured to record what worked, and lessons learned from where I have faced challenges. I wanted to gather it all in this book to try to fill in some of the gaps and share it all with you. My goal is to give you that missing link for some of those things you need to do and to point you in the right direction for how to get started putting them in practice.

You will notice that throughout this book, I leave the level of documentation you need and the formality of your governance process all as a decision for you. After you choose which strategies in this book fit your needs, I will focus on giving you the tools you need to turn those strategies into actions. I took this practical approach to governance because I believe this addresses the most critical aspect of governance: the things you do that have an impact. Documentation absolutely is important, and I encourage you to generate documentation, but this is not a book on or about documentation. Instead, this book focuses on those practical *actions* that you can take right away to make a positive difference in your SharePoint deployment.

I take an agile approach to governance, because I like the idea of making subtle changes frequently and applying practical governance ideas as I go, rather than over-invest in a lot of upfront planning that delays realizing any of the potential governance value. You might have a lot of planning and negotiating for certain policies, but you also have opportunities to make subtle tweaks as you go to unlock some of that immediate value.

Governance can be a huge topic and it can be a little mystifying. As we work through this book together, I will attempt to demystify it for you. In the process, I focus on some core governance areas where I walk you through how to take governance theories and transform them into actions. I am excited to have this chance to share my governance experiences with you. Let's get started!

PART I

Orientating SharePoint Governance

Governance seems to mean different things to different people. For some people, governance involves building out a governance plan, establishing a governance committee, and scheduling recurring governance meetings. For others, it can mean the manner in which one rules a nation. The Oxford English Dictionary defines governances as "the action or manner of governing," or for our purposes, the actions you take in order to govern. In this book, I am going to focus exclusively on the actions you can take to govern your SharePoint environment, and through the discussions and examples we will concentrate on those practical actions that I have found to work well for managing a SharePoint environment.

The chapter in this part focuses on defining governance in the context of the practical actions you can take to govern your SharePoint environment. It will frame the rest of the book and provide an overview of the governance strategies coming in later chapters. Throughout this book, I am going to focus entirely on these actions, these things that you can do and put into practice to help you have a positive impact with governing your SharePoint service. You are welcome to create extensive documentation based on these actions and the examples I provide if you wish, but I will leave this up to your own discretion based on your organization's practice and your own comfort-level.

■ ■ ■

CHAPTER 1

Understanding SharePoint Governance

All glory comes from daring to begin.

—Alexander Graham Bell

In this opening chapter, I introduce the book and define the term *governance*, as used in this book. Throughout this chapter, I will emphasize attitudes and practices as part of a governance process that goes beyond simply filling out a document template. As we progress through this chapter and the rest of the book, I highlight places where I have seen companies benefit from certain processes, and where they have faced challenges. From there, I provide a roadmap of the book by introducing each of the parts and chapters that follow.

This overview introductory chapter frames the book for you and helps set your expectations on how this book unfolds. It also provides you with highlights to help you decide which chapters you might want to jump to right away, if you have a particular problem that you currently face and need to solve.

After reading this chapter, you will know how to:

- Explain why governance goes beyond documentation
- Describe how governance consists of actions, behaviors, and commitments
- Identify who this book is for and how it is organized
- Define governance and decide how much is enough
- Decide where you should start with your governance process
- List new governance-related features in SharePoint 2013

Reclaiming Governance

Governance feels like one of those words that people overuse to the point where it no longer means anything meaningful. It is something marketing departments got a hold of without knowing much about SharePoint, and they put the term to work to support sales of services. Governance became a popular topic at conferences, in blogs, and with customers in general. It became so popular that calling anything "governance" seems to make it easier to sell services, positioning the concept as almost a catchall phrase on which to blame problems or challenges. This diluting of the term governance created the idea that somehow with some governance planning services all of one's problems would simply disappear.

In this book, we are going to reclaim the term: I look at what governance means and what value it brings, what is involved to adopt and embrace governance, and I identify some key areas to govern. Our focus together will be exploring the idea of governance, in all its glory, from the practical to the mythical. I explore what it means when you need to solve a governance problem.

This book explores governance from an action-focus perspective, meaning I share tools and ideas of things you can start doing to make a difference in your SharePoint operations. One outcome you will notice from this book's action-focus is a lack of attention given to governance documents, and this is by design: I want to share actual practices I employ on the frontlines when I am out in the field. As a result, I left out content geared toward a more documentation or theoretical focus, because other books are available that cover those topics well. This book is all about practical things you can put in practice.

Let's expand SharePoint governance from a simple exercise that delivers a document, a cookie cutter "Governance Plan" that sits on a shelf and falls short of all the magic it once promised. Instead, I look at the behaviors you need to adopt, the decision processes, and the people you need involved. Yes, part of governance is documenting, and I look at a wealth of information in this book that you can use to support your documentation initiatives. Yet the majority of governance addresses actual practices used day-to-day on the ground, and this is the primary focus of our exploration into SharePoint governance. Whether you incorporate these practices into your documentation is an option I will leave entirely up to you.

TechNet includes some excellent articles and guides on producing governance related documents and other governance materials, all of which are fantastic resources and do not need to be repeated here. At places in this book, I will refer to this material or other sources of additional online resources, but my primary focus is sharing my governance experiences, and not to provide a systematic process for creating governance documentation. These experiences consist of guiding my customers in the field to apply and use these governance concepts, and I am excited to share with you both the good and the bad of what worked and what did not.

▪ **Note**   For additional resources such as links to planning guides, white papers, and webcasts, see the Microsoft TechNet SharePoint Governance Resource Center: `http://technet.microsoft.com/en-us/sharepoint/ff800826`

The scope of this book captures the practicality of governance, and it can complement another book or website that focuses more on theoretical concepts. This is also not a SharePoint technical how-to guide or a product feature manual. For the most part, this book discusses SharePoint features and functionality in terms that are more abstract and mostly just as they relate to governing a SharePoint service in operations to provide value to the business.

▪ **Note**   For examples linking governance to specific SharePoint features, see the following Microsoft TechNet Site and Solution Governance article: `http://technet.microsoft.com/en-us/library/ff598584.aspx`

I have had very diverse experiences related to SharePoint governance: first as a developer building applications within and on top of the SharePoint platform, going back to SharePoint 2001; then as an administrator responsible for a global multi-farm deployment; and then as a consultant advising a broad range of customers, from governments to large corporate enterprises. I have worked as an independent, inside an IT organization, and for Microsoft directly engaging and helping our customers realize their potential with SharePoint. I have had internal exposure within Microsoft to the product team that develops SharePoint, and I have been involved with several escalations where customers have needed help getting their environment back under control. I have also collaborated with a variety of consulting service delivery firms to assist delivering SharePoint solutions to customers. All these valuable perspectives have given me firsthand experiences solving some interesting governance challenges in different situations, with different priorities, while considering the needs of a variety of different stakeholders.

In the chapters that follow, I share my experience with SharePoint governance: things that have been successful and approaches where I faced challenges, things I have seen customers do well and areas I have seen customers struggle. I have generalized the most common concepts, but one thing I have learned is that no two governance strategies are alike, and this is because no two organizations are alike in their culture and objectives. This for me is why simply downloading a governance template off the Internet or following a systematic process can prove problematic. Most of what makes governance sparkle and shine for me is the process itself; and if the secret is in the process sauce, unfortunately that means to be effective and grasp its value you cannot take shortcuts.

Who This Book Is For

Practical SharePoint 2013 Governance is for SharePoint consultants, administrators, architects, analysts, and anyone else looking for actual hands-on governance guidance. It is an excellent choice for people who like action-focused concepts or who want to go beyond documentation and theory. This book is a fantastic choice for anyone looking for agile ideas to put into practice without necessarily embarking on a lengthy governance exercise upfront.

Ultimately, this book is for anyone who contributes to provide SharePoint to an organization and who is interested in learning how others have found success in their SharePoint operations. Whether you have felt some pain already and need some guidance on correcting the sins of your SharePoint past, are just beginning your SharePoint journey and are looking to be pointed in the right direction, or are somewhere in between, this book is for you.

My hope is that through this introduction I manage to convince you that governance includes opportunities beyond documenting a governance plan, and I hope to motivate you to experiment with some of those opportunities found in the concepts presented throughout this book. Whether you work in the Information Technology department of your organization and want to champion SharePoint governance for your team, or you are a consultant looking for resources to help you better guide your customers, this book has a wealth of valuable information that can set up you and your SharePoint service for success.

I wrote this book in a conversational manner and did my best to design it so the content is quick to read and easy to digest. My goal as I planned and wrote this book was to keep it accessible and direct, so that ideally it comes across as if we are having a conversation together, perhaps over coffee or a "SharePint" on a patio. Throughout the conversation, I will share examples of where I have faced challenges similar to yours and what I did to address them. This book is especially for you if you want a governance conversation where you can pick my brain for action-focused ideas.

■ **Note**   To continue this conversation together, I would love to get your feedback on this book and your experience reading it or trying out the ideas I share. You can find me on Twitter @SteveGoodyear or through my SharePoint blog: http://stevegoodyear.wordpress.com

---

How This Book Is Organized

Part I of this book consists of the chapter you are now reading. It focuses on defining SharePoint governance in the manner that I will use the term throughout the rest of the book. Primarily, governance sets expectations for how a service runs, what the service provides, and how the service may expand. Using governance to define the service in this way clarifies who is responsible for what, what people and system resources are required, and what features and functionality the SharePoint service offers.

Part II focuses on the service description, and it includes chapters on defining a service and service tiers, determining features and functionality, establishing roles and responsibilities, shaping readiness and end-user training, and measuring and reporting on service metrics. A SharePoint deployment can typically spark enthusiastic adoption, generating more and more demand from the business, growing the deployment into new functional areas, and gathering new opportunities for increased efficiencies. Your governance solution will substantiate and support your prospective success if you make decisions on where to go after you launch and how to respond to key scenarios.

Part III of this book focuses on expanding the service, and it includes chapters on creating a roadmap, promoting a feedback process, managing the demand funnel, scaling the farm, and preparing for upgrades. Organizations tend to have the highest satisfaction levels when they customize their SharePoint environments with custom developed functionality and visual interface elements. This satisfaction depends on those customizations enhancing an environment, rather than having them frustrate users by functioning incorrectly or poorly.

Part IV of this book focuses on customizing the service, and it includes chapters on committing sponsorship and ownership of customizations, facilitating user customizations at the site level, designing development standards and testing processes, framing information architecture and user interface design standards, and coordinating code promotion and release processes.

The Rapid Concepts Appendix at the end of the book provides a quick reference synopsis for some of the main concepts that each chapter covers. I follow each chapter's synopsis with an action checklist of decisions to make, practices to adopt, or other actions and next steps to take based on the chapter's topics. My hope is that you find this appendix useful as both a refresher on the concepts and as guidance on what action items to take. I grouped them together in a single appendix at the end of the book to make it easier for you to reference and work through.

I include several areas of governance for you to consider and I include them in this book because they all feel important to me based on my own experience with SharePoint, but they may not all fit your particular situation for whatever reason. For each concept, I have tried to include enough of a description on it and its purpose to equip you with enough background knowledge to make informed decisions on the topic's relevance for you. I organized each chapter to build on or complement concepts in other chapters, yet I contained each chapter independently enough so they do not depend on other chapters, accommodating those readers who want to skip sections that do not apply to their situation or are not yet a priority for them. My goal is to make this book easy and convenient for you to read, either cover-to-cover or to jump around to reference any section you need.

Each chapter has key points at the beginning to frame the focus of the chapter and the main ideas it covers. Some chapters include a "Consultant Comrade" section that discusses some tips specific to consultants and service delivery firms. This is where I share some ideas on SharePoint governance consulting. Chapters also contain an "Inside Story: Notes from the Field" section where I narrate one of my own experiences providing governance consulting for a customer in the field, sharing an example of either a positive or problematic experience that associates with the particular chapter's governance topic and theme.

In some of the chapters, I have invited some of my peers to weigh in on the topic and share their perspectives on a set of general governance questions. In these "Guest Q&A" sections, I selected fellow experts who have diverse experiences to add other voices and share some of their tips. I kept the questions the same for each guest, yet their answers vary quite a bit and this helps to contribute some great ideas for you to think about from different governance perspectives.

What Is Governance?

Before we jump into all these aspects of governance, let's return to the idea itself, and our reclaiming of the term. What is governance? I have already noted how governance is not simply a document you can spend a couple of weeks filling in the blanks, like pressing an easy button on some template you have downloaded and expect to be a magic bullet. In my experience, I have found these types of templates in common use provide a sort of catharsis, a false sense of accomplishment, because they generate a lot of activity but often focus excessively on the task of completing the document itself. They are certainly easier to sell because they fit into a tidy little package, but from the countless customers I have observed, this approach and simplistic view of governance is largely ineffective.

How can we better define governance in the face of it becoming an exploding catchall phrase? For our purposes in this book, governance is a set of actions, behaviors, and commitments that relate to a SharePoint service, and it contributes to a set of established intentional operational processes and procedures, roles and responsibilities, and decision-making protocols.

I used these big abstract categories of actions, behaviors, and commitments to stress that it is something to adopt and do more than just being something to document and file. An action is the first initiative or a response to an opportunity. A behavior is a set of practices that becomes a habit. A commitment is a dedication that evolves into a purpose. Your attitude around these three is a way of thinking that matures into values and eventually becomes second nature. The good habits I illustrate in Figure 1-1 and describe throughout this book can nurture the right environment for success when put into practice with regular action.

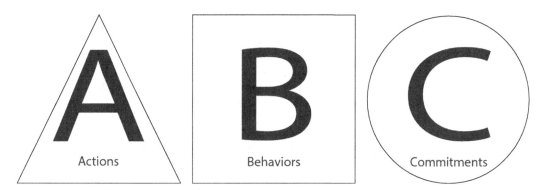

Figure 1-1. *SharePoint 2013 governance building blocks*

"Actions speak louder than words," as the saying goes. In that spirit, actions are the first thing in my governance trinity. I like to think of this as responding to an opportunity that presents itself or taking the initiative to get on top of something that would otherwise begin to unravel or cause you grief down the road. Actions can be things like reaching out to power users and offering guidance to help them maximize their experience using SharePoint while also steering them toward the optimum usage for SharePoint. Actions sometimes are the hardest part, because they often involve the first step toward something, and those first steps can feel like the most work if they are the ones without momentum.

Behaviors consist of actions, but I broke it out so we can think of them more as those routine actions already in practice. Where an action might involve investigating something out of the ordinary, like in conducting a root-cause analysis, behaviors incorporate the more common activities with a regular schedule. These can be things such as your operational procedures, like patching maintenance windows or your site creation process. They can be the way you treat SharePoint, like if you have resources dedicated to managing the SharePoint service or if your responsibilities primarily lie elsewhere but you also need to keep SharePoint available on a best-effort basis.

Commitments encompass your attitude and dedication toward your SharePoint service. Is your SharePoint service a high priority that you are committed to or a low priority that you will get to when you have time? Depending on your circumstances, individual situation, and goals of your organization, either may be valid. Commitments relate to your discipline in taking action and maintaining your behaviors. You also make commitments to your customers: your commitment to offer a service at a certain service level that they can depend on.

You should notice that I have not tied governance concepts in this book to any specific framework or process. My goal is to lay out these concepts based in a generic enough way so you can adopt them as-is, or adapt them to fit with whatever framework you use. My focus is specific to SharePoint with considerations to govern your SharePoint environment by sharing my experience managing SharePoint and consulting with a variety of customers in the field.

How Much Governance Is Enough?

Effectiveness in SharePoint governance increases the further you go in the process. By this I mean it is an additive process, where I find the more my clients put the concepts from this book in practice, the greater the effectiveness they find with their governance outcomes. That does not mean you have to accept everything in this or any other governance book with vigilance, because every governance need is unique. So, take what fits your situation or what you feel your organization would be open to adopting. A greater adoption of concepts and techniques with a greater commitment all leads to greater success in your SharePoint deployment, but the reality is that this ideal comes at a cost, a trade-off constrained by the time and budget required to put these ideas into practice.

There could be other reasons holding you and your organization back from fully embracing the ideas in this book. One big reason you cannot implement many of the ideas we discuss here is that your organization's culture and maturity level is not at a mature enough point. Constraints like this are common ones I have repeatedly experienced firsthand working within an organization and as a consultant working with clients. Another challenge is that you might simply lack the authority to implement many of the processes. I have been there too, and throughout this book, I will share some techniques for building support and buy-in to introduce and evolve these ideas in challenging situations where I could not simply mandate them.

A key message I want you to take away is that each of the governance concepts that follow can have an impact. Although implementing more of them certainly has a greater effect, I also have the mantra that every little bit helps. Look for those low-hanging fruit types of opportunities that you can adopt first; look for those areas you can take an initiative and make a start. This can make that first step easier and can help you build momentum as you get started. There is often no quick fix, and it would be difficult and overwhelming to attempt to adopt everything at once. Nevertheless, I still encourage you to make a start that will slowly cumulate into something significant and rewarding, creating a snowball effect to build your governance momentum.

I like to think less about the scope of governance and more about governance being along a continuum. I typically do not look at a customer's SharePoint situation and package up all the governance pieces they need. For me I usually want to decide what we need to address first, and build momentum from there. Even if we do want to go after everything, there still has to be an order. Something has to come first, and I usually start with the most pressing or what will produce the biggest bang and quickest impact. So rather than thinking about how much governance you need, think about where you want to start.

Where Should You Start?

The best place to start is often to define what your SharePoint service entails. In that description, you are also defining what it does not do. This description gives the service focus, explicitly making it intentional, rather than reactionary. A description like this sets the key foundation for any other governance initiative to depend on and enhance. This has been a crucial component for me, and the foundation on which I use to build all other governance work and initiatives. For that reason, I have arranged it to be at the start of Part II in this book and the very first thing we tackle as we begin our journey into SharePoint governance.

I am not going to flatter myself into thinking I have captured everything about governance and that this is an exhaustive guide. Indeed, there are many great thinkers on the subject with valuable works published. Let me encourage you to explore some of those ideas and perspectives, many of which I reference throughout this book, and you should use them to take the ideas in this book even further than I imagined. My ideas and concepts complement the extensive array of governance resources, both SharePoint related or otherwise. This book just focuses on what I have seen work well specifically for SharePoint governance with my customers, providing some hands-on practical observations for you to consider and try out.

You will notice that throughout this book I keep referring to your SharePoint deployment as the SharePoint service you offer. This is meaningful to me because it creates the right mindset that we deploy SharePoint to fulfill some need, to provide some service to those who use it. If you term your SharePoint deployment in this way, you will find that it also focuses attention toward articulating the value this service provides. Your interest to articulate value may have even motivated you to reach for a book on SharePoint governance in the first place, and you will find several tips throughout this book on how to elaborate on the value SharePoint provides.

Pace yourself: governance can mean a lot of changing actions, behaviors, and commitments. Organizations tend to be slow to adopt changes of this nature because they can affect the core culture of an organization. People can still resist change for a number of other reasons, no matter how possible the changes may seem or how much the changes may benefit people over the long-term. Some people may grow frustrated when they go from being comfortable doing something to feeling unfamiliar with a new process, and as a result, they may appear to resist the changes. On top of that, people only have so much capacity and tolerance for change, so it would be unrealistic to expect your team to rush through this book and transform into a festival of governance as quickly as a travelling carnival sets up tents and concessions when they come to town.

The good news is that people absolutely do embrace change and they can be quite enthusiastic about it. Some examples confirming this are the widespread number of touch screen devices and the ubiquitous nature of social media embedded in people's lives – both of which were largely uncommon for the masses even just a decade or so ago. Change can be good, and some of the changes you may require for the governance ideas and concepts in this book can be for the better as well. Stay open to the possibilities and know that if you position it from the perspective of how your users will benefit, they will be less likely to resist the change you want to introduce. Everyone typically likes things that benefit him or her. The tools in this book will help you navigate this change, whether users resist or embrace it.

■ **Note**   See Chapter 7 for more tips on how to plan for change.

Organizations tend to adopt governance into their culture the most when there is executive buy-in and support. These companies establish strong, long-term sponsorship at the top, setting the stage that governance is important and a priority for the organization. In fact, companies can often correlate the degree of commitment and involvement from an executive sponsor with the degree of commitment and acceptance from the rest of the organization. An organization will find this is the best-case scenario, and one that gives SharePoint governance some weight.

As I mentioned earlier, sometimes governance is just not in an organization's culture, and by extension, executive sponsorship for governance might not be either. The tools in this book can still help, even in these cases. Actually, I have found this scenario is surprisingly common in SharePoint projects where I have tried to introduce SharePoint governance. Let me assure you that if your situation falls into this category, you can still make improvements. I expect many readers to share facing this struggle, as I frequently do myself, particularly given the topic and focus of the book. This book provides several ideas and strategies for actions, behaviors, and commitments you can use to get started with governance, no matter how formal or informal of a solution you require or are capable of adopting for your SharePoint governance.

Personally, I like to think of governance as a level or a sign of maturity. This metaphor resonates because maturity signals growth and a process of evolving over time. It signals experience and wisdom; it signals the passage of time. Maturity does not just happen, it is not something that is just decided, and it does not come from documentation, a couple of meetings, or a workshop. No, maturity is a process, a continuum that is the culmination of life lessons, evolving and learning from the past, and expanding with additional perspectives and new views of the world. It is ever evolving, maturing as the feedback loop cycles and our capabilities grow stronger.

Governance is like that: it grows and evolves over time. Each step sets you up to build on and enhance the service down the road. Your only challenge is to find those first few steps and implement them in some way. In the chapters to come, I share many ideas for you to consider and think about how you can use them to get started with your own SharePoint governance. However, if you still cannot decide, often the best place to start is at the beginning: start with defining your SharePoint service.

Governance and SharePoint 2013

SharePoint 2013 adds exciting new capabilities and it enhances some existing features that aid in achieving different governance objectives, making this a very exciting release for governance needs. I would pick eDiscovery as one new capability in SharePoint 2013 that provides rich governance features, because it provides the infrastructure for managing and governing content from individual items to entire site collections. SharePoint 2013 eDiscovery adds sophistication from a records management and information management perspective, and these enhanced capabilities add maturity to SharePoint itself as an enterprise content management system.

■ **Note**   See Chapters 3 and 15 where I discuss eDiscovery in more detail.

Using eDiscovery in SharePoint 2013, we can govern content retention and other types of policies, globally and across farms. We can also govern legal and regulatory requirements, as well as track and report on our compliance. Site owners or policies can set sites to a closed state instead of simply deleting them, enabling governance strategies to address retiring and archiving content in a gradual process in between a content state that is moving from online to offline.

Apps for SharePoint and the SharePoint Marketplace enable scenarios such as allowing users to purchase and provision their own functionality without modifying or affecting the underlying farm. An organization can also offer an internal catalog of Apps for SharePoint that users can consume and utilize on their site, enabling a centralized catalog and a single access point to provide custom applications and functionality across the organization. This simplifies the process of deploying and managing custom solutions, both for the IT department providing the solutions and for the end-users adding the solution to their site.

■ **Note**   See Chapter 13 where I discuss Apps for SharePoint in more detail.

SharePoint 2013 enhances the self-service site creation feature so that it can now gather more information about things such as how long the site is active and other useful information about the site. You can also customize this process to add additional logic to help govern and manage sites over time. You can use the feature for either site collections or new webs within a site collection, which is a very useful feature particularly for applying policies for either the site collection or individual webs within the site collection.

Site access requests is another long-standing SharePoint feature that SharePoint 2013 has enhanced. These enhancements to the site request process make permission management and request management more straightforward for ordinary users, and this helps make governing access control more straightforward as a result. For one thing, there is an audit trail of permission request activity, so you can trace who granted what permission and when. Another feature useful for governance is the Request Management page, as shown in Figure 1-2, where outstanding access requests and a history of requests are visible for site administrators from the site administration page, rather than in the inbox of a few individuals. Requests also have a place for comments, so site administrators can ask questions to the requesters to understand why they need the permissions they are requesting. This all works toward helping to reduce the number of unnecessary and excessive permissions granted to users, permissions granted simply because in the past the permissions or requests were not clear enough to be understood by the site administrator.

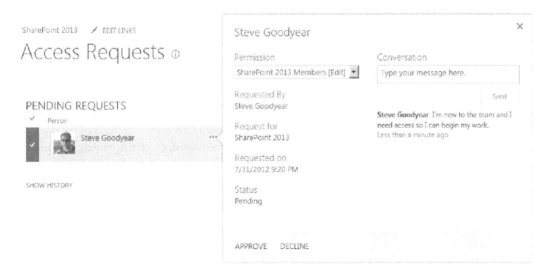

Figure 1-2. *SharePoint 2013 site access request management*

■ **Note**   See Chapter 13 for more details on delegating access controls within a SharePoint site.

Some subtle changes to how you manage branding in SharePoint 2013 can also help to simplify how you govern branding customizations. For one, you can create a branding package by setting up your interface elements, styles, images, and the like, all on a live SharePoint team site and then export them as a branding package. You can then share this branding package with other sites. SharePoint 2013 bases branding on HTML 5 standards, which means your graphic designers will face less of a barrier to entry when it comes to customizing the look and feel of a SharePoint site. More importantly for us considering governance, this also means that you or your site designers can more easily customize user interface elements on sites in a standard and consistent way, and this will help to make maintenance easier to manage.

■ **Note**   See Chapter 15 for more details on how to govern branding.

Continuous crawling in the SharePoint 2013 search engine means the content index continuously stays fresh. Therefore, for those content sources that you enable continuous crawling on, they will no longer require negotiating the freshness of the index with the business users, because it will be fresh in practically real-time. This simplifies scheduling and coordinating the search service. There are performance implications, and in some cases, you may still have to plan an incremental crawl frequency, but otherwise the simplification continuous crawling offers will be nice. For those other cases, you do still have incremental crawling available, perhaps for network file shares or archival media that does not change frequently and does not need a fresh index available in the enterprise search engine.

SharePoint 2013 introduces Managed Navigation, a feature where the site navigation is associated with a term set in the Managed Metadata Service. Now a portal's navigation can easily be managed and stay consistent across many site collections. Using the built-in structure-based navigation was one of the most common objections against implementing an information architecture that consisted of multiple site collections, but now that SharePoint 2013 offers both a structure and metadata driven navigation there is less resistance against going with the more scalable multiple site collection design.

■ **Note**   See Chapter 15 where I discuss Managed Navigation in more detail.

Office 2013 now sets the default file saving location for enterprise users to be their SharePoint 2013 MySite. Although the save file dialog box offered MySites as a location option for several previous versions of Microsoft Office, it was never the default. This change to have the default location as a user's MySite personal documents library is significant because it helps move you a giant leap closer to a centralized content storage. From a governance perspective, having content stored centrally provides you with more opportunity to manage and govern the content, such as when your users store it within their MySites rather than on their desktops. SharePoint 2013 also makes managing and sharing content on a user's MySite easier as well with an improved user experience. MySites only have a single personal document library in SharePoint 2013, so users no longer have to negotiate between the personal and public document libraries the same as they did in previous versions. Now users can use their personal document library to store documents that only they have access to, and documents they share with other users. The library also makes it easy for them to copy the document to other SharePoint locations to collaborate with workgroups in existing sites.

SharePoint 2013 also extends health checks from the farm health checks previous versions of SharePoint made available through Central Administration. They are now also available in site collections to run a health check that validates the site against defined rules. As Figure 1-3 illustrates, there are several categories the health check runs rules against and inspects, including a list of customized system files, missing galleries that a site typically depends on, and references to templates or language packs that are missing. The site collection health check results page displays the results of the health check, providing a visual report on areas that may need attention to alert site collection administrators to what may cause them trouble in the future when they upgrade their site or Apps within the site.

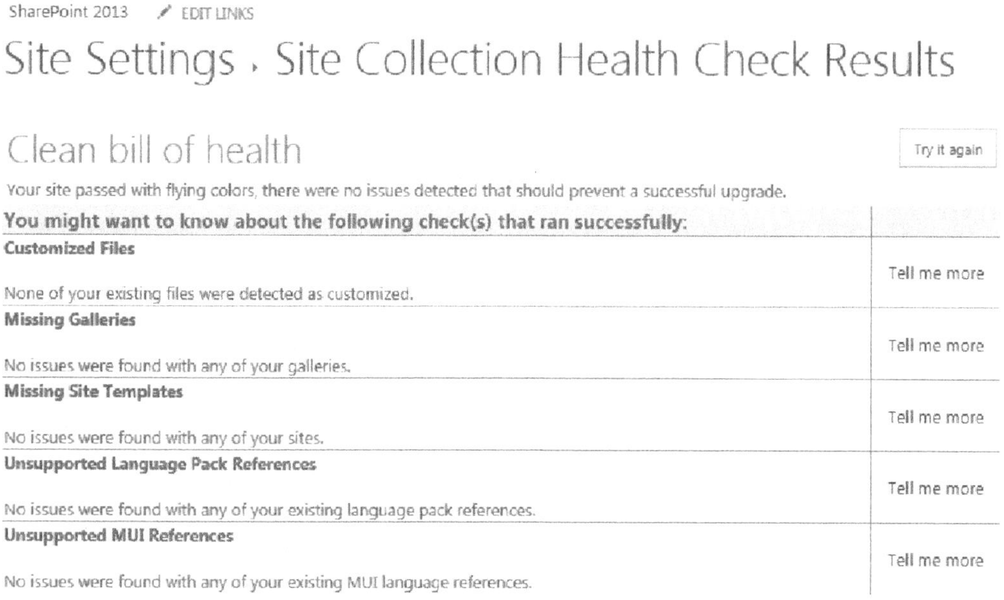

SharePoint 2013   ✏ EDIT LINKS

Site Settings › Site Collection Health Check Results

Clean bill of health

Your site passed with flying colors, there were no issues detected that should prevent a successful upgrade.

You might want to know about the following check(s) that ran successfully:	
Customized Files	Tell me more
None of your existing files were detected as customized.	
Missing Galleries	Tell me more
No issues were found with any of your galleries.	
Missing Site Templates	Tell me more
No issues were found with any of your sites.	
Unsupported Language Pack References	Tell me more
No issues were found with any of your existing language pack references.	
Unsupported MUI References	Tell me more
No issues were found with any of your existing MUI language references.	

Try it again

Figure 1-3. *SharePoint 2013 site collection health check results*

This is not an exhaustive list of what is available in all the new features in SharePoint 2013. I just wanted to offer a quick overview of some of the new features in SharePoint 2013 that contribute to an environment's overall governance capability. I discuss some of these and others as they come up and apply to sections throughout the rest of the book. For now, I just wanted to whet your appetite for some of the new possibilities SharePoint 2013 offers, and some of the existing feature improvements to the user experience that guide users in a manner that has a positive effect on governance.

Consultant Comrade

Periodically throughout this book, I want to share tips that are specific for consultants based on my own experience as a consultant working for other firms and in my own consulting practice. I will use the "Consultant Comrade" section to speak consultant-to-consultant and share any insights or experience I have based on a chapter's topic.

As a consultant, I can see how the idea of SharePoint governance can be a difficult topic on which to advise customers. Governance is a big and complex topic, one that can involve a lot of change and possibly will not show any results right away. On the other hand, governance is a hot buzzword that generates a lot of demand for services to solve. I find it natural for a services firm to engage with a document template to fill out over a series of meetings – a prescriptive document is easier to sell, and certainly easier to contract and track as a deliverable. Nevertheless, I have not seen this approach all on its own actually solve the governance problem for the customer.

So how can a services firm sell and contract a governance engagement? I find the answer to this embodies changing the emphasis from using the verbiage of a governance model contained within a document deliverable, and instead shift the focus to governance activities. Take a series of actions, maybe some taken from this book, and use these in your consulting agenda of governance activities you will help the customer address. Frame yourself or your consultants as a governance advisor or mentor, an advisor who engages to lead and facilitate your customers through governance activities that fit your customer's specific situation.

Governance is a process: adopting, evolving, and maturing over time. As a consultant engaged with a customer as a SharePoint governance advisor, my job is really to guide my customer through a process by providing them with things to consider. Essentially, I lead my customers through a progression of what I like to think of as guided discovery activities. I cannot do the growing for them, maturity does not work that way, but sometimes I can provide answers or direction that steers them in the right direction. Largely the topics I give my customers to consider are the same ideas I have laid out in this book, alongside with any other advice and experiences that may be useful to help you save time and point you in the right direction.

I like to relate typical governance planning consulting engagements to the story *Benito Cereno* by Herman Melville. In the story, Captain Delano encounters Captain Cereno's ship, finding the crew and slaves onboard desperate for supplies after a storm has torn their ship apart. Delano helps by providing supplies and men, leaving him feeling quite content with himself for assisting a fellow sailor. As the story unfolds, (spoiler alert) it turns out that Cereno's real problem is the mutiny on his ship and threat to his life, a mutiny Delano is completely oblivious to despite all the warning signs. While Delano believes he is helping by following the sailor's convention, and he feels pleased for doing so, he is not making any difference on the ship because he is not looking for the real problem to solve. Like Delano, if a SharePoint consultant only focuses on surface-level conventions, they may feel satisfied with a governance plan document they deliver to a customer, and yet not have any effect resolving the customer's real problems and underling issues.

Inside Story: Notes from the Field

Five or six years ago, I was consulting with a government customer – a modest sized government organization with about 40k users or so. My engagement there was to help them establish a governance model and to document a governance plan that would leave them with something they could carry on, build on, and that would set them up for success with SharePoint throughout their organization.

We worked tirelessly for a few weeks in back-to-back meetings, debating options, making decision, and building a gold standard for SharePoint governance plans. At the end, I captured it all in a few documents that included a strategic-focused governance plan and a tactical-focused technical operations guide. We closed out the engagement feeling as if we had accomplished a lot in such a short period, and indeed, we had.

Like any other consultant, eventually it was time for me to wrap up and let my customer carry on without me. This felt okay, because they had all the tools they needed: they made key decisions, their overall direction was clear, and we captured all the details in the governance documents I delivered. I felt quite pleased with our progress and the value I delivered, designing and delivering a new governance model in just a few weeks.

It felt so successful in fact that I often used them as my example to other customers when describing what is possible with the right commitment and sponsorship. I had this prescriptive solution, one that involved a series of workshops and planning sessions, followed by documenting the outcomes in governance documentation. If they were prepared to make decisions and set priorities, I could guide them through the process, and they too would be set up for success. What was not to like?

Imagine my surprise when a year or so later I dialed in to a conference call with my original government customer to discuss governance solutions. To be honest, I was actually a little speechless when they finished describing the challenges they experienced, challenges obviously related to governance. Of course, my first question was around how we had already solved all these problems. Yes, undeniably, they confirmed everything we covered and neatly documented in the governance plan that has since sat lifeless in those original documents, left largely untouched since I had disengaged.

So much for creating a "living document" or for delivering a governance plan they would run with. Frankly, I have seen this scenario repeated frequently with different customers and a variety of consultants. Consultants who deliver valuable governance plans, but ones the customers never act on. Consultants who are very capable and possess the right expertise to produce excellent plans, yet even still, the initiatives fizzle after those consultants roll off their engagement and the customer files the delivered document. Customers who believe they have addressed governance with a plan, yet things are still not running smoothly for them and they do not know why.

The experience has left me fine-tuning governance ideas and reflecting on how to deliver a lasting governance solution in an engagement model that is repeatable, and just as important, able capture the engagement in a service delivery contract. One thing is for sure: the solution certainly goes beyond simply documenting a governance plan. This makes it difficult because documenting a governance plan tends to be the key deliverable consulting firms tend to build contracts around. Yet, it is possible, an effective solution comes out of actions, and you can do those tactical things to drive change and have an actual impact.

Wrapping Up

In this chapter, I discussed how SharePoint governance goes beyond documentation and includes actions that drive change and have an impact on a SharePoint service. I also looked at how the focus of this book will be to cover those actions. I also provided an overview of some of the new features in SharePoint 2013 that support governance. Finally, I noted that this book is for you if you work with SharePoint and have an interest in learning more about my SharePoint governance approach based on actual experiences with customers in the field.

As we move into our SharePoint governance journey, the first stop is to define SharePoint as a service offered to the business. In the next chapter, the first governance action we will take will involve determining the boundary for what the SharePoint environment provides and what it does not. I look at the need for explicitly defining the service offered to operate in an intentional manner rather than constantly responding to crises in a reactionary way. In the discussion, I will also provide considerations to guide an initiative to establish different SharePoint service levels that target different organizational needs. Finally, I will discuss some techniques and tips for designing and implementing a chargeback-funding model for your SharePoint service.

PART II

■ ■ ■

Defining the SharePoint Service

When you adopt a SharePoint operational model that treats users of the SharePoint system as customers, whether internal or otherwise, you not only establish a positive mentality for operations, but you also steer the direction of the whole team towards the users' best interests or what will provide the users with the most value. If you treat SharePoint as a service that you offer, you start to generate this customer-focused mindset. When you define the boundaries and constraints of your SharePoint service, your SharePoint managers are not only able to set expectations with users of the service, but they also benefit from a planning structure that guides budget and resourcing decisions. Your service description also provides a baseline to measure and report against, enabling your SharePoint team to understand the value the service provides and communicate details of it to sponsors and executives, and this potential can only help to justify your team's budget or resource requests.

The chapters in this part cover different areas for defining the SharePoint service you offer. This definition and all of its outputs can take formal forms such as a service description document or a section in a governance document, or informal forms such as a wiki page on a SharePoint site that outlines the service offered and the different processes involved. What degree of formality you choose depends on your specific situation and the comfort levels of your organization and users. I will leave that up to your discretion. The important point is to define what service you offer, what is involved in that service, and what resources are responsible for what actions.

CHAPTER 2

Defining Your SharePoint Service and Service Tiers

It is not enough to be busy. So are the ants. The question is: what are we busy about?

—Henry David Thoreau

Throughout this chapter, I emphasize the idea of operating SharePoint as a service that you offer to internal customers within your organization. I discuss the need for explicitly defining the service you offer in order to operate in an intentional manner rather than constantly responding to issues and requests in a reactionary way.

I provide considerations to guide an initiative you can take to establish different service levels that target different organizational needs. Next, I discuss how to organize your service request tickets, from how to prioritize them to how to set expectations on what the different priority levels mean. Finally, I discuss different techniques and tips for designing and implementing a chargeback-funding model for your SharePoint service.

One essential concept I want you to take away from this chapter is that by treating your SharePoint deployment as a service that you offer to your internal customers, you will find that you will more naturally focus on the value your SharePoint service provides to your organization. This focus will help you determine boundaries for the service and identify priorities for responding to issues and enhancement service requests.

After reading this chapter, you will know how to:

- Make the scope of the SharePoint service explicit and intentional

- Establish different service levels to target different needs

- Organize and prioritize service request tickets

- Design a chargeback funding model

- Establish and schedule maintenance windows

Why Define Your Service?

When I managed a global SharePoint deployment, there were times when it seemed like I was always playing catch-up with SharePoint. My users had a remarkable ability to dream up all the magical things they thought SharePoint should do for them, and they were not shy about requesting more features and new functionality. To add to the complication, users from different business units or departments each wanted different features, and each believed they should be the highest priority.

Who were my internal customers and what was it that I was offering them? This question is different in every situation. To answer it I had to put a box around what SharePoint currently did for our organization and what it did not do. Essentially, I found a solution in treating SharePoint as a service my team offered to the organization, a service the organization could consume if what the service offered met their needs.

This shift in perspective laid the groundwork for a defined, intentional focus – not just for my team, but also for our internal customers who were consuming the service that we were providing. Once we began with defining what we offered and we started associating times and performance levels around the service, we could show how we divided and balanced our limited capacity across our customers. Our operational attention then moved from a reactionary sense, one always under pressure and jumping around between requests, shifting instead into an intentional focus.

Defining the service makes what you offer through SharePoint explicit and intentional. It provides structure and focus, not only for the delivery and operations team, but also for those using the service. A defined service sets and manages expectations, because users will not have to wonder what the purpose of SharePoint is or wonder about all the other magical things that SharePoint can do for them. They can see the strategy and the scope of what the SharePoint service provides, and this gives them a context to frame their expectations. Later in the book, I discuss topics such as how to expand your SharePoint service and how to design a roadmap for it. These topics will build on and expand your SharePoint service description, and this will further help to manage expectations. For now, let's start with a baseline to establish scope and define SharePoint as a service you offer to your internal customers.

By defining SharePoint as a service and what that service entails, you can use this scope to set expectations with system users. In the process, you begin to move from chaos into cosmos. Your first step in this process is to adopt a service focus.

Adopting a Service Focus

When you adopt a service focus, you shift your perspective to consider what your purpose is with your SharePoint deployment. Rather than SharePoint for the sake of SharePoint, a service focus looks at what SharePoint accomplishes, or in other words, its outcomes. You can build a service focus by basing your view of SharePoint on the value it delivers or will deliver to your organization. More specifically, you can adopt a service focus by thinking about SharePoint as the value it delivers to your users.

Your users do not want to constantly face the IT department and hear "no" in response to their ideas or needs. They might prefer to just have the tools they need available or be empowered enough to make adjustments to fit the service to how they want to work. Supporting this can seem overwhelming on the surface. You might wonder how users could survive making their own decisions. You might imagine the possibility and shudder: users running wild, doing whatever they want. I am not talking about opening the floodgates and handing over the keys to your farm, but there are sections in this book that address the degrees that you may want to empower your users to do things on their own.

Whether you are empowering your users with control of their own sites or you are limiting what they can do to manage that control for them, you are still providing a SharePoint service to your internal customers. In both situations, you define a service you offer to the users: one is more lenient and allows users greater control over their own experience, and the other is stricter and standardizes the user experience within a limited range. Of course, your service can be somewhere in between, or even more extreme, depending on your needs and your organization. There is no one correct way to offer a SharePoint service, as long as it is meeting the needs of your organization. The important point is to define what that service looks like.

You can take a few different approaches as you define your SharePoint service. For an existing deployment, conduct a usage audit where you analyze how users are using the system and identify where they are receiving value from SharePoint. Who uses SharePoint and why are they using it? These are your customers, your internal customers who receive value from the SharePoint service you offer them. Through the process of identifying your customers and the SharePoint service you provide them, you will naturally align their needs with the service you provide.

YOUR SHAREPOINT SERVICE AND COMPETING SERVICES

You have competition for your SharePoint service. Sometimes internal customers can simply outsource their need or use an alternative product such as an open source wiki. Even if you mandate and try to block alternative products, you will still face competition. Users seem to have a knack for finding workarounds to any constraints you try to implement. Your users will find creative ways to use things such as using network shares, free email services, outside survey services, and file sharing services. Make no mistake: the workarounds your users find and depend on are your competition.

It may not seem like a big deal on the surface; after all, those alternatives that users find seem to be working for them. The challenge is that through these workarounds, these users are using outside services that are probably not a part of your IT strategy. Do you support any of these free cloud solutions on the market? Are you confident all the data is secure and accessible? What happens when a user leaves the organization? Is there a process to take control of their content stored in these services and protect any intellectual property?

As you can see, this can be a very big deal. You probably do not have the luxury of ignoring these outside systems simply because they are "not supported" or you assume users use them at their own risk. These kinds of things always seem to have a way to come back and bite you – sometimes it is just a nuisance, but other times the bite can happen in the middle of a catastrophe.

This is why I look at these alternative systems as my competition rather than dismiss them with a chancy attitude that IT does not officially support them, and therefore they are not my problem because we do not support them. They are my problem, or typically, they will eventually become my problem. The easiest way to stay in front of them is to focus on providing a SharePoint service that meets your users' needs. It involves offering a better product: a better service.

To provide your SharePoint service, you must also consume services from other groups that underlie or support SharePoint. These other services are things like consuming SQL Server as a database service that the SharePoint infrastructure can utilize. I will come back to this idea of identifying the inputs that run a SharePoint environment, particularly when I discuss roles and responsibility in Chapter 4. For now, just think of those other components of the environment that SharePoint relies on to provide services that support and enable SharePoint to provide its service.

I look at SharePoint as a service that meets the needs of an organization's users in the course of performing their duties. I do not say that it will be everything to everyone, because it will not, at least not all at once. I come back to this idea of your limited capacity to enable SharePoint to be all things to all people, particularly in Chapter 7 when I discuss the process of creating a SharePoint roadmap. In the meantime, you will still need to put a box around what SharePoint service you offer and what the service will entail.

Determining the Scope of Your SharePoint Service

What is the SharePoint service that you are offering your internal customers? What capabilities does your SharePoint service include? I have noticed these can be difficult questions to answer, because SharePoint offers so much to its users that it can be tempting to not want to limit it.

The vastness of the features and capabilities that SharePoint offers can be both a blessing and a curse at times. It is a blessing because SharePoint packs a lot of punch; it provides a single platform for a significant number of solutions. Rather than a hodgepodge of different products and different vendors, SharePoint provides an arsenal of functionality. You might say the curse is also that it offers so much; it taunts you with all the solutions it can deliver. I often find customers in a common situation where so many capabilities in SharePoint entice them, and they end up torn between them all and just do not know where to start.

Often times, the reality is you have to draw the line somewhere. If you are already up and running, there is a chance that you have defined the scope, whether or not it is a desirable scope. Discovering this scope involves looking at the system to determine a list of all the enabled features, observing actual usage to determine what the users use it for, and interpreting this information to understand the nature and scope of your SharePoint service. This information will provide you with an as-is state of your SharePoint service, and you can use this as a baseline for all your other governance actions and decisions.

New projects are a little different. Sometimes someone funds a specific scope and the project has a statement of work associated with it. Perhaps you have a project like this and you reached for this book to help you through your project. I hope that you have not bitten off more than you can chew, but if you have, consider breaking down that project into phases or mini projects.

Now how do you put a box around one of those pieces? My friend Cat once used a saying that I think applies here: "it's hard to only turn the tap on a little bit." Indeed, as I have already mentioned, SharePoint is a wonderfully feature-rich product, and it is hard not to want it all. You need incredible discipline to hold yourself back and remain focused on delivering an initial set of capabilities.

There are several reasons people might want a large scope for their first SharePoint release. The following lists some popular reasons I often see:

- Consulting firms want a large scope so they can secure their own delivery pipeline;

- Project sponsors often want to make a big splash with a wow-factor in a release that they can attach their name to;

- Users are excited about all the different SharePoint features and cannot prioritize between which ones they want first;

There is no shortage of pressure to make your first release huge. I like to think of it as a death by a thousand paper cuts. Each marginal addition to the project in itself does not seem too big, and the value it would add feels desirable. So, what is the harm in allowing these additions? They bloat and delay the project, and that adds risk and slows down the process. Each paper cut might only come with a small sting, but they all add up and work against you. With a regular delivery cycle, you can avoid loading up any individual delivery cycle.

You should deliver quickly, deliver frequently, and deliver incrementally. One of the things I love the most about SharePoint is how it can grow and adapt over time. It is not like other systems that require you to decide on everything upfront. SharePoint does not force you to release the majority in the first pass. You can release the core infrastructure, with a baseline and barebones deployment, and then rapidly and regularly enhance your deployment with very little risk and minimal interruptions.

An evolving approach to your SharePoint initiative carries much less risk than a titanic-type of project. Think of the Titanic for a second: it was huge, well-funded, and supposed to be unsinkable. Even still, there are things you cannot predict, you just do not see them coming until the iceberg is dead ahead. If your ship is too big and you are trying to sail too fast, you practically assure yourself that you will hit the iceberg. Smaller ships might not carry as much, but without all that weight, they can get going quicker and are much more maneuverable when hazards appear in their path. Aim for your SharePoint projects to be less like the Titanic and instead to more closely resemble a speedboat.

Okay, assuming I have succeeded at convincing you to set a scope, how do you set the scope of the SharePoint service? It is a moving target, as I hinted, and you are going to grow and evolve it over time. Therefore, from a big-picture perspective, the grander scope is what SharePoint will eventually become at a point in time, but your initial scope is the first step in that direction. You might start with something easy, something that could deliver a lot of value to your customers in a short period.

■ **Note**   Please see Chapter 3 where I discuss strategies for expanding your SharePoint service by adding features over time.

I use the metaphor of low-hanging fruit: what is on those lower metaphorical SharePoint branches that I could reach quickly and easily? There is no one-size-fits-all answer, as with any kind of design activity, since your choice depends on your unique situation and individual priorities. However, I do not use that as an excuse to brush you off; I am here to give you answers.

Say, for example, that team sites turn out to be that low-hanging fruit for you. Your users currently use file shares, but their file sharing experience is not as rich or collaborative as it could be. You want to offer them the ability to check out documents for editing, to track versions, to comment on changes, and even to set notification alerts when there are changes. SharePoint does this very well, and this scenario makes for excellent low-hanging fruit to pick off.

Now, how do you draw a box around delivering team sites to provide a richer document collaboration experience for your users? First, you need to get servers deployed and SharePoint installed, then you need to generate a website with a URL the users will enjoy, and then you need to decide whether the users can provision their own sites or whether they will request them and have the service desk create sites for them. There you have it: low-hanging fruit that you can deliver quickly and that will provide immediate value to your users.

There is no branding, no site templates, no development, no workflows, and no bells and whistles. You only have the core of SharePoint team sites, and you would have made these sites available to your users in almost no time. Default team sites are already overflowing with bells and whistles built in to them that will excite users who are used to using file shares. Users can assign tasks, create discussions, and they can even blog and send out surveys! There are plenty of features already available to keep them excited, so you do not need to bloat your initial SharePoint service project scope and delay making this value available to your users.

Deliver the value as quick as you can, and then extend and enhance it in a follow-on phase. A phase two for this example might include the following:

- A designer can design the user interface colors and logos, and all that glossy eye-candy that makes users feel good.

- A developer can attach a master page and themes to new sites by using feature stapling.

As you can see, it is very easy to apply branding after the fact when SharePoint sites are already in production. I assure you, you will not damage users of those sites because they have seen their SharePoint site without your custom branding. Instead, you can send out an e-mail to let them know the exciting news that their already excellent SharePoint site is about to get even better – better looking!

The bottom line is the scope you set for your SharePoint offering is going to grow over time. I discuss this growing scope in more detail in Chapter 6 when I discuss how to create a SharePoint roadmap. In these early days, you just need to capture either what your service already offers or the initial low-hanging fruit you plan to offer. For some, that low-hanging fruit can be team sites as in the example I gave earlier. For others, it might be enterprise search or intranets or whatever fits your situation and priority. The concepts are the same whichever SharePoint capability you choose to deliver first.

After you have a scope, you will know what it is you offer. Part of knowing what you offer requires you to understand your customers and to know what they need from your service. What if your customers are diverse in their needs and this diversity makes it difficult to set a scope that works for everyone? In those cases, you might consider designing multiple scopes that essentially provide multiple service-levels to address multiple needs.

Identifying Different Service-Levels for Different Needs

Every customer is different, and that is true whether your customer is an external customer or whether they are your internal users. They all have different needs, different abilities, and different priorities. Each has a unique combination of the three that they bring with them as they consume your SharePoint service, and they have their own expectations that they want the service to accommodate.

Trying to individualize the service to please each of these needs can quickly overwhelm you. If you try to be everything to everybody, you end up risking not being much to anybody. You simply cannot scale the service if you consume yourself with focusing on every individual user, and so you need a way to group users into groups with common needs. At the same time, you do not want to walk away from these customers or develop a militant attitude where they have to conform to whatever you offer. No, you still want to meet the needs of your customers and provide a valuable service that will support them in their daily roles and job functions. Instead of individualizing the service that you offer and making it specific to each person, you can merely give the impression of an individualized service.

How can you give the impression of addressing different needs? You can offer a few flavors of the service where you group together common functionality and usage characteristics into a service tier. This allows you to focus on the heaviest usage to get the biggest returns for the time you invest, while you also provide a repeatable and low-maintenance set of offerings that would satisfy the majority of the needs with the least amount of involvement from you. You can then divide and prioritize your customers by grouping them in appropriate service tiers.

Of course, a typical customer will want to be a tier one customer, because who does not want all the bells and whistles, and who would want to be a lower priority? There are costs associated with this, where the greater the number of customers receiving tier one service, the greater the overall costs. If you have an infinite budget, or at least you have a budget that is sizable enough to accommodate this, then this might not be an issue for you. On the other hand, if you want to limit the scope of your service to fill only a basic need for everybody, considering different service levels might not be an issue for you. However, if you have to squeeze every available means of efficiency out of your budget, then offering different service levels may be a solution for you.

How do you encourage customers to accept an appropriate service tier for their usage? One approach is to charge them through chargebacks based on their usage and their level of service. Later in this chapter, I discuss approaches and considerations for implementing chargebacks. If you charge your customers directly for services they consume, they will naturally gravitate to the most appropriate service tier that meets their needs. Unless, of course, they are the ones with the large budget and they would prefer to subscribe to the whole package rather than invest the time to decide what they actually need. In either case, your service level is funded and sustainable.

I typically find when chargebacks are involved, customers become much more sensible about their needs for the system, and their expectations become grounded within the service definition. For me, keeping their expectations aligned with the service definition provides one of the most significant benefits. Otherwise, they may not realize the costs associated with their requests, which would put the obligation on me to determine if the business value derived from the request outweighs its costs. When you use chargebacks, the customer evaluates and makes their business value decisions directly based on their needs and available budget. Of course, you need to anticipate what types of value to make available and help articulate that value to your customers, because you are the expert that they rely on to provide the service.

■ **Note**   Please see Chapter 3 where I discuss how to map SharePoint features to business value.

Another approach to defining service levels if chargebacks are not an option involves monitoring usage and identifying those heavy users. I typically consider these heavy users of the SharePoint service as my top customers. If I do not have a chargeback model where customers can subscribe and self-identify to their most appropriate service tier, then I identify them based on their actual usage and adoption rates. I use a number of measures to identify these customers. Primarily, I look at the number of active users that use their site and the amount of content they store in the site. These two metrics give me a reasonable indicator on who my biggest and most active customers are. I would identify them by running a script on the server that lists sites by size or activity, ordered with my best customers on top.

In SharePoint 2003, I used a C# console application I wrote that used the SharePoint API to gather site data and produce a list of sites in the farm. By SharePoint 2010, I switched to using PowerShell and began to use some of the built-in analytics reports for this purpose as well. I have been analyzing SharePoint farms like this for ten years now, where I produce a list of the largest and most active sites on which I focus my attention. I typically do not spend my time on any of the other sites until they grow to a size and level of usage to warrant my attention, unless of course a support issue comes up that a first responder escalates to me or if I want to analyze why adoption rates may be lacking. This strategy serves me well and allows me to get the biggest return on my time investment because I spend my time impacting the largest customers.

If I do not have a chargeback model, I start off all my customers with the same basic offering. Usually this means providing a basic SharePoint team site with the core functionality. Then, as their adoption rates grow and they look to expand to consume more features within the service, I increase their site quota and enable more features. This sounds obvious, because that is how any SharePoint site would grow. The keyword in that description was *quota* and how I use it may not have been as obvious. I do not consider quotas as a constraint or a means of limiting my customers. I think of quotas as merely a yardstick to identify what stage a site is at in its growth, or what a site's service tier is. I do not use quotas as a means to restrict users; I use them as a growth signifier and a tool that allows me to adapt to increasing usage. Sometimes I might also use them to alert me where to intervene and provide guidance when a site is growing in an inefficient manner.

The following PowerShell script lists SharePoint 2013 sites in a farm and sorts them from the largest to smallest based on the amount of content they store. I use this as a quick and easy method to get a list of all site collections on a server and their size. Using the output, I can direct my attention to the sites at the top of the list, those sites storing the largest amount of content. I can use this in different scenarios, for example, if I want to audit storage to identify opportunities to reduce any wasted content storage space.

```
Get-SPSite | Select Url, @{Label="Size";Expression={$_.usage.Storage/1MB}} | Sort-Object -
Descending -Property "Size" | ConvertTo-Html -Title "Site Collection List" | Set-Content
SiteCollectionSizeReport.html
```

Designing Your Service Levels

You can name your services levels based on numbers, such as tier one, tier two, and so on. I find numbering becomes pretty generic and boring; but even worse, I find when you number your service levels you constrain yourself within the numbering system. I feel constrained in this numbering system in two ways: numbers imply a hierarchy or order, and this becomes problematic when you want to include parallel tiers that offer the same service level with different feature sets; and the second way is that numbering makes it difficult to insert additional service tiers later on, such as offering tier 1B.

I much prefer names for service tiers, and the most common names seem to be platinum, gold, silver, and bronze. You might use other names that you find more descriptive of their services, such as: basic, extranet, portal, and repository. Alternatively, you might use other names that you find descriptive of their server resource requirements, such as: shared, semiprivate, isolated service applications, private web application, and dedicated farm. You might even mix and match between these naming strategies. All these naming strategies are descriptive and can be meaningful to customers, so pick one that resonates with your organization and the type of service tiers you want to offer.

I generally start with a basic service tier, and this typically includes a default SharePoint team site with my most restrictive site quota applied. I use this service tier to include all the team sites that users create using the self-service site creation built-in to SharePoint. This allows users to self-provision a generic site on demand. SharePoint provisions these sites under a managed path and they share the service applications associated with their web application. Users can grow these sites to several gigabytes in size, customize the visual design, and add additional functionality. They might add custom functionality using a user solution package or a SharePoint 2013 App from the SharePoint Store or from an internal Apps catalog. Depending on how I breakdown the service tiers, I may offer enough in this basic tier to accommodate these types of needs so that I can meet the needs of a majority of my users, particularly if I have a user base who is reasonably self-sufficient and who wants to be empowered to manage their own sites.

The basic service tier can offer a lot of bells and whistles, but in order for it to scale and be largely self-service driven, user sites on the basic service tier need to share the root URL and provision their sites under a managed path. Most users will not care and probably will not even think about this, but some will prefer an easy and short URL. I often call these vanity URL requests. On its own, it is probably not reason enough to break up sites at the basic service tier to start offering individual host names, but you can still satisfy the majority of your customers who do ask about a vanity URL. In my response to these requests, I recommend provisioning the site with a normal URL under a managed path, and then offer a redirector service that uses DNS, IIS, or a simple ASP.NET application that receives requests made to the shorter vanity URL and then redirects them to the site collection's actual URL.

VANITY URLS AND A CENTRALIZED REDIRECTION SERVICE

One option for redirecting vanity URLs to a site collection's longer URL under a managed path involves adding a redirect rule using the IIS URL Rewrite tool. I create the rules to do a redirect to the URL and pass the request on to the SharePoint web frontend server. You can download and learn more about the IIS URL Rewrite tool from the following URL: `www.iis.net/download/urlrewrite`.

I have also seen customers implement a centralized URL redirection service where they create a DNS entry for a simple URL, such as `http://go`. They then build a URL redirection application on the site where they host this Go URL. They design it much like how a public URL shortening service would work and they use it for site or page references, people profile references, map references, and the like. They can advertise a posting in an elevator or a hallway with a short and easy URL like `http://go/102`, and use that to redirect requests to the longer URLs.

You can host this centralized Go URL redirector application in IIS using a simple ASP.NET application. I would create an ASP.NET application to provide a form where users could create their own Go URLs, and store the URL redirection list in a Microsoft SQL Server database to maintain a dynamic list of URLs.

You might be wondering, if the basic service tier covers almost everything, why even have different service tiers? I like to think of the basic tier as the cruise control of the SharePoint service, that part of the service that takes no marginal extra effort to add an extra customer because they just use what is there and it just works for them. We can meet the majority of the demand with the basic service tier while it consumes a minority of our time and service delivery resources. It can deliver a majority of the demand, but it might not deliver a majority of the potential business value. It may keep day-to-day operations running smoothly, but being a basic service offering, it does not go for the gold. For that, a customer needs to opt for a gold service tier.

I find common examples of what a gold service tier could offer would include things such as a dedicated web application to host a custom portal, isolated service applications, a higher content backup frequency, a larger user audience for content, and the like. These higher service tiers are typically for those internal customers who want to build a department portal site or some other type of custom application hosted on SharePoint. They could be for a portal that hosts the expense report forms and processes any workflows, a travel approval and booking portal, or an enterprise learning management system. One could host a Human Resources department portal that contains several custom built applications such as those related to performance reviews and career planning. These are all applications that add rich business value on SharePoint and they might require more of your involvement.

You free up some of your availability to focus on these higher value service offerings by meeting a lot of the more operational or standard demand in the basic service tier. Your basic service tier can consist of those features that SharePoint delivers with ease through its core team site capabilities and the services that support them. This basic service tier can enable your users to receive value consuming the capabilities in their sites – capabilities that can often meet most of their needs. With many of their needs met, you can then focus your attention on opportunities to expand the service.

As your internal customers adopt the SharePoint service, some will have very straightforward requirements, while others will have more complex or more involved service needs. You can provide your customers with a basic service to start, and then offer them different options so they can increase the range of capabilities available and the degree with which they can build a custom application. As Figure 2-1 shows, the service level increases for a particular site based on increases in the following areas:

- A higher number of users using the site
- A larger amount of content in the site
- A wider range of features available for the site

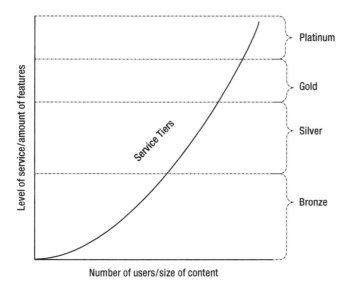

Figure 2-1. *An example of the service tier relationship*

Organizing Your Service Requests

One issue people face with service requests involves a client's service request ticket handling, or lack of handling to be more precise. For example, when a user experiences something or an inkling for something that he or she wants to experience comes to mind, they will open a service request ticket. Of course, a user thinks their service request is important, otherwise, the user would not have bothered to open the ticket, and so they assign a high priority to the ticket. Then the process assigns someone to the ticket, but that resource does not change the priority level, likely because the support resource did not want to insult the requestor. Now you have a high-priority ticket that is active and assigned to a resource, but maybe it is something that is a nice-to-have feature or a request for functionality that is outside the scope of the service you offer.

How do you get around this? Service requests are going to come as people run into issues with the system, and as users imagine all sorts of things that they would like the system to do to support their job functions. If an issue affects a user, he or she is naturally going to perceive it as having a high impact. The user just does not have a global view of the SharePoint service and is typically not aware of the costs behind their request. In the case of requesting new functionality, a user might not even know whether the functionality will solve their problem or even be feasible, as he or she may have just seen a demo and jumped to the conclusion that what they saw would benefit your organization as well. On the other hand, a user may request new functionality that is not the optimum solution for the problem they are trying to solve. If an expert does not analyze the user's actual problem and the team just jumps to whatever functionality the user requested, then the team trusts a user to play the role of a solution architect; yet an ordinary user does not have the same SharePoint expertise as an actual solution architect.

I hate to sound too cynical about service requests that users submit, but I do think users become a little irrational when it comes to filling out request tickets. Whether that comes from their limited perspective of the enterprise SharePoint service or their ignorance toward the costs associated with their requests, I do not know. On the other hand, I do not think those issues should even be user problems, because they have their own jobs to do and they should rely on us to respond to their requests by taking an enterprise view of the system and its costs. We are there to make sense of their requests as the IT professionals, to analyze and understand the business function that they are trying to achieve, and then to design a solution or provide guidance in a way that helps then perform their duties.

I am digressing a little and drifting off into talking about feature requests, which are one aspect of service requests, but service requests also encompass errors with the system and troubles that your users face. The idea

I am getting at is the same for all these types of tickets. Specifically, users rely on IT support professionals to properly prioritize these tickets and to consider them from a perspective of the whole system and all its users rather than having an automatic reaction for each request. The users rely on the service desk to manage the demand and to coordinate all the requests. As such, the service desk needs to be bold and manage the priority level associated with a ticket.

■ **Note**   Please see Chapter 9 where I discuss strategies to manage enhancement requests and prioritize them through a funnel to match your delivery capacity.

Be bold: if a ticket is not actually a high priority, then assign the appropriate priority level to the ticket. This seems so obvious, but it is not as obvious as you might think. You might be surprised at the number of tickets that just automatically go through using the default priority level or whatever level the requestor assigned. A functional service request process includes a triage step where a resource assesses, prioritizes, and routes the ticket to the appropriate group.

Figure 2-2 illustrates an example of a service request workflow for a ticket handling and escalation process. This example uses the frontline service desk to triage tickets and attempt to resolve them if possible. It then routes the ticket to a support team for the application involved and escalates to an escalation team if necessary.

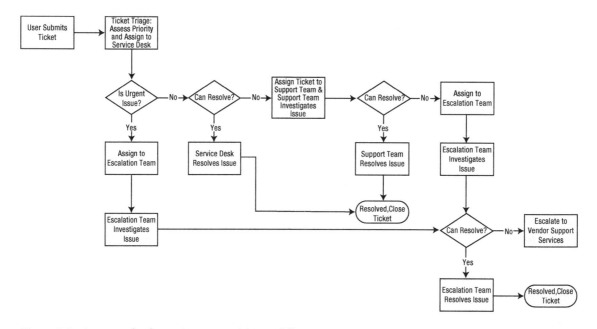

Figure 2-2. *An example of a service request ticket workflow process*

■ **Note**   For SharePoint vendor escalations, my customers use Microsoft Services Premier Support. When they have an issue that they cannot resolve internally, they escalate the issue to a Microsoft support resource by opening an incident with Premier Support. For more information on Premier Support, see the following Microsoft Services website: `www.microsoft.com/microsoftservices/en/us/premier_support.aspx`.

If you are an existing Premier Support customer, you can submit and manage your incidents online through the following Premier Support website: `https://premier.microsoft.com`.

Prioritizing a Service Request Ticket's Priority

If you cannot trust users to prioritize their own tickets, how then can you trust first responders and frontline service desk staff to prioritize a ticket properly? How do you ensure consistency across the team? You need a rubric that defines what each of the priority levels are and the threshold criteria the ticket must fit within in order to assign it to a certain priority level. Your rubric needs precise thresholds for indicators you measure, and of course, those indicators have to be measurable.

One indicator that I find telling of a ticket's priority is measuring the number of people affected by the issue. It could be just the one individual submitting the service request, a small workgroup they are collaborating with consisting of eight people, their department consisting of one hundred people, or the entire organization. When you consider these different thresholds, they should illustrate for you the different impacts a service request has from an enterprise point of view, and therefore provide a consistent way to assign a valid priority to the ticket.

Determining the number of people affected by an issue provides a reliable measure to determine a priority level to assign to a service request during its initial triage. This also takes a global perspective, as its thresholds will be in proportion to the size of the organization. For example, in a smaller organization with fewer than 1,000 users, the thresholds may range from a single user to all 1,000. In contrast, a larger organization with 100,000 users or more will spread those same thresholds over a much larger range. I have found that these proportions also represent the organization's own perception of the priority for a given number of users. That smaller organization would feel the effects of 500 people affected by an outage, half of their total users, and they would prioritize a resolution with much more urgency. The same number of users for the much larger organization would still be important, but the criticality would not be to the same degree because the affected number of users only represents just one half of one percent of their total user population, rather than half like it did for the smaller company.

Another metric I use to determine the priority of a ticket is the potential revenue loss when the service request is in relation to an outage affecting external customers, such as in an example of an ecommerce website. In a similar process as determining measurable thresholds for affected users, I would determine the thresholds of potential revenue loss ranging from none through to having all revenue halted. Any revenue loss is important, so I am not suggesting that you go golfing if there is anything less than a 20 percent revenue loss, but you do need a way to capture the degree of impact. Having these types of reasoned measures and thresholds will help you keep the incident in perspective so you can react appropriately.

It may sound counter to what I have been saying about avoiding subjective or arbitrary measures, but another factor I consider in determining the priority of a service request is the importance of the requestor or the group affected by the issue. I do like to have a list of VIP customers, and these customers typically consist of executive sponsors who provide funding and support to the SharePoint service, other executives who have significant influence over the service, and generally other heavy influencers. The politics of an organization do not stop with SharePoint, so I always try to be conscious of any politics that may affect our service delivery. So if a VIP opens a ticket for a document that he or she accidently deleted, and recovering that document will have a higher cost involved than it would for them to simply re-create it, I would probably still prioritize this higher than if they were an ordinary knowledge worker who was not on my VIP list.

That leads to another measure for priority: comparing the cost to re-create versus the cost to recover content. In a more general sense beyond the production cost of content, you could measure the value of the content's availability. I like to consider both the cost and value, depending on the circumstances. I use cost as a measure for content generated in the daily operations where users can easily re-create it or for content that is not truly mission critical and time sensitive. This provides a straightforward decision metric to use in prioritizing the service request. On the other hand, the content may be mission critical for competitive or other time-sensitive reasons. This type of content fits better with measuring the value it provides rather than the cost to produce, because it is providing ongoing value.

After you have determined the value that the more critical content provides, you can use this in determining the priority of the service request. Now ideally, you have identified that content before an outage or before a user submits an urgent service request, so the triage process does not stall the ticket. Some examples would include disaster recovery or major incident response plans and procedures. These are valuable pieces of content when the users need them, and in the event of a major incident, they will be critical to make available rather than consider re-creating. You can identify that type of content and possibly store it in a designated database for critical content, and this could be the first database you restore in the event of a major incident.

Another case you may use to classify content is by considering the sensitivity of the content itself, and you could use that to help determine the priority of a service request ticket. For example, knowing an incident exposed sensitive content containing personally identifiable information provides an indicator that you might use to determine the priority in responding to the related service request. Content cost, critical value, sensitivity, security, and urgency provide measures you might use to determine the service request ticket's priority, and most importantly, you can measure them all without relying on a lot of subjectivity.

Now that you can prioritize your tickets with a valid priority, you can prioritize your response. When you know the thresholds of ticket priorities and the rubrics that define what constitutes each priority, then you can have confidence in your ticketing system and you will have the right expectations for how it functions. Your users can have confidence in the process, and once you have the priority levels well defined with all the metrics that go into them, you might share this information with your users to help set their expectations as well. However, knowing the priority levels and how they are determined will mean little to your users if you do not also associate what they should expect with those priorities.

■ **Note** You may also use your service request tickets to capture feedback. That feedback might be direct, such as when a customer submits a ticket specifically to offer feedback on the service, or it could be indirect and accessed by analyzing the service requests and their trends. Please see Chapter 8, where I discuss how you can promote a feedback process and use this to capture customer feedback.

Using Service Request Priorities

It is nice to have a high-priority ticket and to acknowledge it is high priority, but what do you do with it then? What does classifying a ticket as a high priority even mean? Does it mean you are going to halt production and bring in whatever outside help is available to resolve the issue? Does it mean you are going to slot it into the queue and get to it when you get to it, whenever that is?

When I first considered this idea of associating some response protocol to a priority level, I decided to include response times and targets for the first responders to respond to the incident. This was a good start, but it still did not resolve the issue. One of my stakeholders, Doug, showed me the limitation of only focusing on a response. He was an operations director, with whom I was negotiating through the details of this new service request process as part of a service-level agreement he would be accepting for the business. The issue, as he expressed, was that it offered him no assurances of when an issue would be resolved, and therefore, did not offer him much at all. "I got it!" an escalation engineer could exclaim, and then they could go to lunch. The response measure only measured how quickly the process would assign a ticket to someone's queue, and not how quickly a resource would work to resolve it.

Measuring how quickly the process assigned a ticket was still an important measure in the overall process, so it is something I include. In order to set expectations on when a ticket would be resolved, or at least what the targets for a resolution are, I found it is also important to include these ticket resolution targets as part of the process. Now, it is hard to predict how long a resolution will take without investigating an issue and understanding the impact, but I can set targets. I cannot always hit the targets, for the same reason it is hard to predict the resolution in the first place, but if I set generally achievable targets for each priority level then I can meet most of them. The ones I cannot bring to a resolution within the target are often indicators of deeper underlying issues the incident has uncovered.

▪ **Note**   Please see Chapter 6 where I discuss topics related to measuring targets in more detail.

My first goal was to have the service request ticket assigned to a resource and have them review the issue within the target time window. When team members felt a sense of importance to take ownership of a ticket in the queue and quickly review the request, the triage process became very efficient. The tickets were no longer getting lost in the queue among a pile of incorrectly designated high-priority tickets. Instead, support resources read the tickets right away, and if the issue had a quick and simple resolution, they were resolved and closed. If the ticket was a valid high-priority or a critical incident, the support resource was immediately active with a response and they would add an initial investigation and resolution plan to the ticket's notes.

With a valid and well-defined priority ranking system, team members know where to focus their attention and when to drop what they are doing when they need to respond to a critical incident. This is what makes the system flow, and without an effective system to process them, the tickets can easily just pile up.

I still treat my e-mail the same way I used to handle service request tickets. I like to process my e-mail as quickly as possible. For many of my e-mail messages I can delete them right away, and I do. Some need a quick response, so I quickly respond and then probably delete them too. Some require more time to plan a response, so I flag them to follow-up later and then get to them in the next day or two. As you might be able to tell, I am a bit of an e-mail-minimalist: I like my inbox to contain very few e-mails, so I delete messages relentlessly and I will quickly file the very few records I need to save. If I still responded to service requests, I would want to close them as quickly as I delete e-mail so I could keep my request queue as empty as my inbox. The only way I can achieve that is with an efficient priority and processing system (and of course, effective routing rules for automated processing when possible).

In Table 2-1, I provide an example of priority levels I have used along with their definitions. I also include the target responses and target resolution times that I set for each priority level. This example comes from an actual service request process I designed as part of a service level agreement I created for a client. You should keep in mind that in this example I have omitted the measurable metrics such as the number of affected users.

Table 2-1. *An example of service request priority levels with target times*

Priority	Description	Meaning	Expected Response Time	Expected Resolution Time
Urgent	Critical Business Impact	Production down, no workarounds, impact is immediate and ceased processing.	Within 2 hours of receiving notification	Within 12 hours
High	Significant Business Impact	Situations where important areas of functionality are unavailable and where the remainder of the system is unaffected but there is no acceptable workaround (e.g. service not available or not performing to standard)	Within 4 hours of receiving notification	Within 2 days

(continued)

Table 2-1. (*continued*)

Priority	Description	Meaning	Expected Response Time	Expected Resolution Time
Medium	Some Business Impact	Situation where important system features are unavailable but a work around is achievable; or less significant features are unavailable but with no reasonable workaround (e.g. Minor database function unavailable); Or, Situations where there is no immediate impact on users (e.g., a request for information or general systems advice/guidance)	Within 3 days of receiving notification	Within 7 days
Low	Very Minor Business Impact	Situation where less significant features did not work correctly and there was a workaround. No business impact; Or, Situations where there is no impact on users (e.g., a request for information or general guidance of the system that is less significant)	Within 5 days of receiving notification	Within 14 days

The escalation team receives notification from the system for Urgent issues. The actual resolution time varies depending on the complexity of the issue, and number of other higher priority issues that are active. The time targets do not cover weekends except for Urgent issues.

As you can see, there are several types of service requests, and it makes the process complex. Yet with a well-defined rubric, you can avoid things such as having the loudest requestor bully their request to the top of the queue, cutting ahead of the patient users. That will still happen, of course, if your place is like most of the places I have engaged. Politics happen in organizations, but using defined measures that take the subjectivity out of your service request process should help make this manageable.

Designing a Chargeback System

If you do not formally have a chargeback-funding model in place, then you have an informal one. After all, someone pays your department to operate. The big difference between a formal and informal funding model is that formal chargebacks bring the decision-making for how the money is allocated down to the department or workgroup level. This can be good and bad. For starters, we already considered how everyone has their own priorities, so this could pull you in different directions if you are not careful. Whereas having the funding come from the top naturally lends itself to distributing it with an enterprise view in mind, rather than having the customer who has the largest budget making the decisions for everyone.

Chargebacks are not as simple and straightforward as they might seem, or at least as how they should seem to me. Every customer is unique and puts a different load on the service. One group may require a document repository to archive scans of their proposals and contracts, and then retain them for up to 15 years. Another group may need minimal storage, yet they may require analytic reporting to slice and analyze their data mart. The first customer requires a significant amount of archival storage space for their repository of document scans, while the second customer requires heavy CPU processing to calculate and process their reports. These are very different needs and would be difficult to group in the same service tier, and likely, they would not even group in the same web application.

Knowing this, what do you base a chargeback on, and how do you enforce it? The amount of disk space and the amount of system resources are certainly good starts. My point is more to illustrate that a chargeback typically has multiple dimensions to it. Some of these dimensions include things such as system resource usage, but others can include the number of users, the degree of customizations that is available to the users, the number and type of features that are available on the site, and the degree of dedicated system resources available to a site.

In addition to the actual functional dimensions that can factor into a chargeback model, you might also factor in offering different degrees of available support resources for different service tiers. Chargebacks can charge for resource usage and feature usage, but they can also charge for support services. Using chargebacks can influence the priority levels you offer to assign to service requests beyond what I already discussed. For instance, an internal customer could subscribe to a higher tier of service to assure their users that they will receive a higher priority from support responding to their service request tickets.

You can base a chargeback model on multiple dimensions. You can base one dimension on the number of features and capabilities available in a tier, and another dimension on the amount of system resources available for consumption within a service tier. You can factor in the number of users using the service and the degree of customization they have available to customize their site. You can also factor in the service level you provide a service tier, ranging from things such as the frequency of backups to the priority assigned to service request tickets. Chargebacks and service tiers are complex because they attempt to address the common needs for groups of users with unique priorities and diverse requirements. How do you address such various needs and priorities among your users if you have groups who both want a premium service level tier, yet one requires a vast amount of archival disk space while the other requires significant amounts of CPU resources? Either you can accept the costs associated with this, or you can offer a means for users to customize their service tier to fit their needs.

You can go to one extreme and offer a generic service in a fashion similar to the famous Ford saying related to their early T-model cars, "You can have any color, as long as it's black." On the other hand, you can adopt a mass-customization strategy. In this strategy, think about a process similar to how Dell handles their customers ordering computers online. Their customers can customize their computers to fit their needs, but there are only a finite number of customization options available. There is the base product, such as the computer tower itself, and then there are customization options available to tailor the computer to the customer's needs, such as the amount of RAM or the CPU processing power. Offering a finite number of customization options is part of what allows Dell to mass-customize computers for their customers, or in other words, they can provide these customizations very efficiently. Dell can be efficient in their manufacturing and supply chain processes, and their customers can benefit from getting a computer tailored to meet their needs. Mass-customization enables both of them to benefit. Now how does mass-customization translate to SharePoint service tiers and chargebacks? Essentially in the same way: design a base service offering, and then design a selection of options your customers can mass-customize to tailor a service that meets their needs.

One option for a base service level could involve the different types of sites available. For example, you might designate a generic team site with the core collaborative functionality for the entry-level tier. The service level behind this site may involve less frequent backups, no customization support, and the default site quota. Other service levels for the site may include limiting it to authenticated users without any external access. Another example might provide additional functionality from a wider set of SharePoint service applications available in the farm, more frequent backups, and end-user customization support that allows them to deploy user solution packages. These are just examples, but I hope they give you a sense of how you can begin to define the base service tiers in your chargeback model. The challenge is to define the tiers with generic and common functionality that you can use as a baseline service offering.

These different baseline service offerings should cover the range of your customer's core needs. Similar to how Dell has several personal computer towers to choose from for their base product, your service tiers should also provide a base to meet the core needs of your different types of customers. In addition, similar to how Dell offers options for their customers to mass-customize their computer, you can offer a variety of options available for your customers to mass-customize their service tier to fit their needs better. You can make these options available *à la carte*, and they can include things such as additional disk space, premium features, and additional support.

Once you have made all these decisions and have defined your different service tiers with their mass-customization options, you can assign chargeback prices to them. You can provide this as a sort of shopping catalog in which your customers can shop for services. Each service tier has a base price, one you set depending on your internal cost structures, and then each mass-customization option has an additional price. Your customers can then select what they need for their desired level of service, and your catalog will provide the chargeback price associated with their tailored service.

Table 2-2 provides an example of base service tiers. This is an actual example of service tiers that Microsoft IT used internally.

Table 2-2. *An example of service tiers provided by Microsoft IT*

Service	Description
Standard (Utility)	The primary SharePoint service that most employees utilize
	Includes My Sites and team collaboration sites
	Offered at no cost to end users/groups
	Employees use a self-provisioning tool to quickly create sites
	Storage above quota limits can be purchased at cost
	Employees can do small customizations for a charge (limited to SharePoint Designer)
	Shares a single host name
	Best for business-critical (not mission-critical) business needs
Custom	Targeted at groups that need more than the Standard service
	Includes vanity URLs and dedicated hardware
	Customizations permitted in addition to SharePoint Designer
	Offered at cost to sponsor; charged quarterly
	Single tenant isolated hosting
	Used for mission-critical LOB applications
	Used by the major portals
Extranet	Service offering for Microsoft partners

█ **Note** For more details on this service tier example, please see the Microsoft IT showcase Quick Reference Guide on Microsoft IT SharePoint Infrastructure and Governance Policies: www.microsoft.com/en-us/download/details.aspx?id=15531

You might notice that my focus for service tiers and mass-customization options centers on measuring the available resource and available features rather than the actual usage. In other words, I have found the best chargeback model involves a customer subscribing to a service tier and issuing chargebacks base on the tier they subscribed to rather than their actual usage. I find trying to measure actual usage in calculating a chargeback involves too much overhead, such as measuring actual disk usage in a period to determine a chargeback level. Instead, I prefer to base a chargeback on the available resources a customer has subscribed to, regardless of their actual usage. In the case of disk space, I would measure the quota available to the customer rather than the actual disk usage for the period. Quotas provide different levels of disk availability for a customer, but having standard quota levels to use in measuring a chargeback level also offers mass-customization because they are standardized.

Essentially, this chargeback model resembles a service in the cloud, but your cloud is an internal cloud. If you ever wanted to use a cloud such as Microsoft Office 365, either for all your services or to augment existing on-premises services, your chargeback model should work well for these scenarios also. Cloud offerings provide software as a service to multiple organizations, in a similar fashion to how your SharePoint service offering will provide SharePoint capabilities to multiple departments and workgroups within your organization. You might even provide the service to enable collaboration with external organizations through an extranet. Whether you are hosting the infrastructure yourself or you are consuming parts or all of it from a cloud service provider, this chargeback model still works.

When you set the price of your chargeback for the different service tiers and the different mass-customization options, you have to factor in the cost of providing the service. If you are hosting everything on-premises, you have to calculate what those fixed costs are and how to spread them out across your different customers, as well any variable costs involved with providing different parts of the service. If you are providing your service through a cloud solution, the cloud provider and the subscription you choose will have already worked out the majority of the costs for you. If your team provides end-user support rather than outsourcing that to the cloud provider, then these will be some extra variable costs to factor in to your chargeback pricing, for example.

I use Office 365 for small business for my own consulting practice, because I do not have an internal IT department and I want to keep my own time available for the core of my business, delivering value consulting with my clients. Not only that, but their pricing enables me to use Lync, Exchange, and SharePoint, whereas for a one-person organization, the costs in licensing and hosting those products myself would be much higher and make them cost-prohibitive. My monthly subscription, or what you might think of as my chargeback, works out to seven dollars and some change every month, in Canadian dollars. For this reasonable chargeback, I can use the same tools that large enterprise and government organizations use, the same tools that my clients use.

Ultimately, the goal of chargebacks is to enable business units and departments to allocate their funding to align directly with their priorities. Its extra accounting overhead comes with the benefit of controlling costs: you can identify granular costs involved with providing the service and factor them in to the pricing of a chargeback model. It gives transparency into the underlying costs associated with different feature areas, and it delegates the cost-benefit decisions directly to the business users who will derive those benefits.

Chargebacks can make for an efficient funding process that has its own natural checks and balances to encourage aligning costs with business value, and they help to guard against run-away costs. Yet, they are not the only option, because funding can still come from above, where finance allocates an overall IT budget that you manage within your group to provide services. I understand many organizations are entrenched with this traditional funding model, and this makes the idea of chargebacks a longer process before you can introduce the change. The first step toward this model is to define the service and its service tiers, and if you can start reporting on the granular costs associated with providing the service, then you are well on your way.

I personally like using chargebacks because of the discipline they offer and the insight they provide into the underlying operational costs. I may be influenced based on all the accounting courses I took in business school, and in particular I am thinking back on my management accounting class that focused on breaking down all the costs, but I do see a lot of value in a chargeback funding model. For this reason, I recommend consulting with a management accountant if you have any who are available within your organization or if you can engage a management accountant from a consulting firm, and use them to help you determine your underlying costs involved with providing the service and what your optimum chargeback pricing should be.

I can offer you no silver bullet pricing levels, because everybody's costs will be different. Understanding your costs will help you determine your pricing levels, because a need for cost recovery largely drives chargebacks. Good management accountants will have expertise in the area of analyzing and understanding costs and they can help guide you as you design your chargeback model.

Identifying Your Maintenance Windows and Availability Needs

I used to have a job as the lead for a global SharePoint deployment, and one of my biggest challenges was finding a window to perform maintenance – apply patches, deploy custom solutions, rebuild database indexes, whatever. The thing about supporting users around the world is that there is always someone working, always someone using

SharePoint, always someone whom I would interrupt. Even at bizarre hours like early on a Sunday morning when I thought that finally people would be asleep or taking a day off.

One of the first things that I needed to do was write a schedule of all the activities in a week at each location and for each SharePoint farm. When dealing with a global schedule, I found it best to have two columns for the time of day: one for the corporate head office time, my time zone, and the other for the server's local time zone. This made it easier to layer on the different activities, especially for those servers located overseas. Then I worked in standard operational scheduled tasks on the local servers, such as database backups and search indexing. Finally, I worked in the global operational scheduled tasks, such as crawling for the global search index. Ensuring no overlap was critical, because some of these tasks are very CPU intensive and can quickly starve a farm of its resources.

My outcome from this activity was having the core operational scheduled tasks captured, including having the global tasks coordinated with the local tasks. I layered all the tasks for a complete picture of activities over a bi-weekly timeline. On the timeline, I then highlighted core operating hours for the high-priority locations around the world. The result was a visual timeline that made all the constraints clear, and it highlighted what windows I had to fit in planned routine maintenance. Eventually I found a small window on Thursday nights for routine and low-risk maintenance. Having the schedule on a visual timeline with all the scheduled tasks made this possible.

Having discussions with the business, I could also determine what their needs were for availability. These needs changed depending on the time of the year. Early in a cycle, they did not have much of a tolerance for downtime. No feature enhancement or upgrade mattered to them as much as being uninterrupted from the work they needed to do during certain months. During other months, their tolerance was the polar opposite.

This certainly depends on the nature of the business, but for my retail clients I have noticed the months leading up to Christmas typically are the months where they have the least tolerance for downtime, while February or March is around the time that they have the highest tolerance. Knowing this makes planning easy: I go into a change freeze for those periods that my internal customers have a low tolerance for change, and plan upgrades or major enhancements for those other periods when they have the highest tolerance. When will making changes to SharePoint have the least amount of negative impact on people's daily life and their daily work? This is when they will have the highest tolerance for interruptions.

You can get into a good routine with regular maintenance windows. Your infrastructure resources can test patches on a regular schedule after Microsoft's patch Tuesday, and then plan to patch the servers during the next maintenance window cycle. I like to have tasks like this become reasonably systematic and operational, so if I can have a regularly recurring maintenance window, I can be more consistent and orderly with my maintenance tasks.

Figure 2-3 illustrates an example of a visual timeline you might use to capture a daily schedule of all the activities that occur on your farm. I typically use a timeline similar to the one illustrated in Figure 2-3 for each day of the week, and then I layer on scheduled tasks for each day and highlight the core operating hours. For my busiest farms, my schedule may differ slightly on alternate weeks, particularly for tasks related to full crawls of large repositories of content. In these cases, I build out a fourteen-day schedule of timelines; otherwise, I build a seven-day schedule. In the Figure 2-3, I added backup, crawl, and Active Directory import schedules. You can start with these and layer on the rest of your farm's scheduled activities to get a complete picture of your farm's activities.

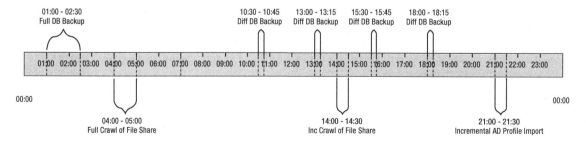

Figure 2-3. *An example of a visual timeline of scheduled tasks*

Consultant Comrade

I often find it easier to establish a service description for an existing SharePoint service already in production. In those cases, I can define the service by analyzing how a client uses their SharePoint environment and what capabilities they have available. They have already made decisions about what services their SharePoint deployment offers, even if they made these decisions implicitly through how their SharePoint deployment has evolved. A service description gives the service order, and the description can help provide a baseline and focus for the rest of our efforts. This also helps me to understand how they are using SharePoint and where they are receiving the greatest value.

Your clients may have SharePoint in production already, and they might bring you in to consult with them on how they could best govern their SharePoint deployment. Although I often find establishing a service description as a good first step in a new deployment, sometimes I have to circle back and help a client to catch up if they have not addressed this yet.

For those new deployments where you are starting fresh, starting with a service description can be a valuable tool to help keep your project delivery on target. I find clients often get excited as they begin to learn about all the capabilities that SharePoint offers while the project delivery progresses. This can be both a blessing and a curse. Their enthusiasm helped drive the SharePoint initiative to begin with, so you do not want that to fizzle out. You want to use their enthusiasm to build momentum and continue delivering SharePoint value beyond an initial delivery. It is a delicate balance though, for if you open the floodgates and try to accommodate every whim that grabs their attention, you risk being overwhelmed with an increasing scope that bloats and drags down the initial delivery.

I like to think of this scenario as having your scope slowly erode away with the addition of all those wonderful extra features that each on their own should not take much for the team to include, but the sum of them all grows to be significant. I call this a slow death by a thousand paper cuts, as I mentioned earlier in the "Determining the Scope of Your SharePoint Service" section.

For this reason, I find helping my clients define their service description before beginning the actual delivery of a SharePoint project enables us to set the baseline and scope for what I am there to deliver. I am extra vigilant at encouraging them to stick with this scope and refrain from getting distracted with all the other little things that come up. My strategy to guide them largely centers on a parking lot list, a list of future items we will prioritize and get to in a future phase and a place where we can capture things as they come up. I remind my clients that our success depends on us all staying focused and committed to our current phase.

We do not want to become inflexible and resist changing requirements. I understand this perspective. Yet, at the same time, if we let ourselves get distracted with every shiny little thing that wows them in SharePoint, the momentum will begin to unravel and the project will be at risk. The reality is that SharePoint is overflowing with great features, so they constantly come up. That is what makes SharePoint so great. I stress this point because I see it constantly and every time I see it, I see it slip into a death by a thousand paper cuts. If the phase is small enough, the changes that come up will be insignificant and probably will not even affect the delivery. For those larger projects that you could not break down into quick phases for whatever reason, your best bet is still to stick with the initial service definition and scope, and allocate everything else that comes up to a follow-up phase.

If you are like most of the consultants I come across in the field, you are probably reading this and can still come up with plenty of reasons to allow scope creep. From my experience, when the consultants are unable to help the client stay disciplined with scope, the project is probably in trouble. They may still deliver, eventually, but these types of projects always seem to wind up being the ones that are like pulling teeth, with no end in sight, with everyone just floating along while no one really owns anything or has any firm commitments. Maybe it is just my experience, where it can feel like I am the only one on the project team who realizes the paper cuts are beginning to add up. At that point, I have to trust my instincts and bring everyone together to give an ultimatum that either we commit to the scope and delivery, or perhaps I am just not the right fit for the project and need to roll off it.

You can avoid this situation, and the solution lies in defining the service. If it is arbitrary or ambiguous, there is more room for paper cuts. If you start with a well-defined scope and have a shared understanding that there will be another phase to deliver more value, but that for this phase everyone is committed to the service definition, then you have a nice chance at guiding your client to success. A strong service definition provides value beyond the initial delivery as well. Therefore, even if your client already has SharePoint deployed, this is still a great place to start.

You can take your client's service description and use that to guide them in planning their service tiers and service request process. It provides that baseline that puts everything else in context, for your clients and for your consulting team.

Inside Story: Notes from the Field

Several years ago, I was working for a company and I took the responsibility to establish a service level agreement for our SharePoint service. It can be a bit of a daunting task, as every little detail needs attention and consideration. I honestly thought that we could quickly document it, make some quick decisions, and establish our service level agreement quickly. I certainly was a little green with service levels from that perspective. I learned right away that they take time, and that everyone involved needs time to process items we were considering before they came back with new ideas and additional perspectives.

As I went along in the process, the process constantly revealed more information to me. It proved to be an invaluable exercise. They say that the best way to learn something is to teach it to someone else. Well, I will take that same idea and say, to best understand a complex SharePoint service with all the different perspectives and priorities for its users, you should work on establishing a service level agreement for it. You would be amazed at how much you learn when you negotiate with all the different areas of the business and try to abstract aspects of the service so that they are generic enough to find common ground among all the stakeholders. I find these to be valuable exercises every time, and every time I learn a little more about how people use SharePoint and what they find valuable.

My involvement with defining service levels and service descriptions helps expand my perspective and provides insights that all help to make me stronger in my role as a solution architect. My experience as a solution architect also helps to make me a better governance advisor. The two complement each other well. You will notice my governance attitude considers the overall solution, because I believe governance is only valuable if it drives the overall solution, if it is scalable, and if it is practical. I feel governance will only truly work if it is adoptable and it will naturally support users in their core job functions. Conversely, I feel solution architectures will only work if they are manageable over time and if users can govern them. My point is that governance efforts will make you a stronger SharePoint resource, because it will increase your other SharePoint skills and broaden your perspective.

While I built out the service level agreement, I started with defining the service itself. We had multiple SharePoint farms with a variety of needs and degrees of cooperation between administrators, so the process of defining a service description for each farm helped identify the focus and purpose of each. This exercise also revealed the politics and the people involved with the farms, from internal competition between groups to gaps in their support coverage. All this was valuable knowledge and it helped to shape the rest of the service level design.

As part of defining the service, I also defined the underlying infrastructure that the service depended on. In some cases, the SharePoint service consumed other infrastructure services from a centralized IT group, such as a centralized SQL Server database cluster or a centralized SAN storage service. Some groups managed their own farm and infrastructure within the farm, while still other groups had a combination of hosting their own and consuming centralized services. I handled this in the service description by listing the service components in a table, and I broke them down into rows to display them in a granular level. I then designated columns for each farm to identify who provided the service of each of those components for a farm. I took what seemed to be complex relationships and I standardized them in a table that captured who provided the service for each component in each farm.

After I standardized the details of each farm and I simplified their relationships to a number of components that resources provided as a service to the farm, I then continued with the service description to define those components and the service expectations around each. For example, with the SQL Server component, I defined a standard for full backups and the minimum frequency they needed to occur to comply with the service level agreement. Once all the farm administrators agreed to the minimum, I then used another table to capture any variances for any farms that require backups more frequently. I broke down each of the components in this way and worked with each of the groups to establish a minimum standard that they would all agree to meet, and then I captured each of their requirements for a higher standard if one was specific to a farm.

The service description took a lot of involvement to analyze processes and standards, and then to abstract and generalize them to find common standards among all the farms. From there I could define a global service definition that encompassed ten SharePoint farms spread around the world; SharePoint farms that six different, and in some cases, competing IT groups within the organization managed. Yet, despite the political challenges and the complexity of so many non-standardized farms, this process still worked, and we were able to agree on a common service description.

The service request ticketing processes varied almost as much between these farms as their service descriptions. Some farms had their own support process, others used a global service desk, and others used a hybrid of their own and the global service desk. My approach to standardize service requests was the same as how I standardized the service description: break down the business process into a set of standardized steps and identify each farm's process for a particular step.

Ultimately, I took a global deployment of disparate SharePoint farms that several different groups managed, and I created a common service description to cover them all. I took a deployed service that we ran in a reactionary manner without a lot of coordination, and I established a set of common standards and minimum commitments among the farms. I navigated some political situations and I helped to reduce some of the service overlap. I also identified gaps in support and coverage, which provided one of the biggest benefits I experienced from the process of defining a service level agreement. This exercise was not just an exercise for my group to come in as the corporate worldwide IT team who wanted to standardize and make everyone conform to the head office way of providing a SharePoint service. Instead, I analyzed each farm at a granular enough level to find commonality among them all, and from there, I built consensus on what would be our minimum standard. In the process, I helped transform their operations to have an intentional focus that we could use to set expectations with our users.

GUEST Q&A: MAXIME BOMBARDIER, MICROSOFT

As I discussed the concept of governance with Maxime Bombardier, a senior consultant in Microsoft Consulting Services, he stressed the relationship between business users consuming the SharePoint service and the IT operations team providing the service as a primary component for SharePoint governance. For him, you can facilitate this relationship between the business and IT if you create a service catalogue that defines the service and its service levels.

He pointed out that the typical IT policies that he sees in common governance templates are simply one of the small outputs of a larger governance process. For him, governance is an ongoing process, not a document. He finds that governance templates and documents are not sufficient on their own, because governance activities need to go beyond infrastructure policies, they need to address the relationship with the business.

His advice is to "build small and build often" as you approach your governance initiative.

Maxime Bombardier works for Microsoft Canada as a Senior Consultant in Microsoft Consulting Services. He is also a Microsoft Certified Master (MCM) for SharePoint. You can follow more of Maxime's SharePoint insights on his blog: `http://blogs.msdn.com/maximeb`.

Wrapping Up

In this chapter, I discussed how to treat SharePoint as a service that you provide for your internal customers. I considered how to make the scope of the SharePoint service explicit and intentional, and how to set up and define different service levels based on different dimensions for different customers. From there, I discussed how to prioritize and triage service requests. Finally, I discussed approaches you can take to design a chargeback-funding model.

Now that you have looked at defining your SharePoint service description, your service request process, and a chargeback model, we will expand and build on these concepts by considering different SharePoint features. In the next chapter, I discuss the core SharePoint functional capabilities at a macro-level. I look at how you can limit features to stay within the scope you define for your service description. I also share some approaches on how to map SharePoint features to business value, through which you may return to expand parts of the service description we looked at in this chapter to include a business case and business value. In the next chapter, I also discuss strategies on how to expand your SharePoint service by enabling additional features over time, and you can use these strategies to expand your SharePoint service definition over time as well.

■ ■ ■

CHAPTER 3

Determining Your SharePoint Features and Functionality

Perfection is the ideal, but the enemy of done.

—Joseph M. Williams

In this chapter, I provide an overview of the key SharePoint functional capabilities at a macro-level: collaboration, social computing, portals, search, records management, business intelligence, and composite applications. I devote my primary focus on the functional capabilities in SharePoint to discussing those new capabilities introduced in SharePoint 2013. From there, I offer strategies that you can use to plan for SharePoint features, and I share approaches that you might take to limit the SharePoint features you make available. Finally, I provide you with considerations on how you can map SharePoint functional capabilities to business value, and how you can plan to build these features onto each other and to enable additional features over time.

One essential concept that I want you to take away from this chapter is the expanding nature of SharePoint. Microsoft has designed the product to provide you with the ability to evolve and expand its features over time, as opposed to having to deploy everything all at once. I stress this idea throughout this chapter so you can see the deployment possibilities in how Microsoft designed SharePoint, possibilities that let a deployment enable additional features and capabilities continuously as it evolves over time. Ideally, this approach can help break down a deployment into manageable chunks rather than leaving you trying to accomplish everything all at once.

After reading this chapter, you will know how to:

- List some of the new capabilities in SharePoint 2013

- Describe the core SharePoint capability areas

- Plan for and limit SharePoint features

- Map SharePoint features to business value

- Enable SharePoint features over time

Understanding the Feature Evolution in SharePoint

SharePoint offers almost an embarrassing amount of riches with its range of features and capabilities. One capability in the product might be what initially attracts you to the platform, and then like a one-two punch, it blows you away with something else it offers. It has a broad range of features and capabilities, and they are getting quite mature in their depth of functionality. All these wonderful things can also make it hard to know which capability to start with, and the vastness of features can make it challenging for you to stay focused on doing your initial deployment well.

Along with the range of features, you might also feel caught up in the hype that builds around considering the different capabilities available within SharePoint, as well as the general hype from the industry around more generic terms that relate to some capabilities SharePoint can support. You might hear industry hype related to things such as social computing, enterprise search, records management, or for our purposes, governance. These are all buzzwords that I suspect you are familiar with, and SharePoint provides a platform that tackles these and other capabilities very well, but beyond the hype, how do they translate into business value?

Are you deploying and enabling features just because they sound cool or are popular in the blogosphere? Did you go to a conference and see a demo that looked promising, and then went back home to start planning how you could deploy the same thing for your organization? I have too; I bet we all have. I think it is easy to find myself caught up in the excitement of everything that SharePoint offers and its potential for an organization. I like having SharePoint fire me up, and I like having the excitement of what is possible carry me away. I find this keeps SharePoint evolving and adapting to meet new business needs. My next step though is to associate business value with whatever feature or capability I am considering.

It is perfectly okay to get excited about something and to want to try it out because it looks interesting; engineers are famous for this, and it is their curious minds that leads them to discover new opportunities or different ways to solve a problem. I am curious and creative in this way, and I enjoy exploring new possibilities to problems. If I want to try out something just for the sake of trying it out, I do it in a development or sandbox environment as a loose experiment or a proof of concept. I do this in a sandbox environment rather than jumping to slot it in as a project for the production environment without any business value associated to it. This helps me scratch that curiosity itch when I just want to experiment with technology, and it lets me do it without gold plating my SharePoint deployment. It also helps me explore new possibilities and prove solution concepts with low risk and minimal investment.

I will come back to this discussion on how to map SharePoint features to business value a little later in this chapter. I am only mentioning it here to put the idea in the back of your mind before we begin to look at the different features built in to SharePoint. This way, I hope you can resist the urge to go and turn them all on right away before you get to the end of the chapter and have read the discussion on associating features to business value or to a business case. Writing this chapter presents a bit of a chicken and an egg scenario for me, because I cannot assume you are familiar with the features SharePoint even offers, and it would be difficult to describe what business value those features offer without introducing them first. Yet introducing the features first contradicts the guidance I will provide later in the chapter when I encourage you to start with the business value and have that business value lead you to the features you need. In the end, I compromised and gave you a quick overview here of both before moving into a discussion on the features in SharePoint 2013.

Throughout this discussion on SharePoint features and capabilities, one thing I hope you will notice is how well they all work together and how they build on each other. I like to think of them as puzzle pieces, building on each other, connecting together, and eventually forming a grander picture. Or, perhaps they form a grandeur picture! You can incrementally build out your SharePoint service, and the beauty is that Microsoft designed SharePoint so that you can incrementally add features and capabilities over time and as you need them, rather than having to tackle them all at once. I come back to this idea toward the end of the chapter where I offer strategies on approaches that you can use to achieve a gradual deployment, after I have introduced the core features available within SharePoint and discussed how you might map them to business value.

I love the Williams quote I used as an epigraph for this chapter, and particularly in the context of this chapter as we look at SharePoint features. This quote comes from a book on writing and style I read and it was mentioned loosely in the context of how perfect sentences might be our ideal, but eventually we need to print and deliver. It resonates with me for this topic as well. I cannot stress this enough: repeatedly I see clients swept up in the vastness of what SharePoint offers, they go starry-eyed and end up consumed with wanting everything, and they want it all at once. It paralyzes them. That perfection is certainly the ideal, but if you want to deliver business value, you need to focus on getting things done. The best way you can do that is by getting things done regularly over time by continually adding features you have mapped to business value.

Now that I have all my disclosures out of the way, I can share my excitement for the tremendous range of features available in SharePoint. This has been true for as long as I have been working with the product. I liked the document collaboration capabilities that SharePoint 2001 offered, but it was SharePoint 2003 when I grew attached to the product. The move to Microsoft ASP.NET was one reason, and another reason that excited me was its architecture that the product team designed for scale. It opened the doors for many possibilities, particularly for me as a developer, where it provided a rich platform on which I could build solutions. I had found my niche around that time where I developed custom ASP.NET controls to help make other developers more productive in the applications they were building; so my transition to building web parts was very easy and came naturally. Everything I loved about SharePoint 2003 got even better in SharePoint 2007, and along with that came some enhancements I craved. In particular, SharePoint 2007 integrated web content management (WCM), added Windows Workflow Foundation, and made some exciting improvements with search, among other enhancements. Then Microsoft released SharePoint 2010 and they introduced of one of my favorite modern architectural designs in the product, Service Applications. SharePoint 2010 also offered a wealth of other enhancements, including the addition of PerformancePoint, FAST Search, and Office Web Apps.

SharePoint continues to evolve and build on its legacy, as it made leaps over the last decade or so with each release. It gave me more reasons to like it with each version, and SharePoint 2013 is no different. As I worked on SharePoint 2013 through beta versions while planning and writing this book, one aspect that struck me is how this release signals to me that it is a sort of maturing of the product. Maybe it is because I have been working with it for so long and watched it grow up, but this release feels like it comes with the fewest radical changes to the overall user experience for working with and administering the product. I have been involved with beta and early adopter programs on several versions of SharePoint so far, and on this version, I noticed it feels as if its overall experience remained consistent with SharePoint 2010. In contrast, other releases involved drastic changes to the user interface on the Central Administration pages and the Site Settings page. Other releases have also changed the model for sharing services, which has typically involved drastic architectural changes. Yet, for SharePoint 2013, it feels as if these aspects have finally matured and settled along with the core architecture for components like Service Applications and the administration model.

Having SharePoint 2013 mature in areas such as its administration interface and its service architecture can help make upgrading and migrating to this latest version easier for administrators and end-users alike. This is because the core experience is largely consistent and does not require a lot of retraining. Even still, the team managed to pack a lot of exciting new features in SharePoint 2013 that still gives it the wow factor for all the new functionality it offers, and so it still has compelling reasons to entice you to upgrade. So, what are all the enhancements that SharePoint 2013 offers? Let's turn our attention to look at what's new in SharePoint 2013.

What's New in SharePoint 2013?

In Chapter 1, I introduced some of the new features and capabilities in SharePoint 2013 as they relate to governance. In this section, I recap a few of those features I already introduced and add on to the list as I point out some of the other new features that I am excited about inside SharePoint 2013.

With SharePoint 2013, we have some very exciting additions that enhance our governance capabilities, and they build on existing governance capabilities carried forward in the product line. Some of these new features are ones that I have craved since SharePoint 2003, and here we are ten years later where these things I imagined would be nice to have back then and would help make governance easier are now a part of the product. First is the managed navigation, resolving one of the commonest objections I faced against going with multiple site collections when I design and propose site structures for clients. This managed navigation feature enables you to base a site's navigation on a term set within the Managed Metadata Service, but you still have the option to use a navigation based on the physical site structure just as you did in previous versions of SharePoint. Alternatively, you can use the managed navigation and have it automatically update relevant terms in the term store when the physical structure changes. I talk about this feature more in later discussions on site structures and information architecture in Chapter 15.

Another new feature in SharePoint 2013 that enhances how we address governance is the eDiscovery capability. The enhancements in eDiscovery overall provides us with excellent information governance options and possibilities. One of my favorite eDiscovery features is the retention policy that you can now set at the site level. This provides a much more feature rich user experience than the long SharePoint tradition of the Site Usage and Confirmation feature that would merely send an e-mail on a regular schedule to request the site owner to confirm that his or her site is still active, without any additional logic or sophistication. Now site owners can specify retention policies for the site and its content that their users create within it. These policies can add a level of sophistication that automatically declares content as a record after a certain period, or the process can trigger a custom workflow to run and take actions against the content.

Similar to records management in SharePoint 2010, SharePoint 2013 eDiscovery also exposes capabilities for designating a piece of content as a record with retention policies assigned to it, whether storing the content in place or submitting it to a records repository. The product team for SharePoint 2013 has enhanced and matured its records management capabilities, making eDiscovery one of the noticeable areas where the team made a large investment and significant innovation for this release. The discovery aspect of eDiscovery provides legal and compliance departments with a tool to locate particular content that relates to a case or an incident they are interested in discovering related content about. As Figure 3-1 illustrates, a user can discover content using query criteria based on dates, keywords, authors, and other metadata. They can run these discovery queries across multiple SharePoint farms and Exchange servers or target a particular site. One of its features includes the ability to set a rule to place content on a legal hold if it matches the search parameters, and you can decide to place a legal hold on content in place or copy it to another location. It provides a rich set of tools for managing and enforcing compliance, whether you are meeting regulatory requirements or responding to a legal case.

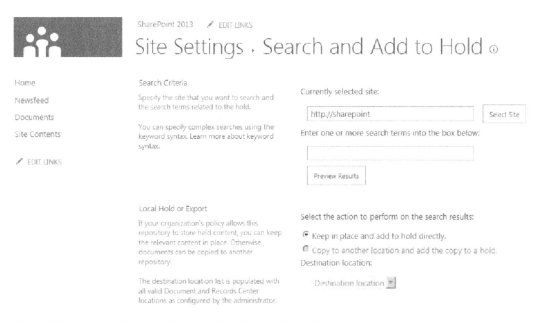

Figure 3-1. *An example of the eDiscovery Search and Add to Hold page*

Apps for SharePoint also presents a wonderful new capability in SharePoint 2013 that provides reuse of services and applications across sites and farms within an enterprise, as well as for consumers from different organizations to procure Apps from the SharePoint Store in the Microsoft Marketplace. Apps provide functionality to a SharePoint farm or just to a site within the farm, yet they do not execute any custom code on the SharePoint servers in the farm and instead can utilize resources on vendor-hosted servers or from a cloud solution such as Microsoft Azure. This provides you with a consistent and low-risk way to deploy customizations and applications, because users can select the App from a centralized catalog and deploy it without affecting the stability of your SharePoint farm.

Speaking of the custom applications you use Apps to provide, you can still deploy your own custom developed functionality through SharePoint Solution Packages (WSP files), and those developers will find new support for debugging issues with the diagnostics available in the enhanced Developer Dashboard. The Developer Dashboard is not just for developers though, despite its name, as I often use it to review logs and page tracing when troubleshooting administration-related issues as well. The biggest change for the Developer Dashboard in SharePoint 2013 is that SharePoint displays the Developer Dashboard in a separate window now, and it has several tabs for activities, such as reviewing a trace of the ULS logs and filtering them for the particular request correlation identifier. You need to use PowerShell to enable the Developer Dashboard in a farm. Once enabled, SharePoint adds a button to the SharePoint pages, and when you click this button it will pop up a separate window containing the developer dashboard. The following PowerShell script provides an example for how to enable the Developer Dashboard.

```
$content = [Microsoft.SharePoint.Administration.SPWebService]::ContentService
$content.DeveloperDashboardSettings.DisplayLevel =
[Microsoft.SharePoint.Administration.SPDeveloperDashboardLevel]::On
$content.DeveloperDashboardSettings.Update()
```

Figure 3-2 shows a screenshot of the Developer Dashboard enhancements. It shows the Developer Dashboard opened in a separate window, where you can see the additional tabs available for monitoring and diagnosing issues on your SharePoint 2013 farm.

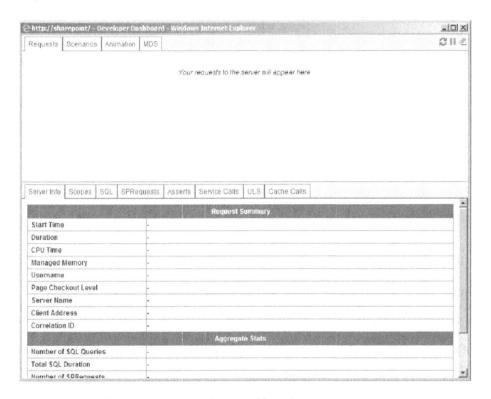

Figure 3-2. *The SharePoint 2013 Developer Dashboard*

SharePoint 2013 makes customizing the self-service site creation process as simple as setting the URL that points to your site creation form. By default, the self-service site creation form asks similar questions as it did before, such as the managed path to create the site, the site name, and optionally, secondary site owners. If you want to collect additional information from users seeking to provision a site, you could create an InfoPath form and update the self-service site creation settings to add the URL for your custom form, and then the process would continue to work by updating all new site links and references to use your custom form. This simplifies the task of customizing the self-service site creation process and it allows you to tailor it to fit the needs of your organization. For example, you could also collect information on the site's expected lifespan and information to set an appropriate policy for retention, or you could capture metadata related to the business impact or sensitivity of the content the site will store.

SharePoint 2013 has updated site policies with the option to set a site to a closed state. With this option, you can have a policy to close a site after a period or a user can close it manually through an option on the Site Settings page. You can close or re-open a site by going to the Site Closure and Deletion page, as shown in Figure 3-3. You can find this page by following a link of the same name on the Site Settings page. With this new concept in SharePoint 2013, you can close a site and use this as a step before deleting it and disposing of its content. When you close a site, it no longer appears in places where web parts aggregate lists of sites, but users can still access the site's content. You can also use the process of closing a site to begin a countdown to delete that site, or you can associate other workflows to the site policy to manage the retention, archival, and deletion of site content.

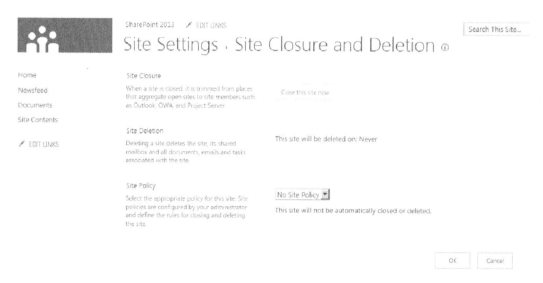

Figure 3-3. *The Site Closure and Deletion page*

One of my favorite end-user features relates to the enhanced user experience for uploading documents. Now document libraries support dragging and dropping a file into the library directly without having to use the Explorer view or having to go through the upload form. For me, dragging and dropping feels like a more natural experience, and it feels smoother without having to switch to Explorer view. This more natural experience means that users will likely understand it easier, and in turn, they will use it more efficiently. It also speeds up the overall process of uploading a document from your desktop into a SharePoint document library.

Mobile users also gain an improved user experience in SharePoint 2013 with the enhanced mobile views in the different areas of the product built to provide a richer mobile experience. In particular, business intelligence visualization offers a rich mobile view with an interface designed for touch interactions when viewing reports and dashboards on a mobile tablet such as an Apple iPad or Windows 8 tablet. Executives can access scorecards and key performance indicators (KPI) on their mobile device, enabling them to keep their fingers on the pulse to monitor the health of the organization, and they can carry that with them whenever they are mobile. SharePoint 2013 has enhanced Excel Services, Reporting Services, and PerformancePoint for general mobile and iPad user experiences with business intelligence.

The social features have improved in SharePoint 2013 with an enriched microblogging experience within the MySite area. Microblogging features now include mentioning someone, such as a colleague, by using the "at" (@) symbol to signal the mention. For example, a colleague could use @stevegoodyear when he or she wants to mention me in one of their posts, and this experience matches how you mention someone on other social networking sites. In this case I used an alias as an example of how my colleagues can mention me in their microblogging posts, and this is the same alias that you would use on Twitter to mention me in a tweet. Your internal alias does not have to match your public social networking alias though, I just had it match here as an example to show the consistent user experience with other public social networking sites. In fact, SharePoint 2013 makes mentioning someone even easier than remembering their alias by offering a little popup when you begin mentioning someone so you can select the person's name from a list of people. This list will include a list of the people you follow as well as a list of people imported into the profile database. You can also see how many posts other people have mentioned you in by using the consolidated web part.

SharePoint 2013 social features are also consistent with the tagging experience users already experience on public social networking sites such as Twitter. A user can add a tag to their post by combining a hashtag followed by the text of the tag. For example, to tag a post with a facilities tag, you would type "#facilities" in your microblogging post, as Figure 3-4 illustrates. When you tag your posts, you make them easier for users to discover them, but you also give users the ability to follow the tag so they can follow the larger conversation related to the tag. You can follow a tag rather than individual people, if you prefer, in order follow posts on a topic that interests you without having to follow all the different people and their other posts that might not interest you. This helps cut down on all the noise and it helps keep your newsfeed relevant to you and your interests. Therefore, in this example, users might follow the tag "#facilities" to keep up with posts from facility managers and real-estate planners for the company, where users may be interested to follow progress on plans to expand office space. They can also see other people's posts related to the expansion process without having to follow all the individual people. In addition to people and tags, you can also follow sites and documents in SharePoint 2013.

Figure 3-4. *An example of the MySite newsfeed post using the tag "#facilities"*

One of the big changes for you to be aware of in the SharePoint 2013 newsfeed involves the change in security trimming. Now most posts are not security trimmed and are visible to all authenticated users. Automatic posts to your feed related to document changes and site changes are still security trimmed based on the permissions of the document or site, but other posts in the newsfeed adopt a more open model consistent with the open and public experience that users are familiar with using on Twitter and other public social networking sites. Retention of posts are no longer limited to 14 days like they were in the past, because now most posts in a microblog are stored in a microblogging list as part of a user's profile and MySite. Some posts are not persisted in this microblogging list, particularly those events that relate to document or to site changes that post notifications of changes to the newsfeed of those users following the document or site. These events are stored in the Windows AppFabric cache, and the cache is not persisted beyond an application restart.

■ **Note**   For more information on Microsoft AppFabric and training resources for using it, please see the following MSDN site: http://msdn.microsoft.com/en-us/windowsserver/ee695849.aspx.

If your profile on your MySite and your microblogging posts on your MySite all make up the presentation of yourself to your company, then community sites are your presentation to a community of practice within your company. SharePoint 2013 community sites are site templates designed for collaboration and idea generation within a community of practice. A community site provides a forum for community members to gather to discuss ideas related to a particular topic. These community sites can serve as a place where people from different areas of the organization gather to share knowledge or to solve common problems, or they can be a place for a particular group or team to brainstorm ideas and cross-pollinate expertise among team members. Community site members can earn a reputation by contributing and actively participating in the community, through automated measures such as having their posts rated or selected as a best answer, or through badges that community managers give them to recognize their expertise or contributions within the community. Your reputation earned in a community site is per community site rather than as a global or enterprise reputation, and it helps present you within a community of practice as an active member, thought leader, or expert, depending on the type of community.

■ **Note**   For more information on SharePoint 2013 Community Sites, please see my blog post where I describe an effective way to use community sites through an example of using a community site to support new employee onboarding and peer mentoring: http://stevegoodyear.wordpress.com/2012/08/02.

SharePoint 2013 search also includes features that are more social. For one, it now has the usage analytics included as part of the search service rather than as a separate standalone service. Including usage analytics in search provides features such as content recommendations to users based on their interests or activity context, usage counts, and activity rankings that capture how active a particular content is to correlate its activity with its overall relevance. The search analytics also uses social distance and social tags in determining relevance in search results, in addition to link and anchor text analysis, click distance, the number of search clicks, and deep links analysis.

Search offers multiple options for Result Sources to use and query for search results. The most notable Result Source for me is the option to select a Remote SharePoint index, which enables the local SharePoint farm to use the content in a remote SharePoint farm's index without requiring the local search engine to crawl the remote content. Using a remote SharePoint index also simplifies the configuration and coordination of remote credentials on remote SharePoint indexes by establishing an oAuth trust between the two SharePoint search applications. Using an oAuth trust requires you to establish a trust relationship between the two farms in the same fashion as you would establish a trust to consume services from a remote farm's service application. Remote SharePoint indexes can effectively allow you to set up an enterprise search portal on every SharePoint 2013 farm deployed in your organization. You can also set Exchange as another option for a Result Source, or you can return results from search engines that implement the OpenSearch protocol. Figure 3-5 provides an example of the SharePoint page for adding new Result Sources.

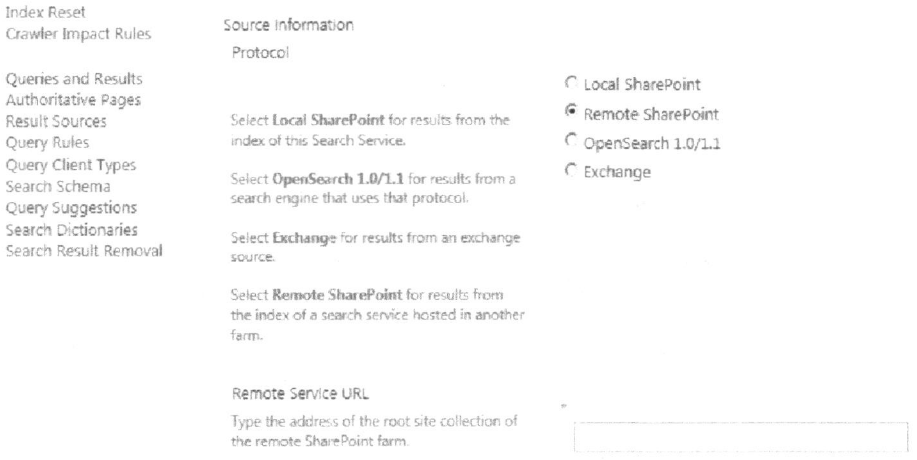

Index Reset
Crawler Impact Rules

Queries and Results
Authoritative Pages
Result Sources
Query Rules
Query Client Types
Search Schema
Query Suggestions
Search Dictionaries
Search Result Removal

Source Information
  Protocol

Select **Local SharePoint** for results from the
index of this Search Service.

Select **OpenSearch 1.0/1.1** for results from a
search engine that uses that protocol.

Select **Exchange** for results from an exchange
source.

Select **Remote SharePoint** for results from
the index of a search service hosted in another
farm.

  Remote Service URL

Type the address of the root site collection of
the remote SharePoint farm.

○ Local SharePoint
◉ Remote SharePoint
○ OpenSearch 1.0/1.1
○ Exchange

Figure 3-5. *An example on the Add New Result Source page*

■ **Note**   For more information on oAuth, please see the following TechNet article:
http://go.microsoft.com/fwlink/p/?LinkID=214783.

Service applications have largely maintained the same architecture in SharePoint 2013 as they did in SharePoint 2010, with some enhancements and a few new service applications added. You will notice one notable change if you are used to SharePoint 2010 service applications, and that change is that the Office Web Apps are no longer a service application within SharePoint 2013. They now are a separate server product, and the reason for this change is to share the functionality that Office Web Apps provides across multiple Microsoft server products without having a dependency requirement for SharePoint to host the service. Office Web Apps now provides Office file rendering capabilities for SharePoint 2013, Exchange 2013, and Lync 2013. This provides a consistent way for these products to render Microsoft Office content, and it provides capabilities to embed web views of Office content in other web pages as well. Separating Office Web Apps to its own server also provides new scaling options for very large deployments where, for example, you can allocate servers specifically for processing Word documents and others specifically for processing Excel spreadsheets. In short, having Office Web Apps as a standalone server product makes it easier to reuse its capabilities across the different server products while also enabling new scaling options.

■ **Important**   You cannot install Office Web Apps on a server that has SharePoint 2013 installed.

This latest SharePoint release also expands Business Connectivity Services (BCS) to support OData, an industry standard for exposing data from a database, which allows for simple no-code solutions against an OData source. BCS also includes enhancements to support handling events triggered from an external data source. This event framework for external notifications also provides alert capabilities for external lists within SharePoint. The external data source must implement the necessary interfaces to raise events to SharePoint 2013 and it must send the event notifications as ATOM feeds or JSON objects. With these enhancements, external data masquerades itself even closer to the user experience of native SharePoint data, and this provides your users with a consistent experience as they interact with list items in SharePoint 2013 without having to be conscious of the differences between a native SharePoint list and an external list.

> ■ **Note** Please see the following TechNet article for more information on these and other enhancements added to BCS in SharePoint 2013: `http://technet.microsoft.com/en-us/library/fp161238(v=office.15).aspx`

One new service application, the SharePoint Machine Translation Service, provides machine translation services for pages, documents, and entire sites. You can use built-in machine translation or you can configure a cloud-based translation service. You can also export the content destined for translation vendors in an XLIFF format, the industry standard translation format you would use to send content to translation vendors. You might send this XLIFF file to a translation vendor manually or perhaps as part of a workflow. You will find this service application particularly useful for portal websites that you need to publish in multiple languages. You will also find the translation service useful as part of your document management process when the document needs to be translated and distributed to audiences in multiple languages. One example might include press releases that you want to distribute in multiple languages to multiple news organizations and news wires throughout the world. In this example, you can create the initial press release in the language your public relations department uses and then use the SharePoint machine translation services to translate the press release into the other required languages. Figure 3-6 provides an example of the Machine Translation Service management page where you can select the different types of file extensions that you want enabled for the translation service.

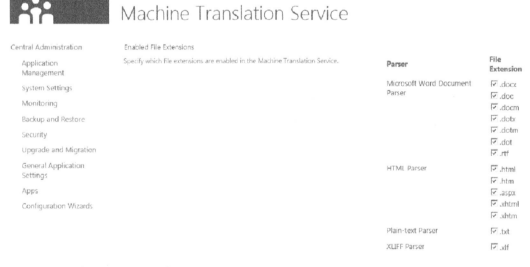

Figure 3-6. *The Machine Translation Service management page*

Another new service application in SharePoint 2013 is the Work Management Service. This service application aggregates tasks for users from across SharePoint sites, Project Server sites, and Exchange mailboxes. SharePoint aggregates these tasks and caches them in a user's MySite to provide a user with a centralized place where he or she can go to view and track their work and outstanding action items. This provides users with an efficient task management system that they can access and manage from a single view, and this saves them from having to hunt down the statuses of all their tasks from many locations. Better yet, tasks are less likely to fall through the cracks and end up missed because a user did not notice it or they forgot to check a certain disparate task list location. For example, rather than having to remember to check the status of his or her tasks in Outlook and then their tasks for a workflow in a SharePoint site, the user can see and prioritize all their tasks from this single view. Figure 3-7 shows the consolidated Tasks view in a user's MySite.

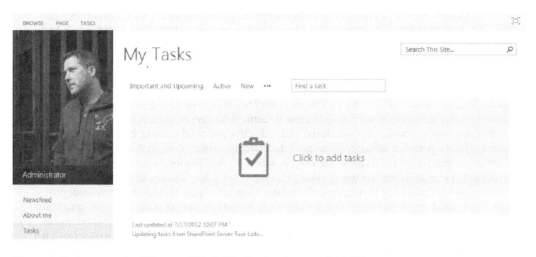

Figure 3-7. An example of the consolidated Tasks view in a user's MySite

Request Management is another new feature in SharePoint 2013, and it is a service that runs to route and manage inbound requests for a SharePoint web application. In contrast to using a hardware or software based load-balancing device that distributes the load evenly across servers, you can apply rules to the SharePoint 2013 request routing and configure an uneven distribution of requests. For example, you can use Request Management to balance requests based on hardware capabilities by providing a higher weighting for newer and more powerful hardware to respond to a greater portion of requests. The Request Management also monitors the health of servers in the farm by assigning them a health score, and it uses this to determine the optimum server for which to route a request. It can also prioritize requests that are more important based on rules you configure, and it can block harmful requests. You might also use it to allocate web front-end servers that you do not want available to respond to end-user requests for administration purposes, or vice versa.

SharePoint 2013 provides many new capabilities, some in new functional areas for the product and others as enhancements of existing functionality carried forward from previous versions. In this section, I have listed several of the ones that I am most excited about, but this is by no means an exhaustive list and I have only just scratched the surface of what these new features entail to whet your appetite for SharePoint 2013. I will come back to some of these features again as they come up throughout the book, and as they specifically relate to governance, but I wanted to digress a little in this section to look at what is new and exciting in this release. I hope this provides you with some context for SharePoint 2013 and for those features that have changed in the latest version. Now I want to shift the focus to a broader sense beyond just what is new and look at what are the core capabilities and functional areas that SharePoint 2013 offers.

Overview of Core Capability Areas

For our purposes, I am going to group the SharePoint 2013 core capability into seven general areas: collaboration, social computing, portals, search, records management, business intelligence, and composite applications. These are similar but not identical to how Microsoft refers to the capability areas within SharePoint in the different marketing material that they use. I am not trying to be different or discredit how Microsoft prefers to categorize the different areas of the product in terms that are more abstract; I just want to simplify them for this discussion so we can look at some particular usage scenarios.

The bread and butter capability of what SharePoint provides is its collaboration capability. This provides the foundation of SharePoint, and it is what I would consider as its core strength. Of course, SharePoint offers so much more than collaborating on documents, but this is where SharePoint found a stronghold and it is still a common driver for organizations to adopt SharePoint. We can trace practically everything else in the product back to collaboration, or at least we can probably find a link from a particular feature area and trace that back to how it builds on and how it complements collaboration. As a result, SharePoint makes the idea of collaborating to share ideas and to create or access new information ubiquitous throughout the product, whether we are participating in community sites, we are viewing slices of data in a business intelligence report, or we are working together to produce new documentation. Collaboration continues to be at the heart of SharePoint and it touches all the other feature areas.

You might consider what the issues with collaboration are as they relate to governance, and you may consider whether you need to address any or make any decisions to govern them. This may range from how open and permissive your collaborative environment is, to how closed and restrictive you need to make it to lock it down and regulate it. Do you want to let the people who are collaborating make their own decisions for how permissive or restrictive their collaboration experience needs to be? Or, do you want to decide this for them? I do not think there is one correct answer that will fit everyone, but it is worth taking a moment to decide where your organization fits on this scale and what approach you want to take to govern the collaboration aspects of your SharePoint environment.

As a capability closely related to collaboration, I want to highlight social computing as another core capability within SharePoint 2013. Users could maintain MySites and their company profile for several versions now; and as in past versions, users can browse an organizational chart, maintain a list of colleagues, or conduct a people search to discover other people within the organization. Users can rate or flag content they like, add comments associated with content, and share links. Other users can discover new content or other types of information through activities of what different users are rating or commenting on simply by being each other's colleague or sharing common interests. Where collaboration allows people to come together, where each can contribute to the process of creating new content or ideas, social computing overlaps and extends this concept by enabling people to discover information through other people and to use those other people to filter its relevance.

Social computing also presents a continuum scale of how permissive or how restrictive you want to make social aspects within SharePoint 2013. Your decision on where you fall on that scale might rest with your degree of trust in your users and the type of content you expect they will post. Your degree of trust might reflect your comfort level with how much you might worry about whether a user will abuse the system, or your confidence that users will mostly act appropriately and that other discipline policies will address them when they do not. Do you care what type of picture your users upload to their MySite or what they decide to write in their profile text? Some people do care and they will want to micromanage this, while others do not and leave it open for the users to manage. Yet other people might fall somewhere in between. You can address this by deciding where you fall and what your tolerance is for social features, and then take the actions of enabling or disabling them.

While social computing can help people discover relevant information, some information could potentially be less social but still important to publish to users. Users need a centralized hub for this other type of information, a portal where content such as organizational announcements, policies, forms, and the like which the portal publishes and makes available to users. A portal might also serve as an entry point for users to initiate processes and workflows, including activities such as submitting their timesheets, status reports, or a performance review. Portals can exist for a specific department, such as a knowledgebase portal, or they can represent the entire organization; and these departments or organizations often brand their portals to give them a branded user experience.

Portals can involve many governance decisions, including who can publish to the portal and who is the target audience for the portal's content. They also involve other governance aspects, such as how to structure them, what are their branding standards, and what are the appropriate types of content. I discuss some of these portal governance issues and more throughout this book, and in particular, when I discuss customizations and information architecture topics in Part IV.

Users typically find content within the portal by clicking through a set of navigation menus and other links, or by searching for content by using keywords related to what they are looking for. An enterprise search can provide users with the option to search within a particular application, such as a portal, or they can use it to search across the enterprise and across content repositories. Users can search for other users, for content that others have generated, or for processes, such as forms that they need to access in order to initiate a workflow process. Users can use search to find specific content quickly from large repositories without having to know the directory structure, such as content stored in a large records repository where a typical user would be unfamiliar with the file plan structure.

As we looked at in the previous section, records management and eDiscovery stands out as a big investment area and a core capability for SharePoint 2013. Once users generate content, some of that content can become critical to the business or have legal compliance responsibilities associated with it. Records management provides additional steps in managing the document lifecycle, as well as the lifecycle of other types of content. It also provides a means for records managers and legal resources to monitor the organization's compliance and to respond to legal cases. One of your governance decisions for records management involves determining if you need a centralized records repository, or if you want to store records in-place within individual sites. Another decision involves deciding how formal you want to make the compliance and retention process and whether you need to enforce any metadata requirements for classifying content.

Besides monitoring the organization's records in a records repository, other monitoring can involve monitoring trends in data, scorecard or performance indicators, and other types of analytical reports. The business intelligence capability within SharePoint 2013 provides this type of monitoring, a capability with services such as SQL Server Reporting Services, Excel Services, and PerformancePoint Services. Users use these services to support decisions and have the services alert them to changing conditions. They may view these reports through a portal, a mobile device application, or through a client application such as Microsoft Excel. Your governance decisions related to business intelligence involve determining who has access to the data, what data you will make available, and how users can request additional reports on the data.

I use the term composite applications as a sort of catchall category that encompasses custom developed applications such as integration solutions that expose data from external systems through Business Connectivity Services, enterprise process solutions that use InfoPath Forms Services and Windows Azure Workflows, or a custom component coded using C# and the SharePoint API. I also consider this category to include those solutions where you provide your own capability to SharePoint by developing it yourself or extending one within SharePoint. These applications can make your SharePoint service shine as they help tailor it to address specific needs.

Governing composite applications and custom development can involve many considerations, and as such, I return to discuss this topic in more detail in Chapter 14. For our purposes in this chapter, you are considering whether you want to enable some or all these capabilities. You might consider what aspect of composite applications you want to enable, whether that includes the Apps from an internal catalog or from the SharePoint Store, user SharePoint solution packages, SharePoint Designer customizations, Business Connectivity Services, and so on.

I hope I have illustrated how all these capabilities provide a specialized set of features and functionality, while also showing the interconnection among the capabilities, as Figure 3-8 illustrates. I wanted to show how they relate to each other, and how they complement and build on each other's capabilities. I find in considering how broad each capability's feature sets are, it helps to illustrate the complexity and size that any one of them entails, not to mention what all of them together entail. For the most part, I consider these capabilities as buzzwords that represent many interrelated concepts and many underlying features. I try to avoid saying things such as "we should implement social computing," because I do not find that perspective to be a valuable one. SharePoint has a bunch of functionality within the product that I grouped into a capability under a common term, but that on its own does not solve a particular business problem, and instead it would leave you chasing features. This idea of chasing features reminds me of the saying where you begin to treat SharePoint as your hammer and you begin to look at everything else like it is a nail. For me, I like to have my focus be less on what capability I am delivering and more on what the outcome will mean for the organization. I achieve this user and business-oriented perspective by mapping SharePoint features to business value, as we will discuss next.

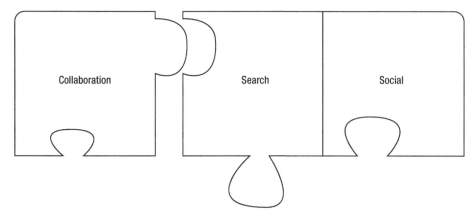

Figure 3-8. *SharePoint capabilities as puzzle pieces fitting together*

Mapping Your Features to Business Value

Before you can map features to business value, you need to to define what business value is. For my purpose here, I consider business value as some degree of benefit that an organization derives from a change or an initiative that I take. You might measure business value using productivity indicators, such as an amount of time saved in a process, or dollar indicators, such as an amount of cost reduced or revenue increased by a process. You might use other factors based on improvements to goodwill, employee morale, or web page click through rates. On the other hand, you might use whatever else is an important measure of value for your organization. For some categories of business value, you might be able to use a precise measurement, while for others you will have to be satisfied with an imprecise measurement.

You do not have to translate every measure of business value into dollars and directly compare the value to the cost required to achieve it, although you might for some measures. Instead, you will look at the business value outcome, whether it relates to dollars or something less concrete, and from there, you need to decide how desirable this outcome is and whether it is worth the cost. I cannot offer you a simplified formula, unfortunately. This process depends on your priorities and how desirable you find a particular outcome is at a given moment. The key place to start is to determine what you want to measure and then determine the actual measurement you need to capture.

A few years ago, I noticed a popular slide that sales people seemed to include in the presentation deck they used to try to sell an enterprise search solution. The slide included a statistic that claimed something that sounds somewhat ridiculous similar to "the average knowledge worker spends 45 minutes per day searching for the information they need." Can you imagine? Picture yourself running a department where each of your people spend almost a tenth of their eight-hour day lost, aimlessly looking for content. You would think they would remember where they saved the documents they were working on the day before, but apparently they come in each day and have to relearn where things are. Perhaps I am too quick to judge, but unless you work in a research role where your actual job involves constantly searching for content, I would expect things to be reasonably constant from day-to-day and that you would be reasonably adept at locating the routine things you work with. I concede that during your first few days, you would be going through a learning curve where you do spend a lot of your time searching for content, but this is not average. What I am getting at is to make sure your numbers match reality and they are not based on some sales stratagem designed to sell products and services.

So, what do you base your numbers on? I find the commonest answer is typically money. How much money can an organization save by using a particular feature? How much extra revenue can an organization earn by using a particular feature? That makes it pretty cut and dry, but not every organization is driven solely or even principally by money. Some simply want to communicate their ideas, such as an environmental activist group whose primary objective is to persuade people to reduce their harm on the environment. Others may want to process as many contacts with clients as efficiently and quickly as possible, such as an outreach-nursing unit delivering a flu vaccine.

If you do not have an immediate need and want to be proactive, I find a good place to start is to look at what are those primary business drivers, those that are crucial to the operation of your organization and its goals. Then I look at the outcomes of a feature or even an entire solution, and I consider those outcomes from the business's perspective. Is this feature something that meets one of those business needs that I am trying to solve? Will it have a positive impact on the organization? From there, I try to quantify the positive impact.

There are no magic bullets to solve this challenge of mapping features to business value; SharePoint does not have a fixed set of business value deliverables because Microsoft designed the product to be flexible enough to fit a wide range of needs and environments. Every organization has different values and priorities, and so the business value SharePoint delivers to one organization might mean very little to another. I do not have a definitive list for you, as you have no doubt noticed through this discussion on how to map SharePoint features to business value. The process involves analyzing the priorities of your internal customers or analyzing what would add value to their job functions, and then projecting where SharePoint features could deliver some of this value. There are several models and processes available for you to use as tools to help build your business case and define your business value, but for our purposes, I will focus on one in particular.

The tool I use to create business cases is to build out a usage scenario that highlights how users will derive value from a particular feature. To do this, I create a use case that describes the task or objective the user wants to accomplish, and then I describe the outcome they derive from going through the process and using the feature. In the use case, I also try to associate what value or benefit the feature adds to the process so that it becomes a narrative about a particular function that a user preform, one that highlights the purpose of the function along with the value derived from the outcome and how the feature contributes to that value. This gives me a usage account from the perspective of the business and it focuses on answering how and why the business would want to use a given feature. I can repurpose this information when I communicate with intended internal users on things such as why they would want to adopt a feature and how it will benefit them.

▪ **Note** One of the best books I have read on how to write effective use cases is Alistair Cockburn's book, *Writing Effective Use Cases*, published in 2000 (ISBN 978-0201702255). I have read this book a number of times, and each time I improve my process for writing use cases. I like to write out use cases in the manner Cockburn describes, and often I like to add in a Visio process diagram to provide a sort of executive summary with a visual view of the use case when it feels appropriate.

I love use cases, but on their own, they do not typically quantify the business value. A quantified measure of business value might be the amount of money saved, amount of extra revenue produced, number of person-hours saved, amount of turn-around time reduced, and other measures of organizational benefits. You might not use a financially related measure though, and instead you could use measures such as increased satisfaction levels with using a system, reduced frustration levels in a process, and the like. Use cases provide a basis to start with determining a measure of business value.

Using use cases, I like to capture the as-is state of the process and take that away to reflect on what the opportunities are. I feel business analysis and solution architecture roles both involve more than simply asking the business what they want; I am the expert they rely on, and my job is to understand their business and then help them understand the possibilities around where the technology can have a positive impact on their business. In sales, I often referred to this as the difference between a glorified order taker and a professional sales resource. A form on a web page can replace an order taker, the same as it can replace the business analyst who only knows how to take orders from business users without understanding or digging into the nature of the business. I try to be the asset who adds value by providing expertise and solutions that solve problems, rather than simply an order taker. After I have captured the as-is state of the process and where users perceive problems with it, I can go away and start to think about where the opportunities are and I can begin to imagine a solution that will have an impact and add a benefit.

It almost feels like a cliché: start with the business problem or business opportunity, and build a solution to address that rather than looking at technology for technology's sake. I mention it though, because it is a step that delivery teams constantly seem to miss or skip or ignore. You need to analyze and understand the business, and then you can identify where the users benefit from a particular feature or an entire solution. You then need to articulate those benefits as outcomes from the perspective of the business and its users. After you have those benefits from the perspective of what the outcomes mean for the business, you have mapped a feature to some specific business value.

Clearly, I am not revolutionizing the process here, as there are other great books written on use cases and business analysis, including the one I mentioned earlier. My hope is not to state the obvious and fill pages with facets of common sense. For those who are experienced, I hope this only serves as a gentle reminder; and for those who are new to the process, I hope this is useful information that points you in the correct direction. I have included this discussion because it is important to mention and it seems easy to miss in the excitement of all the marketing jargon that can distract people when they are looking at SharePoint. Sometimes the hype that builds up around SharePoint can create an illusion that all you need to do is simply turn it on, and as I discuss again later in the chapter, the licensing costs are only a fraction of the total costs involved with operations and support. As useful as a feature might seem, and as easy as it might be to turn it on, my preference is to try to map it to business value first to assure myself that I am not gold plating the SharePoint service and merely driving up costs and complexity.

I feel like this section should not be groundbreaking or one of those tell-all secrets that shocks you, particularly if you have any previous experience working on technology projects. There is no magic, no smoke and mirrors behind the scenes, and nothing different about SharePoint from any other technology project in this sense. I am afraid I do not have a cheat sheet or shortcut or easy button, because the value will be unique for each organization based on their priorities and their unique situation. You can figure out the value though, and you can quantify or articulate value derived from a SharePoint feature or a SharePoint composite application by analyzing your business processes and modeling them using use cases. I hope this discussion has helped you understand how, and perhaps considering an example will help make this more concrete.

One of my favorite examples of quantifying value derived from a SharePoint composite application involves a project to move expense processing from a paper-based system into a SharePoint workflow. I find this is an easy example to relate to, because often with SharePoint, we are replacing paper-based systems and this illustrates an approach to calculate value for those types of projects. At one company I worked for, we introduced an online system that processed employee expenses and their related approvals. Building a use case to understand the process and analyze the steps involved, we could identify the number of people who physically had to touch the paper expense report and receipts, and where someone had to type in data related to the expenses in different systems, such as systems for customer billing and employee reimbursements.

With the use case, we could highlight redundant work and we could capture the total time duration required for different segments in the process. The result gave us a clear picture for how an expense report took an average of three weeks to complete the process of approvals and issue the final reimbursement to the employee. Using the use case with the time durations associated with each step, we could also calculate the cost to process an expense report based on all the cost factors we identified, including the amount of time an individual resource spent working with the expense report. On average, the expense reports cost about $27 each to process and issue a reimbursement. With the new online expense report system we designed, we projected through all the system integration and automated workflow steps we designed and modeled in our to-be use case, that an average expense report would cost around $7 and take only three days to process if everyone was prompt in conducting their reviews and approvals.

I like this example of moving from a paper-based system to an online expense report system because it highlights business value in two ways: the real dollar cost saved by implementing the online system, and the influence it can have on employee morale by providing a quicker turnaround with the reimbursement of their expenses. It also transforms the process so that it now offers one centralized place to go and check the status of an in-process expense report. Those real dollar costs can add up too. The company in this example has about 100,000 employees and contractors, but only about 10,000 of those employees process regular expense reports. On average, those 10,000 employees would process two or more expense reports per month, which gives us a nice round number to work with. If the company processes 20,000 expense reports each month, and expects to save around $20 per expense report, the total projected savings each month would be $400,000. Although this was an expensive project, and one that included significant development costs to integrate a SharePoint application and the set of workflows with enterprise legacy systems, its value was still apparent and easily mapped to this business value. With numbers like this amount of dollars saved every month, it does not take many months for the benefits in savings to add up and outweigh the costs of developing the system.

Although there are no hard and fast rules about mapping features to business value that you can use as shortcuts, I can offer some general guidelines or trends in the following discussion and I summarize some sample considerations in Table 3-1. As you may have noticed in my expense report example, for InfoPath online forms and workflow applications, a good approach is to chart the existing process and calculate how much time and overall involvement it includes, and then translate that into the real dollar costs for the process. Your projected timesaving with the online system can then translate into a projected cost savings similar to how I calculated mine in the expense report example. Document management processes can often follow this pattern as well by calculating the amount of time saved for things like collating the versions or the gains from tracking and managing an approval workflow in a single location.

Table 3-1. *Potential business value considerations for capability areas*

SharePoint 2013 Capability Area	Sample Business Value Consideration
Collaboration	How much productivity can your users gain with a centralized and shared collaboration environment that maintains a single version of the truth?
Social Computing	How many dollars can you save on internal training by facilitating knowledge sharing and peer knowledge discovery?
Portals	How much internal corporate spam can you avoid by standardizing locations and processes for publishing content and communications?
Search	How much wasted productivity can you avoid by using a more efficient and more sophisticated enterprise search engine?
Records Management	What are the risks of potential legal liability involved in your current process that an eDiscovery and records management solution would provide a mitigation strategy to help you avoid?
Business Intelligence	What is the benefit to decision-making and timely reactions that having particular views of data and trends available will enable and support?
Composite Applications	How many people-hours are involved in a process that the application will save, through either automated tasks or a simplified integration?

Records management can build on this document management process and factor in the storage costs for paper-based storage locations in addition to having the workflow history married to the content. For records management, I also like to factor in regulatory and compliance related costs and risks. For example, how much does it cost to prove or audit your level of compliance in the existing paper-based system versus in the online SharePoint system? In addition, I like to consider the exposure risks involved and associate a cost to them as well, such as identifying the potential liability costs an online system can prevent by monitoring and indexing the content, and then alerting relevant resources if it detects something that is out of compliance.

I have already poked fun at common business value metrics for enterprise search that I see in the market, and it is probably typical of something you might have come across. Although I question the validity of the numbers sometimes, the concept and approach feels logical and correct. You could calculate how much wasted productivity you can save by using a more efficient and more sophisticated enterprise search engine, but I often find these numbers suspect and can vary depending on the day and the task. For example, today in my office, I am writing about mapping SharePoint features to business value and core SharePoint capability areas – a topic I am very familiar with and do not need to do much extra research on because this is often my primary job function and a process that is fresh on my mind. Yesterday, on the other hand, I was writing about all the new features in SharePoint 2013. Although I have been using the beta for a few months now and explored many of the new features, I still wanted to cross check my references with the Microsoft TechNet documentation to ensure my understanding aligns with the official documentation. I spent much more time searching for information yesterday than I will today.

What other measures can you use for SharePoint search besides speeding up a knowledge worker's access to information through the search results you provide? I like to think of scenarios and different ways to use search. Sure, it provides search results that help your knowledge workers to find information quickly; but what if they do not know what to search for or if they are unaware that some content exists? Search features have other options to provide business value to knowledge workers, such as the recommendations feature that can recommend content that a knowledge worker might be interested in but would otherwise be unaware of. Information discovery and people discovery certainly add business value, although their value can be difficult to quantify and measure.

I also like other applications for search, such as a dynamic navigation based on a given context to help connect users with relevant information, possibly even in a self-service scenario. One example of a self-service scenario I have developed includes using search as the initial step in a service desk ticketing system. When an end-user submits a ticket, the search engine could parse the request as a search query and use that to search the knowledgebase; it could then ask the user if any of the top results would resolve their problem. The business value derived from this solution would include the faster ticket resolution for the end-users who can resolve their ticket using the knowledgebase, and it would involve the cost savings from not requiring a support resource when the self-service knowledgebase provides a resolution instead.

Search, like all the other features in SharePoint, does not have a magic formula to map to business value. You will find its value is solution specific and you can capture its value by analyzing the solution from the perspective of the business for a use case in the solution. I use this same process for any of the features and capabilities in SharePoint. How formal you make these use cases depends on what you are comfortable with and how much detail you need to document. I vary in my own degree of formal use case documentation depending on the project and the client, and it can range from rough whiteboard drawings to Visio summary diagrams to documenting detailed and descriptive use cases. I leave this decision up to your discretion, and I encourage you to experiment with them all to determine which technique or combination of techniques work best for you and your organization.

After you have mapped your SharePoint features and other composite applications to business value, you are no doubt eager to make haste and start delivering this value. In Chapter 2, I discussed some of the risks involved with losing control on the scope and having your project delivery unravel as it gets more and more features added on to its scope. I find staying focused on the business value helps redirect attention back to the outcome you are trying to achieve with the project, and that outcome is to deliver the planned business value. By maintaining this focus, I avoid having the project unravel into excessive gold plating activities with all the features the team or other project stakeholders can easily get distracted with in their excitement and enthusiasm for what is possible with SharePoint. As a result, this approach involves limiting features you make available, and having a plan for limiting those other features can help your delivery stay focused.

Planning for and Limiting Features

I hate to beat a dead horse, but as I already mentioned, I like to build a use case for major features and have this as my primary planning tool for new features. When I need to analyze business problems or understand the baseline to forecast business value, I like to create as-is use cases; and when I design a solution or plan an implementation, I like to create to-be use cases. This, of course, is a best-case scenario. Not every client will buy in to this process and they might not be willing to fund my time to utilize me in this manner. This does not mean I scrap this step altogether, it just means I scale back on its formality and depth. As I mentioned in the previous section, sometimes my use cases are simply rough drawings on a whiteboard.

As far as planning tools go, understanding how users will actually use a feature will help you set boundaries for it and to understand what it depends on. It also helps you ensure major features you are planning to deploy are features you map to business value. So you have a feature, you know how users will use it, and you mapped it to business value; now what do you do? From here, I also like to consider what a feature depends on. It is fine to say you want to enable a discrete feature, for example something like retention policies. You have a use case that describes how users will use it, and on its own, it does not seem to be overly complex, until you begin to list the dependencies. For something like retention policies to work well, you need to classify the different types of content and identify the retention policies of each. Then you might need a repository to retain content within and you may rely on other forms of enterprise metadata and workflows. On top of all that, you may have a host of other requirements related to enterprise search or the content creation processes. Right away, you can spot some potentially big dependencies on the Managed Metadata Service with an enterprise taxonomy defined, a records repository, and a content type hub with enterprise content types defined. You might find using a roadmap helps you with planning features so that you are enabling them after you have already implemented their dependencies.

■ **Note** Please see Chapter 7 where I discuss strategies and approaches to creating a SharePoint roadmap.

A part of planning for the features you want to enable also involves planning for those features you do not want users to access. You may have any number of reasons why you want to disable features or prevent users from using them. One of the big reasons relates to what I have already pointed out, where you might want to control the release so it does not overwhelm the support team or the users themselves. I have also seen organizations that want to block features because another system already provides similar functionality and they do not want to confuse users or pollute their data strategy. Still other reasons I have seen are as simple as things such as the stakeholders are worried that the users will not understand how to use a feature or that they might abuse a feature.

Whatever your reasons for deciding, the reality is that you will most likely enable parts of SharePoint and leave other parts disabled. My primary strategy for achieving this is through administering and restricting permissions. If I want to enable one aspect of SharePoint and it involves several other features I would prefer to have disabled for whatever reason, I investigate whether there is a permission I can set to block usage of those other features. In many cases, there are permission settings to achieve this, and typically, I can set the permission as a web application policy to deny specific rights or I can control the permission settings through the permission management settings of a service application if it offers permission settings, such as the User Profile Service permissions shown in Figure 3-9. This is not always the case though, and sometimes I have to get a little more creative.

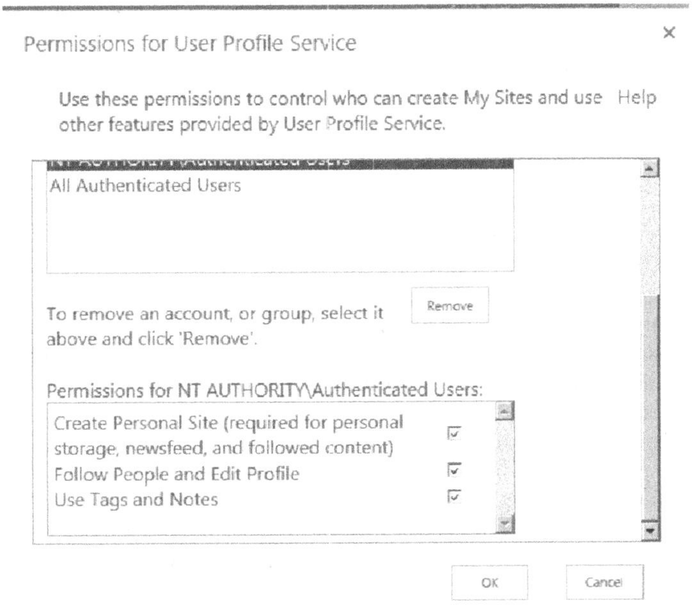

Figure 3-9. The User Profile Service Application permissions settings

For those larger features, I might disable it completely by disabling the service, as long as another feature I deployed does not also depend on that service. If the features are a part of a service application I want to provide to one web application but not to others, I exclude that service application from the default group of service applications, and instead associate it with a custom group for the desired web application. Ideally, I can find a permission setting or a configuration solution such as the ones I mentioned here to limit or disable features. I never like to hack the user interface, as this usually becomes a maintenance headache down the road, but sometimes this is the only solution.

If I do need to block features at the user interface level, my first approach is to see if custom actions will achieve the goal. Custom actions are XML instructions that add or remove items from a menu and you deploy them using the SharePoint feature infrastructure. For this reason, I like them because they are easy to turn on and off, and it reasonably decouples them from the user interface, making them more manageable and maintainable over the product's lifecycle. You can use custom actions to add or remove menu items from locations such as the site actions menu, the site settings menu, central administration menus, list and library menus, and the ribbon.

■ **Note**   For more details on SharePoint custom actions, see the following MSDN documentation: http://msdn.microsoft.com/en-us/library/ms458635.aspx.

As a last resort, I modify user interface elements programmatically. I try to avoid this for performance and maintenance reasons, but sometimes I face strict requirements from clients that call for these types of modifications. I admit that I believe when it gets to this point it is probably easier to just plan for enabling the feature rather than get sucked into the quicksand that developing hacks to prevent them can quickly turn into. Notice I said I accomplish this programmatically, usually by adding a control to the page to make changes during the page's runtime, and never by modifying system files.

Eventually you might want to enable some of those features as you progress in your roadmap and some delivery capacity becomes available. This is the beauty of SharePoint, because you can add to it over time, and you can add to it largely without having to rework previously deployed components or without much interruption to the service. Often this is as simple as turning a feature on. I have a couple of approaches I use to enable features over time I share in the next section, but they largely build on the concepts we have already discussed throughout this chapter.

Enabling Features Gradually

The first step to enable a feature might be as simple as reversing the approach you took in the previous section to limit it. This of course only addresses making the functionality available, but for some features, simply making their functionality available might be your approach. I call these the soft launches, because they occur where I release the new functionality behind these features but I do not broadcast the availability to my user base. This gives me time to ensure everything is stable and the feature is not causing a negative impact, thus avoiding ending up bombarded with support calls or user requests. Some users will naturally discover these released features by fluke or through exploring, but for the most part the initial adoption will be limited. From here, I may invite some early adopters to begin using the new features and monitor their success. Once I feel confident and ready for a larger audience, I may broadcast the availability with some training resources and usage scenarios.

In contrast to a soft launch where I gradually onboard new users, I may have a hard launch that encourages everyone to visit and use a particular feature. These more widely broadcasted releases are typical for scenarios such as new corporate portals or an enterprise search engine. It is expensive to run two systems in parallel while you do a gradual cut over, so these cases often become candidates for a hard launch and a complete switch over. Whatever your launch strategy is, in both cases you ultimately enable the feature and onboard users. This addresses the mechanics of enabling features, but now let me switch gears and share a game plan I typically use when I approach the decision around which features I want to tackle.

I like to build momentum by focusing on continuous and incremental improvements. Sometimes I need to launch a feature set that I would consider a new delivery rather than an expansion of an existing feature area, and

I would call this a *breakthrough* improvement rather than an *incremental* improvement. The initial delivery of SharePoint in an organization is a breakthrough improvement, and introducing a wildly different capability area might be a breakthrough improvement as well.

Despite the occasional need for breakthrough improvements, my preference is for smaller, incremental improvements. Even when I do need to deliver a breakthrough improvement with a new delivery or distinct feature set, I try to limit the size so that it is not so big and radical. For me, the smaller the change, the better. This then allows me to evolve the rest of the feature set using incremental improvements, which ultimately helps me remain in my comfort zone where I can minimize risk while I am constantly delivering value.

This is where the momentum comes from, because many small deliveries of functionality will translate into many frequent successes. I find I generate momentum best by building it on a series of successes, and I build those successes through a process of continuous improvement. The Japanese word for "continuous improvement" is Kaizen. It comes from two words: Kai meaning "change," and Zen meaning "good." This philosophy fits well with how I like to work, as I am constantly trying to stay aware of opportunities to make small improvements; and making small improvements fits particularly well with how I like to deliver and evolve a SharePoint service.

■ **Note** One of the best books I have read on Kaizen is Masaaki Imai's book, *Kaizen: The Key to Japan's Competitive Success*, published in 1986 (ISBN 978-0075543329).

I love the ideas and concepts that Kaizen encompasses: gradual, unending improvements based on many small changes rather than radical transformations. For SharePoint, this means not getting bogged down with trying to implement everything all at once. I have seen a ridiculous number of project delivery teams experience a bizarre twist of paralysis and quicksand that consumes them because they wind up consumed with chasing too much and casting too wide of a net in their SharePoint delivery. I imagine you have also seen a few or could go to any SharePoint user group meeting and hear stories about this experience (assuming the resources are not in denial or they are not afraid to admit that they got caught up in this scenario). This comes up frequently for me, either watching a project team sink or coming in afterward to try and get them back on track, and I have seen it so often that I can usually sense when a project is heading in that direction. You can sense it too if you watch for the signs. Ask yourself whether there is a general commitment toward incremental improvement and small changes, or are you heading toward breakthrough improvements and radical changes.

These are good theoretical concepts and I like how I worked Kaizen into the conversation, but how do you apply all this to SharePoint in practice? I like to use an example of a type of engagement that I have repeated with a few clients. Through this engagement, I began with the breakthrough improvement where I introduced SharePoint. This first step was really to get it installed on some servers and enable its core functionality with some team sites or maybe a generic portal. I did not add any customizations or even any complex configuration settings just yet, as I simply deployed an out of the box web application with basic services. This gave me a baseline foundation to build on and extend; yet, at the same time, it delivered working value to the business. For the next phase, I incrementally improved on this service by adding search capabilities. To add search, I created a search service application and crawled the content. Bam! Now the SharePoint service has search and I have not interrupted the users or caused a drastic change. This delivered more working value to the business. Following on this, I thought, it sure would be nice to search for people. I created a User Profile service application, configured an Active Directory connection, and scheduled profile imports. Just like that, I enabled a simple people search. From there, I looked at improvements I could make in the profile properties for advanced searches, and then eventually I looked at enabling MySites.

These features all build on each other and they offer a natural progression. At this point, I could consider improvements in the branding and user experience, or improvements in search properties, or even improvements in different social features such as introducing community sites. For a couple of customers, I worked with them to take the existing physical office location number attributes associated with a user profile and plotted them on a floor map that I displayed in a web part. User profiles included location information and the facilities department had digital floor maps for each of the corporate buildings, so I could make an incremental improvement by developing a web part to add a visual floor map to the public user profile page. I got this idea from some of my former colleagues who developed a similar solution for their SharePoint deployment. The result: I could improve people's experience incrementally with MySites and people profiles, because in addition to finding their digital location on the corporate network quickly using the people search engine, people search users could then visually see how to find people's physical location as well.

Incremental improvement is not limited to configuration settings within SharePoint and it can include custom development solutions just like my custom developed floor plan web part that visually plots the location of a user's office or desk. It can also include integration solutions, such as those enabled through Business Connectivity Services. This might be as simple as connecting with a database containing a list of all the organization's customers and making that available as external lists for sites to use to tag content.

The trick is to think about these features as things you can introduce over time. I find thinking about them with this perspective helps me work in a mindset of continuous and incremental improvement. My main strategy for this is to run my SharePoint service delivery as a program rather than as a project, especially for the initial delivery. A project has a beginning and an ending; it will live once and then eventually (hopefully) you will complete it and put it to rest. A program on the other hand consists of a series of projects, and so I find it easier to maintain the scope of the individual project streams when they are within a program rather than if they wrap their delivery in a single project that may or may not consist of phases. It may seem like a slight diction difference, but I find this wording can make all the difference with expectation management from project stakeholders and delivery team members.

If we consider the approach that I describe throughout this chapter, those project deliveries within the SharePoint service program each contain a delivery cycle. For each project and for each feature set within a project, I cycle through a set of activities and project phases. I like to work using the Microsoft Solutions Framework (MSF) at the project level, where I go through the five MSF phases of envisioning the solution, planning the solution design and approach, developing the solution, stabilizing the solution, and releasing the solution. For each business problem I am addressing I also go through a conceptual continuous improvement cycle, as Figure 3-10 illustrates. I analyze the problem or opportunity, create the as-is use cases, design a solution, create the to-be use cases, and deliver the solution.

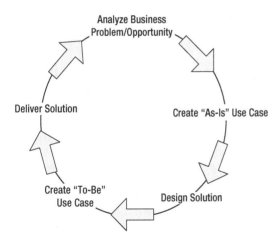

Figure 3-10. *An illustration of the conceptual continuous improvement cycle*

In short, my best SharePoint delivery success strategy consists of running the delivery as a program with a series of small and distinct projects, each concluding with a frequent delivery to production, and each offering a small incremental improvement.

Deciding Which SharePoint Features to Enable

In this chapter so far, I have described how to map the features you need to measures of business value and I have provided you with some strategies to limit features and enable them over time. This still might leave this question unanswered: Where should you start and how do you pick what features you need to get started? This can be problematic, because it drives the focus on features rather than on business value, and it can lead you into a situation where you are looking at a shopping list of SharePoint features rather than focusing on a business opportunity.

I have noticed this shopping list approach can be a popular one where people look at a shopping list of available SharePoint features and then they try to determine which ones they need. It can also resemble writer's block: where too many options or future tasks distract you to the point where your writing stalls. In a similar fashion, your SharePoint delivery can stall when you torment yourself with all the different features, and you end up stuck wondering how you can have it all despite your limited delivery capacity and your scarce resources. Perhaps I can coin a new term for this: SharePoint solution designer's block. When the emphasis is on SharePoint features, I find it near impossible to prioritize a service delivery, and this lack of an effective prioritization process stalls me. It leads me to experience SharePoint solution designer's block!

When the business drives your priorities, you will naturally find the best place to start, and this will lead you to the features you need. If you start with the business case that will deliver the highest amount of value or address the greatest need, you will identify the features you need with ease. So the question of what features do you need is answered by identifying what features are required to fulfill a given business case.

There you have it; we have come full circle in this chapter. As great as all the features are, they are not that great if they are not adding business value. Start with identifying the business value, and your decisions around the features will follow.

Consultant Comrade

This section is a little difficult, or more precisely, a little delicate for me to write. I too am a consultant, so I understand you have conflicting priorities with the approach I presented in this chapter and your consulting business model. Specifically, I am referring to the idea of Kaizen, where you focus on continuously making incremental improvements and small changes rather than going after the breakthrough improvements and radical transformations. Everyone seems hungry to land the big fish, and I have no illusions that a sales representative is motivated to land the big fish most of all – a sales representative who probably receives a bonus based on the amount of revenue sold. Why would they ever scale an opportunity back to deliver small projects and only make small changes?

One typically would not design or incentivize a consulting services business around encouraging smaller projects. From this perspective, I expect the approach I discussed in this chapter to be a non-starter for most SharePoint consulting services organizations, especially those more transactional ones who simply want to plug a hole with a resource for as many hours as they can possibly sell. In all likelihood, your SharePoint consulting practice is in business to make money, just like my consulting practice is in business to make money, and it makes money by billing resources out to clients. We are not on different pages though, and I am not throwing a wrench in your business model. I am merely sharing approaches that have worked for me in my own SharePoint consulting practice, and approaches that have worked for me when I worked for other consulting practices.

My approach is to focus on treating a SharePoint delivery as a program, a program that consists of a series of small projects that each delivers incremental improvements. You can still get commitment for those bigger fish by selling a program. Perhaps part of the program you sell can involve advisors where you embed some of your consultants on your client's team to advise and influence the program. I can keep mentioning this approach until I am blue in the face, but if you are not the decision maker on how your engagements are structured, then I am probably preaching to the choir, and you might feel that there is little that you can do with this information. I run my SharePoint consulting practice and I structure my own engagements, so in that sense it is a little easier for me because I am the decision maker as well as the consultant. What do you do when you work for a consulting firm who will not run their delivery with projects structured in the way I propose? There are many reasons for this, and perhaps it relates to fixed bids or the types of Requests for Proposals (RFPs) your firm gets involved in pursuing. Sometimes your client wants to make a big bang with a huge launch, and you have to align yourself with their vision if you want to win the business.

You can have any number of legitimate reasons why you might have to go with a large project. For example, I have found it difficult to set contracts for consulting using agile practices such as scrum or extreme programming, as the typical consulting business model struggles with adapting to these delivery methods. Adapting to fit Kaizen is no less of a struggle. I think Kaizen closely fits with agile practices, particularly with the principle of delivering value early and delivering value often. My history working in agile software development environments might be the reason I like

Kaizen so much and why I try to embrace it in my life. However, I have also worked in waterfall software development environments where we have a fixed ship date for the next iteration several months out, and the team is only focused on marching toward that date rather than any sort of iteration or quick delivery. I have also worked for consulting firms who deliver large projects in a similar fashion where I do not have any control over the structure of the project or how I deliver; they merely deploy me and I have to run with it.

My most prized approach allows me to adapt to these types of large projects and still feel close to my comfort zone. In my prized approach, I have found that the sooner I can deploy a staging or sandbox SharePoint environment for the team and the stakeholders to interact with, the better. I have been on a few large projects where they are streaming along within the bounds of the contract, yet I have the sense they are not as successful as they might have been if they had adopted the Kaizen approach. In my retrospectives for those projects, I have found a common element that could have helped improve our success, and that common element would have been to deploy SharePoint early for a limited audience of stakeholders and to get these people using the software. If we develop a system of treating this staging environment as our Kaizen-like delivery environment, and we deploy updates to it frequently with subtle changes that the stakeholders can try out, then we can still realize those Kaizen benefits that I like.

A caution though: deploying an unexpected SharePoint staging or sandbox environment does have the risk of pulling you down into a rat's nest as it adds unbudgeted scope to your project. I keep this addition very simple. First, I sell the idea with my clients that they need this environment deployed as early in the engagement as possible. I am actually a little relentless with encouraging them to get this in place, and I simplify the burden it would have on my time by proving them with a checklist to get everything prepared and ready so we can be up and running with a default install in a minimal amount of additional unplanned effort. That checklist includes actions such as a server list that they need to provision, service accounts that I will need, URLs they need to create DNS hostnames for, and the install media. With all this in place, I can usually walk though an install with one of the client's server administrators in a relatively short period.

▨ **Note**   One of the best books I have read on checklists is Atul Gawande's book, *The Checklist Manifesto: How to Get Things Right*, published in 2009 (ISBN 978-0805091748). I find using checklists is an extremely useful tool in project planning, project initiation, and as checkpoints throughout the project. I also like to use them during the pre-flight stage of a project where I provide customers with a list of activities and actions they need to complete to ensure an efficient and effective engagement once I hit the ground and we kick-off the project delivery. You might notice some of what I have learned from Gawande's book incorporated in this book as well.

Having this staging environment also gives the client's server administrators a chance to walk through the install with me early on. Often times, they have not received any SharePoint training or they have only recently been introduced to the product. In those cases, the hands on experience is invaluable for them and it helps set their expectations early about what managing a SharePoint environment will be like. Even if they are experienced SharePoint resources, I can provide them with a significant amount of knowledge transfer in a short period while we go through the install process, both from my pointing out details on configuration settings and from conversations on my experience with other clients.

Once you have this staging environment set up and accessible to the project stakeholders, my next recommendation is to build a schedule for frequent and regular deployments of your deliverables to this environment. I like to deploy these deliverables in a working state, but they may not be feature complete. I try to have a discussion with my project stakeholders about alpha and beta software builds so they know we are continuously going to evolve this deployment on whatever schedule we establish. Personally, I like to deploy to a staging environment every week or every two weeks if possible. Because I am using this to insulate and hedge against the risks involved in a large project, I prefer to have short beta release cycles to get feedback on our progress and to experience the momentum from our deployment successes. Having shorter release cycles also keeps my client's project stakeholders involved in the project delivery, much as they would be in a Kaizen process. This process also fits well with the development team processes I prefer, which include frequent integration builds and regular automated testing. I return to this topic in Chapters 14 and 16 where I describe my preferences for a successful development and release process.

I cannot stress this enough: break your project down into small chunks and then deliver those chunks to your clients frequently. Whether the contract includes this process or not, and whether you are delivering to production or to a staging environment, I have found the potential for success increases remarkably with this approach.

USING CHECKLISTS TO LEAD INTO MORE WORK

You have probably noticed that I like checklists and I find them incredibly useful. I include them throughout a consulting engagement: from the overall project tasks, through to the infrastructure deployment steps and quick start guides. They can keep things on track and moving forward, and they help to make sure things do not end up missed. They also provide a means for me to delegate a set of tasks or action items for someone else to run with.

Another use I find for checklists comes at the end of my engagement. Often, I like to close my engagement by delivering a checklist of next steps to my client. This can include immediate next steps they need to take based on outcomes from the engagement or the project iteration we are closing. I also include detailed steps that lead into the next logical phase for a new project to deliver. I try to make these steps clear so my client can run with them and know what actions they need to take before we kick-off a new project, and then I include more general checklist items that describe the direction and high-level objectives for that follow-on project.

I like to build these checklists in a way so that they give my client clarity on what actions they need to take leading into the next project, and then what general areas they might look at for the next project. I want this to be useful for them so I leave my clients pointed in a good direction and have them set up for success, whether or not they engage me to continue in the next phase. Of course, I usually conclude the checklist with a footnote that encourages my client to contact me if they need help accomplishing any of the checklist items. Often times they do, and this leads to a lot of repeat business for me, but for those other times, I am still happy because this is just good customer service – and it helps me avoid having to help them fix problems they might experience from heading down the wrong path.

Inside Story: Notes From the Field

Years ago, I worked for a company and my focus was on expanding our SharePoint service to meet more needs in the business. I was new and did not have a lot of experience supporting a large number of users, so of course I just wanted to turn everything on and make features available for my users. My manager Micki, thankfully, was a little more experienced and she gently guided me in the correct direction every time I suggested we introduce a new feature. She would respond supportively and ask me to create a business case for it first, and then we could look at going ahead. My first reaction was that the feature was free, or at least it was included in the licenses we already purchased; all I had to do was turn it on – how much more of a business case would we need?

As I learned, licensing costs are not the only costs involved with providing software as a service to the organization. My largest operation costs typically related to support activities, and if I turned something on willy-nilly without foreseeing potential issues, then I could quickly find myself in a support nightmare. Worse yet, if I turned on features that did not offer enough business value, I would then have only managed to add to our budget pressures without adding any value to my internal customers. Finally, without any vision or strategy behind the features I enabled, I would have no plan for how they all work together and how I should prioritize them. If I was unclear on the purpose of a SharePoint feature, then my customers would surely feel hazy around what they should use it for, or why they should even use it.

My internal customers constantly faced time pressures: they had tight deadlines and could not afford any diversions that would pose a risk against meeting those deadlines. The organization measured them and gave them bonuses based on shorter-term cycles and immediate targets, typically within the next year, and they did not have much incentive for longer-term strategic initiatives. I think their focus was typical of many workers in the way their incentive measures how they deliver immediate results and immediate value. Everything beyond that is certainly nice to have, but detrimental if it came at the expense of delivering any of the required immediate value. So the potential business value for them was two-fold: how can I support and speed up their delivery of immediate value, and how can I remove any barriers or blockages that impede their progress?

Time was the biggest business value I could deliver to them. They would find saving money nice, but for them time was much more important. If something delays them in their delivery, their potential revenue loss would be orders of magnitudes greater than the little bit of budget I might save for them. They needed procedures streamlined and automated; they needed technology to naturally fit with their processes and bare some of the load so they could focus their attention elsewhere. Saving them time was the ideal business value to map features to, either by speeding up turnarounds or by automating tasks for them wherever possible.

Often saving budget or increasing revenue is what dominates the activity of mapping features to business value, since for-profit organizations are usually in business to make a profit. In the case of my example, my internal customers were attracted to saving time because it led to greater revenues and ultimately a better profit performance, so their case was no different. However, many organizations do look beyond profit in their measures, particularly those not-for-profit organizations, and they might measure other metrics such as increases in the number of people serviced or increases in the mass-communication of an idea. In this case, I mapped features to the amount of time the features saved, and I used this as the primary measure of business value I delivered.

In this case, I needed one version of the truth in a spreadsheet that supported editing with high concurrency and without the risk of overwriting each other's changes. Rather than e-mailing multiple versions of an Excel spreadsheet around and requiring a resource to collate them all once everyone added their input, I could offer an online and centralized location where everyone edited the same copy. Rather than host the spreadsheet in a file share where one user could unknowingly overwrite another user's edits, I could offer the check-in and out features in a SharePoint document library to control the editing of a single shared spreadsheet. I could provide a real-time and single version view into the state of a team's progress with testing, and provide a controlled manner for editing. However, this became problematic because each tester on the team preferred to have their version of the Excel spreadsheet opened all the time while they worked, which earlier versions of SharePoint document libraries did not handle well.

They were used to storing the spreadsheet on a file share and using a feature in Excel to allow multiple concurrent editors. The file share did not solve the problem either, because user changes could sometimes be lost or overwritten, and hence where my initial focus on checking spreadsheets out for edit rose to address that surface-level need to protect their edits. Once I met with the team and understood the underlying use case, I could focus my business value questions on the real problem: how much time did an average tester waste by double-checking to ensure their changes were not lost, or how much time did they spend merging their changes with multiple versions? If I had SharePoint 2013 deployed, I could map the features in Office Web Apps to this amount of time saved as the business value. In addition, I could map value to how providing a web version of the spreadsheet would allow multiple testers to edit and see each other's edits while they all kept the web version of the spreadsheet open.

Wrapping Up

In this chapter, I looked at some of the new features in SharePoint 2013 and what its core capability areas are. I also discussed how to plan for and limit features, and I shared some approaches that you can take to map features to business value. Finally, I discussed techniques you can use to enable features over time by continuously introducing small changes and incremental improvements.

Now that you have looked at the different features and capabilities that SharePoint 2013 offers, and how to expand your deployment to enable those features over time, I will build on these ideas as I look at how you can ensure coverage and support for these features. In the next chapter, I discuss all the roles involved in a typical SharePoint deployment and I use this list to offer guidance on how to map these roles to specific responsibilities that the SharePoint service requires to support its operations. I also provide a sample RACI chart with some common roles and responsibilities, and then I provide you with considerations for adapting the sample to fit your needs. Finally, I discuss how to ensure you have end-to-end coverage supporting your SharePoint service and what approaches you can take to formalize your communication process.

■ ■ ■

CHAPTER 4

Establishing Your Team's Roles and Responsibilities

The price of greatness is responsibility.

—Winston Churchill

In this chapter, I provide a list of all the areas with roles that a typical SharePoint deployment affects and depends on. I use this list to provide guidance on how to map the roles to specific responsibilities that a SharePoint service requires to meet different needs and ensure availability. I also discuss when you might formalize your communication protocols to ensure that you have a process to notify any relevant people in the case of any disruptions of service.

One key point that I stress throughout this chapter is the importance of ensuring end-to-end coverage, which determines what roles and responsibilities are required for coverage, and thereby identifying what resources you need. To illustrate how to link roles with responsibilities and map them with actual resources, I provide several sample RACI charts and I discuss considerations for tailoring them to fit your own organization's needs.

■ **Note** RACI charts provide a format to map each role's relation to a specific task. The acronym stands for Responsible, Accountable, Consulted, and Informed.

After reading this chapter, you will know how to:

- Identify what roles you require and what their responsibilities are

- Adapt and use a RACI chart as your roles and responsibilities matrix

- Ensure that you have end-to-end support coverage

- Formalize your communication protocols

Understanding the Roles and Responsibilities Need

SharePoint seems to touch everything. It is one of those enterprise applications you deploy that seems to intertwine itself with many other applications and services. Right away, it utilizes services from SQL Server and Active Directory, and it might interact with Exchange. A basic SharePoint service that only integrates with these basic servers already integrates with some significant enterprise applications, and perhaps these are even some of the most significant enterprise applications on your network.

On top of those core systems that SharePoint integrates with, you may also add integration points or dependencies with your other enterprise application software. You may connect with other enterprise applications through Business Connectivity Services (BCS) and then consume their data within SharePoint, or you may output data from an InfoPath form or a SharePoint workflow to another enterprise system. You may even wrap the user interface for an enterprise system within SharePoint to provide a consistent experience for your users.

There are many reasons why your SharePoint environment can grow complex and become intertwined with all these other enterprise applications. Some examples of additional enterprise applications you may integrate with include:

- Enterprise Resource Planning (ERP) systems

- Customer Relationship Management (CRM) systems

- Content Management Systems (CMS)

- Business process management systems

- Business intelligence systems

- Enterprise service bus systems

- Master data management systems

- Order processing systems

- Inventory management systems

- Accounting systems

- Human Resources Management (HRMS) systems

- Learning Management (LMS) systems

This is just a sampling of the popular categories of enterprise applications that SharePoint can integrate with or depend on to some degree. Not many applications have the reach for connecting with other enterprise applications that SharePoint does, and not many other applications provide the value from integrating with all these applications in the same compelling manner as SharePoint does. There are good reasons to integrate SharePoint with all these systems. Hence, the line I opened this section with: SharePoint seems to touch everything.

I find all these touch points are also the danger with how SharePoint can explode in an unchecked and unmanaged fashion throughout the enterprise. Of course, I want the adoption of SharePoint to explode, but I want this to happen in a sustainable manner that I can manage, particularly when it comes time for me to patch or upgrade the environment. Spending some time working through this chapter will help you manage your SharePoint service and keep it in a supportable and maintainable state. A crucial aspect of this process leads you to identify and understand all the systems that SharePoint depends on, and all those that depend on SharePoint. Through this understanding, you will understand your SharePoint service and what the service needs to operate with more confidence and comprehension.

On the one hand, you need to know all the roles that are directly involved and required to provide your SharePoint service, and what are each of their responsibilities. You also need to know all those other roles that are indirectly required with providing your SharePoint service, because your SharePoint service depends on them in some fashion, you need to include their dependence in your roles and responsibilities matrix as well. As such, my discussion in this chapter drifts out broader than strictly focusing on SharePoint resources to help you ensure that you have end-to-end coverage. Before I get into those specific roles, I first want to consider how you can get started with identifying all the different roles and responsibilities involved in your unique environment.

Identifying Roles and Responsibilities

As I mentioned, you can have many different people involved in providing a SharePoint service, some directly and some indirectly. The number of people and how specialized each are will vary depending on your organization and your deployment. I see this number vary and depend on a few factors, such as the type and size of your organization, the size of your SharePoint deployment, the criticality of your SharePoint deployment to the business, and of course, the amount of budget available in your IT department.

The size of a SharePoint team can vary from polar ends of the scale, ranging from a one-person operation where a single generalist is the IT department, all the way up to a small army of IT resources, each specialized in a specific area. I have seen it spread everywhere in between. One is not better and there is no single optimum number or single formula for determining a team size. Often an organization will have people from human resources working with the finance department to plan and set the organization's headcount numbers. Whether or not you feel your headcount numbers are adequate, this is not for me to say nor a debate for me to get involved with. Enterprise resource planning and headcount budgeting are outside of the scope of this book (although I have worked on IT systems I built to support these activities).

For my purposes in this chapter, I want to look at the resources you currently have available and focus on optimizing their allocation first. From there, if you find gaps or if you find certain resource areas are spread too thin, then you will have valuable information on the details, and this can help you articulate what additional resources you need and it can help to justify why you need them. This discussion will set you up well with some valuable tools that can help you build your resourcing case, even though I will not be providing a direct formula for a precise number of people you need.

Although team size varies from a one-person operation to a small army (to a literal army), the concepts and activities remain consistent from team to team. A single IT administrator who supports a small family business and manages the IT services for them is not wildly different in concept from a global services IT outsourcing organization that consists of several thousands of resources. Both these organizations provide a range of IT services for their customers, and their main difference is a matter scale. The larger IT organization operates on a much larger scale, and so it has more roles with specialized resources performing the tasks for which it is responsible. Yet, conceptually, they are both providing IT services, just at different degrees of scale.

I like using this comparison for this topic on roles and responsibilities, because it helps frame the commonality of IT resourcing that is consistent across organizations, even though each implementation will have a difference in their degree of scale. This abstraction helps me begin to standardize and order the roles involved in providing a service, and then to identify their responsibilities that are required. I use roles, because roles are more abstract and I can apply them consistently from one organization to another. Once I have decided on all the roles I require, then I assign them responsibilities, and finally I map actual resources to those roles. For the small organization in the earlier example, I map that one individual IT administrator as the resource for all the roles, while the larger organization will include multiple resources with each potentially mapped to only a single role. By abstracting the roles and then applying resources to them later, I am simplifying the process so that it will work for your organization, whatever its size, and better yet, you can adapt it as the size of your organization changes.

During any initial discussions for new SharePoint deployments, I get a common question from clients and it relates to the number of resources that they will need. Clients usually ask how many resources they need to allocate to the project if I am to deliver a SharePoint deployment, and then they want to know how many resources they will need to budget for to manage the operations and ongoing sustainment of it. Now of course, I have experience as a SharePoint administrator, one who was spread thin at times across support activities trying to maintain an acceptable level of service, so I like to see ample coverage and infinite budgets with infinite resource availability.

Infinite budgets and infinite resource availability sounds nice. Who would not want to live in a world like this? Well, I imagine the finance person accountable for the budget might not want to live in this world if the budget is wasteful and excessive. Sadly, I have no magic numbers and all I can do is help my clients work through what features and capabilities they want to include in their SharePoint service, and what level of service they want to provide. From there, I help them list the roles and responsibilities involved by building their roles and responsibility matrix. They can then take the RACI chart we produce and plan how they want to allocate resources and how much they want to invest in a particular service area.

To build a RACI chart, I take an overall view of the SharePoint service and I look at all the activities and tasks that the service needs to operate. From there, I group these tasks and associate them with a role. Some roles I know about ahead of time, such as the SharePoint administrator – someone has to manage the service unless you are consuming a service hosted in the cloud. Other roles will depend on what features the client enables. For instance, including a data mart architect will only be appropriate if the client includes a business intelligence component that warrants this role.

In naming the roles, I usually stay reasonably consistent with how the market names a similar role, and I do this so my client will have an easier time filling the role with qualified candidates. I also do it because some clients will fill the role using internal candidates they are planning to train and develop, and consistent naming will make it easier for them to identify the appropriate training for their candidates. Sometimes I may break a role into multiple roles if I expect that my client will have different resources who are going to perform the role's tasks. In that case, I get a little more creative with naming the roles.

After I have listed the roles and grouped their responsibilities within them, I then start mapping actual resources to each role. I usually do this in a table following the RACI chart that identifies named resources for each of the roles. In many cases, I have more than one resource to associate to a particular role. This is okay, and usually even preferred. With these cases, I will then identify a primary resource for the role who is ultimately responsible and who is the first point of contact for any of the activities related to the role. Usually this primary resource is the lead for a particular area that you have grouped into a single role. The rest are secondary and are the lead's delegates.

To start, I divide the service into different feature sets or capability areas. I begin this way because I like to group role tasks by similar features or functions to keep their overall responsibility efficient. This division helps when I want to delegate different parts of SharePoint to an administrator or another resource to manage. The more you divide your SharePoint service, then the easier and less complex it makes your process for setting the boundaries for a resource's area of responsibility.

▪ **Note**   For more on SharePoint features and capability areas, please see Chapter 3 where I discuss approaches for grouping features into capability areas.

You decide how granular you want to be with the feature sets or capability areas that you use to define your roles, and you base this mainly on how large and specialized you expect your team to be. On a large team with many specialized resources, you need a more granular listing of the different roles involved with providing the service, and this more granular list enables you to allocate resources to these more specialized roles. On the other hand, you might have a team of one, and in this case, you might not find it necessary to get overly granular with your list of roles because you are allocating a single resource to them all.

Even in the case of very small teams, I still prefer to list multiple roles and allocate resources to several roles. I try to avoid making a one-to-one relationship of roles and resources, or at least I avoid having the number of resources directly dictate the number of roles. There are several reasons for this, and one big reason is that I want to keep my role list flexible and easy to adapt as my team changes. Perhaps the team will grow and add additional team members later on, at which time I may redistribute the roles and areas of responsibility. However, my main reason is that I like to keep the roles granular because having several groupings of responsibilities are easier to manage and comprehend, for resource planning purposes and for the resource themselves.

How specialized you make your team depends on the scale of the service you are providing, and in addition, your team structure depends on how your organization typically organizes teams. Is your organization's culture one with specialized roles where resources have a narrow scope of responsibility, or does your organization prefer more generalized roles with resources who overlap and share responsibilities within a particular domain? Understanding this culture helps you to determine how granular and specialized you need to make your SharePoint service delivery team.

For our purposes, I will assume a modest size team with fewer, more generalized roles. This will keep the examples reasonably straightforward, yet with enough division of labor to help illustrate the concept of identifying roles and their responsibilities. I favor less specialized teams within a capability area where it makes sense, because this approach often helps maximize resource availability where one teammate can take over or relieve another to keep production moving forward. At the same time, I favor a defined list of responsibilities for every team member, and I always want to identify someone and only one person who will hold the ultimate responsibility.

This practice stems back to what I learned in business school about providing team members with a defined list of responsibilities. I remember my management theory and human resources classes, and one point they hammered home is that I should provide a job description to every resource so they will never have to guess at what their priorities should be. Now, like several things I learned in school, this does not always translate into what actually happens in practice, or at least it did not for many of the positions I have held. Yet, whenever I am in a position where I do have a defined list of my responsibilities, whether on a project team or an operations team, I feel more confident in my role and everything just seems to run smoother. Often times I have to define my own list of responsibilities, especially when I engage with a client for a new project delivery, and this gives me a feeling of clarity for my purpose and my objectives. It also gives me the confidence that everyone else shares the same understanding about what I am there to do and for what I am responsible.

One area I often perceive as an underlying reason for opposing this idea of listing responsibilities for each role seems to grow out of a general sense of not wanting to limit a resource. The idea as best as I can tell rests on a premise that a job description might influence a worker in a way that they adopt too narrow of a view of their responsibilities, where their worry is then that the worker would not step outside their own area to take any new initiative or help teammates. There almost seems to be a belief that if one leaves the job description open, then they might avoid constraining the worker's potential. Whether this philosophy is valid does not interest me as much, although I do not buy in to the idea that having a job description would constrain the attitudes and narrow the focus of team members. I find defining a list of responsibilities helps to avoid missing things or leading to situations where team members assume someone else will tend to something. It also gives resources a certain comfort level in clarity of what is expected of them.

I do not think of roles and responsibilities as necessarily a contract, but they do set implicit expectations for what activities need to occur. In this sense, I think of them more as a minimum, and they provide a measure about whether a team member meets their obligations on the team. In a performance evaluation, I would measure my team members against their responsibilities, and those areas where they miss responsibilities will provide me with an opportunity to look at how I can help them improve. Everything they do above these responsibilities serves to highlight where they are exceeding in their job function, which might include activities such as extra initiatives they have taken or cross group collaborations where they assisted a peer. By looking at and valuing these other measures of a resource exceeding expectations, I have found that having defined responsibilities only helps to facilitate this rather than acting as any sort of constraint. For instance, when high achievers know what is expected, they know where they can excel.

Better yet, this process identifies the skills required and it can serve as a career progression map. You might use the responsibility list to help you define what makes a senior resource versus an intermediate or junior resource. Team members can use it to help decide where to concentrate their learning and development activities, and they can base their career progression plan on these descriptions. As such, detailed descriptions of roles and responsibilities not only provide clarity on what you expect from resources today, but they also provide direction for career growth down the road.

If you define a list of responsibilities for a given role, then you are also providing direction and setting expectations for the resource or resources who you assign to that role. This is a recipe for a productive team, and ultimately it is a recipe for success. At this point, I hope I have succeeded with convincing you how valuable this exercise can be – so valuable in fact that I have dedicated an entire chapter to the topic! The biggest challenge I see people face with specifying the roles and responsibilities lies in their potential lack of depth with all the technical aspects within SharePoint. That is okay, because I will get you started. First, let's begin the discussion with those SharePoint specific resources, those whom are directly responsible for providing the SharePoint service.

Identifying Roles for Your SharePoint Service

There are some global roles involved in a SharePoint service, such as a general SharePoint administrator, SharePoint solution architect, and infrastructure architect. At its most basic level, the SharePoint administrator is a common role in most environments. This role might perform SharePoint central administration tasks, such as provisioning web applications and service applications, or it may include tasks such as installing service packs or solution packages.

The architects plan and design the solutions that the SharePoint service provides and the infrastructure it runs on. You might incorporate more application specific tasks as responsibilities for these roles as well, or you may break those out into separate roles based on different applications or capabilities.

Other core roles that are typically global across SharePoint include service desk and support roles. Your service desk might be a separate service from your SharePoint service, but at the very least, they might need some training or someone to write support articles for their knowledgebase. You might also include support escalation engineer roles, where the service desk can escalate service request tickets and have them provide a tier-two or tier-three level of support. Closely related to support, most deployments will also want to include training roles for your end-users to facilitate adoption and productive use of the SharePoint service. Another training role you might consider is one to provide training to the operations team so you can grow its capabilities.

▪ **Note**   See Chapter 5 where I discuss approaches to training and many aspects of activities that you might include as part of the responsibilities for your training roles.

As I mentioned earlier, a convenient area to start and define roles that are more specific begins with considering the capability areas. I like to break SharePoint 2013 into seven core capability areas: collaboration, social computing, portals, search, records management, business intelligence, and composite applications. These areas often provide a useful guide to start thinking about all the different roles I need. I like to start with each area and branch out to identify all the different roles involved with that particular area. Once I have a list and I am satisfied with how comprehensive it is, then I consider whether merging some roles will make more sense or be a better fit for the client I am working with.

The first capability in my list is collaboration, and at its very basic level, this can involve activities such as provisioning team sites or facilitating self-service provisioning, managing quotas, and administering permissions. I usually include this role in the generic SharePoint administrator role, particularly for deployments where these tasks are largely self-service. This role might also be the place where I assign basic SharePoint training or tier-two support responsibilities. For me, I often tend to represent the collaboration capability as the cornerstone of a SharePoint deployment, and because of this, I like to simplify the core roles I define within it.

THE SHAREPOINT CORNERSTONE

I actually used to refer to deploying the initial SharePoint deployment as the foundation deployment phase in a SharePoint delivery program, but I stopped when the product team renamed Windows SharePoint Services to SharePoint Foundation. Out of habit, I often still want to call that initial deployment the foundation phase, but I try not to because I worry it might lead to confusion with the SharePoint Foundation product edition. Instead, I now use synonyms such as the base deployment, or my favorite, the SharePoint *cornerstone*, and I use this to signal I am deploying the fundamentals that I will later build on.

Social computing encompasses another broad category, but for my purpose to define roles related to it, I will focus on the primary social features within SharePoint 2013. To provide and support social computing within SharePoint, I typically start by enabling user profiles, MySites, tags and ratings, and community sites. Some roles you might consider to manage these features include a profile administrator and a folksonomy manager. You might also consider a community manager or community evangelist roles you can use to facilitate communities of practice and seed the social interactions as part of you user adoption strategy.

WHAT IS A FOLKSONOMY?

A folksonomy is a type of system for classifying and organizing content. It does this through metadata that tags the content using a keyword. Folksonomies are similar to taxonomies in the sense that they both use metadata to classify and organize content, but they differ in how users define and apply the metadata. In folksonomies, end-users generate the keywords that they find relevant and they associate them with content in a loose, more organic fashion. In contrast, when using taxonomies, end-users select keywords from a predefined controlled vocabulary, and those keywords are often organized in a hierarchy of terms.

I discuss folksonomies and taxonomies in more detail in Chapter 15.

Portals typically serve as a gateway to other information and processes, or as a channel for communication. In this sense, a portal can include roles such as a communications manager and a content manager for publishing, and it can include an information architect to manage its structure and navigation. They also have a visual identity and style standards, which a brand manager can plan and manage. You might include other roles such as a graphics designer or illustrator, publisher, and a copyeditor, depending on the nature of your portal.

Search overlaps the other capabilities the most because it depends on them to provide content that the search engine will return in search results. Within the search service itself, it requires a search administrator to manage and tune the service, and a search analyst to analyze search queries and other usage reports to identify opportunities for improving the search experience and the value it delivers. Most search engines interface with other systems to index and include their content in search results and a part of planning which systems to interface with and crawl requires a search architect role to plan and design the search architecture.

Records management involves controlling the lifecycle of an organization's content. At the helm, you need a records manager who coordinates and manages policies applied to content stored within the records repository as well as other transitory content stored in other locations. A significant portion of records management entails classifying content, which requires roles such as a librarian or taxonomy manager to design the classification scheme. Another major component of records management involves compliance, and this can involve roles such as a compliance manager and legal analysts or advisors.

Business intelligence (BI) typically involves integrating or interfacing with a variety of data sources to query and report on the data they provide. This can involve developing data marts, data interfaces, and data transformations; these are all in addition to developing the business intelligence reports themselves. The roles that support the integration and data access typically involve a data architect and systems integrator. The BI developer roles typically handle the queries and data manipulation, while report designer roles design and build the BI reports.

Composite applications tend to involve activities that develop and customize an application to host within your SharePoint service. Often with these types of applications, you need a business analyst role to gather requirements and analyze the current business problem, and you need a solution architect role to design a solution. After you have a solution designed, you need roles to build and implement it, such as developers, user interface designers, and user experience designers. Finally, to ensure quality and stability, you need tester roles to verify the functionality, a release manager to control the release, and a system administrator to actually deploy the solution to an environment.

■ **Note**   See the chapters in Part IV, "Customizing the SharePoint Service" where I discuss roles related to customizing a SharePoint service in more depth.

Throughout this section, I looked at some typical roles that are specific to SharePoint and each of its capability areas. These roles should give you a running start as you define what roles you need and group different responsibilities within them. Yet, as I described earlier in this chapter, a SharePoint service depends on more than just the functionality within the software, and so it depends on more roles than just the ones related to its capability areas. Most notably, you may have noticed I did not include a SQL Server database administrator when I highlighted the core SharePoint roles such as the SharePoint administrator. I like to think of these as the roles the SharePoint service depends on, and I have broken those out into the next section.

Identifying Roles Your SharePoint Service Depends On

A SharePoint service can quickly grow complex as it interacts with different systems and acts as a central entry-point for data and processes on the network. It can morph into the glue that holds different enterprise systems together. Because it provides this service, you need to identify what all these different systems are and how the SharePoint service depends on them to fulfill its duties and deliver business value.

One of the first systems you will identify is one that every SharePoint farm depends on: SQL Server and the databases that support the SharePoint farm. In the previous section, I mentioned this idea of treating SQL Server as a service that SharePoint depends on. This may seem weird, because you can deploy SharePoint and SQL Server on the same server, and you can never configure and deploy SharePoint without SQL Server. You might wonder why I would not just include them together because they go together with such a non-negotiable dependence requirement. My main reason is to frame the right perception, because SQL Server is an enterprise system and it warrants you treating it as its own distinct enterprise application.

I am always surprised by how common it is for people to deploy SharePoint and SQL Server in a one-to-one relationship: they deploy a new SharePoint farm, so they also deploy a new SQL Server farm. Some people treat the two products almost as if they are the same product that goes together in a deployment, and this is just a misunderstanding or inexperience with the two products and how they relate to each other. This way of thinking often only leads to an unnecessary bloating of SQL Server deployments where you have an excessive number of SQL Server instances to manage. This has management and support costs, as well as licensing and hardware costs.

Let me clarify if something along the way has led you to believe you need one or more dedicated SQL Server instances for every SharePoint farm: you do not. You certainly may, depending on your expected load and your performance requirements, but it is not a requirement nor is it a set rule. It is easy to get caught up in that way of thinking though, because wherever you see hardware and software requirements for a SharePoint farm, almost inevitability they will also include details on the SQL Server requirements. They are just clarifying the minimum requirements for the database service that the SharePoint service will rely on.

In the spirit of thinking of SharePoint as a service, I also like to think of the underlying SQL Server database as a service the SharePoint service consumes. In consuming these services, I prefer to delegate providing and supporting that service to the database team, including letting them decide how best to allocate the SQL Server resources and optimize the service. You need to provision a number of databases and they require a certain level of hardware and system resources. You might need the database team to provide clustered databases, a frequent backup schedule, and different performance targets. These are all requirements from the database service, and they are parameters you can provide the database team to manage as you delegate the rest of the implementation details for them to manage. Even if the database people are on the same team as the SharePoint people, I still like to treat this as a separate service that SharePoint consumes.

▓ **Note**　Although I encourage you to treat SQL Server as a database service rather than assume that each SharePoint farm requires its own SQL Server instance, remember that you also will want to minimize any network latency between the SharePoint servers and SQL Server. If you are looking to centralize an enterprise database cluster for your SharePoint databases, you should aim to keep the network latency to less than 1 or 2 ms to optimize overall performance.

Once you capture your service's dependency on SQL Server, you next need to look at all the other systems the SharePoint service depends on. The easiest way to approach identifying all the systems SharePoint depends on is to start with your SharePoint service and work your way out from there. List all the different systems that it interfaces with, and note the data dependence and data flow. In this case, I adapt the famous phrase that Deep Throat supposedly whispered to reporter Bob Woodward to advise him on how to find the truth about U.S. President Nixon's Watergate scandal, "Follow the money." Follow the data, and you will find the truth about all the systems that your SharePoint service depends on.

To help follow the data back through the different systems, I use a data flow diagram to map out the flow of data in the enterprise. It is a tool that I find helpful for tracking the data and identifying all the system interfaces involved. These data flow diagrams provide a visual depiction of how data flows throughout the organization, illustrating what systems are involved with what data process. I have used basic flow charts to capture simple data flows, and I have used formal data flow diagrams (DFD) with proper DFD notations. Use whatever diagram format that communicates the best for your audience.

A data flow diagram can support data analysis and it can ultimately help lead to an even more valuable tool for understanding the enterprise data architecture, a data dictionary. These provide a look-up reference that documents and defines every data field in a system, or ideally, across the entire enterprise. Obviously documenting an extensive list of data fields can be a monumental undertaking and a tedious task, but once that information is available in a data dictionary its value quickly becomes apparent. I discuss the idea of creating a data dictionary in Chapter 15.

Throughout this chapter, I pointed out several enterprise systems that your SharePoint service might depend on, and one is your identity management system, such as your Active Directory environment and all of its domain information. Your profile data and authentication process may depend on Active Directory or a custom forms-based authentication application. You may allow SharePoint sites to provision Exchange mailboxes, or you may depend on Exchange or another e-mail service in other ways to provide communication capabilities. These are all enterprise applications your SharePoint service may depend on, and if so, you need to include the applications in your list of what your SharePoint service depends on.

Your security solution might depend on firewalls and proxy servers to secure requests and protect the SharePoint environment. You might depend on a virtual private network (VPN) service where users can securely access the SharePoint service remotely from the public internet outside your corporate network. There are other services related to handling access to SharePoint that you might depend on. For instance, you may have several SharePoint web front-end servers to process requests, and they may depend on a network load-balancing (NLB) service to balance and route the requests among the SharePoint servers. Again, these may be services that you need to include in your list of services your SharePoint service depends on.

Once you have identified all the external services on which your SharePoint service depends, you then identify the roles within each of those services and the tasks grouped within those. You might get this list from the teams directly, if they already have one, or you may have to do some analysis to identify all their different roles in the same fashion as you used to identify the SharePoint roles.

I have now identified all the roles involved in providing a SharePoint service, both those directly involved on the SharePoint service operations and those providing services that the SharePoint service depends on. Now that you have all these roles, you need to link them to the tasks that each is responsible for performing. My favorite tool to accomplish this linking of roles and responsibilities is to create a roles and responsibility matrix, and I create this matrix as a RACI chart. In the next section, I give you an overview on the RACI model and what a RACI chart is, and then I share a few sample RACI charts to help get you started.

Using a RACI Chart

At its core, a RACI chart consists of a roles and responsibilities matrix. I find RACI charts incredibly useful on any team, whether you use them to chart roles on a project delivery team or those roles within an operations team, they add clarity and set expectations for different activities you depend on. Despite its simplicity, a RACI chart is powerful because it organizes activities and the resources who need to be involved, and it communicates this at a glance. It also helps you ensure you have coverage for all the activities you have planned.

There are six basic elements to a RACI chart, which is a grid that relates roles in columns with tasks in rows. The first element is the roles, as I mentioned, and you allocate them each in a column in the RACI chart. The second element captures all the tasks and lists them in rows going down the RACI chart. The final four elements specify the relationship between the role and task where the column intersects with the row. You specify this relationship between the roles and the tasks by using the four letters, R-A-C-I, and placing the appropriate letter in the intersecting cell. Your choice of which letter to place in the cell corresponds to the following criteria:

- R: Responsibility. This identifies the role who will perform the work. There must be exactly one "R" in every row, ensuring that every task has a role and only one role responsible for the work to accomplish the task.

- A: Accountable. This identifies the role who is ultimately accountable for completing the work or making a decision. There may be zero or one "A" in every row, and you should only use it for key tasks or decisions where the role responsible for the task is different from the role who holds ultimate accountability for it.

- C: Consulted. This identifies the role or roles who must be consulted with before completing a task or making a decision. Each task does not need to include a "C" but it can have more than one, as appropriate.

- I: Informed. This identifies the role or roles who must be informed after completing a task or making a decision. Each task does not need to include an "I" but it can have more than one, as appropriate.

Using this description of the roles and how they map to tasks, you can see how RACI charts define clear ownership of tasks and what communication is required for each. I find having both the clear ownership and communication expectations are aspects that are invaluable on any team, and both of these aspects together are at the essence of a RACI chart. I discussed the idea of roles and their responsibilities, and I hope you will see how a RACI chart can help you capture this information in a simple yet clear chart. At the same time, another aspect of the RACI chart involves the other half of the letters: consulted and informed. The main difference between consulted and informed is how a role is consulted as part of the task and that role then has the opportunity to weigh in and influence the activity or decision, whereas a role is informed after the activity or decision completes to keep them in the loop and up to date.

A RACI chart ensures everyone involved in a project delivery or an operations service delivery are all on the same page – literally and figuratively. The physical page allows you to use the chart to ensure you included all the roles involved and you have defined what the expectations are for each role and task. It captures everyone and their activities or involvement in a single place that helps to establish a clear and shared understanding about who is responsible for what.

A TEAM DELIVERING WITHOUT INDECISION OR HESITATION

RACI charts are great organizing tools because they list everyone involved and all the tasks that one needs to address. Overall, they just feel like a great team artifact in and of themselves because they document so much information about a team and its objectives. At their simplest, they are a means for presenting how the roles relate and map to their responsibilities, which is valuable enough, but they reveal their true value with how a team begins to function when they adopt the RACI model.

A roles and responsibilities matrix makes every aspect crystal clear for what a team member's tasks, decisions, and communication expectations are. It shows whom they depend on and what everyone else is in charge of working on. The result is a RACI chart that gives a team direction and team members know what to work on and what they will work on next. It allows them to continue without having to stop and wonder what they should work on next.

In addition to knowing their own areas of responsibility, they also know their teammates' areas. As a result, they do not have to stop and wonder who should respond to a job. I picture having a RACI chart organizing the team is something like having a couple of outfielders in a baseball game coordinating who is going for the ball and will make the catch. If they both run and try to catch the pop-fly ball, they are going to run in to each other as they both run to where the ball is going while looking up at it, and neither is probably going to make the catch. However, if one calls out that he or she has got the ball, they declare their responsibility and the other backs off and allows them to make the catch.

Just like how declaring responsibilities in baseball helps to avoid a collision and removes an outfielder's hesitation from going for the catch, so too will a RACI chart help avoid collisions on your team as the RACI model relieves indecision and hesitation among team members.

You can make a RACI chart in several formats, from informal accounts to formal documentation. For instance, you can write your roles and responsibilities matrix on a whiteboard in a team war room where everyone on the team can see it, and you can even use this to track progress through the project as tasks are completed and communication occurs. You might find this is a nice informal approach that still keeps the team aware of who is responsible for what task and what communication. For me, this is one of my favorite approaches to track a project because it keeps the chart constantly visible for everyone and it is easy to keep updated. I can also watch my task burn down progress as tasks are completed and communication occurs. It morphs into a whiteboard reflection of a functional and effective team.

Another approach you might use to create your RACI charts includes using an Excel spreadsheet or a table in a Word document. Both make formatting and printing a RACI chart straightforward. You can print them, e-mail them to the team, or post the files on a SharePoint site. You can also use a SharePoint task list to create a RACI chart by adding columns to the task list. I like to change the caption of the "Assigned To" column and update it to become the "Responsible" column. I then add an "Accountable" column, a "Consulted" column, and an "Informed" column. I make the Responsible column a required field and limit it to a single person, and I leave the rest of the columns optional, with the Accountable column limited to a single person and the other two unlimited. You can then associate workflows and different views on the task list, set dependencies, add additional notes, and even import the list into Microsoft Project 2013 and then save any changes back to the SharePoint task list. Although I prefer the simplicity and visibility from having my RACI chart on a whiteboard, there are times where I do appreciate some of these added features that SharePoint 2013 and Project 2013 provide, particularly for larger project teams or projects with a lot of cross team dependencies.

■ **Note**　For more details on using a SharePoint 2013 task list to host your RACI chart and to import it into Microsoft Project 2013, please see a blog post I wrote where I describe some of these features:
`http://stevegoodyear.wordpress.com/2012/08/27/`

The best way to understand a RACI chart is often to look at a sample. In the next section, I provide sample RACI charts for an initial SharePoint project delivery, and in a later section, I provide samples for a SharePoint service operations team. Pay particular attention to how I have included communication aspects in addition to the responsibilities of tasks. Remember, these are merely samples to give you somewhere to start and help clarify how a RACI chart works and why I find it so useful and valuable. As such, please do not get too caught up in the specifics of what roles I selected and what tasks I included, and instead focus on how the RACI chart works and the value it adds to a team. My discussions in the other sections of this chapter will help you identify the roles and tasks to include in your own RACI chart.

Sample SharePoint Deployment RACI Charts

In this section, I share several sample RACI charts to help get you started with constructing your own RACI chart. I usually create separate charts for an initial SharePoint project delivery and for ongoing operations of a SharePoint service, but I do not always break down the charts into a series of smaller and more discrete charts such as the ones you will find in this section. The reason I did it here was primarily to fit the pages of the book and keep it accessible for you to read and comprehend. I wanted to contain a chart so it did not span several pages because I thought containing it might make it easier for you to follow and interpret. You are welcome to make larger charts if you prefer, even charts so large that you need a plotter printer to print them.

Another aspect of the following sample RACI charts that I want to make you aware of is how I abbreviate the roles in the chart and then provide a legend in a chart footnote. I have done this to make efficient use of the space I have available for all the content I want to fit in this book. I abbreviate the roles and keep my columns narrow in the samples that follow, so just remember to cross-reference the abbreviations with a legend in the chart's footnote area.

First, I want to start with a sample RACI chart that I might use for a project team delivering the initial SharePoint service. For this sample, let's imagine a scenario where you have a project team who will perform an install of SharePoint, configure the farm, establish web applications for a search portal and MySites, configure a search and user profile service applications, and through the process they will conduct knowledge transfer with the client's SharePoint administrator.

For this example, I am going to simplify the client roles you include in the RACI chart to only include those who will be directly involved with the project team's delivery. I am including the client's SharePoint administrator because they are going to be hands-on and shadow several of the project team's activities to cross-pollinate knowledge and ensure knowledge transfer from the project delivery team to the client. For all the other client roles, I am including the client project manager who I will designate as accountable for any client task and delegate the task for them to manage and resource on the client's side. Finally, I include a generic client resource column to assign responsibility for those client tasks that I delegate accountability for to the client's project manager.

My project delivery team consists of a project manager (Proj. M), a SharePoint architect (SP Arch), and a SharePoint infrastructure specialist (SP Infra). The team delivers to the client and works closely with the client resources. The SharePoint infrastructure specialist works closely with the client's SharePoint administrator (C. SP), and they work on their tasks without involving the project team except when they check-in at key milestones. I also include a client project manager (C. PM) and a generic client role. In Table 4-1, I illustrate a sample RACI chart for this project team's roles and responsibilities.

Table 4-1. *A sample RACI chart for an initial SharePoint delivery project team*

Tasks/Activities	Proj. M	SP Arch	SP Infra	C. SP	C. PM	Client
Provision servers (2 WFE)	I				A	R
Configure NLB for WFE servers	I				A	R
Copy install media to servers	I				A	R
Create DNS hostname entries for web apps	I				A	R
Create AD accounts for service accounts	I				A	R
Identify availability or provision SQL DB cluster	I				A	R
Grant DB permissions for service accounts	I				A	R
Project kick-off meeting	R	C	C	C	C	
Design and document farm architecture	I	R	I			
Install SharePoint 2013 on WFE servers	I		R	C	I	
Provision search service and application			R	C		
Provision MySite service and application			R	C		
Configure user profile service application			R	C		
Configure search service application			R	C		
Configure and schedule user profile import			R	C		
Configure and schedule search crawling			R	C		
Test search and MySite applications	I	I	R	C	I	
Project close-out meeting	R	C	C	C	C	

R=Responsible; A=Accountable; C=Consulted; I=Informed Proj. M=Project Manager; SP Arch=SharePoint Architect; SP Infra= SharePoint Infrastructure Specialist; C.SP=Client SharePoint Administrator; C.PM=Client Project Manager; Client=general undefined client role

Notice how I assigned several tasks for the client to accomplish ahead of the project kick-off meeting. I often assign tasks and provide clients with a checklist of action items that I need them to work through ahead of us kicking off an engagement. I find this helps give them direction on how to prepare, and it helps ensure that they make my time effective and efficient when I engage and the project takes flight. A RACI chart provides a great format to communicate these tasks and to accomplish delegating the activities I need a client to complete, but I also use a simple checklist much like the format of those I include in the appendix of this book.

This sample RACI chart includes granular tasks that you otherwise might roll up into a summary task. You may or may not create your RACI charts with this level of granularity, depending on your preference and what level of detail you prefer for your task list. I always leave the client tasks specified at a very granular level because these are activities I am delegating to them, therefore I would rather err on the side of caution and be as detailed as possible to avoid having them misinterpret the task or miss a crucial piece. My preference is to leave the other tasks as granular as they need to be to identify the single role responsible and the discrete activity area. So in this example, I may have grouped the tasks that relate to provisioning and configuring that the SharePoint infrastructure specialist is responsible for, and summarized those activities in just one or two tasks. However, at the same time, having the activities broken out into that much detail does not bother me and can be quite useful for guiding resources step-by-step and for estimating effort required to complete those tasks.

In the next sample RACI chart in Table 4-2, I am going to add a little complexity to the project and the roles involved. I am going to pretend that you are engaging with a client to analyze one of their paper-based business processes to replace it with an InfoPath form and custom developed workflow solution. I include roles for the project manager (Proj. M), business analyst (BA), solutions architect (Arch), forms designer (Form), developer (Dev), and the client.

Table 4-2. *A sample RACI chart for an InfoPath Forms development project team*

Tasks/Activities	Proj. M	BA	Arch	Form	Dev	Client
Design project plan	R	C	C	C	C	I
Observe existing business process		R				C
Interview sample of knowledge workers		R				C
Analyze existing business process	I	R	I			
Envision solution concept		C	R			
Architect and design solution	I	C	R	I	I	
Mockup solution user interface		C	R	I		
Diagram solution workflow		R	C		I	
Build InfoPath forms				R	I	
Develop workflow activities				I	R	
Deploy solution package to test environment	I			C	R	
Conduct integration and functional testing	I	R		C	C	
Conduct user acceptance testing	I	C				R
Stabilize and resolve form issues	I	C		R		
Stabilize and resolve workflow issues	I	C			R	
Release solution	I	I	I	C	R	I

R=Responsible; A=Accountable; C=Consulted; I=Informed Proj. M=Project Manager; BA=Business Analyst; Arch= Solution Architect; Form=InfoPath Form Designer; DEV=Workflow developer; Client= undefined client knowledge worker roles

I kept this example contained and simplified to illustrate the basic flow of tasks and one approach to mapping responsibility for them to different roles. This provides you with an example that addresses some of the different phases of a custom development without having so many tasks where they consume you and leave you lost in the details. I also limited the roles to save space and not crowd the RACI chart on this book's page, such as where I have the workflow developer who also takes responsibility for deployments and where I only included a generic client role. Normally I would include a release manager and actual quality assurance roles rather than consolidate these functions, but I hope this sample provides you with an example for how you can use a RACI chart to organize your projects and your project teams.

RACI charts feel like a natural fit for project teams, as they take work breakdown structures and transform them into a roles and responsibilities matrix. Their value does not stop there though. All the good they do for creating a highly functional and an efficient project team can transpose to the operations team. Adopting the RACI model for your operations team provides the same benefits as it does for a project team, except with an ongoing and operational focus. They still help to ensure coverage, and they still communicate to everyone who is responsible for what. In the next section, I apply the same concepts that I used for a project team and provide RACI chart samples for an operations team.

Sample SharePoint Operations RACI Charts

Once SharePoint moves from a project delivery into ongoing operations, you need a different RACI chart. You need a RACI chart to outline the roles of the operations team and the regular activities in their ongoing operations. In this section, I provide a few different samples to help get you started.

I am going to start with a simple example in Table 4-3 of a RACI chart that identifies the roles and responsibilities in a service request process. You might include a RACI chart like this with the service request process discussed in Chapter 2. This provides a complete picture of how the process operates, as well as a detailed account of who is responsible for what in the process. I include roles for the service desk (SD), SharePoint administrator (SP Adm), SharePoint infrastructure specialist (SP Infra), support escalation engineer (EE), vendor support services, and the end-user knowledge worker.

Table 4-3. *A sample RACI chart for a service request process*

Tasks/Activities	SD	SP Adm	SP Infra	EE	Vendor	User
Open a new service request ticket	I					R
Respond to tier one routine requests	R					C
Escalate tier two application incidents	R	I				I
Respond to tier two application incidents		R				C
Escalate tier two infrastructure incidents	R		I			I
Respond to tier two infrastructure incidents			R			C
Escalate tier three support incidents	R	I	I	I		I
Respond to tier three support incidents		C	C	R		C
Escalate critical incident to product vendor	I	I	I	R	I	I
Respond to critical support incident		C	C	A	R	C
Resolve and close service request ticket	R					I

R=Responsible; A=Accountable; C=Consulted; I=Informed SD=Service Desk; SP Adm=SharePoint Administrator; SP Infra= SharePoint Infrastructure Specialist; EE=Support Escalation Engineer; Vendor=Vendor Support Services; User=general undefined knowledge worker

This example of the roles and responsibilities in a service request process also gave me a change to make a role accountable for a task but not responsible. You may have noticed the "A" in the second last row. This row communicates that the vendor support services will hold responsibility for carrying out the task, as their support resources will respond to the incident and troubleshoot the service request. However, I assigned the oversight and accountability to the escalation engineer. I did this to keep formal ownership of the ticket within the internal support team even though an external team is leading the actual work toward a resolution.

A process diagram does a great job at communicating the tasks and how they flow from one task to another throughout a service request process. It offers a nice summary view and it illustrates how the different tasks or steps relate to each other. A RACI chart complements this information by adding in details on who is responsible for what. The RACI chart also highlights the communication that needs to take place and who else needs to be involved. Just look at how informed I keep the end-user knowledge workers as team members constantly update them on the progress of their service request.

In the next sample RACI chart in Table 4-4, I provide an example of some of the infrastructure roles involved with the SharePoint service operations. I am going to focus this example on coordinating activities related to disk space, which involves roles from other services that the SharePoint service depends on. For this sample, I take just a subset of backup and restore activities to highlight the communication and coordination of tasks among these different services and roles. I include roles for the SharePoint administrator (SP Adm), SharePoint infrastructure specialist (SP Infra), SQL Server database administrator (DBA), SAN storage disk administrator (SAN), backup administrator (BU), and virtual machine administrator (VM).

Table 4-4. *A sample RACI chart for infrastructure roles involved with SharePoint service operations*

Tasks/Activities	SP Adm	SP Infra	DBA	SAN	BU	VM
Recover document from site recycling bin	R					
Restore site collection	R					
Schedule backups of Machine.Config and Application.Config		R			I	
Restore Machine.Config and Application.Config	I	R				
Schedule SharePoint database backups	C		R	I	C	
Restore SharePoint databases	C		R		I	
Test and validate database restore process	I		R			
Schedule virtual machine server state backups	I	C		I	C	R
Restore virtual machine server state	C	C		C	I	R
Test virtual machine restore process	I	I				R
Schedule capturing backups to tape	I		C	I	R	C
Recall backups from tape	I		I	I	R	I
Manage off-site backup storage process					R	
Manage available disk space for backups	C		C	R	C	C

R=Responsible; A=Accountable; C=Consulted; I=Informed SP Adm=SharePoint Administrator; SP Infra= SharePoint Infrastructure Specialist; DBA=SQL Server Administrator SAN=SAN Storage Disk Administrator; BU=Backup Administrator; VM=Virtual Machine Administrator

You can see the different activities and the different roles responsible for them, and yet again, you can see the communication that coordinates each of the activities for the different roles that depend on the task or have its outcome affect them. For instance, the SAN disk administrator needs to plan the amount of disk space needed to meet the demands for their disk storage service in any of the backup activities, and therefore he or she needs the other resources to inform them or consult with them on any key backup and restore activity that impacts storage. You can identify who is responsible for what, and just as importantly, what coordination and communication you need.

In the final sample RACI chart in Table 4-5, I provide an example of an application within the SharePoint service. A popular application is a corporate portal, and it makes a great example because it incorporates a variety of roles from within the organization, users who interact with and manage the application without any direct IT involvement. For this example, I cover a series of tasks that a typical portal might include in its process of publishing corporate communications within an organization. I include roles for the communications manager (Comm), copyeditor (Edit), content manager (CM), information architect (IA), branding manager (BM), and graphics designer (GD).

Table 4-5. *A sample RACI chart for roles involved in a portal application*

Tasks/Activities	Comm	Edit	CM	IA	BM	GD
Define brand and style standards	C		C	C	R	C
Design corporate portal user interface	C		C	C	C	R
Design or touch-up portal images	I		I			R
Manage portal styles						R
Design portal site structure	C		C	R		I
Design portal navigation structure	C		C	R		I
Write portal corporate communications	R	I	I			
Edit corporate communications	C	R	I			
Publish corporate communications	C		R			
Manage aggregating web parts on portal pages	I		R	C		
Manage information web parts on portal pages	C		R			
Manage other portal content storage	I		R	C		
Manage user input forms on portal			R	C		
Configure portal permission rights	C		R			
Configure content deployment schedule	C		R	I		

R=Responsible; A=Accountable; C=Consulted; I=Informed Comm=Communications Manager; Edit=Copyeditor; CM=Content Manager; IA=Information Architect; BM=Brand Manager; GD=Graphics Designer/Illustrator

This example provides a snapshot of some popular roles involved in a portal and the tasks that they are responsible for completing. You may have additional roles or you may use different role names, and you probably have more tasks involved, but the idea is the same. You have roles responsible for how the portal looks, how it is structured, what content is published, and the polishing of that content. These roles all have to coordinate their tasks and coordinate how they hand off work for the next role to complete their tasks. We could even use a RACI chart such as the one in this example to design and develop a custom publishing workflow that enforces all the responsibilities and automates some of the communications.

Sadly, I only have a limited number of pages in this book to fit in all these ideas, and so I have to limit my samples. I also think that the RACI charts start to become repetitive after a few examples, and therefore I do not want to bore you with too many repetitive examples. Instead, I want to provide you with just enough examples to get you started with creating your own RACI chart to fit your operations team. Otherwise, I could end up writing the entire book on RACI charts. As you can probably tell by how passionate I am about RACI charts, you can guess that is a book I would enjoy writing! For now, I have this chapter for you with these samples that you can use to introduce the RACI model to your team.

These samples are just that, samples to help get you started. Think of them as a working template that you can build off, with some roles and responsibility information already seeded to give you a head start. You can adjust which role holds the responsibility for a given task and which roles you want informed or consulted for the task. You can add additional tasks and additional roles, and you can start fine-tuning the RACI model to fit your organization and your SharePoint service team. In the next section, I give you some considerations you can use when adapting these samples and the RACI model for your team.

Adapting the Sample RACI Charts

I have provided you with a great start. Your next step is to start your own RACI chart and add all your roles that you need to provide your SharePoint service, both the direct SharePoint roles and all the ones that the service depends on. After you have added your roles across the chart, you need to add all the tasks and decisions down the chart. Once you have your roles and responsibilities laid out, your next job is to map them to each other.

One important point that I want to stress is that the sample RACI charts I share in this chapter are not golden rules for how you have to organize your team. Take them as an example, but tweak them to fit your organization. Use them to judge the level of detail you want, and think about all of the service areas you want to establish a RACI chart to cover. You can make a series of small, relatively contained charts, much like the samples that I shared in this chapter, or you can consolidate them into one or just a few charts.

If you are starting with a project for an initial cornerstone SharePoint delivery, then start with creating a RACI chart for the project team. Do not list out your roles based on the resources you currently have allocated to the project. Instead, build a list of tasks and define your roles based on a logical grouping of tasks. This slight change in perspective makes all the difference in capturing a RACI chart that reflects what you need rather than one that you constrain based on what you have. It also lends well to help you focus on all the required tasks rather than just the ones that individual resources are working on, and this helps ensure that you have coverage.

Once you identify the roles in your project team, or if you are starting with addressing an existing SharePoint service, it is time to build an operations RACI chart. You need this to incorporate the activities of the core SharePoint team in providing the service. You also need to capture all the activities from other teams that the SharePoint service depends on. This helps you to build out a complete picture of all the roles and their responsibilities that you have involved with your SharePoint service.

As you identify systems that your SharePoint service depends on, you continue to dig deeper and identify the different roles involved and what tasks they need to accomplish to provide the appropriate level of service to your SharePoint farm. This can be a lengthy process, and it takes time to uncover and capture everything that is involved, but the payoff is big.

Once you have your tasks and your roles, the next obvious step is to begin mapping responsibilities and communication expectations in your roles and responsibilities matrix. At this point, you will have a detailed RACI chart or charts, and you will have an incredible amount of valuable information that will support and drive the rest of your activities. However, you still do not have any named resources allocated to any of the roles, and no one holding any of the responsibilities for any of the tasks.

After you have done all that other work in the RACI model, it is time to look at what resources you actually have and start to allocate them to one or more of the roles. Roles do not equal job titles; they are just a description I use in the RACI chart to group a number of tasks within a common function. It is fine to have one resource span multiple roles, but if you struggle with two resources directly overlapping in responsibility or accountability for roles, then maybe you need to make either the role more granular or break down the task into a set of more detailed tasks. You can allocate two or more resources to a single role, but you can only identify one resource as the primary for the role, which is the resource who is ultimately responsible. Typically, in this case, you would identify the lead for a role and their backups if you were allocating resources on a large enough team with many redundant team members.

I usually have a resource list that maps each to their respective roles at the bottom of the RACI chart, or as an attachment. You can make this as a simple table with a named resource listed in one column and their roles in another. Alternatively, you may want to map job titles or formal workforce positions to the roles and use this for your workforce planning and job descriptions. I do not mind either way and have used both, but I find mapping to workforce positions rather than named individuals avoids having to amend the table when people change jobs. Other bits of information I often like to include in this table includes contact information, working hours, supervisor(s), and who fills in as their backup.

Having all this information laid out in a chart makes it easy to also ensure that you have end-to-end coverage, especially if you built your RACI chart by starting with the tasks your service needs to accomplish rather than with looking at the resources you have available and what they do. In the next section, I discuss this idea of ensuring end-to-end coverage in more detail.

Ensuring End-to-End Coverage

Coverage can mean support coverage, delivery coverage, or service coverage. Essentially, it looks at whether you considered and incorporated everything necessary to provide the overall purpose behind all the tasks in your RACI chart. You can use coverage as a means to look at where you over-allocated resources and where you have gaps.

The first step you need to take is to ensure that you have included all the tasks and the roles in the process. This involves a closer look at your RACI chart, and often you can discover where you omitted tasks or roles by having your team review the RACI chart and provide feedback. You can also have someone like a business analyst audit the RACI chart to validate that it incorporates all the tasks and roles. Once you are reasonably confident that your RACI chart includes all the necessary details, the rest of the process is easier and relatively straightforward for ensuring end-to-end coverage.

Next, you need to go through each row and ensure that each task has one and only one role specified as being responsible for the task. This ensures that you have coverage with a role identified as responsible for every task. In the process, you also need to ensure that each task has the appropriate roles identified to consult and inform, as well as any role who holds accountability for the task but is not responsible for performing the work on the task. Once you are satisfied with the coverage in your roles and responsibilities matrix, you are ready to ensure resource coverage.

You map resources to roles, so through this, you can ensure coverage by validating that every role has a resource allocated to it. You need to look beyond just whether or not you mapped a resource to a role though, because if a resource is over allocated or not available during some hours that you need them, then you have a gap. You can determine how utilized a resource is by determining what proportion of their time and how much of their time that they spend on each of the tasks or each of the roles you allocate them to. If you find you are not satisfied with the amount of time a resource can spend on the tasks of a role, then you may have over allocated that resource.

The working hours of a resource indicate what hours he or she provides coverage, and so if there is only one resource allocated to a role or all the resources maintain the same working hours, then your coverage for a particular role is limited to those working hours. There may be off-hour exceptions, but these are exceptions and not the standard coverage times, otherwise utilizing resources during their off-hours provides another indicator of over allocation, and therefore would not be a sustainable coverage plan.

Not every service requires around the clock coverage, so if you are limited to a resource's working hours then that can be perfectly acceptable in many cases. The point is to go through this process and be aware of what your coverage window is, and if this meets the window for the service level that you want to provide, then you have coverage. If it does not meet the window that you want to provide, then you have gaps.

Building out a RACI chart solidifies the coverage of your team, whether that is a temporary project team or an ongoing operations team. It helps to understand the expectations around what your team needs to deliver and where each team member contributes toward the overall delivery. It also identifies communication requirements among the different roles, which can be formal or informal, depending on your needs and the needs for the task involved. In the next section, I cover some considerations and approaches to establish formal communication protocols.

Formalizing Your Communication Protocols

Your RACI charts identify some types of communication that need to occur, with expectations for resources to consult or inform other resources on their activities and decisions. What form should that communication take? In some cases, the form that a particular communication requires is probably evident or is fine to leave to the discretion of the resource performing the task. In other cases though, you might want to formalize what form this communication must take and what its process must be.

SharePoint and other ticket management systems do a good job handling formal communications and automating the processes around them. In one approach, you can design a workflow to implement your formal communication protocols and associate that with certain tasks in SharePoint. Your service request ticketing system might also provide workflow capabilities that allow you to follow a formal communication procedure. A workflow, as in both of these examples, can automate some of the communication, but they can also enforce the procedure and capture an audit history.

You could use a workflow procedure for tasks related to approval decisions and change management processes. This ensures that you involve everyone who needs to be involved. The workflow makes the procedure for these types of tasks largely routine and systematic, and it remains consistent from one instance performing the task to the next.

Creating a workflow and standardizing the communication protocol within it sounds like a nice solution, and it is, but it is probably overkill to implement this solution for every task. For some task communication, you may opt for just an informal e-mail or a team meeting. You might use this communication technique for those tasks that do not require approvals or similar types of formality. Remember, formalizing the communication protocol does not necessarily mean you need to formalize the communication channel; you can use an informal channel such as e-mail with some guidelines around when to send the e-mail and to whom.

Your communication requirements may extend beyond a small group of roles related to your task, and it could even involve mass communication to the entire organization. For example, in a support RACI chart, one of your tasks might relate to informing the organization about a planned outage for system maintenance or upgrades. You can take one of several approaches to notifying the organization, and one of those might be to send out a mass e-mail to everyone with the details that you wish to communicate.

Another option for handling mass communication requirements of this nature could include adding a message to the portal ahead of time to announce the planned outage. You may publish a news article to the portal or use a standard announcement list and web part, or you could create your own web part for mass communication alerts of this type and include that on all of your site master pages. This way, when you do post an alert, all those web part instances will subscribe to the alert message and display a notification on each SharePoint page so that users are likely to see it and be aware of its content.

During the actual maintenance period, you could also set up a temporary web redirection to a page that explains the maintenance occurring and when you expect to restore service. I use this process of enabling a temporary web redirection to these types of maintenance notification pages to provide users with information during planned maintenance windows and during unplanned outages. Providing this type of communication can often help reduce the number of service request tickets that users open while the service is unavailable.

Creating a Service Level Agreement

A service level agreement (SLA) typically involves a formal agreement between the service delivery provider and the service consumer, and it includes topics such as the terms of the service, minimum availability, and expected performance levels. In Chapter 2 I briefly touched on the idea of an SLA and I discussed topics that are relevant for you to include in an SLA, especially those related to defining your SharePoint service boundaries, service request process and prioritization, and chargeback-funding models.

You will find useful aspects in every chapter in this book that you might want to include in your SLA, but Chapter 2 combined with this chapter provide the fundamentals of an effective SLA. While Chapter 2 covers the bounds of what the service entails, this chapter covers who provides and supports that service. You can use these chapters, as well as the others in this book, to guide you in making decisions about what you want to incorporate in an SLA for your organization, and you can take and adapt the topics that fit with the degree of formality you need to capture.

Often an SLA is an agreement between an IT department and decision makers from the business. It serves as a contract between those providing the service and those consuming the service and it defines the official policies and procedures involved with the service operations. An SLA can be strictly formal and bureaucratic, particularly in cases where it may need a lot of formality such as when a business unit depends on it for its own business operations. Indeed, this uncovers the purpose of an SLA: it defines the level of service that a customer can depend on and consume with confidence, and without having to get involved with any contingency details or any complexity around how the service might perform at different times. The SLA commits to a consistent and minimum level of service that the customer can rely on, while they trust and delegate to the service provider to worry about any contingencies to maintaining that level of service.

To gain this trust and build the confidence to rely on your service, this may require a formal and even contractual agreement that you both sign and establish as a commitment together. When you both commit to an agreement and to each other, you need to make the relationship and expectations official, and this can mean working through many details as you find common ground. Throughout the process leading up to an agreement, you will likely find a lot of effort goes into working through the details and finding that common ground. Your agreement has to represent both the service provider and service consumer, and any process that has to reconcile interests from two or more parties will always involve trade-offs and compromises. You negotiate towards balance and a settlement for an SLA that works to address everyone's essential requirements.

Your negotiations will involve more effort working toward common ground as you increase the number of people included in the process and the different interests they represent. It can be a lengthy process where you address many different aspects of a service and comb through minute details involved in the service. Depending on the significance of your agreement, you may need an exhaustive account of every aspect of the service and address every expectation. You may require extensive text detailing different aspects of your service within your SLA, because you cannot leave grey areas in contracts that people depend on or else you could quickly find that this leads to misunderstandings and possibly even disputes – exactly the types of things you are trying to avoid and mitigate with an SLA.

Not every organization will be at a stage where you can introduce a formal SLA. Your service delivery team might not be mature enough in its processes to be at a point where you can commit to a certain service standard, or your organization might not be familiar enough with their own needs to feel comfortable enough with committing to a certain service level. Everyone may just be anxious with making any sort of formal commitment. They might worry that a formal agreement will introduce rigid processes that make IT unresponsive to change, or they may just worry about whether they have thought of everything.

This worry or resistance against a formal commitment can obstruct your ability to establish an SLA, and I find this type of reluctance toward an SLA is very common. You can address everyone's uneasiness through techniques such as working in contingencies for changes, agreeing to a time limit or a trial period, gradually amending the SLA to cover additional areas rather than making it comprehensive for the service all at once. Even after hedging the SLA with these types of techniques, you may still face some resistance. Perhaps your customer lacks any interest for even going through the process or for committing to a service level. Perhaps you are just not comfortable enough yet with what service level you can provide and maintain.

Whatever the blocker to establishing a formal service level agreement, if you want to establish something of this nature regardless of whether it is formally agreed to, then one solution is to consider a service level objective (SLO). A colleague of mine, Arlene, suggested this to me years ago when we were working on an SLA initiative and found ourselves lacking enough involvement from the business to really consider the output as an agreement. Instead, we treated the entire process the same, but we called it an objective we targeted and against which we held ourselves accountable. The business was disinterested with getting involved with negotiating any service levels or committing to an SLA, so we made our best efforts putting a stake in the ground to define our service levels and to then hold ourselves accountable against them.

Documenting a Governance Plan

Throughout this book, I have left any formal governance documentation up to your own discretion, and I will leave the formality of your service level agreement (SLA) documents up to you as well. Some people swear by the need for a documented governance plan and they slot this on the critical path as one of the first things you need to do, making a blanket claim that they suggest should cover every case. I am not opposed to this nor am I saying it is wrong. I am merely suggesting that you first ask the question: is extensive documentation the most effective approach and optimum solution for the current situation you face?

Every situation is different, and every organization has their own comfort level for how formal they need to record things. Some relate governance to some sort of bureaucracy, maybe because "governance" sounds like "government" and governments can infamously involve a lot of bureaucracy. This can be valid if it fits an organization's situation and it works for them, but at its essence, SharePoint governance embodies the actions and manner in which you manage and administrate your SharePoint service.

Whether or not your actions and manner for governing SharePoint involves rigorous policies and procedures detailed in governance documentation will depend on your needs and your situation. On one extreme, if actual lives depend on a certain order of things in SharePoint, well then I would say you probably require more thoroughness in your SharePoint governance documentation. Over on the other end of the spectrum, if you use it for simple ad hoc collaboration and no lives depend on how SharePoint functions, then I might not expect you to require as much diligence in your documentation efforts.

Certainly, I feel having good documentation can communicate expectations to the team well, but not every team member will study and frequently refer back to a lengthy document. You can communicate and ensure a shared understanding using other less formal methods as well, as I frequently point out in this book, but sometimes an organization just needs the formality as part of their process.

An SLA is a good example of when you will typically require formality. Different parties are involved in a formal sign-off and they are agreeing to the service level, and you might then establish it as a contract between everyone. I find this type of situation almost always requires a lot of formality because of the nature of having different people with different needs, all of which is a recipe for misunderstanding and conflict when you do not clearly define things. With a degree of formality and thoroughness in the SLA documentation, you can establish a shared understanding and set common expectations for how the service will operate.

Of course, governance plan documentation can serve this same purpose: it gets everyone on the same page with a shared understanding and sets common expectations. You might wonder why I have a preference to formally document any SLA while I am more nonchalant and neutral when it comes to deciding how formal to make the governance documentation. The answer is because an SLA has some weight to it; people have committed to meeting targets and they actually hold each other accountable for them.

For me, a degree of accountability makes the difference for how effective documentation will prove to be. Service providers and service consumers in an SLA hold each other accountable, and they specifically hold those accountabilities around each other's expected actions. Documentation can serve to capture knowledge and archive it for the future, but if you want it to be effective today, it needs to have actions that lead toward an outcome, and you need to hold someone accountable for those actions. Otherwise, you are just archiving something for the future.

You can typically have two main objectives for documenting your governance plan. One serves to capture the knowledge and decisions that encompass your actions and manner for managing your SharePoint service, and you want to save it for future reference. The other serves to hold people accountable for those actions you expect from them. This book overall, and this chapter especially, identifies many of those actions for which you might consider using to hold people accountable, and this information can assist you as you establish the appropriate level of documentation for your situation.

Consultant Comrade

This topic is very exciting for a consultant, because you can help answer those mysterious questions your clients face. You come as a SharePoint expert and you get to be the hero who guides them and who helps them work through the design of their SharePoint team. Trust me, this is no small matter.

The RACI model arms you with a tool you can use to drive the process and with it you are set up with a deliverable around which you can build out your consulting engagement. I listed many roles and provided several sample responsibilities to get you started. As you build out the rest and tailor it for your client, think about what the role will entail and follow my advice in the section in this chapter on adapting the sample RACI charts to your situation. The process will largely be the same, except your client has you as their expert to guide them and help them make sense out of what the roles mean.

I enjoy these types of engagements because they look closely at how a client structures their teams and how their IT department is structured. Often this allows me the chance to reveal structures and dependencies that my client did not even realize existed. It brings potential issues to light and uncovers overlap or gaps that otherwise might remain hidden and be difficult to detect when related problems arise. Not only do I get to learn about my client's environment, but also I facilitate them learning about themselves.

Going through this process helps differentiate you as a professional, because most other SharePoint consultants probably will not provide this level of detail or insight. I hope more will now that I detailed the main steps in this chapter, but you still have a lot of room to add value and differentiate yourself. As you probably noticed, there is no standard RACI chart to fit every client and every SharePoint service. Although the process of developing one is straightforward, it is not systematic enough to go through using a simple survey. If it was, I would have just included that in this chapter and moved on.

For me, I find the best time to address this is at the beginning, before you kick-off an engagement delivering SharePoint or a solution that you are deploying to their SharePoint environment. Whether they have a SharePoint team already or are looking to establish one, this is still a valuable step. You might sell this as an engagement all on its own or as part of a planning phase leading into a project delivery phase. When it is leading into a project delivery, the primary activity should be an extended project team RACI chart, extended to include the client resources the project depends on as well as any stakeholders or occasional project members from your team or from the client.

Once you have a project RACI chart, a project plan, and a pre-project checklist of activities that need to occur before you kick-off, I like to then move into planning what the operations team will look like. Building an operations RACI chart, at least at a high-level, will help set expectations with your client and help them begin to plan for what they will need when it comes time for you to hand over the delivery of an operational SharePoint service.

If your client has an existing SharePoint operations team, this is your chance to learn about who all the players are, who is responsible for what, and whether there are any gaps in coverage. This is often invaluable information to have throughout the lifecycle of the project, and it can help make your hand-over a smooth transition, as you will have all the right people identified and ready to involve. It also gives you an opportunity to raise warnings if you are delivering to gaps in the RACI chart that you need the client to fill. The information is useful, and it can help solve problems before you even get started!

I mentioned earlier in the chapter how I love to have the project RACI chart on a whiteboard where everyone can see it and use it to track our progress. If you have this option, I encourage you to try it out and experiment with it. This can be a powerful tool, for the client and the project team to monitor progress, to understand expectations, and to manage scope. It is more difficult for anyone to try to introduce any scope creep into a project while they are facing a whiteboard of tasks and fully utilized resources. This makes the consequences and required tradeoffs much more visible and readily available. Scope creep is not just simply about a change request and additional billable hours; it affects the plan and upsets the balance of the project. Sometimes it is necessary, but with your RACI chart on a large whiteboard in the project war room, you can see and prepare for the ripple effects that the change will cause.

The RACI model is one of my favorite tools to mitigate risk and optimize my chances of success. I cannot stress enough the degree of how clear it makes expectations for everyone. Everyone can see what is expected of them and what they can expect from everyone else, and not just with what tasks will occur, but also with what communication is required. It takes a little upfront effort, but it pays off in dividends through the awareness it instills.

Inside Story: Notes from the Field

I could almost take my pick from any of my projects that had success challenges, and no doubt, it could serve as an example of the dangers when projects do not have the roles and responsibilities defined. All my strong projects included a RACI chart, and all my more problematic projects seemed to also be the ones where they omitted the RACI chart. Nevertheless, I trust you can probably imagine scenarios where projects can drift off course or they have too much overlap in resource responsibilities that only lead to frustrations or conflicts.

Truth be told, I have a couple of examples in mind, and I thought about sharing one of them in this section as a great example of how dysfunctional a project team can become when no one knows who is responsible for what. You may not have experienced this situation, and in that case, I will have to ask that you trust me when I tell you that there was plenty of people working completely uncoordinated with each other, they made an excessive amount of assumptions, and they hardly had communication with the rest of the team. The project sponsors initially thought that everyone is a professional and should know what to do; they did not want to babysit or micromanage because they felt the team was competent enough to manage on their own.

You got me, I still wanted to work a little of the bad in before I got to the good. My point is that even with a team of some of the best resources, you still need to define the roles and responsibilities. Every team needs some coordination and direction. Even elite hockey players on an NHL team have a coach who lets a player know what their role on the team is and what responsibilities the team expects from them on a given shift. If a coach wants a player to be a checking forward during a game to shut down an opposing team's line, the coach will assign what the player's responsibilities are to keep that opposing line from generating any offense. Elite and championship hockey players need a coach to work out the roles and responsibilities on the team before they can function as a team, and long before they can reach success. As far as I know, every sports team functions in this way. Establishing your roles and responsibilities is never something to skimp on or try to skip, because they are part of the fundamentals that allow a team to function.

Now I want to get to the good and provide you with an example of a RACI chart working and laying the fundamentals for a highly functional team. One example I like was a few years ago when I engaged with an office services outsourcing company to deploy a SharePoint cornerstone phase with collaboration team sites. We did not have much time or margin for error; we needed to get SharePoint deployed and functioning quickly and hand it off to the operations team. We took the project approach that I always prefer, which was to have an initial planning engagement where we worked through the project objectives and the operations handover plan. Most importantly, we worked through the list of all the roles we needed involved for the project delivery and the operations roles the service required for a successful handover. From there, we built out a list of all the responsibilities for each role, and what communication needed to take place.

Some people broke down their tasks into minute detail while others just focused on the highlights. Both worked well, and better yet, both worked well together. The more detail we had for a role, the easier it was to reallocate resources for portions if we needed to, but for the most part these were experienced domain experts who were quite familiar with their tasks and the requirements for each task. Capturing all the tasks helped us ensure that we missed nothing and that we made everyone who needed to be involved available and a part of the project delivery team. A business analyst could then take and audit this task list to ensure we had coverage before we kicked off the project.

With our RACI chart in hand (or more precisely, on a whiteboard in our project war room, just the way I like it), we kicked off our project. Everything unfolded like clockwork. Team members knew when we required their contributions and they could easily stay aware of the team's progress. Just like a hockey team where everyone knows the position they need to play and can rely on where their teammates will be, we cycled through the tasks as if they were routine. Everything and everyone fell into place in a perfect orchestration of activities and outcomes.

When you have the fundamentals in place and your team is functioning in a healthy state, you can rely on these pieces to carry your team through tough times or difficult challenges. If everyone knows what role that they play and what they are responsible for, then they can feel confident that they are working on the right things, and that their teammates are also working on the right things. The whole process can almost feel routine, even if there is nothing routine about what you are tackling, and this is all because we have it all laid out and everyone has clear direction and coordination.

Wrapping Up

In this chapter, I discussed what resources you require for your SharePoint service and how to identify their responsibilities. I also looked at RACI charts, how to adapt a RACI chart for your team and your organization, and how to use the RACI chart to ensure that you have end-to-end support coverage and defined communication protocols. All this leads to a functional team that knows who is responsible for what and who depends on each other's tasks. It leads to a team that delivers without hesitation and indecision, as each team member knows what they should be working on and where to go next. The RACI model with its roles and responsibility matrix looks after the fundamentals so a team can focus on providing value.

I just looked at all the different types of roles that a SharePoint deployment depends on and what responsibility those roles often hold. With all the people who are involved with the SharePoint service, you need to ensure they possess the technical knowledge and skills to meet their responsibilities that you identified. In the next chapter, I discuss technical readiness strategies you can use to train and prepare your resources to support your SharePoint service. I also look at approaches to end-user training that you can adopt to enhance your user adoption strategy.

CHAPTER 5

■ ■ ■

Shaping Your User Readiness and Training

Ability will never catch up with the demand for it.

—Confucius

In this chapter, I address the need for training for both the SharePoint operations team providing the service and the end-users consuming the service. I provide considerations for setting up internal self-help resources such as quick start guides or peer mentors. I also reference the roles and responsibilities I covered in Chapter 4 and I relate those to training requirements that you will need to ensure the operations team has the right skills to support the SharePoint service.

One crucial takeaway that I want you to get from this chapter centers around how your adoption success depends heavily on readiness: readiness for your end-users consuming the service, and readiness for your service delivery team providing the service.

After reading this chapter, you will know how to:

- Plan for readiness

- Decide between classroom and online training courses

- Establish peer mentors

- Plan for end-user training

- Prepare quick start guides

- Explain why user adoption depends on adequate readiness

Planning for Readiness

Readiness and training are critical. In the previous chapter, I looked at the value of having people know what they need to do, know their responsibilities, and how making these roles and responsibilities clear to everyone will help to make everyone more productive. There is a caveat to that though, namely that people also need to know how to do what they are responsible for completing. If they do not already possess the skills they need to complete their responsibilities, then having a readiness strategy can help bridge the gap and provide direction. Without a readiness strategy, you risk leaving people unsettled, particularly in the following areas.

- Not knowing how to do something can be stressful, and this stress will grow in proportion to the complexity of the task and the pressure to complete it.

- Not knowing how to do something can also be frustrating and this frustration will grow if there is no support or training resources available to figure out the task.

We are not born knowing everything. In fact, we are born knowing very little beyond natural instincts such as how to breathe and how to move our body parts. We spend the rest of our lives learning and absorbing knowledge, much of which we receive from thinkers who worked through problems before our time. This is what makes humans special compared with other beings: we can record knowledge and pass it on to future generations. Imagine if we had to figure everything out from scratch and we had to relearn the simplest things without access to a body of knowledge or a teacher. Training and learning provides us with unbelievable amounts of productivity.

Your SharePoint team and your end-users can both relate to this need for training. If they have not done something before and they have not received any training, then they may experience stress or frustration. Some things may be obvious or relatively consistent with what they do have experience with, and so the stress or frustration they experience with these tasks will stay minimal. You might be safe with not addressing those things in the training and you can instead focus your training efforts on those things that would lead to greater amounts of stress and frustration. You can make these training decisions as you plan and identify your greatest training needs.

In the following sections, I look at what types of training are available and how you can plan readiness strategies for your SharePoint service operations team. Later in the chapter, beginning in the "Preparing Training Specifically for End-Users" section, I shift focus and look at how you can address the training needs that are specifically for your end-users.

Understanding the Types of Training Available

The great thing about technical people is that we enjoy learning about new technology or new possibilities with technology. I love to learn, about all kinds of things, but especially about new technology. This learning can take many different forms from formal classroom training to peers sharing advice to independent reading, and on and on. We face no shortages in the ways we can acquire new knowledge, and in this section I look at some of the popular types of training that you can provide.

A part of your planning for readiness will start with considering the possibilities and the different avenues that your team can take to acquire the knowledge and skills they require. What is available and does it match what you need? You can use the RACI chart that I described in Chapter 4 to help you identify any gaps in skills on your team, and you can use this information to identify what training your team will need. If SharePoint is new to everyone, then any training will match what you need on some level, so you also need to consider which approach will give you the most value and the best return on your training investment.

For me, I have always found that books provide the biggest return on my training investment. An average technical trade reference might cost me somewhere around $30-$50, and each book has a bunch of ideas packed in its pages. Spending $50 to generate a couple of great ideas is quite cheap in my book! Some of these books take a how-to focus with a series of steps that you can follow, and these directly transmit the skills required for specific tasks. Again, I find the cost quite cheap compared to the value received. You can also start a team reference library with the books your team acquires, and you can then reuse that book investment across team members to generate discussions and garner new ideas from the same book. I love books, and maybe that is why I am writing one. I also take advantage of other training materials, including:

- Reading blogs and message boards

- Watching how-to videos on YouTube

- Attending a conference to generate new ideas from speakers

- Enrolling in formal classroom training

- Signing-up for online e-learning courses

- Joining a user group and attending meetings

- Finding a peer mentor

- Working through self-paced online virtual labs

Sometimes there might not be any training available or what is out there just does not meet your needs. In these cases, you need to create your own training to acquire these skills. For example, while I am writing this book, SharePoint 2013 is going through a series of betas, and as I write this section, the final version is still two or three months away. Without general availability of SharePoint 2013, there is almost no training or references available either. I have to train myself. Lucky for me, I have an extensive background with SharePoint, so I am not starting from scratch. I like to think of this type of training as one of exploration and discovery.

Discovery can come in a couple of flavors. You can have a self-directed discovery, where you set out to experiment with ideas and see where your exploration takes you. Sometimes this is fun, but sometimes you need a little more structure to shape your expedition and keep it relevant. In these other cases, I like to use what I call *guided discovery*. Guided discovery in SharePoint might take the form of peer mentoring, where one experienced peer guides a mentee to help develop his or her skills. This is an especially valuable form of training and I discuss peer mentoring more a little later in this chapter. You could also align guided discovery with a book or an online virtual lab. Virtual labs walk you through a series of steps to teach you how to perform certain tasks, but they also provide you with a wonderful opportunity for guided discovery, where you can also experiment on your own. You can experiment with some of the tasks that the exercises lead you into without risk or worry about ruining your own environment.

■ **Note**   Microsoft offers an extensive array of online virtual labs for many of their products. For a list of SharePoint administrator virtual labs, please see the following TechNet site:

http://technet.microsoft.com/en-us/virtuallabs/bb512933

And for a list of SharePoint developer virtual labs, please see the following MSDN site:

http://msdn.microsoft.com/en-us/cc707678.aspx

With so many types of training available and so many ways to learn, you can start planning your training strategy to include any of the training options. You have options between formal or informal training, paid or free training, and group or individual training. Your best training will involve a mix of all these to help maximize the training's impact. For instance, your team might each go and explore a particular area within SharePoint through independent discovery, but then the team members come back together as a group to present and share what they each discovered with the rest of the team.

All these types of training are options that you can employ for your end-users as well as your operations team. The content of the training changes depending on the audience and the learner's objectives, but the process of how you can deliver training is not wildly different. There are some limiting factors, such as your ability to scale and deliver personalized training to a massive user-base, but the basic training concepts are consistent. First, I look at how you can plan and deliver readiness more specifically for your operations team, and then later in the chapter I look at how you can adopt these approaches and how you can design custom training for your end-users.

Planning Readiness for Your Operations Team

If you built a RACI chart for your team, which I covered back in Chapter 4, then you can use that list of responsibilities to determine what areas where you need to focus your training. You can go through the list of tasks with each of your team members and highlight any area that they are not already proficient in. This draws attention to what your current training needs are for your team to meet the responsibilities for the roles you have allocated. You might discover this gap when you assign a role a new task as you expand the service to include a new feature area, or you may just discover a previously missed task through your analysis in the RACI modeling process. The good news is that either way, you will be aware of where your weaknesses and gaps are, and you can build a plan for how to provide the appropriate readiness and move toward filling in those gaps.

You might recall me mentioning in Chapter 4 how you can use a RACI chart to facilitate career progression planning, because a RACI chart can lay out what skills a resource needs in order to take on a particular role and grow their career. You can align your training plans to this idea as well, and in doing so you can provide training to expand the skills of your team members beyond their immediate role. This will not only help you grow your team's capabilities, but you can also increase your team's support coverage as you increase the number of resources who can fill in for a role. Your RACI chart will help you to identify immediate training needs as well as potential strategies to expand your team's capabilities.

When you list all the training that you would like to provide to your team, you are off to a good start. The next step is to prioritize this list. I like to work with a prioritized list because my training needs or training desires can often exceed the amount of training that is available or the amount that I can consume over the next planning cycle. I would prioritize as the highest priority for any of those skills that I identify as lacking proficiency and are pivotal to the core roles required to provide the service. I would continue my prioritization from there based on how immediate the training need is and how crucial it is for maintaining reliable operations.

I like to compare the training I need with all the different training types that are available. If a resource is starting from scratch and he or she needs to develop most of the skills to fill a role, then perhaps classroom training in a course that offers broad SharePoint skills will give them the best start. If there are only a couple of tasks that require training, then they might find opportunities in the virtual labs or an online self-paced tutorial. I always like to work some degree of books into a training plan, because they offer both self-paced learning and ongoing reference capabilities, and they afford one of the few training resources that you can reuse without any extra costs. Once you look at the training needs and survey the training options, you can begin to form a plan that balances your priorities with your budget.

Technology constantly changes, and this is both a blessing and a curse. For someone like me who loves learning and exploring new things, the ever-changing technology landscape makes a nice environment to always keep me stimulated. However, at the same time, it is constantly changing and constantly demanding that I keep up. Sometimes it feels as if everything is changing all at once, almost as if every technology vendor got together to plan a new release at around the same time. Even just with Microsoft, my primary technology vendor and my previous employer, every so often on their release cycle it feels as if they are refreshing practically the entire product line with a new version, and all within a period of just a few months. I get excited to try out all the new software and to start thinking about new possibilities for my clients, but I also know I cannot tackle learning it all at once. I need to prioritize a training plan based on my highest priority, my budget, and the availability of training resources.

Somehow training needs to fit so that you can continue operations, or at least not interrupt operations to any unacceptable degree. By this, I mean it is not viable for you to dedicate your team to training indefinitely. Eventually they need to come back to work and deliver the benefits from the new skills they have acquired. Therefore, depending on how extensive your training needs are, your training plan may have to include compromises so that you can continue operations and stay in business. It may include compromises for less dramatic reasons as well, which could be a limited budget or a predetermined rotation of training opportunities to ensure you can spread them equally across the team.

In my experience, it is often difficult to build a multi-year training plan. This is for a number of reasons, mainly due to the uncertainty about the future: people develop new interests as they lose interest in other things, and technology changes can be hard to predict. Instead, I prefer to build plans around a quarter or around a year, and I set targets and goals within this more immediate timeline. I can park the other potential training opportunities and revisit them the next time I revise the training plan, either for the next quarter or for the next year. This lets me check in and ensure the training activities will still relate to business needs and I can then prioritize them along with all the new training needs that arose since the last check in.

As you build out your training plan and you consider where you need training to focus over the next cycle of time, you ought to include a mixture of the training types. For your training plan to have an impact and drive new skills for your team, you need to approach it from different angles. Not all your training should come from classroom workshops, just as it should not all come from independent discovery. You need a balance and a mixture. When you include different training methods, you accommodate different learning styles and different approaches to learning, and unless you have any expertise in adult learning theories, you should probably hedge your bets and incorporate many different approaches.

My main reason for encouraging you to include many different approaches is to allow for the cross-pollination of ideas. Different situations will stimulate different ideas, while different experiences will also stimulate different ideas. You allow for creativity when you plan for a diverse range of training experiences and learning methods. You just cannot predict when that *ah-ha* moment will come, when the learner will have an epiphany and things will become clear to them. I do not know of any theory or technique to reliably script this experience with consistency for different learners; I can only create an environment that facilitates and cultivates an opportunity for those moments.

I enjoy building lists and organizing them; that is just how my mind works. Yet, at the same time, I do not stay rigid in my plans and instead I adapt when new opportunities come up. Things come up, conditions change, and new possibilities present themselves. For example, your team members might change jobs before the next planning cycle, or a training provider might offer an irresistible discount on training that you cannot pass up. There are many valid reasons why your training plans may need to change, and that is okay. You can treat your plans as if they are the way things will unfold up until one of those valid reasons presents itself, and then you can adapt.

I go into more detail on how you might balance the mix of training types in the next couple of sections, where I discuss actual training options. For now, I wanted to stress this approach to plan your training by creating and prioritizing a list of skills that your team needs to develop to meet its operational duties or expand its capabilities. You can use this as a checklist that you and your team can work through, with some items aimed at formal classroom training, while others are destined for less structured learning initiatives. In the next section, I discuss some of these types of informal training along with other types of training you might offer internally for your team.

Approaching In-house Training Initiatives

By referring to in-house training initiatives, I primarily think of those internal activities that you can offer your team to facilitate their learning and skill development. For the most part, I consider these as internal initiatives, or those activities that stem from knowledge within the organization, and they often are informal, but they do not have to be. Internal training can be just as structured as any formal training you enroll in from a training provider, particularly if you have corporate trainers who offer internal workshops and courses, or if you formalize a peer mentoring process for your team.

This division between internal initiatives and external training opportunities forms a bit of a grey line, because you can have external training providers or trainer consultants come in to offer customized training, or your internal training initiatives can eventually become commoditized and sold externally. I do not need a definitive description for my purposes in this discussion though, as I am being much more arbitrary in my division. In this section, my focus is on initiatives based on what is available within the organization and how you might take advantage of them to support your training needs. In the next section, I share some of my considerations for when I shop for classroom or e-learning courses, either for myself or for my team. After that, I return to the topic of internal training initiatives and discuss peer mentoring as I go full circle in the discussion.

I have already mentioned some of the training resources available, and in particular, those that are low-cost or free. These include books, online virtual labs, and the like. You now know they are available, and you have a prioritized list of skills you need your team to develop, so how do you actually approach putting these initiatives into practice? Your greatest impact will come from the degree of importance you associate with training and these initiatives. If you truly believe in developing your team's capabilities and you look for ways to take initiatives in all your processes, then training will habitually be included as a priority. Alternatively, if one merely pays lip service to training without designating time or actively facilitating learning opportunities, then the approach will depend on how much initiative individual team members will take on their own.

One of my favorite approaches to in-house training is to divide and conquer. This is where each team member or pairs of team members take on a topic and learn it well enough so that they can later present it and teach it to the rest of the team. You can plan to invest in an off-site retreat with a full day workshop that everyone participates in to both teach and learn. Or you can schedule brief team meetings in the boardroom to cover a single topic as a type of lunch and learn session. You might also have team members present over an online web conference, especially if your team is distributed or mobile and you want to include everyone.

People learn best those topics that they try to teach others. There is something motivating about knowing you will have to explain a concept to someone, motivating in the sense that you will need to know the topic well yourself if you are to explain it well enough so that someone else can also understand it. It is also motiving in the sense that you probably feel a sense of responsibility to learn the topic well, because your team is depending on you to teach it to them. Your team members are often more respectful and attentive to your presentation, both because they will eventually present to you and because you are a colleague who is trying to share knowledge with them. This divide-and-conquer process generates good energy and is full of positive reinforcements for productive team learning.

The main challenge you might face with this divide-and-conquer approach is if your team feels stress or anxiety with the idea of presenting or they are overwhelmed with all the learning that they need to do to teach. If you sense this is the case, often times just pairing up team members will help to relieve some of this pressure. In that case, they can rely on each other to learn and understand the topic well enough, and they can present it together as a duet. This technique can also help further their learning as they bring their different perspectives and bounce ideas off each other.

Another option for paired or even group learning is a book club. You could also make this a lunch and learn session where perhaps every week the group discusses a chapter in a book that they all agree to read ahead of time. Each teammate can then offer their perspective or whatever insights they gained from the chapter. This is a great way to get the team talking and sharing ideas as they build out their skills, particularly if they are meeting to expand people's skills for future career growth or to expand support coverage.

FINDING ANSWERS IN FORUMS

The old bulletin board system (BBS) from years ago is still holding strong, as it provides a place where people can gather to discuss like-minded topics. A forum is another name for this, and it just means a place or medium where people can meet to exchange their ideas on a topic. Their essence has not changed much over the previous 20 years or so, as someone posts a topic and people post replies to the topic. Some forums have additional features, such as measuring a contributor's reputation and rating the value of different posts, but their essence remains constant.

Forums are especially useful when you are new to something. You can do a search and find that someone else may have faced a similar problem, and there you might find your answer to the problem. If you do not find your answers or if nobody has posted this problem before, then you can post it and pose the question to the community. You might find this is a great way to get started, and it is a handy resource where you can draw on the collective knowledge and collective problem solving from the community.

Podcasts and blogs are another great resource that is freely available on the web, and they both give you access to other people's raw thinking and ideas. They provide a means to stay on the cutting edge as people share their insights into new or evolving technology. They might even offer posts that describe what they observe in software on the same day as a vendor releases it. The software developers might even post some insights into a particular feature or how they intended people to use it, or they can share their plans on features that they are thinking about adding. Technology blogs can help you stay current with what is trendy and they can help you discover things you might not otherwise discover on your own. I find they often help add to and inspire my creative process.

Blog posts might give me creative ideas directly, or they may simply suggest things to try out, and those things then lead to creative ideas. When I try out ideas, then this only leads to additional experimenting of my own. They give me new questions that I can wonder about, new ideas that I will want to explore, and this all leads to new creativity and new possibilities with the software. Indeed, I find anything that leads to getting hands-on and trying out ideas, or anything that gives me something to practice ultimately leads to new possibilities.

Practice is one training option that feels obvious but that might not be so obvious. Online virtual labs provide a viable option for practice, with little risk and no real investment in infrastructure or extra software. You can also deploy your own environments for the sole purpose of practicing. Then, before every deployment or every change, you can set a policy that you need to first run through the deployment process a few times in the practice environment. You might even practice aimlessly, and just explore the possibilities or experiment with different settings in the practice environment. People solidify their learning by trying things out, getting hands-on, and practicing what they have learned. Whatever your approach is to practicing, the more opportunities that you make available for practicing, the more learning you can cultivate on your team.

This discussion shared some of the ways that you can facilitate learning on your team. You are not limited to these choices; they are just some popular options I have come across in my practice and with my clients. However, you might not be able to meet all your skill development objectives using internal self-study methods. In addition, you may need to send people away for more dedicated or more structured training, or you may need to send them to conferences to add new perspectives and generate new ideas. Alternatively, you might subscribe to an online e-learning course. In the next section, I discuss some considerations for making these selections and the ways that you might maximize your training investment in these courses or conferences.

Considerations for Classroom and Online Training

I like every type of learning; I am sort of a nerd that way. Classroom and online training are no different, and I find that as in reading a book, courses offer a structured way to learn the essence of a topic quickly. They save time, because someone else has already thought through the connections between topics and how they build on top of each other.

Classes can be expensive though, both from the cost to register and from the time away from work. For me, the time away is my biggest cost, as I am usually pressed for time or have other commitments that make it difficult to clear a block for classes or conferences. This is where online training is helpful for providing the structure and the advantages of having someone else organize the content in a manner so that one concept builds on another. However, I find the online training usually lacks the interaction between the instructor and students, which is where I can ask questions to explore a topic deeper or get an extra explanation if I am having trouble following the concepts. While online training does allow me to fit the training to my schedule and minimize the amount of time I have to sacrifice for it, I often find my experience with it is more limiting than in a classroom, even though sometimes this tradeoff is necessary.

Conferences can generate a ton of ideas for different possibilities, different approaches, and different solutions that I can apply to whatever technology the conference focus surrounds. They are often fun and can feel quite social, and sometimes it is the social aspects that makes a conference worthwhile. I usually pick up new ideas from speakers in their prepared sessions, but I also garner valuable insights through those informal discussions as I meet other people to chat with during coffee breaks. I can see the attraction why some people get on conference circuits to attend them frequently. Even though the sessions might not deviate much from one conference to the next, the people might, and better yet, your experience and the ideas that come up certainly do.

I have noticed that when a team has to travel to attend a conference or classroom training, the experience offers a team building opportunity while it solidifies the learning that they are doing. They might attend sessions together and then chat about them afterward, or they might go to different sessions and then share what they each learned. Often attendees will eat together and generally spend their time as a team rather than as individuals in each of their own hotel rooms. Sometimes you can measure the value of a conference for a team beyond just the direct knowledge presented in sessions.

You might look at maximizing the investment in any courses or conferences by having these folks share what they have learned with their teammates. You might plan a workshop for knowledge transfer or a series of lunch and learn sessions. It could just be a quick presentation on the highlights of the topics that they learned, and where their teammates can find more information if they are interested. Remember, people learn something best when they have to teach it to someone else, so this knowledge transfer not only spreads the knowledge around, but it also deepens the level of understanding of the topic for the course or the conference attendee as well.

I mentioned several benefits from taking classroom training, but there are some drawbacks. One is that classroom courses target a wide audience, making the material generic. Often this means it will include over simplified examples that may or may not apply to your industry. For instance, when my government clients attend training or a conference, they often point out how irrelevant the examples or demos are, especially when the examples and demos are sales focused. The government workers might not sell any commodities, and so a series of examples and demos that focus on bicycle sales or something similar might be difficult for them to relate and apply to their organization.

For all the reasons that I mentioned in this section and the previous sections, no single training method provides an ultimate and exhaustive solution. Your optimal solution will encompass a mix of these training approaches, such as a book study group combined with classroom training, and followed up with team training in a divide-and-conquer strategy. When you plan for and adopt a healthy mix of training, you hedge your bets against different learning styles as I mentioned earlier, and you maximize the return on your training investment.

TRAINING METHODS AND THE LAW OF DIMINISHING RETURNS

The law of diminishing returns is a theory in economics that states that for each additional input, the additional amount of extra output returned on that input will continue to decrease. If I apply this theory to training methods, then for each additional investment in a particular training method, the amount of return garnered from that investment would yield less and less additional amounts of knowledge.

Think of this in the context of art school: if you constantly just take art theory and art history classes without any studio classes, then you will continue to learn a little bit more about art without learning how to apply it. Conversely, if you take all studio classes, you might learn technique but you would lack fundamentals related to composition and criticisms. Each class would teach you a little more, but by combining the two training methods, you could gain greater amount of total knowledge from the additional classes.

I like to apply this theory with learning technology as well. If you only took classroom training, then you would continue to learn some additional general SharePoint skills, but if you mixed in a peer study group or peer mentoring, then you can expand and apply your learning to your specific situation. This can generate ideas specific to your organization, and ultimately it can increase the total amount of learning.

Peer Mentoring

Peer mentoring is another one of those topics I could probably write an entire book about, and one day I might. This broad topic can involve things such as onboarding new employees to help them quickly settle in and feel comfortable within the organization or it can involve knowledge transfer where an expert mentors a novice in order to help develop their skills. It might even involve two people at the same level who give each other an alternative perspective. For my purposes in this section, I will consider the aspect of peer mentoring where a more experienced resource mentors and shares that knowledge with a less experience teammate.

The *peer* in peer mentor is crucial. This concept does not work with supervisors and subordinates, because that is a different type of relationship and it involves a different style of coaching. I know people in several organizations who believe in their open style of management, where they believe that they cultivate a supportive environment where supervisors and subordinates can have open discussions. While this may be true for the most part, I do not fully buy in to the idea. It does not matter how open and supportive of an environment I am in, I will still censor or hold back some things from my supervisor. It may just be instinct, but I always want to paint the best picture for anyone who is evaluating my performance and who has input on what type of bonus or salary increase I may receive. I am generally a confident worker and usually feel secure in my abilities, but even still, I may have an easier time talking about any shortcomings or frustrations with a peer. For instance, perhaps my issue is with my supervisor.

Having a peer mentor is different than having a career supervisor who evaluates your performance and has influence over your career, and it is different than having a project manager who plans and tracks your progress on a project. A peer mentor is someone who does not hold influence over your career fate, someone who can offer objective guidance and advice. Those other roles serve a valuable purpose, and they too can offer valuable advice, but they hold a position of authority, and this is true no matter how friendly you make them and no matter how open you design the relationship. It is still a superior and subordinate relationship.

You might even consider a peer mentor from a different functional area of the organization or a different geographical location, such as a foreign branch. This type of peer mentoring can widen your perspective on your organization and its operations, it can help you grow toward a different role, and it can give you a completely detached and impartial point of view. Peer mentoring in this fashion facilitates cross-group collaboration and it contributes to everyone's career development support and progression. You can explore and experiment with this type of peer mentoring on your own, as I shift focus now to how you can adopt peer mentoring and use it specifically for SharePoint team members.

Fitting Peer Mentoring into the Team

Peer mentoring is a broad topic and it can fit a variety of scenarios where you want to develop a team member or to better integrate them on a team. For my purposes in this section, I focus on the potential of peer mentoring for a SharePoint team and how you can use this technique to smooth transitions of team members and to be more effective as you onboard new teammates. I also discuss how you can use peer mentoring for existing team members as a tool to help maintain the team's health, to further develop and grow team members, and to cultivate a collaborative and cohesive team.

This gives you two flavors of peer mentoring: one that is short-term and specific for onboarding new team members, and the other one is ongoing for sustaining and developing your team members. To start, you need a process for welcoming new teammates, helping them get settled and comfortable on the team, and most importantly, providing them with all the support that they need to start being productive right away. A peer mentor for new hires can help a teammate settle in to the team and to feel welcome in many ways. You might create a checklist to help prime the mentoring relationship and to help it be effective right away.

To use peer mentoring to help orient and welcome new teammates, I found that starting with a checklist helps to facilitate the process and it ensures that some common tasks are addressed. You can use this checklist for predictable tasks, such as introducing the new teammate to everyone on the team, and then later reminding the mentor to help refresh the new teammate's memory of everyone's names. You might also include processes on the checklist, such as walking through expense report submissions or the travel booking processes, submitting hours or scheduling time off, and filling in status reports. You should also include more informal checklist items to begin to lead the new teammate peer mentoring relationship off the checklist, such as going for lunches or coffee breaks together, and discussing any team practices. Of course, you need to cover those role-specific topics as well as all these team-specific topics on the checklist as well.

When you onboard a new teammate to a SharePoint team, your peer mentoring process has to help them fit in and feel a part of the team, but this is also a good time to offer any additional clarity to help them understand their role. I do not have the space in this book to go through every possible SharePoint role, so I will just focus on mentoring a generic SharePoint administrator. When you have a new administrator joining the team, some of the things he or she will need to know are basic things such as where all the servers are and how to connect to them, what software you have deployed, and what your processes for making any changes are. You can build this in to a checklist and add other informal discussions such as who the key internal customers of the service are and what is the roadmap for your SharePoint service.

Essentially, a peer mentor who helps onboard new teammates is there to help their teammate quickly feel a part of the team and understand how the team operates. They remove some of the mystery and anxiety involved with joining an unknown team, and they provide answers in an informal setting without any hierarchal or political pressures. In short, they welcome the new teammate and make a great first impression of the team.

PEER MENTORING AND FIRST IMPRESSIONS

I have heard that first impressions mean everything, and I find this is true. Every time I joined a team where we got off to a bumpy start, this experience has always set the stage for the rest of my experience there. Conversely, when I joined Microsoft, I was lucky to get a great peer mentor right from day one. My mentor, Manjeet Lidder, did the typical things such as introducing me around the office and he showed me where to find the printers. He also took me to lunch or for drinks and checked in on how I was doing and how I was settling in. I shadowed him on a couple of projects, and then eventually I started delivering projects on my own while still having him to connect with and ask any questions.

> I felt welcome and supported from the very start. The experience integrated me on the team, it quickly helped me to understand my role, and it helped to build my confidence as a new services consultant in a giant software company. It also made a great first impression, as I felt valuable not only seeing Microsoft invests so much in my onboarding experience, but also in having a peer I felt connected with. Thus, I felt more connected to Microsoft and started off my time there with a wonderful impression – a positive impression that I still have today.

Once teammates move past the new phase and you have finished onboarding them, they become regular members of the team. At this point, you shift from a new and onboarding peer mentor focus to an ongoing peer mentor. This may be the same peer mentor and the relationship just develops beyond integrating the mentee into the team, or the peer mentor might change to involve someone new. Peer mentors can also change over time, as people look to change roles or as interests change.

When you move to more of an operational mentoring focus, the relationship will consist less of first introductions and following checklists, and it instead moves more to one of inquiry or support. The mentor will need to ask the mentee how their work is going, what they are thinking about working towards, and where they may be struggling. Sometimes these things are obvious, but other times they need an objective party to notice them or draw them out. This is the value of a peer mentor, because they have an objective perspective and often can notice things that you might not be aware of when you are in the thick of your daily grind.

A peer mentor at this stage can include a range of mentoring goals. For instance, when you are unfamiliar with the technical aspects of a piece of software and you want to learn how to manage it well, then a senior technical resource who is familiar with the software could provide you with direction and insights based on their experience. Through this mentoring relationship, you can build your technical skills through your hands-on practice, and at the same time, you can rely on your mentor to help steer you in the right direction when you face challenges or you have questions. They can also point you toward training references or other types of material to support your growth with your skills in the technology. Someone who possesses the skills you hope to develop can help you understand how it all works and the most efficient ways to do things.

The important concept here is that a potential mentor has the skills and experience in the area you seek to develop. They do not have to do the same job or even the same type of job, they just need to have expertise in an area where they can offer you coaching and feedback to help you develop in that area. Now you might ask, how does this apply to a SharePoint team? A SharePoint team is no different. If you need mentors to help develop technical skills in SharePoint, then you need SharePoint resources to serve as mentors and to help build one's skills. Otherwise, you are more open and flexible. Some technical skills may come from other technical team members, such as from those who administer other products. Perhaps they can coach a new resource on change management, stability, and other general IT administrator concepts. This provides a great way to grow and mature your SharePoint team as a disciplined IT team by cross-pollinating with other more mature IT teams.

You may also have team members you want to develop in other, nontechnical areas. Whether you are building leadership skills or consulting skills, you can use a peer mentor from another area within the organization to share guidance on this development. You may also use a peer mentor as a general support structure, where the mentee is not in any specific track for career development, but who you just want to facilitate an alternate communication and support structure to aid in their career. This may or may not focus on topics directly related to what a mentee's supervisor will measure in their annual performance assessment, or it could focus on work-life balance. It could also focus on frustrations or anxieties the mentee experiences at work. Better yet, it could focus on all of the above.

The value from peer mentoring comes from this diverse range of mentoring relationships you can adopt. Whether you use it to welcome and onboard someone who is new, to help a teammate develop skills in a new area that will help grow their career, or to provide a support structure that encourages job satisfaction, peer mentoring fills a gap that none of the other formal supervisor-subordinate or informal teammate relationships address. Now that you understand what a peer mentor is and what are the ways that you can leverage one on your team, I will shift focus to look at how to be a peer mentor.

How to Be a Peer Mentor

The first challenge with becoming a peer mentor is connecting with a mentee. Where do you find someone to mentor, or how do potential mentees find you? In a small team or a small organization, this can be easy, but in a large organization with many locations where not everyone knows everyone, this may be more challenging. You might use managers to identify potential peer mentors in their career discussions, and then when other managers mention a need, they can bridge a connection. Alternatively, you may expose options through a MySite or a community site to help facilitate these mentoring connections.

Once you identify your mentee, you can begin the mentoring process. The first step, and probably the most crucial, is to set objectives. Your objectives may capture what the point of the mentoring relationship is, what you are working toward, if you know, or at least the issue or area that you both want to address. These are the bigger picture objectives that guide the focus of the mentoring sessions, and you can use them to set objectives for each mentoring session when you meet. Objectives help to bring focus, but if you find yourself in a mentoring situation where your mentee wants a new direction, yet they are not sure what that direction is yet, then you might set the objective to identify the aim and ultimate direction of the mentoring relationship. Perhaps the objective is to identify what is causing the mentee to feel discomfort or conflict, or it could be to explore ideas on where they might take their career next. Setting those overall objectives, at least setting them for now, gives you a nice place to start and focus the mentoring sessions.

OBJECTIVES IN A MENTORING OR COACHING RELATIONSHIP

I feel a little hypocritical saying that setting objectives might be the most crucial step. I say this mostly because sometimes in the thick of things, I am not always the best at setting these objectives. For example, a couple of years ago when I felt a little stagnant with my own consulting direction, I hired a professional coach, my good friend Nicole Leighton. As she would no doubt confirm, I can sometimes be evasive when it comes to setting specific objectives. Luckily for me, she is a talented coach, and even though I made her job a little more difficult, she began with setting objectives for our individual sessions. She then set objectives for homework that she wanted me to work on or think about between sessions.

Objectives are important, because they give direction and focus for a mentoring or coaching session, as well as the overall relationship. As my friend Nicole said, "Otherwise it's just coffee talk." Coffee talk is nice, but you might not actually accomplish anything. If you find yourself in a situation similar to mine, where you know you want to change something, but you are not sure what it is just yet, then you might not be able to name long-term objectives. In this case, just start with the short-term or immediate objectives, and set objectives for each mentoring meeting, and then build from there.

One technique she used that helped me focus on longer-term objectives was to create a vision board. Since I am a visual person, this helped me to organize my thoughts and interests by visually laying them out on a page. I could see logos or sketches on the page and they included things that I wanted to accomplish or experience, such as writing a book, taking some classes, and focusing on a particular type of work. This vision board helped me visualize, and then later articulate my objectives.

Your first meeting with your mentee should cover establishing the overarching objectives you both agree on for the mentorship, or at least for the initial mentorship. As I discussed, these objectives can be to onboard and help a new teammate quickly get familiar with life on the team, they can be to develop technical or soft skills, or they can be to explore some general career growth options. With objectives in place, you next need to cover the ground rules, the essence of how the mentorship will work. How often will you meet? What is the protocol for communication outside those scheduled meetings? It is important for you both to create a shared understanding for how the relationship will work, what you each can expect from it, and how you both prefer to communicate or connect.

Understanding each other's communication preferences helps to set boundaries for when you will be available and how you want your mentee to contact you. For instance, when I am in a groove and in the middle of working on something, I usually close my e-mail and ignore my phone. There are these times when I just do not like interruptions or distractions, and during those times, I will close chat and e-mail software to completely avoid any interruptions. Even when I have Outlook open, I change the settings so that it never pops up a desktop alert when any new mail arrives. I set up my mobile phone in the same fashion so it does not display any alerts when new mail arrives. I never let e-mail run my day or act as if it has precedence. I process my inbox when I get to it at different times, such as when I am about to take a break or switch tasks. I am a little funny that way; and it gets worse, because I am also the type who can completely disconnect and not check my e-mail after work hours or while I am on holidays. My mentee needs to know this, because some people are conditioned where they expect instant responses, and they get this expectation because many people always have their e-mail program open and they jump on any alert that pops up. Not me, so I need to set this expectation up front so everyone knows that it will often take some time before I respond.

Once you both agree on the overarching objectives for the mentorship, you establish the ground rules for how the relationship will work, and you set expectations for any other preferences that you may have, then you are ready to begin. You also need to organize your individual meetings to ensure you stay productive and work toward your overall mentoring objective, and you can do this by setting objectives or an agenda for each meeting. Each meeting or mentoring session needs an agenda to keep discussions on track and to make sure nothing ends up missed. In fact, I think every meeting, mentoring or otherwise, should have an agenda and meeting outcome objectives explicitly specified. Depending on the length of your mentoring session, you might not break down the agenda by time, as a bullet list with the key points that you both want to address will do. Lead the mentoring session by asking your mentee leading questions for each of those points, and then discuss them freely.

Sometimes, things come up that were not on the agenda, and this is why I keep the mentoring agenda fairly loose and flexible. It has structure with the key points that you want to cover and address, but it is flexible in that you can explore topics or follow where the discussion leads when it is helpful. Building on this idea, you might find it useful to end your session with an open question, such as asking what else your mentee wants to discuss or is wondering. I get this from the process that doctors use when they meet with their patients. Apparently, many patients who visit a doctor wonder about other things or have other questions that they do not bring up. So a doctor will often ask an open-ended question to inquire whether there is anything else he or she can help them with, and this prompts a patient to bring up these other issues the patient may be wondering about before the doctor leaves. This is a great way to encourage your mentee to open up and it provides a chance to have the mentee share any other issues they are experiencing.

You may not get to every issue in the same session. Your sessions may have a scheduled time limit, which is a good idea. As issues come up, you should write them down, so that as you get to the end of the session you can recap what you both discussed and what is still outstanding. If you want your mentee to do some thinking about one of the topics, this is a good time to let them know, and then you can add the topic on the agenda for the next session for you both to follow-up on. This creates a great routine of inquiry and follow-up, where you can offer advice and your mentee will bring feedback on how it works.

Your job as a peer mentor is to offer support and guidance, and you need to provide this consistently and in a manner so that the relationship works for you both. With some structure for a shared understanding and direction toward objectives, you both will likely find the mentoring relationship and overall process rewarding and productive.

Now that I shared ways to build readiness on the operations team, I want to shift my attention to the end-users. End-users can adopt many of the same approaches to readiness that works for the operations team, such as classroom training, online labs, or peer mentoring. Whatever the approach, training your users is critical to facilitate strong user adoption and appropriate usage. In the coming sections, I discuss the types of training you can offer, as well as training considerations for user adoption.

Preparing Training Specifically for End-Users

The biggest challenge with training end-users is often one of scale. How can you train everyone effectively given a limited budget? People might be located all over the world, or you might have thousands of users within your organization. In these cases, perhaps it is just not practical to have one-on-one training sessions with each of them.

They still need training, so you have to either consider compromises to the amount of training, or consider training techniques that will scale.

Later in this chapter, I discuss using what I refer to as quick start guides. These one or two page reference sheets walk a user through key tasks and they can offer just enough support to help an end-user understand how to perform his or her primary job functions. I find these guides incredibly handy because they can reach a large audience right away and they can take some pressure off. They are also contained and direct enough that service desk resources can provide users with a copy when a related support request comes up. Quick start guides are effective when they address a few key tasks, but users can become quickly overwhelmed if you provide them with too many of these sheets, in which case, the quick start references will lose their effectiveness. As such, you need to select just the most common tasks for each type of user. For everything else, you will need to take advantage of one of the other training options available.

Sometimes the best way to train end-users is to train them in-person through classroom training. This option obviously does not scale as well as the quick start guide, but it can be effective for those users you can reach. I found that breaking down this training into short workshops helps to enable training on any of the basics of using SharePoint as an end-user without overloading them with too many details. For example, I usually aim to create a four-hour workshop with a particular focus, such as the basics of collaboration or content management. This allows me to build their basic skills in a particular area of SharePoint, and it complements the quick start guides. With this approach, I can reach a wide audience in a short period and get them reasonably competent with using SharePoint.

Although I do not feel anything beats face-to-face, I do compromise at times to achieve scale. In this case, I would offer the training workshops, and I would offer a recorded version of the workshops and make it available on the network for on-demand viewing. I do not find the recorded workshops to be quite as effective as the in-person training can be, but they still build skills that will help users adopt the application. I might even augment this with additional self-paced training resources online, such as other how-to videos or presentations. This achieves scale because reaching those extra users does not incur any extra training delivery costs.

■ **Tip**   Organizations that subscribe to Microsoft volume licensing often have access to e-learning vouchers that they can use for training. Microsoft offers e-learning courses not just for IT professionals and developers, but also for end-user SharePoint site collection administrators and power users.

`www.microsoft.com/learning/en/us/business/volume-licensing.aspx`

Short videos available on-demand combined with quick start guides can provide a solution for training that scales to the masses of users. Your users can access a discrete topic just in time and as the users need it. If the content is direct and concise for that topic, a user can digest it quickly and then they quickly become productive with performing the task. Again, this can complement the other training offerings you make available and it can provide support resources with content that they can refer end-users to when users open training-related support requests.

Designing Custom Training

When I create any type of training, I like to break it down into small units that address specific learning objectives. The main tool I use to organize these units is a DACUM chart, which stands for *Develop a Curriculum*. I first learned about these charts when I took an adult instruction design and development program at our local community college, which included a range of courses from lesson planning to how to evaluate learning, to incorporating technology in a classroom. One of the courses was specific to establishing learning outcome objectives and using those to design the curriculum for a training course or workshop. The learning objectives drove the entire training and all its content. Each part of the course I create relates to a desired outcome I intend for the learner to learn. Since that process was so valuable and effective, I included this section to share with you some of what I learned in that course and from applying its concepts in practice.

You can apply this process whether you are designing classroom training, online videos, or another type of e-learning or self-paced training resource. These concepts are all about how to organize the content for the eventual instruction. How you implement that instruction can and will vary. Better yet, you can use these techniques to design and organize the training, and then implement the instruction in multiple ways, such as a training manual, classroom training, and an e-learning component. Think of this first part as organizing what you want to teach and you can later decide how you want to teach it. You identify what you want to teach at a high-level by establishing the overall learning objectives, and from there you can work your way down into the details of different learning tasks and activities that will lead a learner toward the learning objective. The tool I use to organize the learning objectives and their associated learning tasks is a DACUM chart.

A DACUM chart consists of columns and rows. You list the learning objectives down the left column, and then for each learning objective you list the tasks or activities involved across the row beside it. Typically, the left column consists of rectangles that angle out along their right sides to form a sort of arrow that points to the row of tasks. The rest of the columns in the row consist of rectangles that contain each task or activity associated with a learning objective. In Figure 5-1, I provide an example of a compact DACUM chart with two learning objectives that relate to learning how to use collaboration team sites.

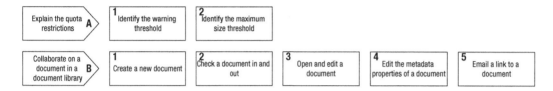

Figure 5-1. *An example DACUM chart that illustrates two learning objectives with their associated tasks*

The first thing that I want you to notice in the chart is the learning objectives. Notice that I wrote them using a verb in an action statement. These objectives are things the learner will be able to do after taking the training, and you want to write them using a verb phrase as in my example. You are not writing a novel with these objectives, so it is okay if you repeat some of the verbs you use to start your objective statement. Do not get caught up worrying about the style or with needing to vary how each statement sounds; just focus on creating an objective that uses an action phrase. If you capture something more abstract or that is more of a statement, add a verb and turn it into an action.

The process I use to create objectives with an action phrase begins with thinking about what the learner is going to do with the new skills that they learn as part of the objective. If they are not going to do anything with it or are not going to use it, then this is a good time to question whether the topic belongs in the training. Learners only have so much capacity to learn and I only have so much space within a training session to include content, so I have to make decisions and cut content that I do not expect will add any value to the learner. When I stay focused on what the learner will do or how he or she will later use what they are learning, the training naturally aligns itself with what the learner will find relevant, and it will therefore add value. In contrast, if one just bombards learners with a stream of content, learners may or may not grasp parts of it, but the learner will have to do all the work to relate it to what is relevant for them. Put in the work now and think about the outcomes that your learners will take away from the training, because good learning objectives can make or break how effective your training is.

Often times I come up with learning objectives that are simply to know some aspect of the material, such as when I want a learner to know something that does not relate to anything they will do or use. For example, I may want learners to understand that a particular limitation exists, such as with their site quota. One learning objective might be for them to know how to request additional quota space, but if that is not an option then I will need an objective for them to be aware of the quota restriction. One phrase that often comes to mind is to *understand* the quota restrictions, but understanding is not a strong action, at least not one that I can measure and evaluate their learning using the same action. A stronger action phrase would be one where I can also use it to measure whether the learner has achieved the learning objective. In this case, a stronger action phrase might be to *explain* the quota restrictions.

Considering what the learner will do and using a strong action phrase highlights the essence of how you can write effective learning objectives. It also aligns well with evaluating a learner's learning by checking whether they can do an action identified in a learning objective. In a classroom, you may ask questions to check whether they learned what you intended to teach them before you move on to the next topic. For online learning, you might include a quiz to assess whether the learner learned. You could also include labs at the end of the unit where the learner actually performs tasks on a SharePoint site. However you measure learning, this is where the learning objective you write comes full circle.

Once you have the learning objectives listed in the left column in your DACUM chart, the next step is to list the tasks or activities involved in each objective. Here you analyze each objective and deconstruct its parts to identify what are all the parts making up the objective. For example, I created a learning objective to collaborate on a document in a SharePoint document library, and with that, I added some of the tasks involved in the objective. My list of tasks for that objective includes: create a new document, check a document in and out, open and edit a document, edit the metadata properties of a document, and e-mail a link to a document. These tasks all contribute to the learning objective and they provide a list of topics I need to include in the training resources for the learner to achieve that learning objective.

With a task list, you can begin to visualize the training resources. Some tasks may fit well as a hands-on lab or exercise, while others will work better as an example or case study. I like to think of this as the learning activity associated with the learning task. What I try to avoid here is making too many of the learning activities a presentation slide with bullet points projected on a screen. I try to include variety with the learning activities to keep the training session fresh and interesting, and to keep the learner engaged, but I especially try to avoid summarizing verbiage on presentation slides wherever possible.

New trainers and novice instructors might find it easy to rely on a presentation slide to walk them through their training materials, but this can be very boring for the learners. Where I have seen this approach fail the most frequently is when there is a large amount of content to get through. Actually, I raise a flag anytime I hear about a trainer who focuses primarily on getting *through* content. Sometimes I catch myself digressing into these types of attitudes, as if my job is simply to touch on a topic quickly so that I can check it off a list and feel good about everything I covered. I notice this comes up when I have too much content that I am trying to fit in a training session or when I am not prepared enough to deliver the training. Whatever the case, rushing through content just so I can say that I covered it will not do anyone any good. I need to either cut content or spend more time preparing.

As you look at your DACUM chart, you may have listed a lot of learning objectives, and each may have a large number of learning tasks. This is where you might find it tempting to summarize them all in a presentation slide so that you can include everything. You may not have time to cover everything. Everyone has their own style and their own preference, and my preference is to avoid overloading training like this. For me, I find that if I include content simply so that I can feel as if I did my job as a trainer, whether or not the learners grasp the content, then I failed as a trainer. I wasted my time and the learners' time by covering topics that the learners did not grasp or take away. I would rather cover a few things, cover them well, and be sure the learners comprehended them all, as opposed to covering a lot of topics and hoping that the learners do their job and absorb as much as they can. Effective learning does not work that way; it only works when the focus is on the learner and what the learner actually learns, not on how much the instructor can cover.

This brings me back to the learning objectives: before you move on to the next objective, you can check how well your learners meet the learning objective. Have they met an adequate proficiency level and can they do the action as the objective describes it? If you stop to check this, then you can confirm that you were effective in delivering the training. If you were not effective and the learner does not understand, it is time to review and maybe explain it in a different way. You now have the basic formula to teach an adult something: describe the learning objective in an action phrase that you can later measure, teach them using a variety of training styles and techniques, and then measure how successful the learner achieved the learning objective. Once everyone achieves the learning objective, then you can move on to the next one.

The teaching formula is a simple formula, almost too simple, and the trick is to keep the learner as your primary focus – they are the point, the whole point, and your primary reason for delivering the training. As soon as you catch yourself slipping into placing the focus on the instructor and what you need to get through, remind yourself that the instructor already knows the content and your whole purpose is to help the learner to learn it. Writing the learning objectives is the first place you put the emphasis on the learner, and you can continue the process by breaking up the objectives into modules that you may use as individual workshops or training videos or with other training materials. Several modules make up your curriculum, and they generally consist of one or more of your learning objectives.

You can divide a module into units, and within these, you can address one or more of the tasks that make up a learning objective. I like to use these structures to organize the learning materials because they break it down into chunks. At the end of each unit, I can ask questions or include some way to assess how well my learners have learned the topics in the unit. This breaks everything down into manageable chunks, manageable for the learner to learn and for me to organize the materials. A unit might be a video or a quick start guide, or it may be a workshop or just a part of a workshop. I like this flexibility because it lets me use different mediums and different training delivery methods to help the learner learn. To build out the content for the unit, I only have to focus on those tasks that the unit includes, and the units will all come together cohesively.

When I find that I have too many learning objectives that I would like the learner to achieve but I cannot fit all the content in the time available, I like to create appendix units. These appendix units often take the form of self-paced training videos or quick start guides that supplement the core training. I find this approach is especially effective for classroom training where you may face a limited amount of time, yet you would still like to make extra topics available for those who want to continue with their learning at their own pace.

Delivering training can serve several purposes. You may just feel a duty to teach users how to use a new system you are deploying, or you may want to make sure users know how to be effective and productive with the system so they experience all its value. Perhaps no one would use the system if you do not show them how, or maybe more people will use it if training is available. Effective training can have a positive effect on user adoption, and in the next section, I share some of these considerations for user adoption.

Considerations for User Adoption

If people do not know how to use your application, then they will go with something they do know how to use. People do not resist change as much as one might assume they do. They just take the path of least resistance or the one that looks the most attractive. A good example of this is the behavior changes in recent years where many people stopped going to video stores to rent videos and instead adopted new ways to rent videos by streaming them from an on-demand service. The service made it easy to figure out how to rent videos, and they made the purchase immediate and convenient right from a customer's home. This offered less resistance than the previous process of having to go to a video rental store to rent the video, and then having to go back to return it. It also solved the problem of scratched disks that one might occasionally face when renting a DVD.

People flock to new changes and embrace them when the change offers less resistance than the current way of doing things. If the change you are introducing is not improving the user experience, then you might want to ask yourself why you are making the change in the first place. Perhaps you are making the change for other reasons, such as to standardize on a platform or for cost reductions, but whatever your ultimate reasons are for introducing a change, it is still worth improving the user experience in the process. Find those areas that your change will improve and think about the benefits from the end-user's perspective. I often use the following questions to help identify how a change will benefit an end-user.

- Will it save them time?

- Will the process become more logical or transparent for them?

- Will it automate redundant or meaningless tasks?

- Will it make information more open and available?

- What does your change offer that benefits the end-user and motivates them to adopt it?

Once you have a good list of how your end-users stand to benefit by adopting a new application included with the change you planned, then you have the material you need to paint a picture to show this change as the path of least resistance. I also build training materials around this information, because it can reinforce people's motives to adopt the change. Even if my ultimate motive is to save money by consolidating licensing costs, I still try to find a reason to benefit the end-users. It may feel like a public relations' spin, but it is still better than forcing a change down everyone's throats and generating a lot of resistance.

By taking an end-user focus on the change, and examining it from their perspectives, I can also predict where the most common stumbling blocks are. This helps me determine what kinds of training I should include, and how extensive I need to make the training I offer. It is all about making this change the path of least resistance, so every little snag I can predict and mitigate with training or with some other way, the more likely it is that users will adopt the new change. This can involve significant upfront planning and analysis, and ongoing adjustments to the training you offer, but its payoff is in the support it saves and how it mitigates any resistance to change.

There are other considerations for user adoption beyond just mitigating any resistance to change. How do you deal with your users adopting a new application to use it inappropriately or inefficiently? People are creative beings and if something is not clear, then they may come up with their own answers. For example, if they face resistance, such as an unknown process, then they will search for the path of least resistance by creating their own process. The process they come up with may or may not fit with how you intended end-users to use the application, and this might even create more challenges to support down the road. On the other hand, sometimes when users use their creativity and discover new ways to use an application, you can discover new value in the application. Therefore, I usually do not want to be overly restrictive with how I let users use an application to find new creative ways to solve problems with it, but I also want them to use it efficiently and in ways that will not cause a burden on support.

Internal classroom workshops provide a great way to help your users learn an application and how to use it in the manner you intended. You might also use computer-based training to show users the proper usage of an application. Another very effective process involves providing your users with a one-page reference sheet that includes the steps for how to perform a particular task. I call these reference sheets quick start guides. In the next section, I describe how you can offer these reference sheets to complement your other training efforts and support user adoption.

Offering Quick Start End-User Guides

I think of quick start guides as summarized and concise reference material that address specific tasks that a user needs to perform. In this sense, I think of the guides as a type of cheat sheet that an end-user can follow to accomplish the most popular processes for interacting with their SharePoint site. They are detailed enough that they can walk a user through the steps without requiring that he or she possesses much background knowledge, but they are concise enough that users can use them as references to refresh their memory later.

There is a balance between how much detail to include and how concise to make a guide. My own rule of thumb limits the detail I include for a specific task to where I can cover the steps of that task in a single page. Think of a recipe in a cookbook. These are often contained on just a page or two, and they rarely contain much background information or explanations. They get right to the point and list the ingredients you need and the steps you need to follow. I like to model my guides after recipes in their level of conciseness, but I also like to include a visual summary wherever possible, which may be a screenshot or a flow chart diagram.

Your purpose for providing these quick start guides is to arm your end-users with enough direction on how to perform some of the key tasks so that they do not stare blankly at a SharePoint screen and wonder what to do. You might provide them as laminated sheets that you provide to everyone when you launch a new application. In this case, a laminated sheet can provide two benefits: it can guide your users and help make them familiar with how to perform certain tasks, and the sheets make your users aware of the application and its key functions. Alternatively, you might e-mail a PDF of the guide to everyone when you launch or to new people as they join the organization.

I design these guides as a one-pager, so they are an at-a-glance reference that addresses the majority of an end-user's questions or their struggles for a specific task. It is critical to design and write these with the end-user's perspective in mind, because the whole point of the quick start guide is to facilitate their learning and productive use of an application without involving additional support. This is how I scale a deployment and enable mass adoption while also providing guidance to each user. If you supply your users with a few sheets outlining their primary tasks, you should help to alleviate some of their anxiety around the new system because they will have the reference material that they need. However, I like to limit the number of guides, because they will lose their effect if you overwhelm each user with a binder full of quick start guides. You will probably find that a few laminated sheets will be welcome to get them started, while a binder full of tasks can feel intimidating.

Another trick I like to include in these guides is a link to a video on the network. In the video, I might do a screen cast where I walk through the task covered in the guide, and I might even add a discussion or provide additional tips that I did not have room to include on the guide. On the same page as the video, I might also include a series of screenshots that provide a visual example of each step listed in the guide. This is a great way to keep the guides concise, while also providing additional information in a self-service fashion.

Consultant Comrade

Training is expensive, and I often engage with departments who do not have the budget to send their people for a lot of training. They also might find it difficult to spare people if they are already operating at capacity. It is tough to make major investments in people for the future when you have immediate needs. This was especially true in 2008 and years following, where I saw training budgets slashed or frozen as companies struggled to balance their budgets and maintain operations. These are tough decisions for a manager to make, but sometimes they are necessary ones.

During those tough recessionary years in North America, where practically every budget seemed frozen or slashed, I realized that many of my clients were not going to get training that year, nor did they have any plans to attend any conferences. Yet there I would be, engaged with a client to drive a new SharePoint deployment that I would hand over to a couple of future SharePoint administrators, none of whom had any SharePoint experience or training, and there was no budget for any immediate training.

It was around that time when I changed my engagement model. I realized the value of knowledge transfer and the impact I could make in lieu of any formal training. As a result, I started emphasizing a knowledge transfer component within all my engagements, where I tried to share as much expertise and informal training as my client could absorb. Acting as a peer mentor with my clients helped to fill part of the training gap, at least the short-term training gap and for those mentoring objectives I would identify as priorities.

Another thing happened as well, and that was the effect of emphasizing knowledge transfer as a component of the engagement. Now instead of simply delivering software or architecture diagrams or whatever, my engagements also included learning and knowledge transfer objectives as part of the deliverables. This gave my clients another reason to engage with me, particularly because their training budgets were limited and they could get this benefit from a consulting project instead, one they already planned and allocated budget.

Do not underestimate the value of knowledge transfer in your own consulting. I have taken several workshops on training and mentoring, but even if you do not have a lot of experience with this, you can still provide your clients with plenty of learning opportunities. You bring a broader perspective than they get, because as a consultant you get to see different environments and different uses of SharePoint. Going to user groups and conferences helps with broadening your perspective, but it is not the same as actually getting hands on in all of these different scenarios with different clients. You can share product expertise and your experience on all the different practices that you have encountered.

Another side benefit from consulting is that some tasks become routine for you. Where a client might only perform certain tasks a few times, such as deploying SharePoint itself into production, you might perform this activity repeatedly on your engagements. You may have worked out the kinks and fine-tuned the process, and this is valuable knowledge that can save your client a lot of time, and it is also an opportunity to share knowledge with them to help them understand more about the deployment process than just watching you click through a series of wizards or configuration steps.

If you are not sure where to start or how to conduct any sort of knowledge transfer with your clients, then this chapter will point you in the right direction and give you some of those answers. Pay particular attention to the peer mentoring section and adopt some of those practices, because that is essentially what you will be, a peer mentor to your client. I also recommend that you make your client aware of the extra value they are getting from you by setting learning objectives, just as you would if you were a peer mentor to someone on your team.

Inside Story: Notes from the Field

Several years ago, I joined a SharePoint team to deploy some SharePoint farms and an enterprise search engine. I joined midstream in the project's delivery, after they made most of the decisions and the infrastructure was largely deployed. My focus at the time largely centered on custom control development, and particularly web parts, which was what they hired me to contribute to the team. What I immediately discovered was that my new team did not have anyone with any SharePoint skills, there was no SharePoint administrator, and they were largely learning on the fly through trial and error (mostly error, it seemed).

My new team's approach meant two things: one was that I would have to take over and act as the SharePoint administrator to stabilize the environments, and that I had my work cut out for me. They contracted inexperienced consultants, a team of consultants who were largely student interns, and this comprised the extent of the outside help that drove the SharePoint initiative. This presented another problem, where we relied on consultants who lacked any kind of enterprise experience, which means their decisions lacked any foresight for sustainability, scalability, and maintenance.

Both my team and these consultants were learning on the fly and making amateurish decisions that would haunt me for some time after as I tried to reverse some of the different directions that they explored. This seems challenging enough, but the real bite came from not acquiring any knowledge transfer from these junior consulting resources. My team was only marginally more inexperienced than the consultants; no wonder they needed to hire me, and in a hurry.

Our training issues did not end there. The project manager on my team had a poor attitude when it came to training. I could see how little he valued training with the team itself, as no one had received any readiness training nor did anyone have any training slated in their plans. In addition, no one could expect to gain adequate knowledge transfer from the consulting vendor he selected, as the consultants also lacked experience and expertise. Apparently for him, he thought true experts were overrated and we could all figure out SharePoint on our own, including our end-users. That was the real kicker for me: he actually said the words, something to the effect that if a user cannot figure out how to use SharePoint, then they probably should not be working here.

You cannot know what you do not know, and so I try my best to appreciate that everyone is at a different level. I try to be patient and tolerant that I am not always going to arrive at the correct solution the first time around and that everyone will not always show up with all the right answers, me included. However, this project approach was a recipe for disaster, where a green team of consultants led by an inept project manager were simply throwing technology over the fence and expecting users to just figure it out while SharePoint would somehow magically just run itself.

It is frustrating to inherit these problems, but you can work through them and correct these sins of your SharePoint past, whether you inherited them or you found that you unknowingly took a wrong turn somewhere along the way. In this example, I took the helm and began steering the ship back on course. With me carrying the weight from the operations side of things, I was confident in our ability sustain the service in the short-term. My priority was to start training users so I could guide and influence their usage and adoption.

My first task was to rewrite an end-user training manual. We had a token training guide, but it was subpar. Over my holidays, I had a few lengthy flights and I decided to use that time to create the training resources. I wrote a beginner training guide that would introduce SharePoint, while addressing some of the most common support questions that had come up. I then wrote an advanced training guide as well that would cover some techniques for customizing a team site.

I paired these training guides with four-hour training workshops and delivered them regularly to most of our locations around the world. I also posted the training guides on the intranet along with recorded videos and quick start guides that walked through different tasks, and I created an internal user group community to start facilitating different types of support. The outcome from these initiatives was dramatic and the impact was practically immediate. This significantly reduced the burden on support and my users found productive value from using SharePoint.

Wrapping Up

Throughout this chapter, I discussed the need for training and readiness, both for your end-users and for your operations team. I shared some approaches that you can use as part of your training and readiness strategy, including formal options for classroom and online training, and informal options such as peer mentoring. With the right training, your operations team will have the right skills to support the service, and your end-users will be better able to maximize their productivity using your SharePoint service.

No matter how well you train your users, if the service is not stable, then you will struggle in any effort to drive user adoption. In the next chapter, I look at measures that you can use to monitor the health of your service. You can use these measures to help you identify where your problem areas are, which can signal things such as where to focus your readiness efforts for support issues related to unfamiliarity or inexperience. I also share an approach for investigating issues to identify their root cause as opposed to just addressing the symptom of the incident.

■ ■ ■

CHAPTER 6

Measuring and Reporting on Your SharePoint Service Performance

Success is not permanent, and failure is not fatal.

—Mike Ditka

In this chapter, I cover how to take the pulse of your SharePoint service and measure its vitals against defined targets. To achieve this, I provide considerations for the types of metrics to measure that will indicate the overall health of your SharePoint environment and what thresholds to compare the measures against. To link the service metrics to a proactive service philosophy, I introduce the value and the process for conducting a root-cause analysis when the SharePoint service is trending negatively or an incident occurs that negatively affects availability.

After reading this chapter, you will know how to:

- Establish time targets

- Measure and report on performance and availability

- Plan your incident response

- Investigate an incident and perform a root-cause analysis

- Conduct retrospectives on incidents for proactive prevention

- Monitor and tune your service

Measuring and Reporting

You can capture a measurement on practically anything; however, you cannot measure everything. Some potential measures provide meaningful insights into the state of the service, while others are simply a piece of immaterial information. Some of your measures may be harder to quantify, while others are readily available. This is the challenge with determining what to measure and what to include in reports.

What people choose to measure is what they prioritize, whether this was what was measured and graded on in school or what contributes to one's bonus at work. This is true for what I prioritize in SharePoint as well. The opposite is true too: when I do not have any measures then I might not know what to prioritize. If I do not have explicit measures to target or if the measures that I set are too vague or unclear, then this can lead to a situation where I feel as if I am constantly chasing incidents. To avoid this, you can use measurements to help focus attention on the priorities that matter the most.

On the other hand, measurements are not very useful if you do not do anything with them. Primarily, you need to know whether the measurement you capture is good or bad, and then you need to report this information so you can make decisions and respond to changing conditions. Reporting on the measurements is the second half to the equation, and the two go hand-in-hand. Essentially, measuring an aspect of the system captures the event, and reporting when it reaches a threshold raises potential issues to your attention.

If you have a measure and you want to report on it, you need to make it meaningful. You need a filter to only alert you to what needs your attention, and to filter out the rest. I like to establish thresholds, where if the measure is within a healthy threshold, a report or alert does not raise up to me and I can safely ignore it. This way, when a measure falls outside a healthy threshold, I will notice it and I can direct my attention to it. Throughout this chapter, I share some of the thresholds that I use in my measurements to filter out some of the noise in service monitoring and reporting.

I cannot stress this enough: one critical aspect of measuring and reporting for me is to filter out and ensure that the noise does not consume me. I do not want false positives or false alarms, and I do not want to be inundated with reports or alerts with such frequency that I begin to ignore them. I set thresholds so that only events that need to come to my attention do so. By minimizing any irrelevant noise, I stay focused on those measurements that affect the health of the SharePoint service.

You might base some measurements on processes or workflows, such as how long a service request sits in the queue or how long it takes to resolve an incident. I break out these measures into what I refer to as *operational metrics*, which involve processes in the service that are not completely system-automated. For those system-automated or system-contained processes, I refer to them as *performance metrics* that you can use to measure system performance levels.

One great aspect of the SharePoint platform is that it exposes many of the technology-related measurements that you might want to capture and report on. I come back to these measures later in the chapter in the section on performance metrics. In that section, I also discuss other tools to measure performance that you will find in the underlying infrastructure that supports SharePoint, and in particular, I focus on Performance Monitor in Windows Server 2012.

You can use all these ways to measure and report on different aspects of your SharePoint service to stabilize your SharePoint environment and maximize its availability. This is not just an academic exercise. Ultimately it lets you keep your finger on the pulse of your SharePoint service and it gives you early warning signs if its health is deteriorating. With those early warning signs, you can then respond with preventative or corrective actions, and this will help to keep your SharePoint service running stable.

Before I get too far into measuring and reporting, let me take a step back and look at your quintessential purpose to incorporating them into your SharePoint service measuring and reporting to maximize the service availability. At the end of the day, you want to maximize the availability of your SharePoint service, and for me, this is the main driver behind why I measure and report on different aspects of my SharePoint service. I come back to measuring and reporting later in this chapter, but first, let's understand its purpose: let's understand availability.

Understanding Your System's Availability

In its simplest meaning as I use it in this book, availability relates to how available the system is for use. Is something preventing users from accessing their SharePoint site and interacting with it? If they have access, has their experience degraded below an acceptable level? If so, users are experiencing reduced system availability.

In the following sections, I give you suggestions on how to set targets for specific things that you can measure to understand what your availability is and how to monitor it. I like to think of these as early warning signs or early detection systems, something I put in place to see the overall availability of the service. It also allows me to respond quickly to events that interrupt service, such as when an event causes a measure to go outside the threshold for its healthy range. For me, I can only define availability in the context of thresholds.

You will face a trade-off when it comes to defining your availability targets. In an ideal and imaginary world, you would always be available and you could seamlessly handle any spikes in demand. In the real world, this aspiration might grow prohibitively expensive, and it could be an illusion you might never be able to achieve. The closer you get to 100% availability, the higher the price you will have to pay.

Even if you had an unlimited budget, could you even achieve 100% availability? I once heard this referred to as *the fallacy of infinite availability*. Some things are just beyond your control, such as the network beyond your data center. What if for political reasons or for censorship reasons, a foreign country decides to block the public Internet and instead the country runs its own private network? If its citizens were regular users of your system and who have then lost access to it, would you count this as a loss in availability?

Availability is complex. It may feel as if you have to achieve some minimal level of availability, because that is what the architecture diagrams look like on TechNet and that is how people talk at conferences, but it might be overkill for your situation and usage. I think that more availability is always better in the sense that it will meet the needs of end-users better, but it might not be better in the sense that if it costs more to achieve the higher availability than the value that the added availability produces, then it probably does not serve you well in the long run.

How available does your SharePoint service need to be? To answer this, you need to consider your tolerance for downtime and data loss. When you consider your tolerance for downtime, you might hear this referred to as the "nines" of availability. This refers to your percentage of availability and Table 6-1 lists common availability percentage levels along with their equivalent amounts of downtime per day, week, and year.

Table 6-1. *Availability Percentage and Calculated Downtime Matrix*

Availability %	Downtime per Day	Downtime per Week	Downtime per Year
90% (one nine)	2.4 hours	16.8 hours	36.5 days
95%	1.2 hours	8.4 hours	18.25 days
97%	43.2 minutes	5.04 hours	10.95 days
98%	28.8 minutes	3.36 hours	7.3 days
99% (two nines)	14.4 minutes	1.68 hours	3.65 days
99.5%	7.2 minutes	50.4 minutes	1.83 days
99.8%	2.88 minutes	20.16 minutes	17.52 hours
99.9% (three nines)	1.44 minutes	10.08 minutes	8.76 hours
99.95%	43.2 seconds	5.04 minutes	4.38 hours
99.99% (four nines)	8.64 seconds	1.01 minutes	52.56 minutes
99.999% (five nines)	0.864 seconds	6.05 seconds	5.26 minutes
99.9999% (six nines)	0.086 seconds	0.605 seconds	31.5 seconds
99.99999% (seven nines)	0.0086 seconds	0.06 seconds	3.15 seconds

I like to break this down in several ways, rather than trying to define a single availability need. Primarily, I consider availability from two perspectives: normal operations and extenuating circumstances. I also like to divide availability requirements by service level or application. This gives me a tiered availability measure and it lets me adapt it to fit the situation.

During normal operations, you might face outages or reduced availability that relates to server or network failures, over utilized hardware, local area network issues, or similar problems. Your tolerance for these categories of downtime may be low, particularly during the peak hours of a workday. After hours, you may or may not have a greater tolerance, and as such, I often further divide the availability needs into peak versus non-peak times. I consult with some large retail customers whose availability needs are seasonal, where their tolerance for downtime significantly diminishes in the fall months. It is important to understand these different availability requirements so that you do not go overboard trying to achieve availability where you have no requirements driving you.

For extenuating circumstances, I consider these as larger scale incidents that affect availability, such as natural disasters, major acts of terrorism, or other catastrophes. I redefine the availability needs in light of these potential situations because often the availability requirements change or are different from those during normal operations. The organization may have more tolerance for downtime when there is a major outage that affects an entire region.

I live in Vancouver, Canada, on the West Coast of North America, which is along an area known as the Pacific Ring of Fire. We face a constant threat of natural disasters that we have to plan for here. I live near the Juan de Fuca Plate's fault line, and although I hear most of our buildings can withstand earthquakes up to around a seven magnitude, if a major earthquake strikes, it will still cause a serious disruption. The Pacific Ocean to our west frequently experiences earthquakes on the ocean floor, and if one strikes with enough force, it will cause a tsunami. As if that was not enough, Vancouver is along the Cascade Mountain Range where to our north is Mount Garibaldi and to our south is Mount St. Helens – both are potentially active volcanoes.

My region may seem like a natural hazard zone, but other areas face other types of threats. When I consult with clients on the East Coast, they face different risks for natural disasters. Some of them have to plan for potential tornados, hurricanes, floods, ice storms, and the like. Every area seems to face risks for events that will interrupt availability. These events may also include political unrest, civil conflict, labor disputes, or a number of other causes beyond your control.

One solution you might consider for maintaining availability is to design geographic redundancy, where you replicate your data and services across multiple data centers located in different regions around the world. You might find a cloud provider that offers this type of hosting, or you might implement it yourself. However, just because you can does not mean that in every situation you must do this.

For example, if Vancouver has an incident that causes a wide scale loss of all connectivity and power, how much will I care if my timesheet application is unavailable while someone works to restore service? My tolerance for downtime is quite high for extenuating circumstances in my region. However, in my normal consulting operations, I need this timesheet application available at least occasionally throughout the month so that I can generate invoices. This is a simple example, but it illustrates how needs shift and how an organization's downtime tolerance will vary depending on the situation. This is why you need to consider these different perspectives and your different service levels as you determine your availability requirements. Every situation is unique because every organization is unique.

I have done consulting work for a client whose deployment includes mobile data centers onboard Humvees, where they need to be available in a temporary location with a select cache of the data and with occasional connectivity to synchronize with a permanent or semi-permanent data center. My client wanted a constant and real-time connection between the permanent or semi-permanent data centers and the mobile data centers, but they only needed an occasional connection. As such, I would strive to maximize connectivity, but I met their availability requirements by ensuring at least occasional connectivity.

My point is that availability will vary, depending on the situation and other external factors. Your availability needs will also vary as you face those situations and as you weigh you tolerance for downtime against the cost to mitigate downtime. As you identify your availability needs and your tolerance levels, the next step is to establish thresholds. One useful threshold you can set is a time target, and because time is such a popular threshold to set for your targets, I discuss that in more depth in the next section.

Establishing Time Targets

There are different types of time targets you can use, depending on what you want to measure. Time targets are useful because time is a popular unit to measure and report on for different metrics. You could use response times, the duration an incident affects service, or the amount of processing within a period. You can apply time to measure and report on metrics in several ways.

Sometimes you might know exactly what time targets you want to set. For example, you might know that for the inner-farm network communication among the different SharePoint and SQL Server instances, your minimum supported latency time is eight milliseconds. You might set an optimum latency threshold target somewhere between one and two milliseconds, and if latency begins to trend beyond this time then your monitoring system will alert you.

Other times, you might find the time targets are much less prescriptive. Maybe you do not know how long something will take or what time targets you should strive to meet. What do you do then? I discussed some of these types of time targets in Chapter 2 when I looked at priority levels for service request tickets. As I indicated there, sometimes you have to set an initial time objective, and then adapt it as you learn more about how long things take. This is the equivalent of licking your finger and holding it up to judge the wind: it is not exact, but it will give you an indication and a place to start. It might be close enough that it works for you, or you might need to make adjustments later.

I usually start out with a time target that feels reasonable and achievable. At the same time, I do not want to treat them in the same fashion that corporate budgets can often feel like. That is, I avoid any measures that give an impression of arbitrary targets or any measures based on a blanket annual percentage increase. I try to ensure that the numbers are meaningful and that they directly relate to a service driver. I adapt the measure as needed to set appropriate expectations and to fit changes to their underlying driver.

Some questions I may ask myself to determine the target for a measure include the following:

- What is the ideal time to strive to reach?

- What is an acceptable or minimal time I can meet?

- What influences the amount of time something will take?

- Are there any exceptions to the time measure or targets?

With this information, I can begin to envision a range or a bearing to set the initial target. I may set a tentative target to review and revise later when I know more about the measure, but I do set a target to get started. You can apply time to many aspects of your service that you want to monitor, and you can combine it with other measures. In the following sections, I look at specific aspects you can measure, first for overall operational measures and then for system specific performance metrics.

Measuring and Reporting on Operational Metrics

In this category, I measure and report on operational aspects that support the SharePoint service. These aspects typically measure activities that involve human input, such as a person's response time to a task. I also include other big picture system measures, such as the total amount of unplanned system downtime. The primary output for these measures report on the discipline and effectiveness of an operations team and their activities.

You might include different metrics that report on service requests, which can give you a good indicator for how well your users are receiving the SharePoint service you provide and how well your team is responding to user needs. Metrics that I find useful in this category include the following list:

- The current number of open service request tickets for the team or individual team member, grouped by priority or severity.

- A weekly count of the number of new service request tickets opened to report the historical trend.

- A weekly measure of the average time service request tickets remain open for the team and by team member, grouped by priority or severity.

- A weekly count of the number of service request tickets resolved within and outside the SLA objective for the team and by team member, grouped by priority or severity.

Reporting on unplanned system downtime and service request metrics provides valuable indicators for the health of a service and the maturity level of an operations team. For those tasks that surround responses to events or support requests, I like to categorize these as *run activities* when I measure them. I think of the other tasks that are more proactive in nature as *investment activities*, or those measures that invest in and will contribute to some aspect of the service in the future. Metrics I find useful in this investment category include the following list:

- A quarterly measure of the total number of training and readiness hours completed for the team and by team member.

- A quarterly measure of the number of usage audits and proactive health checks performed.

- The number of end-users who attend an internal training workshop during a period or the total number trained to date.

You may find other measures relevant for your organization as well. These are only a few examples that I find are the most useful. One point to keep in mind is that whatever measures you use and report on will become the priorities for your operations team. People focus their attention on what the team measures and reports. As such, this can be an effective approach to introduce change or to motivate new priorities across a team.

As you identify the operational areas that you want to measure, your next challenge becomes how to capture the actual measures and report on them. For some metrics, you may have a system that already monitors this information. For example, your service request ticketing system likely stores the tickets in a database that tracks whether or not a ticket is open, the priority or severity of the ticket, and whose support queue the ticket is in. The system likely also records timestamps for events such as when a user opens the ticket and when a support resource closes it.

Other measures may not be as readily available in a database. For example, if you do not have a learning management system, you may not have a database to query training data. One solution you might consider is to create a status report process for your team. You can use SharePoint 2013 and InfoPath forms to collect the status report data. Questions in the status report can relate to measures you want to capture, such as the number of training hours that a team member attends or the amount of proactive work they perform in a period. This can provide you with a data source for the data that you want to report on and monitor.

If you do gather operational data within SharePoint, you can build reports using the built-in web parts such as the Key Performance Indicator (KPI) web part. You can also query external systems by creating an external list through a Business Connectivity Services (BCS) model, and you can report on those metrics within SharePoint as well. You can create a scorecard or a dashboard within a SharePoint 2013 site that reports on the state and efficiency of the service operations team. You can also configure workflows and alerts within the SharePoint site to notify the appropriate people, such as to other managers or escalation engineers, when metrics begin to trend outside their target thresholds.

Monitoring an operations team helps you to identify whether any areas are heading off track or need attention. This provides a view into how effectively the team provides the SharePoint service and how proactively the team invests and prepares for future operations. To complement this information and provide the rest of the picture, I also capture the more transactional system-level performance metrics, which I discuss in the next section.

Measuring and Reporting on Performance Metrics

You can capture farm and system performance using built-in tools, such as the Windows Server 2012 Performance Monitor or the SQL Server 2012 Profiler. With these tools, you can capture performance levels and resource utilization levels of the servers at specified intervals. This gives you performance data for the different resource aspects that enable a SharePoint service to run.

There are many performance counters you can use to monitor performance, and which ones you choose will depend on the application load and the resource characteristics that you want to monitor. For example, when you want to measure CPU utilization, select the CPU counters. When you want to measure an application specific counter, such as the unhandled exception counter for ASP.NET applications, you can select one from a category that relates to your needs. Figure 6-1 provides an example of Performance Monitor graphing sample CPU and RAM counters.

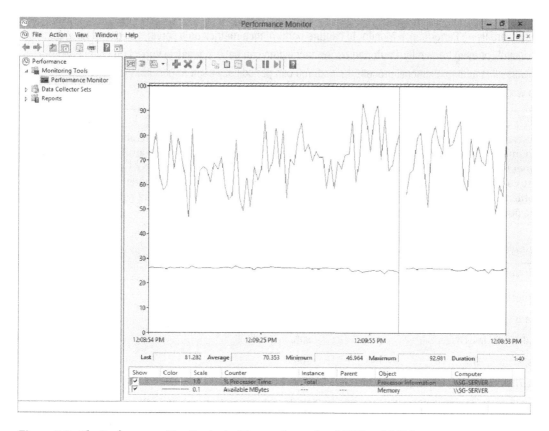

Figure 6-1. *The Performance Monitor tool with sample graphs of CPU and RAM counters*

In addition to connecting to a server using Performance Monitor, you can also use System Center 2012 Operations Manager or another type of operations management and monitoring software. If you use Operations Manager, you also need the System Center Management Pack for SharePoint Server 2013. This type of software can provide you with an end-to-end view of the performance across the servers and applications that make up your SharePoint service. If you are running your SharePoint farm using virtual servers, you might also have additional performance monitoring and analysis tools as part of your virtual machine management software.

■ **Note**   For more information on Microsoft System Center 2012 Operations Manager, please see the following TechNet site: `http://technet.microsoft.com/hh205987`

For our purposes, I am going to focus primarily on the monitoring and diagnostic tools that come with Windows Server 2012 or are typically available without additional licensing requirements. My goal here is to share techniques that you can use to assess the performance and health of your environment and to make those techniques relevant to everyone, and so I chose to focus on those tools that are available for the least common denominator. If you have other tools, you are welcome to adapt this guidance to fit your environment and your toolset.

■ **Note** When you are using Performance Monitor to capture performance metrics on a server, you do not need to capture data constantly or even frequently. Capturing performance data can have a negative impact on your server's performance because it is adding additional processing load. You can periodically capture performance data and still get valuable data to work with.

Table 6-2 lists the most common counters that I use in Performance Monitor to get a general state of health for a server. These counters capture the core resource areas, and these can help to quickly identify any bottlenecks or over-utilized components. As you can see, I focus on disk, memory, CPU, network, and some ASP.NET specific measures. Along with these counters, I also include their thresholds that I target as indicators to signal potentially over-utilized resources or bottlenecks. Once a measure goes beyond its threshold for any sustained period, I typically treat this as an indicator of a potential issue to investigate.

Table 6-2. *Example Performance Counters with Sample Thresholds to Monitor*

Performance Counter Object	Target Threshold
Processor\% Processor Time_Total	< 75%
System\Processor Queue Length\(N/A)	< # of CPUs x 2
Memory\Available Mbytes\(N/A)	< 80%
Memory\Pages/sec\(N/A)	< 100
PhysicalDisk\% Disk Time\DataDrive	< # of Disks x 2
ASP.NET Applications\Request/sec_Total	Trends with sharp declines can indicate a problem
ASP.NET\Worker Processes Restarts	Any number above zero can indicate problems exist
.NET CLR Memory\% Time in GC	< 25%
Logical Disk\Avg. Disk Sec/Read	< 20 ms
Logical Disk\Avg. Disk Sec/Write	< 20 ms
Logical Disk\Average Disk sec/Read	1-4 ms for logs (ideally 1 ms on a cached array) 4-20 ms (ideally below 10 ms)
Logical Disk\Average Disk sec/Write	1-4 ms for logs (ideally 1 ms on a cached array) 4-20 ms (ideally below 10 ms)
Logical Disk\Current Disk Queue Length	< 20
Logical Disk\Average Disk Reads/sec & Logical Disk\Average Disk Write/sec	< 85% of disk capacity

Another important performance measure is connectivity, or how much latency your users will experience when they try to load a SharePoint page from their location. You may have tools to monitor your network with a rich set of features that can analyze network latency for you, and this is probably the ideal. However, if you do not, you can still do manual tests and manually time a page's load time. This may be as simple as using ping, where you open the command prompt and ping the servers from different areas of your network and then measure the response.

There are other web load testing tools that offer richer features than a ping from the command prompt, and depending on which tools you have access to, you might prefer one that offers scripting or automation capabilities.

One tool I use is Visual Studio 2012 with the Web Performance and Load testing capabilities. I find this tool useful for latency tests as well as for simulating a load on the servers. Using this tool, I can stress test the SharePoint service by simulating a heavy user load from multiple network locations and then monitor how the servers respond. It also provides useful reporting capabilities on the characteristics of the load test.

■ **Note** For more information on web performance and load testing in Visual Studio 2012, please see the following MSDN site: http://msdn.microsoft.com/dd293540

One valuable monitoring tool built in to SharePoint is the SharePoint Health Analyzer. This tool runs predefined rules at regularly scheduled intervals to evaluate the security, performance, configuration, and availability of the SharePoint farm. When the Health Analyzer detects a problem, it reports it in Central Administration and it provides guidance on how to correct the issue. You can even have a developer create your own custom rules for the Health Analyzer to evaluate and notify you when problems arise in those areas that your custom rules evaluate. Figure 6-2 shows a screenshot of the Site Collection Health Check Results report after analyzing the health of the site.

SharePoint 2013   ✎ EDIT LINKS

Site Settings › Site Collection Health Check Results

Clean bill of health
Your site passed with flying colors, there were no issues detected that should prevent a successful upgrade.

You might want to know about the following check(s) that ran successfully:	
Customized Files	Tell me more
None of your existing files were detected as customized.	
Missing Galleries	Tell me more
No issues were found with any of your galleries.	
Missing Site Templates	Tell me more
No issues were found with any of your sites.	
Unsupported Language Pack References	Tell me more
No issues were found with any of your existing language pack references.	
Unsupported MUI References	Tell me more
No issues were found with any of your existing MUI language references.	

[Try it again]

Figure 6-2. SharePoint Site Collection Health Check Results

■ **Note** To learn more about creating a custom SharePoint Health Analyzer rule, please see a following blog post I wrote where I provide a sample: https://stevegoodyear.wordpress.com/2011/04/09

All these measures give you insight into how healthy your servers are, and by extension, how healthy your SharePoint service is. They can provide you with early warning signs to signal where problems are developing, and this allows you to proactively resolve an issue before it escalates. These measures can also provide historical information where you can trace growth or different events over time.

Unfortunately, even with extensive performance monitoring, you still might not catch a potential issue until it occurs. If an incident does arise, having a good performance monitoring process in place will help you identify it and respond to it quickly. Planning for an incident will help prepare you for an efficient response. In the next section, I build on the uses for the data I discussed capturing in this section and I look at how you can use this information to help you respond to an incident.

Planning Your Incident Response

At some point, things will go wrong, even with system health measurements and reports in place. How well you get through it will depend on how much you plan and prepare to respond to an incident. You do not necessarily need to plan every possible scenario, and you might not even create a detailed plan for your response, but having some sort idea for how you want to respond will help.

You might group types of incidents into general categories, such as regional disasters or server hardware failures. One option might be to associate these categories with the service levels and service request priorities that I discussed in Chapter 2. This way you can plan your response based on the tier of service and criticality of the incident. It is good to have this type of information available and to consider the criticality of different incidents for different service levels. Otherwise, every incident will feel like a high-pressured catastrophe, even the ones that are not.

At the very least, I find it useful to plan and make the following information available before an incident occurs:

- How and when do you communicate the incident to affected end-users?

- What other groups do you need to notify?

- How do you communicate the resolution progress or status updates?

- At what point do you escalate the incident and to whom?

- How do you identify what servers and services the incident affects?

- Who has service account and password information for the service?

- What is the latest backup available and how do you initiate a restore?

When this type of information is readily available, you will reduce your stress level when a serious incident occurs. When systems are down or you are in the middle of a major catastrophe, you need all the help you can get to take some of the pressure off and begin a response. You also need a systematic process to help keep everyone from over reacting.

In the heat of the moment, it can be difficult to stay objective and to assess the issue. People feel pressure to resolve the issue and return to normal operations, so much so that they often want to rush into a resolution. One trap with this is they can begin to chase symptoms, and multiple people can start making changes without anyone keeping track or coordinating the response. Chasing symptoms is not effective, and having multiple teammates searching the web and applying every idea that they find in random forums is dangerous and amateurish. Investigate and gather the facts of the incident first, and then take a step back to determine your resolution plan, especially when you are in a code red situation.

If you have captured measurements for some of the areas I noted earlier in this chapter, you can check this information for any clues. For example, if you are investigating a non-responsive server, you might check your performance reports and discover that the CPU utilization continued to increase until the server exhausted all available CPU resources. You might then correlate this with service schedules on the server and discover that an overlap of your backup job conflicted with the search crawl job, which consumed all available resources and left the server unresponsive.

Proactive measures and reports are incredibly valuable in reactive situations. This is why I designed the chapter this way where I included proactive and reactive topics together. As you plan your incident response, think about how you want to design your proactive measurements and reporting to help give you those types of clues when you need them. Every little bit of insight into an incident and what might be causing it will help you as you respond to an incident.

At this point, as you consider your incident response plan, picture the process you will adopt for a disciplined and systematic response. This can help you get through the situation without having excessive stress and panic blind you, and more importantly, it can help you avoid freezing like a deer caught in the headlights of an oncoming vehicle trying to decide what to do. The more rational and methodical you can remain as you work through an incident, the clearer your mind can work and the more open you are to potential solutions. You might consider some practices such as gathering a standard list of information you require and deciding on the types of notes that you want to take as you respond to an incident.

For any incident, I generally keep notes in Microsoft OneNote where I begin a detailed log of our response, capturing any information and assumptions as we progress. This, of course, helps to keep track of our progress, but it also helps me to stay objective and focused, rather than jumping around chasing symptoms. Gathering notes is a systematic process and it enforces a certain amount of discipline. The following lists the type of information I like to capture in my notes:

- Servers involved or affected by the incident

- Symptoms of the incident

- Any suspicions or assumptions on underlying causes

- Causes I rule out

- Any thoughts of things to investigate or verify

- People who get involved and when

- Every change I make

- Links to any sources I reference, such as blogs, message boards, or preferably, documentation

As I progress in a response and with my notes, I keep what I like to think of as a rolling resolution plan. While I collect intelligence and note ideas of potential solutions in my notes, I start thinking about an approach to test as a possible resolution. With details of the incident, I make a hypothesis for a potential resolution, note a resolution plan, and then attempt the resolution while noting the results. I call it a rolling resolution plan, because I continue this cycle until I reach an actual resolution to the incident.

I am generally a calm person, and I have been through a few high-pressure incidents now, so as a result I usually feel a level of confidence that I will get through the issue and find a resolution. I just stay focused on the process and trust that it will eventually lead to a resolution. One of my primary techniques is to use information to manage the pressure and avoid senses of panic. When I have preplanned and gathered good information, such as answers to some of the questions I noted earlier, then this helps me to remain levelheaded and focused on working through the incident. When I find myself deployed to respond to an incident where the team there did not preplan and gather this type of information, then I begin to gather it right away.

My initial response to an incident is to assess the situation. I do not look for blame, but other people involved may already be on the offense trying to divert blame. It is critical to keep everyone focused and to gather facts about the situation. When people get defensive or trend toward looking for blame, I stress that this is not the time to look at how things went wrong. In those moments, I only want to look at what *is* wrong and how I can resolve it. I can return later to investigate the cause during the root-cause analysis, which I discuss in the next section.

Approaching a Root-Cause Analysis

A root-cause analysis can transform your SharePoint service, just in the nature of going through the process and uncovering the root-cause of incidents. It is a thorough investigation into the underlying causes and everything involved in an incident. The process identifies all the contributing factors that led to the incident. It can also capture any of the symptoms or warning signs that failed to detect an issue as it developed.

The point of a root-cause analysis is not to find fault or to assign blame – it is not a witch-hunt. The point of it is to understand what went wrong so that you can prevent the issue from reoccurring in the future. You also go through the process to ensure that you identify and treat the actual problem rather than attack surface-level symptoms with hacks and patches. As you confirm a resolution to the underlying problem, you can also rest assured that you have not simply implemented a temporary fix and left the problem to reoccur at some point in the future.

Personally, I enjoy conducting root-cause analyses, because they feel like I am an investigator solving a mystery. I let my imagination turn it into a mystery to add excitement, because the process might be a little tedious in parts with reviewing logs and retracing events. These are all clues, pieces of the puzzle that will reveal more of the root-cause and all of its contributing factors. Investigating all those tedious areas will reveal the clues you need to solve the mystery.

It can be time consuming to gather all the information and extrapolate what went wrong, so it would not be practical to perform a root-cause analysis for every issue. I generally invest the time for an outage or a recurring issue, since taking a closer look at these issues will often provide the biggest return for improving the service. For the other types of issues or service requests, they are often more routine or less serious, so they do not warrant my investment of time for a closer investigation.

Similar to my process that I described in the previous section on planning your incident response, I ponder questions and take detailed notes as I work through a root-cause analysis. Some of the details I note do not provide any insights, but I capture as much as I can because some will end up offering clues that will eventually lead me to uncover the root cause of the issue. In my notes, I also like to capture all my assumptions and any questions that come to mind, because this helps me keep track and can lead to additional questions that I want to answer.

I start with trying to understand what went wrong, and part of acquiring this understanding is to build a timeline of the sequence of events. As I build this timeline and uncover additional events to add to the timeline, the picture builds with what happened leading up to the incident. Each event I can add to the timeline can lead me to more pieces of the puzzle, which eventually will lead me to a clear picture of the incident, and this will ultimately uncover its root-cause.

Some questions I try to answer or and use to build a timeline of events leading up to the incident include the following:

- What were the exact times when specific events occurred?

- What are all the scheduled tasks that run in the farm?

- What areas of the service did the incident affect?

- What were the specific servers or server issues involved?

- What were the symptoms of the incident?

- What errors do the Windows Event, System, and Application logs report?

- What errors or exceptions does the SharePoint 2013 ULS log report?

- What errors does the SQL Server Error Log report?

As I gather this type of data, I continue to build out the timeline of the incident and identify clues about its underlying cause. Logs can provide a great deal of information about where a problem originated, or at least when it first surfaced. They can also reveal patterns such as the occurrence frequency or what other errors occur as the timeline leads up to the incident. Logs give a historical record of events, but sometimes, depending on the problem you are troubleshooting, you need to augment them with a real-time view of events as you interact with an application. To address this, I use additional diagnostic and monitoring tools.

One tool available in SharePoint 2013 exposes a real-time view of logs and other request details as you load a page. This tool is the SharePoint Developer Dashboard, an instrumentation framework that provides diagnostic information for page components and the page execution lifecycle to assist developers and administrators troubleshoot issues. An administrator can easily overlook this resource and forget they have it in their toolbox, due mostly to its name. It certainly helps developers and the idea grew out of practices that developers use to debug their applications, but it also provides a wealth of insights for an administrator troubleshooting a page or the entire application.

I first mentioned the Developer Dashboard in Chapter 3, where I described some of the logs and tracing information available. Since it is short, I have repeated the PowerShell script again here that you can use to enable the

Developer Dashboard. Run the following PowerShell script to add a button to your SharePoint pages, and then you can click the button and pop up a new window containing the Developer Dashboard.

```
$content = [Microsoft.SharePoint.Administration.SPWebService]::ContentService
$content.DeveloperDashboardSettings.DisplayLevel = [Microsoft.SharePoint.Administration.
SPDeveloperDashboardLevel]::On
$content.DeveloperDashboardSettings.Update()
```

The Developer Dashboard is great, particularly for tracing SharePoint and ASP.NET events. I have a range of other tools I use to build on the information that the Developer Dashboard provides. Other diagnostic tools that I use include the following list.

- *Microsoft Message Analyzer (Network Monitor)*: I use this tool to monitor server connectivity, the request/response communication between servers, and the data transferred on the network to identify any network or server communication issues.

- *Windows Server 2012 Performance Monitor:* I use this tool to monitor each of the servers in a SharePoint farm to understand how the servers utilize their resources and identify where bottlenecks exist.

- *SQL Server 2012 Activity Monitor:* I use this tool to monitor queries and processes executing on SQL Server to obtain information about how they may affect performance or availability.

- *SQL Server 2012 Profiler:* I use this tool to capture traces of queries and processes to analyze later.

- *Internet Explorer Developer Tools:* I use this tool to troubleshoot page components and to troubleshoot network or page request issues.

Note   For more information on Windows Server 2012 Performance Monitor, please see the following TechNet article: http://technet.microsoft.com/cc749249

For more information on SQL Server 2012 performance and activity monitoring tools, please see the following MSDN article: http://msdn.microsoft.com/ms191511

With all of these tools and by working through this process of discovery, the information you gather should eventually provide enough clues to identify the root-cause of the incident. It reveals a ton of information about the farm and you may find this process is a useful exercise even if you have not experienced an incident. You might consider this type of analysis activity as a type of preventative health check for your SharePoint service, and I discuss this idea more in the "Consultant Comrade" section later in the chapter.

After I identify the root-cause and complete my investigation, I then prepare a Root-Cause Analysis Report. I use this to document the incident, what led to the incident, and the underlying issue or contributing factors. Most importantly though, I want to answer a single question: what corrective actions and changes will I implement to prevent the problem from reoccurring?

A Sample Root-Cause Analysis Report

In this section, I share an actual root-cause analysis from the wild. I performed this root-cause analysis several years ago in response to an outage. Although the incident itself was not major, it illustrates how useful the information can be that you get as an output from the process, even for a straightforward incident such as in this sample.

My team did not investigate every incident or every service request. Generally, I would only perform a root-cause analysis for major incidents that tier-one or tier-two support resources escalate to me. However, I would perform a root-cause analysis for every unplanned outage, whether or not there was an escalation to my team. This sample is the output report from my investigation of an unplanned outage, with the same headings and the same level of detail as the original report.

SharePoint Outage: Root-Cause Analysis

When did the Incident occur?

- Date & time of issue: September 26, 20XX 7:00 PM PST

- Locations(s) affected: Asia-Pacific Region

- Service request ticket number: N/A

- Time service was restored: September 26, 20XX 7:00 PM PST

What was the Incident?

- **Issue description:** AP-SPSQL exhausted all available disk space, resulting in SQL Server unable to grow any transaction logs. Therefore, SQL was not able to save data for the affected SharePoint sites.

- **Business impact:** Lost ability to save new data to SharePoint sites on AP-SharePoint that use AP-SPSQL as their database server (some of the SharePoint sites on this server use the HQ-ITSQL cluster as the database server for their content databases).

Why did the Incident occur?

- **Root-cause:** Database backup maintenance plans have failed since Nov 23, 20XX 12:00 AM PST due to insufficient disk space on drive E:, and as such the jobs were unable to back up and truncate any transaction logs. Disk space on drive F: (the drive that stores the log files) ran out of available space as the SQL transaction log grew until it exhausted all the drive's space.

- **Other contributing factors:** N/A

How was the Incident resolved?

- **Action taken to resolve the issue:** Steve Goodyear performed a shrink database operation to shrink the largest databases to free up enough space to immediately restore full service. Following that, he performed a full backup of system and user databases to an available network share, he backed up and shrunk all the transaction logs, and he reallocated logs to available disks.

- **Recommended changes moving forward:** Steve Goodyear will engage the SQL DBA team to review SQL Server stability and ensure System Center monitoring of backups and disk space correctly sends alerts as a server reaches a threshold. Additionally, he recommends renewing the farm consolidation initiative to consolidate all these affected sites onto the more stable HQ-SharePoint farm and retire the AP-SharePoint farm.

Conducting a Retrospective on Incidents

After you conduct a root-cause analysis and produce a report based on the findings of your investigations, your next biggest learning opportunity comes from conducting a retrospective. A retrospective looks back on the events and considers what you might do differently next time or what processes you want to change.

Similar to the root-cause analysis, I like to conduct retrospectives without focusing on assigning blame. This is an opportunity to learn, and the goal is to learn to improve in the future. Assume that everyone is trying to do their best given the circumstances they face, and try to identify parts of the process that broke down rather than simply pointing blame at any individuals. For instance, perhaps the process broke down with assigning resources to the team without providing adequate training or direction, or perhaps the process lacked an adequate assessment of skills to match the right resource with the right role. Look past any individual resources and try to find something in the process that will improve the outcome next time.

Retrospective meetings held in person are the best approach to conducting a retrospective. When the team gathers to discuss the issues and brainstorm ways to improve, they work through it together. Mass e-mail chains just do not have the same effect, at least not in my experience. Video conferencing can help, but the idea is for the team to meet in person and work through the retrospective together.

A meeting needs to be timely, meaning you should schedule it close to the incident so that it is still on everyone's mind, but not so close that the team has not had a chance to give it some thought. At the very least, I usually like to give a team a few days to read through and digest the root-cause analysis report before I conduct a retrospective. This also helps relieve any emotional connections or defensive feelings to the incident.

You need to set everyone's expectations for the retrospective meeting, especially for the first retrospective you conduct. The team needs reassurance that it is not a witch-hunt, and that your goals are to improve processes in the future, which should help to make their jobs easier. Ahead of the meeting, possibly even in the meeting invite e-mail, establish the learning and improvement objective for the retrospective and ask all the participants to think about the incident to prepare for the retrospective.

One option you might consider is to create an anonymous survey before meeting for the retrospective to collect thoughts and concerns from the team. You can ask questions to everyone about what part of the process they feel broke down, reminding them to focus on the actual process and not on any individuals. This information can help spark discussions when you conduct the retrospective.

Some other questions I use to help spark discussion when I facilitate and conduct a retrospective include the following list. I like to work with the team to brainstorm answers for each of these questions, because they can provide valuable insights into what areas the team can improve for the future.

- What went well that we want to continue in the future?

- What areas were problematic or challenged that could have gone better?

- What caught us off guard or that we did not plan for having to address?

- What were frustrating experiences or moments?

- What were satisfying experiences or moments?

- How extensively did we define the roles and responsibilities?

- How clear were the project objectives and timelines?

- What could we have done differently to experience a better or more positive outcome?

Our meeting objective and ideal outcome from the retrospective meeting is to generate a prioritized list of action items that the team can use to implement change. These learning artifacts will help the team improve in the future and they will give the retrospective participants a feeling of accomplishment when they come out of the meeting with them.

As I indicated, a retrospective is not the place to shame or criticize any individual's performance. This is about identifying those processes that are less than ideal and then looking at how you can improve them in the future. When a team member's performance is inadequate, their supervisor is the appropriate channel to manage and discipline them, whether through a performance review or a one-on-one meeting. Another option might be to conduct a private meeting between the supervisor, the team member, and the project manager to review and discuss issues that are specific to the individual's performance. You just need to keep it out of the retrospective meeting, because that is the place to go after processes, not individuals.

Most of my focus centered on responding to an incident, where something has gone wrong. You might also conduct regular retrospectives even if your team has not experienced a major incident or had a serious break down in its processes. You might conduct a monthly or quarterly team retrospective meeting, and use this as an opportunity to uncover risks or any potential issues before they escalate into an incident that derails the project or the ongoing operations.

Conducting regular retrospective meetings can also contribute to a culture of continuous improvement. It helps to build and strengthen teams as everyone regularly comes together to discuss ways to improve their shared processes. Team members grow encouraged to invest themselves into improving the team and its processes as they engage in retrospectives. It also reinforces the notion that you measure success by the success the team achieves, not simply by individual achievements, which is another reason you focus on processes and not on individuals during retrospectives.

With ongoing retrospectives, you can fine-tune your team's processes regularly as the team grows and evolves. In the next section, I discuss other aspects that you can monitor and tune over time to maintain a healthy SharePoint service.

Monitoring and Tuning the Service over Time

In the sample root-cause analysis report I shared in an earlier section, you might notice that one of the changes I implemented to prevent the issue from reoccurring was setting an alert in the monitoring tool to notify the database team if the available disk space ran too low. Setting alarms for different thresholds is one way to apply the concepts from this chapter, and I recommend you do this. This will alert you as problems arise, often while they are still developing and before there is an interruption to the service.

Depending on the type of infrastructure management and monitoring software you use, you might be able to specify thresholds and create alarms within the tool you use. This provides you with an enterprise view into the system and a consistent way to manage notifications. If you do not have tools of this sort in your environment, you can look to achieve a similar goal of automatically notifying you when a condition deteriorates by using the tools you do have available. For example, SQL Server 2012 Alerts can monitor events and performance conditions for the database and the operating system, and when something matches a rule for an alert you define, the system can send an e-mail or pager notification to you.

This strategy allows you to set the criteria for when you want the system to notify you, allowing you to forget about it until a notification comes up. As a result, you do not have to check routine aspects of the system, those things you probably do not have time to check regularly anyways, but if something does come up then it will not fall through the cracks or end up getting missed. When you choose your thresholds for alerts, just choose ones that are relevant and that truly demand your attention so when they come up you can respond. For all other types where you are merely interested, choose a different monitoring strategy so it does not create noise and drown out your more important alerts.

For some monitoring of the service, including a web part that aggregates the information on a SharePoint page will do. By using a web part like this, then you will have the information available on demand, so whenever you are curious you can simply load the web part page. You can report on a lot of useful information here without creating an excessive amount of alerts or notifications when there is no urgency for your attention. When you design a combination of these two approaches, you get the best of both worlds.

Some aspects that I often want to monitor and set alarms for include the following list.

- I use a network utility to periodically ping the servers and trigger an alarm if a server is unreachable or unresponsive.

- I use a disk utility to monitor the amount of available disk space and trigger an alarm if a server runs below a predefined level.

- I use a backup utility to verify that backups complete successfully and trigger an alarm for any backup errors or failures.

- I use a database utility to run the SQL Server DBCC CheckDB command to verify the logical and physical integrity of each database and trigger an alarm for any corruptions.

So far, I looked at what you can monitor and respond to, but I also run other jobs to automatically tune different aspects of the service. To optimize the disk storage, I like to schedule the Windows Server 2012 Defragment and Optimize Drives utility to run periodically. I schedule this job during non-peak hours for every server in my SharePoint farm to keep all the disks optimized and defragmented.

■ **Note**   Modern versions of Windows Server offer the capability to schedule disk defragmentation, but if you have an earlier version without scheduling capabilities, then you can create your own schedule. For example, you can create a scheduled task to execute the following command to run the defrag utility on all disks: `Defrag/C`

Another tuning job that I like to run regularly is to defragment the database indexes. In SQL Server 2012, I create a scheduled job to defragment and then rebuild the statistics for indexes in each database. Like the disk defragmentation, this helps to keep data organized in an optimized manner. It is like washing your dishes and then putting them back in the cupboard so they are easy to find when you are preparing your next meal. It keeps the database page files optimized on the disk so that SQL Server can quickly locate and access each one.

One aspect of the farm that I monitor is the size of content databases. I personally like many smaller content databases rather than fewer large databases. Smaller databases are easier to tune, quicker to backup and restore, and they reduce the surface of risk and exposure in the event of a database corruption. When I create new web applications, I typically create a few content databases so that SharePoint will use a round-robin process to create site collections in alternating content databases. This spreads out the data and is generally effective, but sometimes a content database can end up with a few site collections that are growing very large. In those cases, I prefer to break up the site collections and move them into multiple content databases manually.

■ **Note**   For more information on moving site collections to new content databases, please see the following TechNet article: `http://technet.microsoft.com/cc825328`

For most collaborative applications, I generally target a content database size of around 25-50GB. This is not a hard rule, but this is the range that I find I am the most comfortable with. I often make exceptions though, particularly for those content databases that archive content, such as archival or records repositories. For those, I have targeted sizes as large as 400-500GB. It depends on the application and your data needs. By default, I use the smaller size as a guide and make exceptions where they make sense.

This leads me to another database-related task to regularly perform: validate the backups. By this, I mean actually go through the process and attempt a restore to another test environment for each database in your farm. Ideally, I would like to do this once each quarter or at least semi-annually, but because it is a manual task it is easy to get lost in the pile when I get busy. It is important to go through and verify the process as well as the integrity of the backup as part of your routine preventative maintenance. Trust me, you will appreciate discovering issues at this point rather than when you are trying to recover from a disaster.

Patching is another routine manual task you need to plan and schedule. I include this as part of monitoring and tuning because you have to monitor the patch levels and when you apply a new patch, you are effectively tuning the farm. Whatever your change management process is, I hope at the very least it includes testing and applying regular security and other update patches to the environment.

■ **Note**   Please see Chapter 11 where I discuss other considerations to help you prepare for patching and apply service packs. Also see Chapter 16 where I discuss custom developed component testing and release processes that you can also apply to your process for testing patches and security updates.

Finally, I also include archiving sites as part of the ongoing monitoring and turning activities. This can be a manual process, but it works best if you automate it. Content can grow so large that it will overwhelm you if you try to manually manage the process. In SharePoint 2013, you have the option to assign site policies to sites, and in the site policy, you can specify rules for deleting a site. For example, you can first configure the policy to set the site to a closed state after a given duration and then to delete the site after an additional given duration of time. With little effort, this policy configuration can address the rudimentary needs of those more basic sites that you want to simply dispose of after a given duration.

A basic site policy can be useful, but sometimes you might want to add more sophistication to your process. Perhaps you do not want to simply delete everything after some predetermined time elapses, and you need some automated way to inspect the content or assign tasks for people to review it. In these cases with more advanced requirements, site policies can still meet your needs by adding custom workflows in place of the simple delete option.

Rather than simply delete the site, you can assign a custom workflow to execute. The actions you develop within this workflow can include logic to check additional rules or to take additional actions with processing the content, such as moving certain pieces of content to the records repository and assigning tasks for users to review the remaining content before you delete it. You can even create a workflow action that will move the content to a designated archival area. In an archival area, you can store the content on cheaper disks and you can allocate fewer system resources for processing it.

Note   To learn more about site policies in SharePoint 2013, please see the following TechNet article:

`http://technet.microsoft.com/jj219569`

Consultant Comrade

Being a consultant, you have no doubt already caught on that clients often bring consultants in when things are not going well. I sometimes find myself on the first day arriving on site to discover and solve their problems. Sometimes I feel like I am The Wolf from the movie *Pulp Fiction*, where he says, "I'm Winston Wolfe; I solve problems." Like him, I often engage with clients who need my help to clean up a mess they find themselves in, and like him, I solve problems – SharePoint problems.

My approach is one of the main reasons behind why I can be so effective at solving these problems, and I shared my methodical approach with you in this chapter. This approach works whether you are an IT administrator responding to an isolated SharePoint incident, or you are a consultant engaging with a client whose SharePoint environment has unraveled and has become problematic. The process identifies any underlying issues and any contributing causes, whether there is one or many, and it guides you to develop a resolution plan based on what you uncover.

You can use this process to investigate and audit a SharePoint deployment that has grown problematic over time. For example, if your client chose a chain of shortcuts and applied a series of hacks, and this eventually left them feeling stuck or painted in a corner, you can use the process in this chapter to get a complete picture of the situation. I find this can be a common scenario, as clients do the best they can with the limited information and experience they have. Now that they are aware of the long-term effects from some of their decisions and they are ready to get back on track, you can help them correct the sins of their SharePoint past.

I like to structure this type of engagement as a type of audit and analysis of my client's current state. My main output and deliverable from the first phase of this engagement produces a root-cause analysis report, one similar to the sample I shared earlier in the chapter. I work through the process and analyze as many aspects of their SharePoint environment as I can, looking beyond the symptoms of what causes them pain, and instead looking down to identify the underlying issues and contributing causes. Once I identify the problems, I then move to document a resolution plan.

The final part to the report identifies all the changes I need to work through with my client to resolve the issues. Depending on the situation, this can be quite an extensive list. Therefore, I like to prioritize this list and address the more immediate needs first. There often will not be a quick fix, but there are usually immediate actions you can take to relieve some of the pressure. These will get your client on the road to recovery, and the rest will come as you get to them.

One example I relate this process with involves my chiropractor and my treatments with him. Years ago, I found myself travelling somewhere every week, and between the different hotel beds and the awkward seats on airplanes, my back developed some discomfort and what felt like a constant kink between my shoulder blades. To get my back healthy and comfortable again, I needed regular chiropractic treatments with adjustments to gradually get my back on track, but he relieved some of the pressure right away on my first treatment – although hearing the crack as he adjusted my back was not as pleasant as how I felt immediately afterward.

As you identify your client's symptoms and their underlying causes for discomfort with their SharePoint environment, work with them to develop a resolution plan. Maybe they can take on many of the resolution action items on their own, but they will often need your help. You will want to write the resolution plan with as much detail as you can so that it will provide your client with direction on what they can do, and this is mostly so they head down the correct path and take the proper steps.

You do not need to hold back and horde information in hopes of forcing their dependence on you. This strategy simply does not work because you cannot solve all their problems on your own, and without the right information and direction, your client might make things worse. I encourage you toward a full disclosure and to offer your clients clear direction on what needs to be done, whether or not they engage you to do the work. This helps them budget and prioritize the resolution, and you will continue to be the expert that steered the ship back on course.

I find there is a lot of opportunity to engage with your clients in this process. It is not that everyone is doing it wrong or that SharePoint causes discomfort, not at all. Instead, this type of consulting engagement uncovers opportunities. Not everything has to be in a disaster zone, and usually it is not. Even if your client holds their environment together with duct tape, it is still working to some degree – SharePoint is surprisingly resilient. Your clients might want this type of engagement as part of a continuous improvement process to identify opportunities to improve, or they may simply want it to validate that everything is still on track and no issues have crept up. Whatever the motive, you can probably find some benefit that you can deliver your clients with this type of engagement.

Take a moment and consider your different clients and how this process can help them. Also, take a moment to consider how these types of engagements can benefit your consulting practice as well. You can find benefits in the follow-on resolution work, or in any number of other opportunities that you uncover through the process. Too often I find consulting firms just jump right to the big upgrade project as a magic bullet to start over and to try to simply pave over any problems, but you and your clients do not have to wait for the next version to help you merely mask problems. Better yet, if you go through this process and actually resolve the problems first, your upgrade will typically go smoothly and you can be confident that you are not simply delaying these problems.

Inside Story: Notes from the Field

I am quite passionate about conducting a root-cause analysis, as you can probably tell. Perhaps I just like the feeling of the investigation and solving the mystery about what went wrong, or perhaps I like the impact the process has on the stability and availability of the SharePoint service. It brings a level of discipline that seeks to resolve underlying issues rather than patch symptoms, and I like that. I like it most of all because as I treat the root-cause, I prevent other symptoms from coming up and I generally reduce the amount of reactive support that the service demands.

Just through the nature of incorporating a root-cause analysis in a team's culture raises the bar. For me, it seems to transform how I operate and provide the service, because it focuses heavily on taking proactive actions: the corrective actions and changes I plan to implement to prevent the problem from reoccurring in the future. I find that this proactive nature also has a transforming effect on the SharePoint service itself – namely, the service becomes more stable as the operations team spends less time putting out fires.

In the root-cause analysis example I gave earlier in this chapter, this was one in a series of analyzing the root-cause of outages in our SharePoint farms. Usually, I would uncover issues beyond just what directly related to an incident, as I often find an incident is just the outcome from a series of operational process failures, whether they relate to monitoring or hardware planning or something else. In the case of the root-cause analysis sample in this chapter, I uncovered the monitoring process failures.

Several years ago, I used to work for Pepsi, a beverage company. One of our principles that we adopted was to always *fix it right the first time*, and we adopted this as part of an initiative to improve our customer service. We dispatched service technicians to repair equipment such as vending machines and soda fountain machines, and when we analyzed the data through business intelligence analytics, we found that technicians often repeated visits to a customer shortly after the initial visit, sometimes to re-address the same problem but more often to address a new problem. We found that by putting too much emphasis on resolving the reported issue as a measurement, we missed an opportunity to ensure no other problems were developing at a particular location.

With our focus on fixing it right the first time, we put an emphasis on looking beyond the reported problem and using the incident as an opportunity to be proactive and perform any preventative maintenance. Of course, we wanted to restore sales of cold soft drinks that day, but we also wanted to minimize the potential for another outage. It took an upfront time investment for our technicians to assess the equipment for any other potential issues and take proactive measures, but this paid off by saving more time later when we did not have to re-dispatch a technician to that same location. It also paid off in the increased availability of the equipment to sell cold soft drinks and the extra customer service we delivered.

This philosophy stuck with me. After I moved on from Pepsi, I continued to incorporate this philosophy into my other software development processes and into my IT operations processes. A few years later, when I joined Electronic Arts, a video game software company, I applied the principle to service outages as I began to fine-tune my root-cause analysis process. This little bit of background information also gets to the heart of what a root-cause analysis is for me: fixing it right the first time.

I always thought about writing a script that could assess common issues in a SharePoint farm, and for some aspects I did. I never got time to write an extensive health analyzing utility, so lucky for me the product team eventually built one into the product. I mentioned it earlier in the chapter, the SharePoint Health Analyzer, which automatically checks different aspects of the farm and draws your attention to potential problems. It also allows you to extend the rules by adding your own custom rules. I bring this up again here to mention that if I find myself responsible for a global multi-farm SharePoint deployment again, I would consider what long-term corrective actions I could create as custom rules to automatically test in my farms and to warn me if the problem is reoccurring. Automatic tests of these custom rules can be your insurance for the future, and you can delegate them for SharePoint to monitor for you. Fix it right the first time, and then automate a way to warn you if it is reoccurring.

GUEST Q & A: CHRIS IZQUIERDO, DEVFACTO

As I discussed governance with Chris Izquierdo, a SharePoint consulting and technology leader, he stressed two key aspects that are a part of his governance philosophy: you need a way to measure governance and you need a way to automate governance. When he addresses governance, he looks to establish a consistent framework that includes automated measures that he can report against a defined service, such as one covered by an SLA.

In his experience, governance plan documents with hundreds of pages of policies can often simply end up collecting dust on someone's desk – a client pays for the document's production without later realizing any of the benefits. For Chris, these governance plan policies are easily prescribed and somewhat standard, but they are not practical unless you apply them to the SharePoint service with some automated way to enforce them.

His advice is "what gets measured gets managed." He finds that success comes from having a way to automatically measure and report on a service level's effectiveness.

Chris Izquierdo is the CEO of DevFacto Technologies Inc., a SharePoint consulting firm based in Edmonton, Alberta, Canada. He has worked with SharePoint since 2001, starting as a developer and eventually moving into architecture and management. Over the last five years, he has concentrated on growing DevFacto to 70+ SharePoint consultants in Edmonton, Calgary, and Regina. To learn more about Chris, please see his company website: www.devfacto.com.

Wrapping Up

Throughout this chapter, I discussed techniques for monitoring and reporting on the health of your SharePoint service. I shared some sample metrics that I use to measure and what targets I typically set as thresholds to warn me about any potential problems or degrading levels of service. I then considered how you might use that information to proactively respond and tune your environment to avoid issues. From there, I looked at how you can respond to an incident if one occurs, and how to conduct a root-cause analysis to identify why it occurred. Finally, I discussed how to conduct a retrospective to learn from what went wrong and how you can avoid having it reoccur in the future.

Defining what your SharePoint service is will provide your team and your internal customers with a shared understanding about what the service provides, and it gives us something to set targets against and measure. This second part of the book covered broad topics such as how to define the service and the team that provides the service. With this information, you can set expectations about what needs your service will address and how it will operate. However, eventually new needs will arise, and when they do you need to expand your SharePoint service.

In the next part, chapters focus on topics related to expanding your SharePoint service for things such as adding new capabilities, handling demand for new features, and upgrading to new versions. I start in the next chapter with how to plan for an expanding service by creating a roadmap. A SharePoint roadmap will set the course for where you plan to take your SharePoint service, and when. This can help you manage expectations and pace the demand so that you can approach expanding your service in a methodical and appropriate manner.

PART III

Expanding the SharePoint Service

One constant with SharePoint seems to be it is always evolving, both as a product itself and in the scope of capabilities an organization chooses to adopt and implement. As a result, any SharePoint service definition is also constantly evolving to deliver new value and meet additional needs. Having a process for how and when the service expands helps set current and future expectations. This process facilities a disciplined and intentional approach, as opposed to a reactive one that is continually in response to random requests.

The chapters in this part discuss related topics centered on common activities and considerations involved with planning and preparing for expanding your SharePoint service. These chapters highlight key points that I have found to work well when approaching a SharePoint initiative and how to break it down into manageable phases. Again, like in the other parts of this book, the formality of documentation that you produce will depend on what suits your individual situation to best communicate the process with your team and your organization. What is paramount is designing and implementing a process that sets expectations for when (or even if) a capability is planned, and to use this to protect a project or an operations team from getting pulled off track with chasing feature requests.

CHAPTER 7

Creating Your SharePoint Roadmap

A goal without a plan is just a wish.

—Antoine de Saint-Exupery

In this chapter, I focus on the process for creating a vision and a roadmap that describes what a SharePoint service will evolve into over time. I discuss approaches to building a timeline view of enhancements that provide an at-a-glance view of plans and the timing for the SharePoint functional capability areas. From there, I offer you some considerations for prioritizing and identifying dependencies between capability areas. Finally, I provide a sample visual roadmap that builds on each of the core SharePoint capabilities to continuously evolve the service and enhance the value it offers.

One key point I stress throughout this chapter is the need to pace rollouts and transformations, because your team only has so much capacity to deliver and your end-users only have so much capacity for change. A roadmap can help you set that pace and provide direction on where to go next.

After reading this chapter, you will know how to:

- Eat the SharePoint elephant

- Describe the value in a roadmap

- Assess your maturity level as an IT organization

- Plan your big picture feature areas

- Understand your users' capacity for change

- Pace changes and transformations

- Create a roadmap for your SharePoint service

Eating the SharePoint Elephant

One especially beautiful aspect of the SharePoint architecture is it can expand and adapt to changing needs and situations. As an organization's needs evolve, they can also evolve their SharePoint deployment. This capability of the product is particularly helpful to support organizations that take a phased approach to deploying SharePoint in smaller manageable chunks over time. A big portion of the value SharePoint delivers is the vast degree of capabilities that address a diverse set of business needs, yet achieving this value can often feel overwhelming for anyone who tries to do it all at once.

Taking on the breadth of SharePoint feels like the adage of eating an elephant. Like an elephant, SharePoint is smart and it has a fantastic memory, and it is also quite large. The best way to eat an elephant is to cut off smaller pieces and eat those. Then, when you are ready, cut off the next piece and eat that. As you continue that cycle, eventually, you will have eaten the elephant. Likewise, rather than trying to tackle every aspect of SharePoint at once, it is best to focus on smaller pieces.

When you try to eat an entire elephant, you will eventually hit a wall that will drag you down. It will eventually sink you. Plus, it would take a long time before you deliver any value, if you eventually make it to delivering value. You can take a divide-and-conquer approach and break it up into different work streams where different teams attack different parts, or you can break it down into phases that focus on delivering incremental value.

This advice sounds a little obvious, but I see it constantly on projects: customers of the SharePoint service get so excited after looking at all the capabilities and value available in SharePoint that they start wanting everything right away. Sometimes the hunger for the range of benefits available in the product grows too tempting and you end up trying to swallow everything all at once. Before you bite off more than you can chew and end up choking, pace yourself; you will get there. Hold yourself back and do not blind your better sense by the delicious buffet in front of you. Even though people will push for more, and your mind might play tricks on you as it tries to talk you into overloading your plate, you need confidence that the rest will eventually come. You will eventually cut off another piece of the SharePoint elephant and enjoy that too.

When you find yourself caught up and pulled in different directions, it not only distracts the delivery team, but it also compromises the probability and the degree of success the team can achieve. That is not to say that you should ignore all the value from those capabilities. After breaking it down into manageable chunks, small discrete phases with a beginning and an end, you can then schedule the individual phases. Over time, you can eat that SharePoint elephant and eventually you will realize all its different benefits.

For me, it is critical to break up larger SharePoint ambitions into chunks. You might have a bureaucratic process or your procurement department just might not want the added overhead to deal with smaller chunks, but you can work around these concerns. You might bundle a series of smaller phases into a larger funding budget, and this will allow you to secure the budget but still treat each part as smaller distinct phases. Or, you might just push back and accept the added administrative overhead because of how valuable a smaller phase can be to you. However you get there, the more focused and discrete each chunk of work is, the greater I find the chances of success.

Often you just cannot work around an amalgamated procurement process or you only have the nerve to ask to procure consulting services once. I sometimes refer to this as not wanting to go back to the well again. Another reason is that you might be trying to upsell your internal customer or your client to commit to a larger project. There are many motives pushing you toward piling too much on your plate, but they do not have to drive individual phases (or courses). One approach is to set a master budget for a larger program and then establish the scope of a limited, focused phase that has both project objectives as well as a defined shutdown point if things veer too far away from the plan. This approach can provide the same structure as a series of smaller projects.

I find structure helps to deconstruct the process into manageable pieces. Just like how a dinner menu helps to divide and pace courses of a meal, you need a structured way to divide and pace how you will approach SharePoint. Enter the SharePoint roadmap. A SharePoint roadmap sets the priority of functional areas that relate to business value, arranged on a timeline or through some other organization strategy that coordinates activities and work streams.

■ **Note**   I actually love elephants and do not think I would ever really eat one.

Understanding a Roadmap's Value

A roadmap's value stems from building a clear picture of where you are going. Think about a paper roadmap you would unfold and use on a drive across the country: it lets you know which highway to drive, what turns are coming up, potential checkpoints to track your progress, and the like. You can unfold it and see the big picture, or fold it up to just have an immediate view of the route. You can also have several roadmap versions to provide different levels of detail to view the journey, such as city maps with neighborhood details and country maps with only the main highways.

When I was a child, my family drove across Quebec, a province in Canada, and I remember tracking our route on a roadmap. I could see where we were going and I could talk about the highways coming up, and I traced our progress by marking the route we travelled with a highlighter. We could see our progress at a glance, as well as how much driving remained (it is a large province and takes a full day to drive across). When I build SharePoint roadmaps, I like to model them on this same concept and have them communicate where the SharePoint service is going, what I can expect, and how far I have progressed already.

Your SharePoint roadmap provides value in a similar fashion: you can track your progress from where you have been and set expectations on what to expect with where you are going. Most of all, it helps to set the pace at a time when you do not face the pressure of delivering everything at once – you can take a step back and build a roadmap with a clear understanding about what the priorities are and what your team can reasonably deliver in a phase. You can use it then to relieve any pressure by pointing out when you plan to address any particular needs and why you slated them for when you did.

A roadmap highlights priorities of activities that you want to address and feature areas you want to release. In addition to its value as a planning tool, it communicates these priorities well. It calls attention to dependencies between phases, which can have a significant influence on the order you approach development activities and releases. It also points out how any changes will affect plans for other phases, either in the trade-off you have to make in your limited delivery capacity or in the workarounds for any dependencies. Often with this information, what might otherwise seem like a small change that requires little effort instead enables you to properly assess the impacts.

You just cannot be everything to everyone, and having a roadmap will help keep you from drifting off into the abyss trying to be everything to everyone. I find a common scenario involves an internal customer who somewhere along the way developed a tendency to try to yell the loudest or exaggerate the urgency of their request to have the IT service delivery team address their needs. If a team is used to trying to be everything to everybody, then it bounces from issue to issue without any triage process to handle requests. As a result, they train their customers that they need to stress everything with urgency and yell loud to get the team's attention; otherwise, they may just fall through the cracks. A roadmap helps to prevent you from having customers pull you in every direction as you try to respond to what sounds important.

Roadmaps give you and your team focus and direction by helping you to avoid falling into short-term reactionary and chaotic situations. They set the bigger picture context for the rest of your governance strategy and operational priorities. They make budgeting and resourcing convenient because they can give you a sense of the required effort's rough order of magnitude. You might even find that roadmaps contribute to a team's motivation as everyone can see where the service will eventually go and how different pieces build on each other to get there, rather than a misguided impression that a piece of work is unnecessary or a lower priority. This transparency and insight into where the service is going can be beneficial to support your planning process, your customers' expectations, and motivate your team. It can even be beneficial to share with your vendors.

Why would you share your roadmap with your vendors? Often I find an outside consulting firm will have a beginning and an end to an engagement that you contract them to deliver, and this set duration and set deliverables tends to limit their perspective. Although they are probably interested in your long-term direction, their primary focus is on what they are delivering in the short term. By sharing your roadmap, you help them to avoid making any assumptions about your direction and your priorities. It can help them provide you with the best advice, and of course, it can also help them plan how else they may be able to offer to help you.

Another area your roadmap can help with your vendors is through a Request for Proposal (RFP) process. Often times I see an RFP process is less effective than it could have been because they tend to concentrate on functional requirements. By sharing your roadmap, potential vendors can see where you are going and what your ultimate goal is. They do not have to make as many assumptions about where your priorities lie and what will depend on the work they deliver for a particular RFP. They can also help you as you plan your RFP, because you will know more about the desired outcomes rather than a vague sense of configuration tasks. You will also have a better sense of the constraints to specify for your vendors so that they do not make incorrect assumptions in their pursuit of a low-price bid, which could ultimately limit your SharePoint service. Without a roadmap to help ensure vendors have the full picture, these shortfalls might not be apparent until later.

On top of all this, your roadmap can serve as a baseline and something everyone can turn to and share a common understanding about the direction and goals of your SharePoint service. It is a reference point for future requests or enhancements because it communicates the plan as well as the trade-offs necessary to adjust and reprioritize the plan. It can also help to focus attention and to help you think through opportunities with the product – perhaps there are hidden uses that people can use it for that you will discover in the process.

The other thing I like about roadmaps is how they communicate the big picture with all the dependencies and required capacity. People have their own agendas, and a roadmap will help manage their expectations in a way that can help reduce the motive to bloat an earlier phase with things the roadmap slated for later. It also helps your team see your ultimate direction with the SharePoint service, and this helps them avoid making decisions that will limit you later.

I have found that roadmaps offer value in so many ways. They help give you and your team direction, they help to set everyone's expectations, and they can help your vendors and partners provide you with better service. In the next section, I look at where to start with building a roadmap and then I discuss other considerations for your roadmap planning throughout the rest of the chapter.

ROADMAPS AND VISION DOCUMENTS

Often times I extend roadmaps to include additional context such as the overall vision. Roadmaps are often visual representations to show where you are going. They can communicate this in a general sense, such as a generic series of arrows, or they can communicate this in a specific schedule, such as on a timeline. Their final output is often simplified to communicate what is happening and when.

When I extend this concept, the document I produce still begins with this simple visual representation, but I include other aspects, such as background information and other points I discuss in this chapter. I also might include use cases to describe the expected user experience and vision-related documentation that describes solution objectives and overarching visions.

Starting with a Roadmap

Sometimes, you might find it obvious where to start with a roadmap, particularly if you have a series of feature areas that will build on each other. Your roadmap could be as simple as putting them in order on a timeline and that is as much as you need. In this case, your roadmap strictly focuses on features you want to deploy and you are using a roadmap as a scheduling tool. This is a perfectly legitimate and useful roadmap, and I return to this approach later in the chapter, but first I share some other aspects that I often include in roadmaps because of the value that they can add.

I usually start by assessing the IT organization's capabilities, and I do this by determining their maturity level in a range of categories. This comes before listing the major feature areas, because I often find dependencies between a capability level and a feature area. For instance, if the maturity level of the organization is still early in a developing stage for a category such as enterprise search, then the roadmap will need to reflect a plan to evolve enterprise search from what is possible in their environment and with their capabilities currently to the maturity level they want to reach.

The capability and maturity model that I am most familiar with is the Infrastructure Optimization model that Microsoft uses. For SharePoint, Microsoft has the Business Productivity Infrastructure Optimization (BPIO) model, and this includes capabilities listed at different maturity levels. This model is a bit dated now as it was more popular a few years ago, but I find its concepts are still useful. They have divided the maturity levels into four stages: Basic, Standardized, Rationalized, and Dynamic. Understanding what your maturity level is for a particular capability will help you identify your roadmap plans to evolve and mature your organization for that capability.

■ **Note** For more information on the Business Productivity Infrastructure Optimization model, please see this Microsoft optimization site: `www.microsoft.com/optimization`

I find there is a danger in building a roadmap driven by the feature areas you want to deploy. This approach can risk leading you into a situation where you find yourself deploying aspects of SharePoint just for the sake of deploying SharePoint. Whereas when you start with a capability assessment and use your desired maturity level to drive the roadmap creation, you maintain a business focus. This leads to a roadmap that links to organizational goals and business value. Start by building out a chart that models different maturity levels for capabilities that interest you.

One option is to use the BPIO model from Microsoft, as it already has a list of SharePoint-related capabilities and their maturity levels. Microsoft based the BPIO model on other maturity models, particularly on the work Gartner did. Table 7-1 lists a few common maturity models and their respective maturity levels.

Table 7-1. *A List of Common Maturity Models*

Maturity Model	Maturity Levels
Microsoft Infrastructure Optimization	<ul><li>Basic</li><li>Standardized</li><li>Rationalized</li><li>Dynamic</li></ul>
Gartner IT Maturity Model	<ul><li>Reactive</li><li>Basic</li><li>Emerging</li><li>Expanded</li><li>Pervasive</li></ul>
CMMI Maturity Levels	<ul><li>Initial</li><li>Managed</li><li>Defined</li><li>Quantitatively Managed</li><li>Optimized</li></ul>
ITIL Process Maturity Framework	<ul><li>Initial</li><li>Repeatable</li><li>Defined</li><li>Managed</li><li>Optimized</li></ul>

MATURITY LEVELS AND GOVERNANCE DOCUMENTATION

I would like you to notice that in the maturity models in Table 7-1, the detailed governance documentation for processes, policies, and procedures occurs in the latter portion of each: in Microsoft's Rationalized phase, in Gartner's Emerging phase, and in CMMI and ITIL's Defined phase.

I find too many approaches to governance try to skip the necessary work in the early phases and jump right into sophisticated documentation. In this book, I focus on those actions you can take to make a shift from the Initial or Chaotic phase into one that is more proactive and intentional, and from there you can continue maturing your organization by building out any documentation.

I discuss how to assess your maturity levels more in the next section. For now, you can consider which maturity model that you would prefer to work with. Once you pick a maturity model, then you can assess your organization's maturity level for each of the capabilities that interest you. Your next step is to recognize the desired maturity level that your organization would like to mature to for each of the capabilities, and then identify the gap. You can use your roadmap to build a plan to fill any gaps.

When assessing different capabilities, I prefer to be pessimistic rather than being overly optimistic about which maturity level a capability fits. This is not a performance assessment to pat myself on the back and calculate how much of a bonus I deserve. It is a situational assessment that serves as a baseline for the growth and development plans in your roadmap. For the progress and maturity you achieve on the other hand, you can and should use this to assess performance and to pat yourself on the back once you achieve your target maturity levels.

In a capability assessment, I like to consider the gaps. What maturity level does my organization fit, and what is the gap between the current state and the desired maturity level? Most of these gaps relate to business processes and some relate to technology feature areas. These gaps are the tactical capacities that the roadmap addresses, and you can use the maturity model to prioritize and identify dependencies while you design your roadmap. As the gaps identify the major activity blocks on the roadmap and a sense of their priority, they also provide insights into the business value they can provide.

Estimating business value for capability gaps helps you to prioritize them on your roadmap. Along with the business value, I also like to estimate a rough order of magnitude for how much effort the piece of work will take. This information gives you a sense of the cost involved, and you can compare this cost with the business value you anticipate. This in turn offers even more help as you prioritize your roadmap.

I find it is sometimes useful to involve potential sponsors at this point. You might not seek their commitment as sponsors, but you can share your roadmap and solicit their feedback. You might interest them in the maturity assessment and gaps that you identified so far, and they might have valuable insights to contribute. Your potential sponsors might be managers within your IT organization or managers from the business. Even if you are not ready for formal sponsors at this stage, this is a good chance to get your initiatives on their radar.

This probably feels like a strange time to bring up sponsorship considering I am this far along in the book. Sponsorship is important and I devote Chapter 12 to additional aspects of sponsorship. That is in the final part of the book, and that probably feels even stranger because I noticed that sponsorship is usually one of those topics people seem to bring up first. I avoided bringing up the topic earlier because I did not want it to stall any of the governance progress that you can make before you have a sponsor established.

I have found that sometimes facing the daunting requirement to establish a sponsor can bring governance progress to a halt because it feels like a prerequisite you need to fill before you can make any progress. Sponsorship is valuable and can help substantiate your roadmap or any other topic I cover in this book, but as I hope you are discovering, there are actions you can take to build governance momentum even before you establish sponsors. For now, I just want to point out how you can use your roadmap as a good opportunity to engage potential sponsors.

I return to discuss sponsorship more in Chapter 12. In the next section, I look at how to assess your maturity levels and how this can help design and prioritize a roadmap.

Assessing Your Operational Maturity Level

The process to assess your operational maturity level is largely consistent across the different maturity models. Although each have their own approaches and practices that you may find useful, I focus on working through the core concept of maturing along a progression from a state of reaction into a proactive and intentional state.

To start, you might consider performing the type of assessment that I discussed in Chapter 6 when I looked at how to perform a root-cause analysis. You can use those assessment techniques to get a sense for how your SharePoint service is operating and where the trouble areas are. This also provides you with a handy reference for identifying your maturity levels for different capabilities. I find this can also help to give teams a dose of reality, particularly if they are blissfully oblivious to how basic and chaotic their operations are.

For my purposes in this chapter, I have adopted a hybrid of maturity levels and I use them for this discussion. You can use whichever model you find fits well with your organization. Personally, I like the naming convention of this hybrid for the maturity levels, because I find they are descriptive and less abstract than the others are. They do a good job describing the state of maturity for a particular level, so much so that you can often identify with just the name alone.

However, "feeling chaotic" is probably not scientific enough as an assessment. As such, the following lists the maturity levels and I have added a rubric for each that describes your general state of operations. Note that I largely base the rubric descriptions on my own blended process for assessing maturity levels with my clients, and these may deviate from how Microsoft or Gartner or CMMI defines their model. This rubric should help you recognize and identify your operational maturity level. Remember, this is not an exercise in trying to boost our egos; this is an assessment to understand a baseline and highlight the focus areas for improvement.

- **Chaotic**: You operate in an ad hoc, unplanned, and unpredictable manner. You do not have a complete inventory of deployed software and infrastructure. You do not automate your processes and you have not documented your procedures. You manually manage your infrastructure on an individual bases. You manually distribute desktop software. You discover and respond to problems by user call notifications.

- **Reactive**: You operate in a fire-fighting manner. You do not have business sponsors and your IT executive drives decisions. You have an inventory of deployed software and infrastructure. You have limited automation for your processes and you have documented some procedures. You have a centralized system to distribute desktop software. You discover and respond to problems through an alert and event management process. You implement a problem management process and you measure system availability.

- **Proactive**: You operate in a predictive manner. You set thresholds and predict problems. You have moderate automation for your processes and you have documented many procedures. You centrally manage your IT infrastructure. Your problem, configuration, change, asset, and performance management processes are mature. You measure application availability.

- **Managed**: You operate as an IT service provider. You have defined services, service levels, and pricing. You understand costs. You have maximum automation and integration for your processes. You have fully documented Service Level Agreements and you have linked them to business value. You have a capacity management process. You measure and report service availability. You have fully defined your governance policies and you have automatic reporting to enforce them.

- **Optimized**: You operate as a strategic business partner. You collaborate with the business to improve business processes and engage in business planning. You have fully automated the management of your infrastructure. You have real-time infrastructure management and provisioning. You measure and report on IT and business linked metrics.

Once you recognize the operational maturity level you most closely identify with, you will begin to get a sense of what your roadmap will entail. The rubric itself can uncover phases in your roadmap, such as moving from chaotic to reactive to proactive and beyond. You can use descriptions such as your level of automation, and build a plan in your roadmap to develop and evolve the types and amount of automation in your operational processes. This alone can help give you a sense of the high-level topics you can mature and progress.

As you progress through these maturity levels, your operational focus also progresses and matures. At the chaotic level, you primarily focus on leveraging tools. As you mature to the reactive level, you begin to focus on engineering operational processes. As you mature to the proactive level, you focus on engineering service delivery processes. As you mature to the managed level, you focus on service and account management. Finally, as you mature to the optimized level, you focus on managing IT as a business.

Again, I want you to notice that rich governance documentation comes later in the managed maturity level. Of course, you can generate documentation as you progress through the earlier maturity levels, but I want to stress that this is not the driver, and you should smash any expectations for jumping right to the detailed and sophisticated documentation and skipping the evolving nature in those earlier maturity levels.

I regularly see IT organizations and consulting firms try to "solve" governance by skipping the groundwork that will mature an organization. They seem to try to jump right to establishing an executive sponsor and detailed governance documentation. It reminds me of when I used to teach snowboarding at a local resort in the mountains near Vancouver, Canada. At the snow school desk, we had a menu of different types of lessons that correlated to different levels of ability. A level one would be someone new to snowboarding, and a level two would be someone who could link a few sliding turns with some success on a green run, and so on. Guests would come and they would want to skip the basics to jump right into the advanced skill they wanted to learn. The result would be a beginner snowboarder who lacked any balance and control signing up for a class to learn how to take jumps. They just were not successful and did not get anything out of the group lesson because jumping required that they had balance and control on the ground first before they achieved it in the air.

This is true for your SharePoint governance as well. You will have an easier time documenting procedures once you mature out of a chaotic or reactionary maturity level, when you can begin to look at your processes and procedures with an intentional emphasis. This change in perspective will allow you to act in a strategic manner where you align your operations with delivering business value, rather than simply attempting to adopt generic SharePoint policies that are popular on the web. The policies and procedures may be the same, but how you apply them and the value you derive from them will depend on your maturity level.

Your overall operational maturity level will give you a good sense about where you are operationally. It can also reveal where you would prefer to be. My clients often find it revealing when we meet and I present where they fit in this maturity rubric. They can recognize it and usually affirm they had suspicions but they now have a clearer picture of their maturity level. More revealing still is the other maturity levels, particularly the latter ones they can mature to and achieve. You might share their experience as you recognize your organization on one of the earlier maturity levels and visualize the operational excellence you can achieve in one of the other levels.

You can take this description of where you fit in the maturity model and the potential for operational excellence by maturing to another level, and you can use it to solicit buy-in and support for your SharePoint governance initiative. You can present a vision of how your operations can run at a more mature level and how that can benefit everyone. You can show where that will make a team member's job easier or how it can make an IT manager look good. You can show how this can make your internal customers and end-users more satisfied. You can show how a progression of incremental improvements can lead you to achieve these benefits. Most of all, you can highlight how maturing your operations can lead to saving money.

Ultimately, I think that this maturity model can and should frame your roadmap and your entire SharePoint initiative. It highlights where you are and your potential opportunities and it provides direction on how to approach a progression. The different maturity levels can serve as wayfinders in your roadmap – they can establish major points along your journey to help you get your bearings and orient yourself.

Transforming the operational maturity level of your IT organization is an ideal, but it might be beyond your influence. Perhaps your reach is limited to the SharePoint operations, or maybe even just a subset of that. It is still good to assess your organizational maturity level to get a sense of the limitations and constraints that you will face. This could lead to change down the road, or it could just serve as a benchmark to guide your own SharePoint service planning.

Once you have a sense of your overall operational maturity level, you can begin to assess the maturity level for individual capabilities. You may have noticed that you fit with some aspects of a maturity level, but with other aspects, you are more mature. This is particularly true once you break down an application into areas of more granular capabilities. Every organization has its own priorities and may have matured particular areas more than other capabilities. In SharePoint, this can highlight different areas you want to mature and include on your roadmap. With our operational maturity level in mind, I next move on to identifying the capability maturity levels.

Assessing Capability Maturity Levels

As I mentioned in Chapter 3, I focus on seven core capability areas within SharePoint: collaboration, social computing, portals, search, records management, business intelligence, and composite applications. In this section, I step through each of these and look at some of the characteristics of each for each maturity level. This will help you identify your current state in a particular capability and where you would like to mature it. For now, I focus on assessing the maturity level, and in the next section I walk through how to understand the maturity gap and translate that into your roadmap.

The first core capability area is collaboration. With this, you assess the maturity level for how users collaborate with each other. Primarily, I focus on their process of creating and sharing documents as an indicator of a client's overall collaboration maturity level. You can add other characteristics to this table, such as versioning and alerts. Table 7-2 lists the maturity level characteristics for collaboration.

Table 7-2. Maturity Level Characteristics for Collaboration

Maturity Level	Collaboration Maturity Characteristics
Chaotic	Your users create and then share documents by email. You have multiple versions of the same document scattered across local drives, email folders, and network shares. Your users use external cloud and peer-to-peer file sharing services.
Reactive	You have a large network share or collaboration site with a deep folder structure hierarchy to store files. Your users segregate collaboration activities in different unconnected enterprise systems such as email, task lists, and document repositories.
Proactive	You provide collaboration sites for departments and business units. Your collaboration sites provide a single repository to support collaboration activities.
Managed	You provision collaboration sites for each workgroup and project. Your collaboration sites integrate with an email distribution list. You assign a quota policy to collaboration sites. You assign an archival and disposal retention policy to collaboration sites. Your users can apply rights management protection to sensitive content they share internally.
Optimized	Your users self-provision collaboration sites with automatically assigned quota and retention policies. Your users can apply rights management protection to content they share with customers, suppliers, and partners.

The second core capability area is social computing. With this, you assess the maturity level related to people information. Primarily, I focus on how well users can discover each other as an indicator for a client's overall social computing maturity level. You can add other characteristics to this table, such as colleagues and online presence indicators. Table 7-3 lists the maturity level characteristics for social computing.

Table 7-3. Maturity Level Characteristics for Social Computing

Maturity Level	Social Computing Maturity Characteristics
Chaotic	Your users maintain a contact list of people in disparate spreadsheets or individual contact lists. You have no centralized capability to search for people in the organization. Your users have no internal system to discover people or another's expertise.
Reactive	You can search for people based on their name, but you have no capability to search for people unless you already know their name.
Proactive	You can search for people based on attributes other than their name, such as their department, responsibilities, or expertise. You provide basic static people profile pages. Your users can rate and tag content. Your users can discover and join communities in the organization.
Managed	You can search for users based on social or organizational distance. You provide dynamic and self-managed user profile pages. Your users can update their profile attributes and these updates propagate across enterprise systems.
Optimized	Your users can self-manage their group membership.

The third core capability area consists of portal sites. With this, you assess the maturity level related to portal publishing, including intranets, extranets, and public websites. Primarily, I focus on the publishing experience as an indicator for a client's overall portal maturity level. You can add other characteristics to the table, such as standards and accessibility. Table 7-4 lists the maturity level characteristics for portals.

Table 7-4. *Maturity Level Characteristics for Portals*

Maturity Level	Portals Maturity Characteristics
Chaotic	You have a basic web server that is web-master controlled.
Reactive	You have a dynamic portal where business users can manage their content using a WYSIWYG web content editing form.
Proactive	You have a common multi-tier publishing process with authoring, staging, and production environments. Your portal menus are dynamic and security trimmed.
Managed	You have a publishing workflow and approval process for content publishing. You can schedule publications. You personalize content to target only relevant users. Your users can personalize their experience and the content displayed on the portal. Your users can access the portal using a mobile device.
Optimized	You have a multi-lingual translation and publishing workflow to target different languages. You have related page suggestions based on analytics and context.

The fourth core capability area is search. With this, you assess the maturity level related to the search experiences and capabilities. Primarily, I focus on enterprise search capabilities as an indicator for a client's overall search maturity level. You can add other characterizes to the table, such as search analytics reporting and featured search results. Table 7-5 lists the maturity level characteristics for search.

Table 7-5. *Maturity Level Characteristics for Search*

Maturity Level	Search Maturity Characteristics
Chaotic	You have no enterprise search. You have disparate search capabilities.
Reactive	You have enterprise-hosted search available within a single workspace or portal.
Proactive	You have an enterprise-wide metadata driven search across collaboration sites, portals, and line of business sources. You have search capabilities from mobile devices. Your search results are security trimmed.
Managed	You have a single centralized enterprise search experience that searches across multiple sources, such as line of business, third-party, web, and desktop. Your users can take actions and preview content within the search results. Your users can set alerts for specific queries as the search engine indexes new content.
Optimized	Your users can vote to tune the relevancy of their search results.

The fifth core capability area is records management. With this, you assess the maturity level related to records management and its related processes. Primarily, I focus on assessing the records repository as an indicator of a client's overall records management maturity level. You can add other characteristics to the table, such as legal hold and auditing capabilities. Table 7-6 lists the maturity level characteristics for records management.

Table 7-6. *Maturity Level Characteristics for Records Management*

Maturity Level	Records Management Maturity Characteristics
Chaotic	You have no records management policies defined or a records repository for storing records. Your users store records on local drives or network shares. You manually archive records.
Reactive	You have disconnected departmental or business unit records repositories.
Proactive	You have a framework for managing distributed repositories and content metadata. You have forms embedded in documents to capture metadata and workflows. You have automated retention policies.
Managed	You have enterprise policies defined. You have an enterprise set of structured authoring templates based on content types with metadata, workflow, and retention policies attached. You have a content classification schema to identify different sensitivity levels.
Optimized	You have automated retention policies and workflows associated with any content users generate. You automated processes to discover content in different systems on the network. You can apply and enforce retention policies to content stored in backups.

The sixth core capability area is business intelligence. With this, you assess the maturity level related to the business intelligence reporting and scorecard solutions you develop. Primarily, I focus on how standardized the data and the centralization of business intelligence are as indicators for a client's overall business intelligence maturity level. You can add other characteristics to the table, such as notifications and self-provisioned reports. Table 7-7 lists the maturity level characteristics for business intelligence.

Table 7-7. *Maturity Level Characteristics for Business Intelligence*

Maturity Level	Business Intelligence Maturity Characteristics
Chaotic	You have data chaos and spreadsheet sprawl. You build one-off business intelligence reports.
Reactive	You have data inconsistencies and data redundancies across the organization. You have silo business intelligence solutions within departments or business units.
Proactive	You have business units and departments funding business intelligence projects as needed. You have isolated pockets of users realizing business intelligence value.
Managed	You drive business intelligence and scorecard strategies based on business objectives and business value. You build analytics into and around business processes.
Optimized	Your users trust data and information across the organization. You extended business intelligence to suppliers, customers, and partners.

The seventh core capability area is composite applications. With this, you assess the maturity level related to the composite applications you build and deploy. Primarily, I focus on how advanced the forms and related processes are as an indicator for a client's overall composite application maturity level. You can add other characteristics to this table, such as web part development and Apps from the SharePoint Store. Table 7-8 lists the maturity level characteristics for composite applications.

Table 7-8. *Maturity Level Characteristics for Composite Applications*

Maturity Level	Composite Applications Maturity Characteristics
Chaotic	You have paper-based forms and redundant data entry.
Reactive	You have departmental electronic forms with transactional workflows.
Proactive	You have electronic forms integrated with line of business systems and processes. You have forms that are accessible from mobile devices.
Managed	You have enterprise forms and workflows. You have forms and workflow orchestration across departments and systems.
Optimized	You have automatic retention and auditing policies associated with forms.

These maturity levels and their respective characteristics for each core capability give you a place to start with assessing your current maturity levels. Remember, these are guidelines based on what I use to assess my client's maturity levels and they do not represent an exhaustive list of characteristics. Depending on the client's priorities for their organization and its operations, I will adjust these characteristics. Sometimes other characteristics will be more relevant to their business. This should give you a start and a good baseline, and you can use it as is or you can apply it to another maturity model.

With the SharePoint capability maturity levels identified for both the current state and the desired level, I move on now to look at the gap between the current and desired state, and how to apply this to your SharePoint roadmap.

Understanding Capability Gaps

As I mentioned earlier in this chapter, the gaps can reveal the details for your roadmap. Taking this perspective centers your roadmap on maturing your operations and your capabilities to align them with your organization's goals, and this helps you to deliver business value.

You can identify the gaps by comparing the characteristics of the capability at different maturity levels between the level you are at and the level you want to attain. Although you do not have to step through each maturity level, you do have to address all the capabilities in a level on your way to the next level. Thus, if you want to move from a paper-based forms system to an electronic forms and workflow, you need to address departmental forms before you can reasonably achieve enterprise forms and workflow. You will also need to integrate your forms with line of business systems and processes before you can enable an enterprise-wide orchestration of forms and workflows.

Some gaps are larger than others are, and the gap size depends on how sophisticated and optimized you want a particular capability to be. This is a useful place to start listing any dependencies or existing constraints that affect filling a gap for a particular capability. Along with these dependencies and constraints, you can also look at whether you can break up a gap into phases to fill smaller portions of the gap at a time. At this point, it is also useful to estimate a rough order of magnitude for how much effort and how much related costs would be involved with each portion of filling the gap. In addition to effort, I also like to estimate any expected durations the work would take. Finally, and probably most importantly, I like to identify the expected business value that filling a certain gap will deliver or an anticipated business problem that it will solve.

■ **Note**　Please see Chapter 3 for more discussion on how to map features to business value.

Once you have these details, you can list the gaps you want to fill. Basically, this makes up the substance of your roadmap. When you have it in a list, you can begin to prioritize the order you want to address the gaps. You may address a portion or a phase of a gap at one point and then come back to the rest later in your roadmap. This helps to keep it flexible and it allows you to make some progress on a mixture of capabilities rather than having to over-invest in a single capability.

Other factors contribute to how you prioritize these pieces of work on your roadmap. Some relate to the importance of the customer or the wider business opportunity it will support beyond the immediate business value it delivers. Some relate to issues such as your users' capacity for change or your infrastructure upgrade cycle, two considerations I come back to and discuss in more detail later in this chapter. At this point, you should have a working priority of opportunities for the different capability areas. As you work through the rest of the chapter, you can continue to reprioritize this list until you finally have a working roadmap that you and your team can use as a guide to mature your SharePoint service.

These capability gaps map to product features within SharePoint 2013. Next, I look at the big picture feature areas and how you can use the maturity model assessment and capability gaps to determine where to slot them on your roadmap.

Determining Your Big Picture Feature Areas

I first discussed determining your main SharePoint feature areas back in Chapter 3. One thing I discussed was how business value consists of the outcomes that a particular feature, capability, or composite application provides to end-users. I also discussed the technical aspects you can use to limit and later evolve your features over time. That discussion becomes useful again here, because part of your roadmap may include features that you limited back in Chapter 3 and you still need a plan to enable them over time.

How you decide which features to enable relates to the priority list of capabilities you began in the previous section. I chose capabilities that encompass SharePoint feature areas on purpose, and I discuss these capabilities consistently throughout the book. This is why I divide the maturity assessment into capability areas and used this to help you consider the maturity level of each. Now you have a prioritized list of capabilities mapped to business value, and you have already associated a set of features to each capability.

As I go through this process, I look at the maturity levels separately and then I look at the SharePoint capabilities from a product perspective. Some things in SharePoint just go naturally together or build on each other with little extra effort, depending on what your goals are. These relationships might not be as apparent when you strictly look at maturity levels, so it helps to consider them from a product perspective as well. For example, a portal would probably benefit from including a search component. Adding search within SharePoint 2013 in a subsequent phase can enhance and complete the portal; and if the search phase only delivers a lightweight search with limited content sources, then it can enhance the portal without a lot of added effort.

These kinds of product decisions can help you reprioritize or fine-tune your priority list of capabilities and phases for your roadmap. At this point, you can review your list of capabilities and consider which are complementary to each other in SharePoint and how one can enhance another. You might consider breaking a capability gap down into smaller phases to deliver some lightweight functionality early, and then address the rest later when you reach its priority on the roadmap.

A constraint you face is that you usually cannot simply enable every feature, or at least you cannot expect wide-scale adoption rates if you do. One aspect of this constraint is your users' capacity for change, and I discuss this more in the next section.

Understanding Your Users' Capacity for Change

I mentioned the idea about people's limited capacity for change when I discussed training and readiness back in Chapter 5. People can handle change if you make it easy on them and you set it along the path of least resistance. But too much change can stress people out, particularly if they are ever confused or unsure how to do something. Stress can erupt and cause a backlash if you do not relieve the pressure from time to time.

People can grow frustrated after a while of being in a constant state of change too. Everyone needs a break to settle and experience some stability at some point; otherwise, it eventually leads to fatigue, and this eventually leads to frustration. In my experience, I noticed this is not a gradual decline either. Things seem to be going well and everyone seems to be tolerant of the changes, and then all of a sudden it seems people are upset. Once you reach that point, you will have a harder time getting people motivated again.

It is a balance. On the one side, you do not want to change things too quickly because this causes stress. Yet, on the other side, if you drag the change out too long, this leads to fatigue and then to frustration. This balancing act depends on how dramatic of a transformation you are planning and how much tolerance your users have. It also depends on the nature of the transformation.

If you have planned to make extensive training and support resources available, then your users will likely have a greater capacity for change. Some of the strategies I discussed in Chapter 5 will help increase the capacity for change and can accelerate your timeline to implement a successful transformation. A successful transformation is usually one that is accepted and adopted, and you typically can only achieve these things with sufficient training and support.

Another consideration to understand your users' capacity for change involves identifying priorities in the business cycle and how the job functions of your users relate to those priorities. For example, if your users earn bonuses and it is a particularly crucial time of the year to earn those bonuses, they probably will not have much capacity or tolerance for change. If your business is in the retail industry and it is sometime in early December, your users are not likely to have much capacity for change. If your organization is in the middle of a labor dispute and your users are considering job action, then your users will probably not have any capacity for change.

These are just some random examples, but they highlight the need to consider what is going on in the world of your users. The more you can understand about what else is vying for their attention and consuming some of their capacity, the better sense you will have with how much change you can successfully introduce. You may need to pace your changes to avoid interfering with their actual job duties.

As I mentioned earlier, you may also pace your changes to help ease the amount of stress the transformation causes your users so that they have time to adjust and get comfortable with one change before you introduce another. You might also pace the changes to give your project team time to deliver and implement those changes. There are many reasons why you might want to pace your changes, and in the next section, I discuss some strategies to help you set a pace.

Pacing Your Changes and Transformation

When I looked at capability gaps and feature areas, I suggested breaking some gaps into phases. The more you can break things into smaller chunks that you can spread across phases, the more flexible you will find your prioritization and scheduling of your roadmap. You will also find this handy for when you want to pace changes and transformations, whether to accommodate your users' limited capacity for change, your team's limited capacity for change, or your team's limited capacity for project delivery.

One technique that project managers often use is they add lead or lag time to a task when they build a project schedule in a Gantt chart. Figure 7-1 illustrates the different between a lead and lag time. Lead time means a certain amount of time needs to elapse before work on a task can begin, usually an amount of time between a task and a preceding task. Lag time means a certain amount of time needs to elapse after work completes on a task before work on the next task can begin. When a project manager enters lead and lag time information in a project plan stored in software such as Microsoft Project 2013, then the Gantt chart can automatically update the schedule when earlier task durations change.

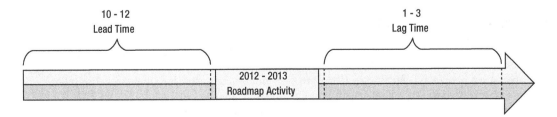

Figure 7-1. *An illustration of lead time and lag time surrounding a task*

You can use this concept of lead and lag times on your roadmap to set a pace for changes. You also might leave a block of time to accommodate user training and adoption activities. As you review your list of capability gaps and phases, consider where you might include lead or lag times to accommodate any pacing requirements you suspect. You can use this information to help schedule activities.

This is also a good point to consider any busy periods in your organization's operations that you might prefer to block off and avoid implementing any major changes. You might also consider popular vacation times when many of your users will be away, making this either an ideal time or a poor time for major changes, depending on the nature of your change and the level of user involvement you require. Gather these more global and enterprise-wide schedule impacts and requirements to help you further prioritize and refine the schedule of your roadmap.

As you build a list of schedule and delay requirements and align those with your prioritized list of activities, you will begin to get a preliminary sense of your roadmap's schedule. This can serve as the basis of a SharePoint program schedule or a schedule for a series of projects. Alternatively, if you do not want to commit to dates on a schedule, it can be your roadmap for what comes next when you get time or budget. It can but does not necessarily require a scheduled date for when the work will take place if the majority of the roadmap is still tentative or requires approval. Sometimes you might use milestones or checkpoint gates to pace the roadmap, and if you have effort and duration estimates, then you can schedule the work tasks when you activate the next phase and you prepare to deliver its work activities.

I looked at capability areas and their respective maturity levels as priority drivers in many of your roadmap activities, but some activities might not be included in maturity characteristics. Some activities might relate to the underlying infrastructure maintenance and replacement schedules or the software upgrade cycles. In the next section, I look at considerations for capturing these activities in your roadmap.

Considering System and Infrastructure Upgrade Cycles

Eventually vendors release new versions of their software and hardware. Servers break down or newer models begin to look more attractive. This upgrade cycle is the nature of technology, and how frequent the upgrade cycle affects you depends on how cutting edge your organization is with respect to technology. For some, the cycle might be barely noticeable as you find yourself still content with using Windows XP for a little while yet. While for others, as soon as a beta version becomes available they start to think of the last version as now legacy software.

Whatever your upgrade cycle, it is important to include that in your roadmap. You might recall my discussion in Chapter 4 when I looked at all the roles and responsibilities that SharePoint depends on, and not just those directly involved with SharePoint. Similar to that, you also need to consider the upgrade cycles for all the systems that SharePoint depends on as well. For example, consider the coordination complexities you might face if you plan a major document repository migration without realizing it is at the same time the database team has planned to upgrade SQL Server or the storage team is replacing the SAN.

All this information will prove to be very useful. It can reveal additional dependencies or constraints that can help you prioritize the order and schedule of your roadmap, and it can save you headaches in the end. It can also serve as a check to help you verify that you plan for these work items and maintenance tasks. The following lists some examples of these types of external system considerations:

- Known system upgrade or replacement plans

- Infrastructure and network support agreements

- Infrastructure consolidation or virtualization projects

- Known software upgrade plans

- Expected software version release dates

- Expected system requirements for future versions

- Software support agreements

These can all help give you a good indication that you have not overlooked anything or overbooked a delivery as you build your roadmap. Sometimes you already know the upgrade dates for the foreseeable future, and they can slot right in on your roadmap, but other times you have to infer dates based on support agreements or changing minimum system requirements. On the other hand, you might be aware that you have to upgrade a piece of software, but identifying the date for its end of support lifecycle will help ensure you are not planning an upgrade after the software falls out of support.

■ **Note** For more information on the product support lifecycle for Microsoft software, as well as details on support dates, please see the Microsoft Support Lifecycle site: `http://support.microsoft.com/lifecycle`

Your team's available delivery capacity is another reason you might include a major upgrade work stream on you roadmap, even if it does not relate to SharePoint and SharePoint does not depend on it. If another upgrade project utilizes part of your team or resources that your team depends on, then they probably will not have capacity to contribute to the planned activity in your roadmap. Planning for these upgrades, or any other major project for that matter, can help you design a dependable and realistic roadmap. This is just another dependency or another set of constraints that will help you plan a realistic roadmap.

Often I will represent this information as an infographic, usually with a chart listing the software and infrastructure vertically and time horizontally. I then add lines in the chart for each row to represent the support window and I add milestone diamonds to the line for activities that I will notate. Figure 7-2 shows an example of an infographic that details mainstream support dates for software.

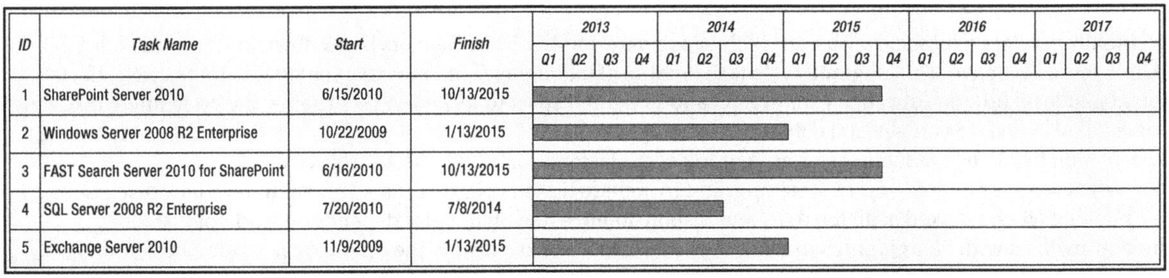

ID	Task Name	Start	Finish	2013				2014				2015				2016				2017			
				Q1	Q2	Q3	Q4	Q1	Q2	Q3	Q4	Q1	Q2	Q3	Q4	Q1	Q2	Q3	Q4	Q1	Q2	Q3	Q4
1	SharePoint Server 2010	6/15/2010	10/13/2015																				
2	Windows Server 2008 R2 Enterprise	10/22/2009	1/13/2015																				
3	FAST Search Server 2010 for SharePoint	6/16/2010	10/13/2015																				
4	SQL Server 2008 R2 Enterprise	7/20/2010	7/8/2014																				
5	Exchange Server 2010	11/9/2009	1/13/2015																				

Figure 7-2. *An example of software mainstream support dates*

I usually like to include an infographic of the upgrade and support lifecycle as supplementary information. In the next section, I describe a visual summary infographic that I like to create for the roadmap. I usually keep the upgrade and support lifecycle infographic separate because it can clutter and distract from the roadmap. Sometimes I will combine it if I need to stress an impending end of support date, but not often. Typically, I use the visual summary to communicate the roadmap with its details as concise as possible for effective communication.

Creating a Visual Summary Infographic

A visual summary might be the only part of your roadmap that most people read. People are busy beings, and they might not be interested in all of the details in your roadmap; perhaps they just want a synopsis of what affects them. Even your team, who are more likely to be interested in the details of your roadmap, will still find a visual summary useful since the most important information is available at a glance and they will not have to search for it in the document.

The other thing I like about a visual summary is how you can color-code it. Colors can add some energy to the roadmap, but they can also help organize information. You can put different phases in different colors, you can separate capabilities by color, or you can emphasize different priorities with different colors. You can even track progress by highlighting completed phases in a specified color. A few years ago when we on a project together, I noticed that my colleague Annie Kalfayan used this technique in her status reports, where she had a visual representation of the project stages and she highlighted completed stages in yellow. Ever since, I have liked this visualization as a progress communication tool and it can fit particularly well for tracking progress in your roadmap.

Inside a modern version of Microsoft Word, there is a feature where you can insert a "SmartArt" graphic. (Look for it on the Insert menu/tab). This does a great job at creating a visual infographic for your roadmap, particularly with the SmartArt in the "Process" category. I often use the Vertical Chevron List or the Staggered Process. I also like the Increasing Arrows Process when I create an infographic for onboarding. Figure 7-3 provides an example of a visual roadmap that I created using a SmartArt graphic in Word.

Figure 7-3. *A visual summary roadmap created using a SmartArt graphic in Word*

Visio also offers similar capabilities with richer features for diagraming your roadmap infographic. I find it easier to edit the styles and the structure of a graphic in Visio, and this is probably because I am more used to editing diagrams in Visio while I am more used to editing text in Word. You can also attach a Visio diagram to a data source, so if you are feeling extra keen, you can make your roadmap data driven and dynamic. You can also render a Visio diagram as a web page using Visio Services in SharePoint 2013. This makes it easy to add a visual summary infographic of your roadmap to your SharePoint site by rendering the Visio diagram directly.

Your roadmap documentation might consist solely of this visual summary. If you find this is all you need, then you are all set. Sometimes a visual summary fits my purposes just fine and then that is all I will use. Other times, I find a more detailed document is necessary to share information across the team or for funding purposes. Although even in those cases when I need to produce a roadmap with more details, I still include a visual summary. I like to include an infographic of the roadmap early in the document as a type of executive summary, and then continue with the rest of the document.

Once you move beyond a visual summary, what should you include in a roadmap document? In the next section, I discuss an approach to create a roadmap document.

Creating a Roadmap

In my roadmap documents, the visual summary is the essence of the roadmap. As such, I put it at the front of the document because this is often all many people will care to read. As you build out your visual summary of your roadmap, use the lists you created throughout this chapter to determine the priorities and scheduling requirements.

The visual summary carries most of the communication weight for a roadmap. Most people can grasp what you are planning and when each activity occurs after they look at your visual summary. Nevertheless, some people will look a little deeper and will want to understand why you prioritized it the way you did. Following the visual summary, I find it is useful to include a description and list of your constraints and limitations. You can also note any of your assumptions and any other information you used to prioritize your list.

After the visual roadmap and the supporting information, I like to include relevant schedule information such as the software and infrastructure support lifecycle schedules. You can also include expected vacation schedules and anticipated peak business periods. This is where you can discuss any lead and lag time you built in to your roadmap activities, as well as any adjustments you have made to accommodate your team or your users' limited capacity for change.

One aspect that I find useful to include in a roadmap is use cases. These can describe the expected user experience for different facets and capabilities of the system as you progress through your roadmap. They can help to articulate any expected business value and they communicate expectations for the experience the roadmap is working toward delivering. You can include use cases for different types of users or different usage scenarios.

Another aspect I like to include in a roadmap document is a parking lot of deferred features or requirements. Here I can describe what I am not planning to address in the scope of the roadmap and I might explain why. Perhaps it is because I do not have the budget or there are higher priority opportunities. Whatever the reason, there were features I considered or requirements that were raised, and I excluded them from the roadmap. It is important to capture why, but I find it is especially important to capture the items themselves so I have an artifact to consider in future incarnations of the roadmap.

As you build your roadmap document, include any supporting information you capture or use to assess maturity levels or to make decisions about priorities. This information will provide others with background details on the roadmap and it will help to justify the roadmap itself. With the visual summary being the essence of the roadmap, the rest of the document provides supplementary and supportive information.

Consultant Comrade

Creating roadmaps is one of those activities that can benefit everyone. In earlier sections, I described ways that it benefits my clients, where most notably it helps provide direction, manage expectations, and pace transformations. It can also benefit a consultant, because it involves you as your client's long-term advisor who can also help them deliver a lot of the work in their roadmap.

Sometimes I find in the course of delivering what I like to call the *SharePoint cornerstone* – that initial SharePoint deployment phase – I can generate many ideas with my clients for addressing all of the opportunities that arise. It can often feel as if all those potential follow-on engagements will keep me busy for a long time; yet, once I roll off that initial phase, the momentum seems to fizzle. What happened?

People generally need direction on what specifically the next steps are. It is one thing to say how valuable social computing will be as a follow up to the current deployment, but this can sound abstract and vague, particularly with identifying what is the first step and what it will involve. It leaves questions, such as how big will it be, and who needs to be on the team? When anything leaves more questions than direction, then momentum can instantly stall. Of course, lack of budget or competing priorities are among the other reasons that progress comes to a standstill, but when it becomes a permanent hiatus, it is usually relates to a lack of a roadmap and direction.

A roadmap provides that direction, it illustrates what comes next, and it produces a master checklist. I am especially fond of checklists in their many forms, as you no doubt can infer from my organization throughout this book. As such, this might explain why I value roadmaps so highly. Another benefit is that they leave a legacy of your expertise, so even if the client works through some of the roadmap without you, they still have a reminder of you. When they reach a part that turns out to be over their head, then you are probably their first call. Roadmaps are win-win and benefit consultants as well as your clients.

Another thing that I like about roadmaps as a consultant is that they give me the chance to leave my client with expert guidance they can refer to even after I roll off the project. Whether or not I can engage to help deliver a later phase, they have the direction they need to keep going, perhaps building on a SharePoint cornerstone deployment that I helped them deliver. This allows me to roll off an engagement with a client and feel confident that they have the direction they need to be successful. Otherwise, I might feel nervous as if I am abandoning some dependency. Best of all, if I do engage with them again down the road, I will not have to help them backtrack from heading too far in the wrong direction – these engagements are never as exciting as the ones where I can focus on new possibilities and delivering new value.

Because they offer so much value, you might consider how they can fit with a consulting service you offer. I recommend packaging it with an initial assessment, perhaps an assessment that includes some of the evaluation approaches I discussed in the root-cause analysis section in Chapter 6. Your assessment can also encompass a capabilities assessment where you analyze and identify what your client's maturity level is for different capabilities. From there, you can help them identify potential business value that they can realize from filling the gaps. Finally, you can help them prioritize and create a roadmap that can guide them to mature their operations and practices.

I consider this type of consulting as one where you engage as a strategic advisor. Roadmaps are about building a strategic plan for the future, and as you can see, the effective ones involve more expertise and insight than simply listing the specific technical features for your client to deploy. As such, this also offers the opportunity for premium consulting or a closer partnership with your clients.

Inside Story: Notes from the Field

Several years ago, I engaged with a client to deliver a SharePoint cornerstone project and help them get started with SharePoint. I scheduled the final portion of my engagement to focus on building a roadmap to point them in the right direction for where they could go after I rolled off the project and I had to leave them to continue on without me. This is the nature of consulting relationships; unfortunately, I will eventually have to move on and let my clients swim on their own. Knowing this, however, I usually try to leave them with enough direction on where to go next so that they have what they need to continue making progress on their own.

I went through the process I described in this chapter, starting with identifying capability gaps they wanted to fill as they matured to another level. I identified scheduling constraints and other priorities that would affect their roadmap. Finally, I built a visual summary of the capability and feature areas, prioritized based on the order they would address them.

This left them with some direction: a prioritized list of work activities they could chip away at while they enabled new features and delivered new business value. Often this seems as if it is the most difficult part, as SharePoint is so vast it can be difficult to determine where to start and what to address next. When it is broken down into a prioritized list, then I have addressed the hard part and all that is left is to slowly chip away at the list of activities on the roadmap.

When I have left a customer with this level of direction, I feel comfortable disengaging and moving on to my next project. I feel confident that I left them with the right information so that they can be successful as they continue working their way through the roadmap. I know some initiatives fizzle after I wrap up, and I often catch up with those clients down the road and discover that momentum was lost. This happens for many reasons, but I try to make sure that it does not happen because they did not know what to do next.

It was great catching up with the client in this example a couple of years later and seeing them diligently working their way through the list of activities on the roadmap. Sometimes I can return to a client and time has stood still since my last project with them, at least as far as their SharePoint initiative is concerned. Other times, such as with the client in this example, I can return and it seemed as if time has sped up for them since I was there. In these cases, I usually have to play catch up.

In this case, I created the roadmap and I included it as part of a project close out report. I like to wrap up my client engagements and leave them with a close out report – sometimes it is an informal email report, and other times it is a little more formal in a Word document, it all depends on the project and the client. In my engagement close out reports, I like to include a recap of all of the key activities I performed and the planned and extra (value-added) deliverables that I delivered. I like to highlight how I performed compared to the original budget and what knowledge transfer activities I managed to accomplish.

Finally, in my engagement close out report, I like to include a section on next steps. These can be immediate next steps or a longer range of next steps that my client can take. I usually list these in the form of a checklist and I append a note on the bottom encouraging them to contact me if they have any questions or if they want to plan to engage me again if they find they need some help addressing any of the next steps. This can serve as a short-term roadmap of activities.

Sometimes I also include a longer-term visual roadmap of capabilities to augment the checklist of next steps. Again, I include a reference to engage me again if they need help enabling capabilities in the roadmap, and to update me on their progress if not. This is how my client reconnected with me, to update me on how well they were working through the roadmap and how useful they were finding it, and this is always satisfying to hear.

Wrapping Up

Throughout this chapter, I discussed techniques for planning and building a roadmap for your SharePoint service. I shared some considerations for what makes a roadmap valuable and how you can get started. I then looked at the concept of maturity models and walked through how to identify maturity levels for different capabilities. From there, I looked at accommodating your users' limited capacity for change and your upgrade cycle requirements that both affect your roadmap's activities and schedule. Finally, I covered how to combine all this into a visual summary of your roadmap and other elements you can include in a roadmap document.

Even with a well-thought-out roadmap, you will still discover new opportunities you can add to your SharePoint service. One source of discovery is by capturing feedback from your users. In the next chapter, I look at ways you can capture user feedback and how this can help you stay allied with your users. Finally, I also look at ways you can drive adoption by utilizing the feedback you capture.

CHAPTER 8

Promoting a Feedback Process

It's never crowded along the extra mile.

—Dr. Wayne Dyer

In this chapter, I provide guidance on capturing users' feedback on their experience using your SharePoint service, as well as any frustrations or shortcomings that causes users to struggle. These topics offer considerations to keep your SharePoint team connected with your users and in tune with their needs. From there, I introduce approaches to create connections with potential internal evangelists who can help grow the service.

One key point I stress in this chapter is the opportunity that capturing feedback and user requests will present: handling potential adoption issues early, often by connecting end-users with the training resources or guidance that they need to consume the service effectively and in a way that meets their needs. I also provide guidance on implementing a SharePoint survey that captures feedback.

After reading this chapter, you will know how to:

- Capture user feedback

- Handle potential adoption issues early

- Build internal evangelists to promote your SharePoint service

Valuing Feedback

Too often, I have found myself falling in a trap of assuming what users need and what their experience is like. I have to catch myself and avoid this, because I have experience engaging with business users and this can often compensate for missing any of their actual requirements with my general knowledge. My risk is that I will carry over my previous requirements or previous experiences, and I will then unconsciously project these on a new situation where I miss the opportunity to uncover any of their business needs.

This can be a tempting situation, one especially tempting in light of business users with limited availability or who have a hard time articulating what they need. With my experience in a variety of SharePoint scenarios, I find I can anticipate several core requirements that do not change from situation to situation. My clients are reasonably consistent with the value they seek and how they want to deploy the product, although some have had wildly unique requirements and constraints. Overall, I can predict many requirements and be within a reasonable range. As a result, I make an extra effort to check on the process to ensure I involve the voice of the business - the voice of those end-users whose productivity I will affect and who have valuable requirements of their own.

Feedback can come from upfront requirements for a new deployment, or from ongoing usage. When you are gathering requirements, it can often feel natural to gather requirements from your users, because project plans typically include these activities and they allocate business analysts to conduct user interviews to gather these requirements. These requirements are valuable feedback from users, and as I just mentioned, they are a step I pay extra attention to in order to avoid projecting my anticipated requirements into the solution I deliver. The other type of feedback comes after that: feedback about the ongoing operations of the service and whether it continues to meet their needs.

This ongoing feedback can validate that your initial delivery meets the known requirements as well as their other needs. I am a firm believer that once users start using a system, they reveal more requirements as they gain a better understanding about what the system offers and how it will fit with their processes. These requirements are difficult to foresee, simply because no one can imagine every detail while the system is still conceptual. Once the system is in production and users are using it to do their work, then you will discover whether you met planned requirements, whether all those requirements are still valid, and where there are opportunities to enhance the system from new requirements.

Discovering unexpected or unknown requirements is not a failure, and it does not indicate that the analyst missed anything during the requirements gathering phase. Instead, discovering these opportunities comes as you and your users learn more about the system and what is possible with it. Requirements will evolve as these new opportunities present themselves to deliver value to your users. This is why I prefer to scope projects in small incremental phases, phases that allow everyone to learn and continue to enhance the service through ongoing enhancements.

By delivering value incrementally in smaller phases, you reduce the need for extensive upfront requirements planning. I find by addressing fewer requirements in more frequent cycles, users reveal proper requirements and you will face less resistance to adoption because these requirements will more closely match what the users ultimately need. In contrast, I find when I conduct an extensive requirements planning activity early in a waterfall fashion, I miss possibilities that I find myself later resisting as I try to manage project scope. There is a danger in having a business analyst work to document requirements too extensively ahead of time – the greater the amount of time, the greater the risk of changing requirements.

I always get worried when I see business analysts documenting what they believe is every detail of a system before users have even been exposed to SharePoint. I often see these types of requirements focus on minute details found in the existing system's functionality, systems that I am going to replace end up introducing legacy requirements simply because they exist and they are what the users are used to. SharePoint requirements then end up resembling simple built-in functionality such as checking in documents, and then because of a lack of any other requirements, this massive list of feature requirements goes into a Request for Proposal (RFP) without anyone vetting them with what else may be possible.

If you are deploying SharePoint to replace an existing service or process, I recommend starting with a pilot deployment where your users begin to use SharePoint and provide feedback. Through their feedback, you will gain valuable insights into what types of requirements are important and what legacy practices you can replace. Through this approach, you can gather the same type of user feedback that will contribute to initial requirements for a deployment and to requirements for enhancements.

User feedback can reveal the business value you can deliver to your users, and these insights can help you make your SharePoint service more relevant to them and their business processes. As I discuss later in this chapter, user feedback can also help you respond to adoption issues and engage potential evangelists who help promote the service. I return to discuss those opportunities and the value they offer in later sections of the chapter. First, I want to look at how you can approach capturing user feedback.

Capturing User Feedback

If it is convenient and easy enough, users are usually happy to share their experience and offer feedback, particularly if they had a negative experience or they wished something worked better. This is good, because this type of feedback will give you insights into what changes are necessary and what opportunities exist. Users generally know if something does not feel right or if a process feels inefficient, and these are often clues into where you should focus your efforts.

You can approach this in several ways, from automated system forms that populate a database to interviewing users about their experience. You can even capture usage statistics and monitor how users interact with the system and analyze that data to determine whether this reveals any usage patterns that indicate where users struggle or where users have invented their own solution to a business problem that you were unaware of. Usage statistics and other techniques that analyze actual usage help to reveal how users use the system beyond expectations such as how they are supposed to use it or what the actual intentions of the system are.

Data forms such as surveys provide an ideal tool to aggregate data across a large number of users. This approach works best for questions that do not require further probing. Questions that work well for this format include true or false questions, multiple-choice questions, rating questions, and other fixed list questions. You can also include open-ended questions that gather input, such as asking for the user's suggestions or comments on the SharePoint service. These types of questions are more difficult to aggregate to analyze trends, but they can capture unstructured feedback where a user has a specific complaint or suggestion and they have details to provide about it.

Interviewing users offers the most flexible approach for gathering feedback because you can probe users for additional details based on their reactions or feedback in a more personalized fashion. A branched survey can probe for some questions, but you have to know ahead of time what will come up that you will want additional details about. In a personalized interview, users can reveal unexpected information that can lead the interview in an unanticipated direction. The downside to this is that it does not scale very well – you cannot reach as many users as quickly as you can with a survey or another system of data gathering methods. This approach is best for closer analysis with a limited sample of users who are adequately representative of the whole user population. The remaining users can provide input through an automated approach such as system data collection.

I prefer to frame user feedback in the sense that they are offering suggestions or pointing out things that bother them; they are not there to design solutions. This distinction is important for me, because I am there to interpret their feedback and design solutions, not simply collect a shopping list of features to build. After all, I am the expert there to help them discover possibilities. I often like to think of Henry Ford's comment that if he gave his users exactly what they wanted, he would have designed a faster *horse*. Instead, he focused on their needs and abstracted their requirements to recognize what they desired was a faster transportation method. He interpreted their feedback and he used his expertise and creativity to design a solution.

This Henry Ford example highlights something I literally try to remind myself as well as my project teammates on every project: do not just give our users a faster horse. As I mentioned earlier, I pay special attention to ensure I include the voice of my business users in solution requirements, but as I collect this feedback, I also keep in mind that my job is to interpret their feedback and think in the world of possibilities rather than fill the order with a faster horse. This engagement and creativity is what I love the most about my job: I love envisioning possibilities and designing optimum solutions to solve business challenges.

My approach focuses on user feedback and how I collect it. I try to avoid leading the user with questions that ask what they want. Maybe I do not give them enough credit, but I just assume they are not SharePoint experts and therefore they cannot know what they want. I especially try to avoid leading questions such as, "Would an InfoPath form and workflow help?" It is tempting to start throwing SharePoint features at your users, because after all, they are exciting. However, this type of questioning jumps into solutions too quickly and will miss the larger opportunities to influence your users' productivity in unexpected ways.

I like to ask questions about their work and their processes, and in the process, I steer them away from talking about features. When they start saying things like, "I think I need a document library and a workflow," then I suggest we take a step back and discuss what they are trying to accomplish. It could turn out that this is exactly what they need, but I want to get there through analyzing their actual business requirements and processes. So the short answer is I try to keep my questions focused on their work.

The following lists some examples of work-related questions I use to probe my users for insights into their requirements:

- Can you step through the tasks you do in your process?

- Do you experience any interruptions as you work through the process?

- Is there anything about the process that frustrates you?

- What feels like a waste of time in the process?

- Can you describe the different types of information you interact with or manage?

- Who depends on this information?

- Who else gets involved in the process and what do they do?

- Is there anything extra that you do in the process as a backup or workaround?

- What is the ultimate goal or overall point to doing this process?

Depending on the type of problem you are analyzing, these specific questions may or may not fit, but these will still be the types of questions to ask. They get users talking about how they work and why they do the things they do. They also uncover what bothers users or where the process is the least effective. These questions mostly fit with gathering requirements for a new deployment, but you can still use them to audit the effectiveness of an existing deployment.

Open questions are useful, particularly for in-person user interviews. They probe the users on their work and they stimulate discussion on the details of their processes. As I mentioned earlier, they make it harder to aggregate responses when you use a tool such as a mass survey. For these survey approaches, closed-ended questions work better (although I like to leave room for some open-ended questions in case the user has something to add). The following lists some examples of these types of closed-ended questions:

- Can you get your work done without finding workarounds?

- Do you feel adequately trained in how to use the system?

- Does the system meet your needs?

- Do you use any of the following solutions? (Follow this question with a checklist of externally hosted solutions, such as peer file sharing, email, surveys, and the like).

- On a scale of one to five (one being hard/poor, five being easy/great), how has your experience been with sharing documents with your colleagues?

- On a scale of one to five (one being rarely, five being frequently), how often do you visit the intranet homepage?

These types of questions can gather answers from a mass number of users, and because the answers have a fixed selection, they are easy to aggregate to see trends and patterns. Again, I try to steer these questions away from feature-specific questions, so I would avoid asking questions such as, "Would you like a MySite?" Instead, I might ask something related to how they find information about people – especially people whose name the user might not know.

Lucky for you, SharePoint has rich survey capabilities built in! This makes it easy and convenient to poll the masses and capture user feedback. If you are gathering feedback for an existing deployment, then you already have somewhere to host your survey; but if you are gathering feedback for a new deployment, then you might not have SharePoint available yet. These new deployments are a great opportunity to deploy a pilot and host the survey there. (I always find that the sooner I can get a pilot deployed and get people trying SharePoint, the better, and surveys can be a great motivator toward a pilot).

Whichever way you approach hosting SharePoint surveys, the process to design them is the same. In the next section, I walk you through how to design and use SharePoint surveys.

Designing and Using SharePoint Surveys

SharePoint has powerful tools built in that will support your efforts to collect feedback. However, there is a tolerance level for how much information you can ask users to provide. There is no optimum number of questions or duration of time, because the tolerance depends more on a relationship with the users' perceived value from the survey rather than some fixed number. For example, if users are frustrated with a current system and feel heavily invested in influencing the future system, their perceived value will be much higher. The higher the perceived value, the greater the number of questions you can ask and you can expect a higher involvement from users in answering them.

Think about it: research firms and marketing departments constantly inundate people with requests for information about their lives. Polling firms, telemarketers, customer satisfaction surveys, customer loyalty cards, and a flood of other examples bombard people with requests for information. These requests chip away at their valuable time and can lead to what I like to think of as survey fatigue. Participating in many of these types of survey activities may not and probably does not offer me enough value to warrant allowing it to chip away at my scarce time availability. I hear statements such as, "but your feedback is important to us and it will help us better serve you in the future." Too often, my response is that I simply do not care, or at least not enough to warrant spending the time to help them sell things to me more efficiently.

Your internal SharePoint survey for user feedback may not face this same disinterest and cynicism, but it does have to consider the value question. Why will it be worth a user's time to participate in the survey? How much of their time will be worth investing in completing the survey? (How much of their time will be worth investing for *them* – I already assume that an infinite amount of their time will be worth their investment for you). In answering these types of questions, you will get a sense for how much you can fit in a survey and how involved you can make the survey questions. With this in mind, you can begin to prioritize your survey questions.

It seems much of my process in a SharePoint project is prioritizing, and designing surveys are no different. You constantly face limitations and constraints, and prioritizing helps you to uncover the opportunities and reach achievements available in the face of any constraints. As such, you will face trade-offs for how much information you can gather from your users, and so you will need to focus on your top priorities and the most valuable topics where you need a greater understanding or deeper insights. One approach to prioritizing and designing your survey questions is to organize a worksheet.

Table 8-1 provides an example of a survey question worksheet. Excel is often a great tool in which to build your worksheet or you could use a SharePoint custom list. Use whichever format you are comfortable with for organizing and prioritizing tabular data. This example provides a nice start for what different aspects you might comprise and how they can help you prioritize which questions to include in the survey.

Table 8-1. *An Example of a Survey Worksheet*

Priority	Time	Topic Area	Question	Potential Formats
High	Low	Adoption	How frequently do you visit the intranet?	Selection list with ranges
High	High	Challenges	What experience frustrates you the most?	Comment field
Med	Med	Impression	How do you rate these portals for ease of use?	List with star ratings
Med	Med	Impression	Which features do you use every week?	Checkbox list
Med	Low	Readiness	Do you feel adequately trained?	Yes/No
Med	Med	Adoption	Do you use any of these other systems?	Checkbox list
Med	Low	Impression	Are you satisfied with the system?	Yes/No
Low	Med	Design	Which layout do you find more appealing?	Selection list
Low	High	Process	What departments do you depend on?	Comment field
Low	High	Challenges	Do you have any other suggestions?	Comment field

Of course, your priority levels and time involvement estimates may vary. You might extend this worksheet to also incorporate things such as branched questions, optional questions, questions for particular categories of users, and whatever else that will help you design your survey. You might even look for ways to auto-populate questions and include that here. Some are readily available, such as the user's name, but others might require more creativity on your part to automatically capture. Once you have this list, then you can begin to build your survey with the questions that you prioritize to include.

My example focuses more on gathering information for a new solution. You can use it for ongoing operational feedback as well, but users generally prefer to answer shorter and fewer questions when they provide ongoing feedback. Those types of surveys should focus on a couple rating questions that rate a general aspect of the service and a comment field for other suggestions or complaints. These are handy to monitor the pulse of how your users perceive your SharePoint service. You can report on weekly trends and follow up on evolving issues. You can promote this feedback survey by including a link to it in follow-up emails to users after your team resolves their service request, or you can post a link to the feedback survey on your intranet homepage.

For those more involved surveys that you use to gather detailed feedback from users, you might email a link with a description about how you will use their feedback and the value it will provide. The email can describe the project and your team's goal of aligning with business needs, and how business value drives your decisions. You can articulate this so the users know that their feedback will help you make the best technology decisions and solution designs, which in return, you want to design to benefit the users. You can state how valuable their information and feedback will contribute and help to influence the solution, as well as mentioning any direct value that users can expect for participating.

This returns to my initial discussion on value. Sometimes you just need too much information, where the number of questions and their required involvement outweighs any perceived value that your users will recognize. In these cases, you might consider including a contest as part of the feedback survey process. You could have a random draw for a gift certificate or some other prize that would add perceived value and entice users to invest the time to submit their feedback.

The thing I love the most about surveys is how they can aggregate responses to questions from a huge range of users across the entire organization. This can give you a clear picture about what the perceived priorities should be and what are the more important issues to your users. This information can help you identify business value and build a business case for a particular initiative. It can also help you manage expectations, for instance when you have competing requests then you can use the widespread interest from across the organization to justify why you prioritized one over another.

As you choose your question format types, think about how you want to report on the results. If you choose a field for free text entry for every question, then not only are you adding overhead to your users' involvement in their responses (and thus reducing their perceived value), but you are making it difficult to aggregate and report on the answers as well. When you have selections, ratings, checkboxes, or the like, then you have a range of options that you can aggregate across all responses.

■ **Note** For details on how to create a survey in a SharePoint site, please search for "create a survey" on the following Office help site: `http://office.microsoft.com/en-us/windows-sharepoint-services-help`

Designing Custom User Feedback Solutions

I found that an effective way to collect user feedback can be through custom solutions that extend the ways that you can gather feedback from users for your SharePoint deployment. One of my favorites is to add a feedback control to the SharePoint page. If you have tested a beta version of SharePoint during the last couple of releases, you may have noticed a smiley face that users can click on to submit feedback directly to the SharePoint product team. I like this idea and I like to include something similar in deployments to collect feedback for my SharePoint team.

Basically, I build an ASP.NET web control, which is just a "Give Feedback" link button. When a user clicks the button, I show a modal window with a form that gathers information on their experience. You can make this form submit the user's feedback to whatever data source you like, such as a database, an InfoPath form library, an email address, or even a SharePoint survey. What I like about it is I have it in the location to allow a user to submit feedback without leaving the context of where they are and what they are doing.

You can use this type of custom feedback control at the top of pages and you can submit the current page URL as part of the feedback so that you can trace the context back to the page that motivated the user to provide feedback in the first place. You can also include this type of control in functional areas such as search results, in which case you can also submit the query the user entered as part of the feedback. This information can help alert you to poor experiences in different areas of the service, or it can reveal new opportunities as the users think of them in the context of whatever they are working on.

As part of this solution, I also like to generate an email to the user to thank them for taking the time to share their feedback, and this is a good chance to assure them that someone has received their feedback and he or she will act on it.

I find this simulated connection helps to encourage users to submit feedback again in the future, but if you can have a real team member reach out to them personally then this will have an even better effect. This could be simply to thank them for the feedback or to gather more information, or you can use this as an opportunity to try to remove any roadblocks they faced by offering training materials or some additional support. Whatever the case, often the follow-up can reveal additional user feedback that this custom solution sparks.

You can add whatever magic and pizzazz to this solution, as you see fit. I kept it simple in this example just to illustrate the possibilities for collecting feedback. The more effortlessly you can make providing a response and the more pervasively you make opportunities to provide a response, then the greater the likelihood is that you will generate responses and feedback. Similar to the line in the movie *Field of Dreams* – "If you build it, he will come" – if you make it easy for your users to submit feedback, then they will. This means that you should avoid an excessive list of required fields on a form, and that feedback form should be available from as many different access points as possible (without being too intrusive, of course).

When you look at developing a custom component to collect user feedback, the limits are really of your own imagination. You might stick with options within SharePoint, or you might explore other access points with your users. For instance, if you have Windows 8 deployed in your organization, you might consider adding a custom feedback component as a tile on the start menu. You can incorporate this tile to include other features, such as reporting on service health metrics or providing the ability to submit a service request, or you might keep it simple and use it just for feedback surveys. If you have Lync deployed, you might develop a similar customization add-in that your users can access through their Lync client. You might also consider developing an add-in for Office programs such as an App for Word or Outlook, where you enable your users to submit feedback directly from the Ribbon or an App panel. You might provide a mobile application for smart phones or tablets. You really do have a wide array of potential survey channels.

For this example, I focus on an ASP.NET component, and you can integrate this solution into a SharePoint site. I return shortly to discuss how best to integrate this component on a SharePoint page, but first, I share the code that makes up this component. The following code snippet displays JavaScript that you can use to display a modal window using Ajax on a SharePoint page. You can add a button or link that says something to the effect of "Submit your Feedback" and include this within the component. You can include a method call to the following JavaScript function so when your users click the link a modal window displays with the survey form.

```javascript
// JavaScript function to open a new modal dialog window
// Pass the URL of the new item form (the survey response form) and a title
function OpenModalDialog(url, title) {
    var dialogOptions = {
    url: url,
    width: 800,
    height: 600,
    title: title,
    dialogReturnValueCallback: ModalCallback
  };
  SP.UI.ModalDialog.showModalDialog(dialogOptions);
}

// JavaScript callback function to close the modal dialog window
function ModalCallback(dialogResult, returnValue) {
  SP.UI.ModalDialog.commonModalDialogClose(dialogResult, returnVal);
}
```

You can wrap this JavaScript in an ASP.NET control that you add to the SharePoint page. As part of that control, you also add a way for the user to click and open the feedback form. Because it is an ASP.NET control, you can use the page context and the SharePoint API to gather additional data you would like to include as part of the survey response. In this case, you might create your own custom survey page to display in the modal window and populate hidden fields with this additional information.

There is a feature within SharePoint that I absolutely love as a developer. I use it frequently when I develop solutions, and especially when I develop solutions that interact with the user interface in some way. What I love about it is that I can add elements to the page without modifying the master page, layout page, or pages in the site definition. This makes it easy to add or remove components from a page, or even override and replace other components on a page, all from activating or deactivating a custom SharePoint feature.

I have built up the suspense long enough. This feature is a delegate control. Essentially, a page or master page embeds a `DelegateControl` with a `ControlID` attribute. You then specify that identifier, a control template to use, and a stacking sequence in a SharePoint feature definition. Once you activate the feature, the SharePoint runtime then determines which candidate control template to render on the page based on the sequence numbers. When you deactivate the feature, the SharePoint runtime no longer renders the control.

Using delegate controls, you can add and remove functionality to pages at different scopes, depending on the scope of the feature. This decouples your component development from your user interface pages and site definitions. Ultimately, because you decoupled it in this way, this approach has the highest degree of maintainability and upgradability. Web parts and Apps for SharePoint have a similar decoupled design, but delegate controls are a way to add components on a wider and more automated scale.

■ **Note** For more information on developing a delegate control and adding one to a SharePoint page, please see this MSDN reference: `http://msdn.microsoft.com/ms478826`

CUSTOM FEEDBACK AND A NOTIFICATION BAR COMPONENT

I like to add this custom feedback component to the header area of the page – somewhere at the top where users can see it and easily provide feedback from wherever they are. This makes it consistent for the user experience, and easy to deploy. Rather than a delegate control, you might deploy it as a Custom Action. A Custom Action is another XML element you can deploy and activate as part of a SharePoint feature, and through it, you can add or remove menu items from different menus within SharePoint.

Personally, I usually go with the delegate control I described earlier. The reason for this is that you can combine a few things into the control template you add to the page. For example, you can add a feedback web control, as well as other web controls that can add to your user experience and provide functionality you want to add to your SharePoint pages. One of these controls that I find especially useful is a notification bar.

Think of the notification bar as similar to the yellow notification bar you might get in your browser to warn you about different events on different sites. Figure 8-1 illustrates an example of the SharePoint Health Analyzer notification bar in SharePoint Central Administration. I find that having a notification bar like this within SharePoint is particularly useful for mass communication. Perhaps you are scheduling system maintenance and you want to let everyone know. Picture adding a notification to the top of every SharePoint page to effectively communicate this. Perhaps there is a new feature or a new service you want people to be aware of, or perhaps you need to quickly communicate about a major incident.

Figure 8-1. *The SharePoint Health Analyzer notification bar*

E-mail, of course, can communicate these things. However, the trouble is an e-mail is out of context, where as a notification bar about SharePoint in a SharePoint site is in context. E-mail can also get lost in the pile.

You might extend the functionality of this notification bar even further and add informational notices regarding the sensitivity or confidentiality of the content in a site. You could even add terms of use notices and other types of statuses. This functionality lays the framework that you can continue to take advantage of for effective communication across your organization.

On the topic of notifications, this can be a way for you to provide feedback to your users. Keeping them informed will help you head off any potential issues. It can also draw their attention to things, such as a survey that you want to use to collect their feedback and participation. SharePoint Central Administration has a great example of one of these notification bars that draws the administrator's attention to actions they need to address. Figure 8-1 illustrates the notification bar that the SharePoint Health Analyzer displays when it detects issues.

SharePoint includes other types of notifications you will notice as well. For example, Figure 8-2 shows a screenshot of the notification that SharePoint displays after you share a site with "Everyone" on the People and Groups page within the Site Settings. Notice the little notification in the top-right notifying you that "Everyone" now has access to the Search site.

Figure 8-2. *The notification alert displayed in the top-right after adding "Everyone" to the site*

Gathering System-Generated User Feedback

Not all feedback has to come from a survey or direct user responses to questions you ask. You might have heard the adage, "vote with their feet." This describes people's ability to walk off and find more beneficial solutions elsewhere. A store's customer might vote with their feet by shopping at a new store where they find better service or lower prices. Your internal customers might vote with their feet by deciding which system to use and how much they adopt it. In voting by using and adopting the system, these users are providing you with feedback.

Back in Chapter 6, I discussed some measures you can use to capture different usage metrics. Those will help give you a sense of usage and how your users might be voting with their feet. One tool in particular that will help you to collect feedback based on how your users are using SharePoint, and that is the Site Usage Analytics reports. Figure 8-3 shows a screenshot of the View Usage Reports available for a site collection. You can access these reports by navigating to Site Settings of a site, and then under the Site Collection Administration section, click the Popularity and Search Reports link. In these reports, you can gather information related to user actions or user events, such as viewed items or clicked links. You can see what the most popular site is and which of your users interact with which types of sites.

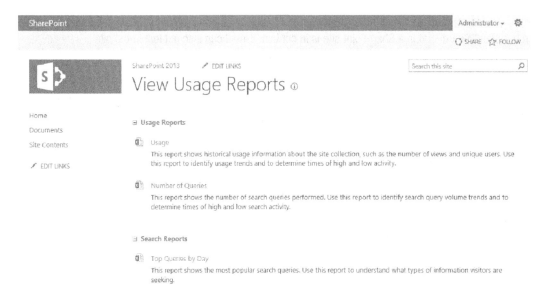

Figure 8-3. *The Site collection Usage Reports*

You can also use the search analytics in the Search Usage Reports to discover what your users are searching for and what they find. Figure 8-4 shows a screenshot of the View Usage Reports available for the search service application. You can access these reports by navigating to the Search Administration page for the service application, and then under the Diagnostics section on the left, click the Usage Reports link. These reports can give you insights into how they search for information and the terminology that they use for particular types of information. It can also reveal what users could not find, either because it does not exist or because the terms they use to search are different from the language of the content itself. This can also help you discover different types of popularity for information that interests your users as well as how they interact with search.

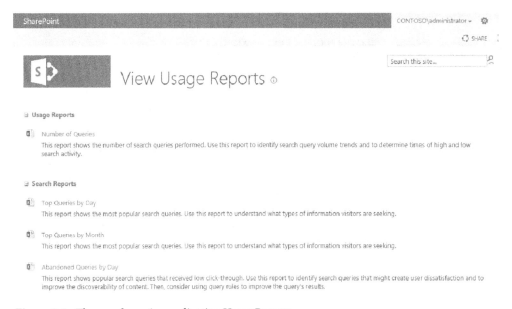

Figure 8-4. *The search service application Usage Reports*

These analytics reports can reveal how your users use SharePoint. As you look at the reports, try to answer questions that will help you to build a profile of your users. Some questions might include the following list:

- What is the most popular use of SharePoint?

- When is SharePoint the most popular?

- What do users come to SharePoint to access or accomplish?

- How do they achieve these goals?

- Does anything indicate a part of SharePoint does not meet their needs?

- Is there functionality or information available in SharePoint that users are overlooking?

- Which features are users ignoring?

- What sites have users abandoned?

- Have users designed their own workaround for something?

- What other customizations have users made to their sites?

These types of questions can help you paint a portrait of your users and how they use SharePoint. To answer some questions, you will have to go beyond the analytics report and look at the site itself. I usually focus my attention on the most popular sites, because they have the highest adoption and therefore they can provide the most insights into usage. The other sites offer useful information too, but depending on the size of your deployment, you may not have time to manually review each site beyond their usage analytics reports.

Gathering all this information can answer many questions before you even survey your users. Do not burden your users with providing you with information that you can discover yourself. That way, you will know more ahead of time about the information you do have to collect from them, and you can collect it by making the most efficient use of your users' time.

With all this information in hand, you can identify what you still need to learn from your users. Usually, this type of information is more specific to their business processes and the reasoning behind why they do some of the things in a particular way. This type of information is not apparent in usage analytics reports and surveys will usually end up missing it as well. This type of information is what you need to engage with your users to discover. You will discover this information by either interviewing them and have them explain their business processes, or by shadowing them to directly observe their business processes. In the next section, I share some tips on how to interview your users and in a later section, I look at how to shadow your users as they perform their tasks.

Interviewing Users for Feedback

It may seem as if interviewing users is an easy task and maybe should not warrant a prominent section in a chapter on gathering feedback. After all, you talk to people every day and ask them how they are doing and what they did over the weekend. I do not doubt that you know how to interact with people and ask them what it is that they do. Nonetheless, interviewing users for feedback is a little different and it requires special care if you want it to be effective.

The biggest trap you can fall into is to rely on your knowledge of SharePoint and the capabilities it delivers and to use this knowledge to drive your discussion with your users. By this, I mean that as a user tells you a problem, you begin to think right away about what that means in SharePoint, or while the users are describing what they want or how they want it to work, your mind wanders to think about how you can enable that in SharePoint. I refer to this as *solutioning*, or jumping prematurely into a solution design before you have fully understood the problem.

I call this a trap because it can be very easy to drift into designing a solution as you hear a problem. People inexperienced with SharePoint do this in their quest to understand SharePoint and where it might fit – perhaps they have a mandate to deploy SharePoint and they are trying to match the features to some requirements. However, this is not limited to novices with SharePoint, as experienced solution architects can often fake or bypass business requirements because they know the product and its capabilities so well. It is an easy trap to fall into, and one I try to be conscious of to avoid falling into it myself.

Jumping to a solution too quickly will blind you. You will miss opportunities that you would have uncovered by staying disciplined and focused on analyzing the business problem in depth. Ultimately, this means that you will deliver a solution that does not align tightly with specific business value. Instead, you will deploy features that are loosely associated with a symptom of a business problem. You do not want that and I doubt it is ever intentional, but from what I can tell, this is how it creeps in and happens on projects.

For me, I think this stems from my innate desire to please people, so when a user explains a challenge they have, I want to jump to a solution and give them some happiness by describing how whatever idea jumps into my mind will solve their problem. My mind wanders and I cannot control that, so I am going to get these ideas and flashes of solutions as users describe their business needs. My process then is to recognize these ideas without distracting the user with them. I usually add a quick note so the idea is not lost, and then I continue with actively listening to the user describe their processes and challenges.

Active listening is the key there. If you are actively listening to your users and asking them to expand on issues they bring up or the ways they are doing things, you will discover a lot. I try to take notes and write questions I have or things that I am wondering so I can come back to them later during the interview; this way I do not have to interrupt the user but I also will not lose ideas I can later explore. This also lets the user drive the interview while I merely prod them with questions.

As you ask your users questions, try to frame them so that the questions are both open and broad. I particularly try to avoid asking any technology-specific questions or leading questions that lead to a solution. For instance, I would consider this as an example of a poor question: Which of these SharePoint 2013 features do you think will benefit you the most? If you ever hear me ask a user this question, then you know it is time to break for lunch. Instead, I try to frame my questions so that they are more general and open, and so they are more about the user and their business needs. For example, this is a question I ask users: What frustrates you the most in your work processes?

There is certainly an art to framing effective interview questions. A good rule of thumb that I use is to keep questions focused on the user and their business processes and business needs. The following lists a few of these types of questions that I use when I interview users.

- What challenges or frustrates you?

- What do you think is unnecessary?

- What do you do that you feel is inefficient or redundant?

- How do you find things or people on the portal?

- What shortcuts do you take to speed up a process?

- What part of your day runs the smoothest?

■ **Note**   One of my favorite books on interviewing users and gathering their business requirements is *Software Requirements*, Second Edition, by Karl E. Wiegers and published in 2003 (ISBN 978-0735618794).

As users think and answer these questions, they can give you ideas on areas you want to inquire about deeper. Keep asking open questions and practice active listening as they answer. This is what gives you deep insights into the business problem. User interviews are not for designing solutions; they are for gaining a deep understanding of business processes and business problems. Once you have collected all this information, you can go away to analyze it and begin to envision a solution.

Even with brilliant questions that are open and that focus on the user rather than the technology, you still may not fully understand all the intricacies of a business problem. One reason for this is that maybe the user is unaware of an aspect of their process that they do not think to bring it up. It could have always been that way, and because it has become almost second nature to them, they do not even think about bringing it up to you. To uncover these types of details and help yourself form a broader picture of the business problem, you can shadow users performing their job. When you shadow a user and analyze their processes, you will typically spot things they did not think to mention.

Shadowing Users and Analyzing Business Processes

Your first challenge when you shadow a user is to blend in – you do not want to interrupt or interfere with their work. Usually when you shadow someone, you are shadowing them for a period of time, such as an entire shift. Since your presence could include a large proportion of their day, you should try your best to make yourself unobtrusive. This is not only to prevent the user you are shadowing from regretting that they are allowing you to shadow them, but also because the more invisible you can make yourself the less you will influence the business processes you are analyzing.

Unlike conducting an interview, shadowing a user works best when you merely observe. As such, you should minimize your questions and focus on capturing notes. This ensures that you do not distract the user from the tasks they would normally perform, and therefore it will help you get a more accurate picture of how they work. If they do things that you wonder about, you might make a note and then schedule a debrief session with the user later to gather more details.

Although, it would probably be awkward for both of you if you did not say anything, so it is okay to have some conversation. I try to keep this conversation light and a little more informal as opposed to an interview. Typically, I would have a user describe the tasks that they are performing, but I would avoid prying into details of the tasks or anything that would slow down performing their normal job. This approach seems to strike a good balance between staying engaged with the user you are shadowing while avoiding causing any interference.

When I shadow a user, I like to make a lot of notes about their activities, business processes, and people or departments that interact with them. I usually draw rough diagrams about any processes or interactions, and later I can polish them in Visio. I might review the diagrams with the user later during a break or a debrief session to ensure that I understood the process correctly and that I did not miss anything. Usually, this can reveal even more as the user thinks through their processes and mentions any exceptions or alternate paths it could take.

I find shadowing users often produces several diagrams and pages of notes. It generates a ton of information and insights into the business problem, and this is a good thing. After all, you are on an information gathering expedition when you shadow users. This provides detailed, granular data about the business problem – data that you collect by observing and analyzing. I find this process is beneficial and the insights into the business that shadowing provides are valuable. However, at the same time I realize that this is not always practical or even necessary.

Admittedly, shadowing users is a time consuming activity. If you want to gather information at this level, you have to prepare for a time investment from you and the user. You also have to select a representative of the users, because shadowing every user is probably not practical or even worthwhile. Shadowing is a tool you can consider, but you will have to weigh whether the feedback and information it will collect will outweigh the time costs involved with conducting a shadowing activity with a user.

Directly observing your users provides the closest level of user feedback. You may find this approach useful for when you want to gather feedback before expanding your SharePoint service into a new capability area. This is also a useful technique to employ when you are gathering requirements and preparing to replace another system with your SharePoint service. Because it is so involved and it requires a significant time investment, I usually save it for gathering feedback I can use for major projects, such as new system deployments or service expansions.

DETECTING AND HANDLING POTENTIAL ADOPTION ISSUES

One side benefit of regularly collecting user feedback is that it can tip you off when there are potential adoption issues. If everyone submits negative feedback to a survey or you notice that usage patterns suddenly shift, then this can indicate that there probably is a problem having a negative impact on your users. With an ongoing feedback process, you can detect and handle these problems quickly before they grow into a major adoption issue.

Detecting adoption issues might not be as obvious as a sudden change in survey satisfaction levels. Trends in usage or survey responses can provide insights into whether adoption rates are trending down, holding steady, or increasing.

Users might also put up with something for a while before it bothers them enough to complain about it or to find a workaround. These types of potential adoption issues are harder to detect early, but you can still include survey questions that can reveal user frustrations as they develop.

Resolving potential adoption issues helps you offer a service that your users continue to find useful and relevant. User feedback provides early warning signs, and these signs are available at all levels of user feedback, from surveys to usage analytic reports to user interviews. As you build your approaches to gathering user feedback, think about how you can also detect and alert your team to potential adoption issues.

Building Internal Evangelists

If you are providing a service that truly addresses business value, then your users will have plenty of reasons to help evangelize your service. By addressing business value, I mean that you are providing a technical solution that really addresses something that helps your users do a better job or it makes their job easier. This solution probably goes above and beyond their basic needs and it strategically adds something to the process. When you deliver that kind of value, then your internal evangelists will almost form naturally, but you can do things to help facilitate the process.

First and foremost, evangelists need a reason to get excited and be passionate about whatever they are going to evangelize. If you are following along with my guidance in this book, and particularly in those areas where I discuss offering a SharePoint service that you align with business value, then this should position you well for internal evangelism. When you offer a great service, then finding people to promote and speak passionately about it should be easy.

I am not talking about a stereotypical portrait of a used car salesperson. (I do not mean to offend all used car salespeople; just the shady ones). Your users are not walking on to a car lot and hearing, "what will it take to get you in this car today?" Your job is not to push lemons – cars that will soon break down and will only cause the owner headache after headache. You are not there simply to push numbers, or at least I am not and I assume you are not either. My process is all about driving the right solution: a strategic asset that contributes value to the business.

Internal evangelists are your power users and early adopters. The main difference between being a power user and an evangelist is that the evangelist has added support from the SharePoint team to carry the message to the masses. When you pair the evangelist's passion for the SharePoint service with communication tools and other information that will support their efforts, you unleash an extension of your team. Some refer to these individuals as product champions, while others might just stick with calling them power users. I choose evangelists because this is a good descriptive term for what I hope to facilitate through them. It is also a consistent term with how many software companies market and promote their products in the market.

Think about product evangelists from software companies. Part of their job, of course, is to communicate and engage with the community. However, a bigger part of their job is to create other evangelists in the community – non-employee evangelists who are so passionate about a software product that it drives them to share that passion with others in their community. There are many motives for this, such as a desire to feel part of a community or a longing for recognition, but the underlying motives is their passion for the product itself.

A great example of establishing successful community evangelists is the MVP program at Microsoft. Microsoft does not pay an MVP, but Microsoft builds a relationship with them to provide them with extra product information and support, all to help facilitate the MVP's passion for community evangelism. Microsoft has formal product evangelists, and then they have many more informal product evangelists sharing their passions in the community through events such as user group meetings. Other software companies are similar in their approach to community evangelists, and the reward for the community evangelist is a closer connection to information from the product team on the thing they are most passionate about. It is win-win.

I find this is the ideal model to base an internal evangelism program on, mostly because it has been so successful. At its essence, you need to connect with those users who are the most passionate about your SharePoint service. They want access to information and other experts who can answer questions when they are stuck. They enjoy being the voice of the service as they share their experience and insights with other users. Most importantly, they want to connect you with the frontline where they can provide suggestions or feedback to influence future directions.

Here is where you tie internal evangelists back to this chapter's topic: feedback processes. For one, they are users from the business and they have their own feedback to share. For another, they hear feedback from their peers and can share that as well. They can see opportunities with the SharePoint service that others will miss, in part, because they have such a close connection to the business and a level of domain expertise as a business user. They may be passionate about the potential for your SharePoint service, but make no mistake, their motives underneath that passion is because they recognize how the SharePoint service offers value to their domain of expertise. In order to enable and encourage their passion, you need to provide them with tools that will support their connection and sharing with other business users.

Some tools you can use to support evangelists and promote community-based knowledge sharing include creating a SharePoint community site forum or a wiki or a blog. These sites are also a place where you can discover potential evangelists within your organization. You can even use them to harvest a lot of feedback from the comments or forum posts that different users contribute. Whether it is trouble they experience using the SharePoint service, or new ways they found to realize value from the existing service, their posts can provide precious feedback for your team.

Community-driven sites and processes offer the ultimate potential for a feedback process. Internal evangelists can seed these sites with ideas or they can moderate discussions, and ultimately these evangelists can champion any issues or opportunities back to the service delivery team. This builds on and extends the other feedback processes I discussed in this chapter, but it also likely offers the richest form of feedback that aligns with business value.

USER GROUPS AND USER FEEDBACK

User groups may augment your user readiness plan, as I discussed in Chapter 5. They can provide support and help drive adoption, and they can also provide a valuable venue to gather user feedback. Typically, a user group is a peer-to-peer knowledge-sharing group who meets and discusses topics that relate to a shared interest. Often with technology user groups in the market, vendors and other experts participate in the user group to help share additional knowledge and gather feedback from their power users.

You can use this same concept and establish a peer-to-peer knowledge-sharing SharePoint user group within your organization. Your team can act in a similar manner as a vendor would with a public user group, and you can participate to help share expertise with your power users in your organization. This can help you collect ongoing feedback from an influential group of users.

Consultant Comrade

For the full-time business analyst consultant, collecting feedback is probably how you fill most of your days. I hope some of the ideas in this chapter added tools to your business analysis toolbox. More importantly, I hope that this chapter reinforced the notion that you cannot simply go and ask users what they want from technology; you have to go and understand what makes them tick, and then use your expertise to interpret that into a technology solution.

Business analyst or not, any consultant engaging with a client to deliver a technology solution has to involve him or herself in some level of gathering feedback from the users. You can add even more value by teaching your clients how to continue to gather feedback after you roll off your project. This can be actual tools you deploy, such as the SharePoint surveys and custom web parts I discussed in this chapter. It can also involve you mentoring their processes so your client knows how to monitor usage patterns and interpret feedback from the data logs and usage reports.

One great thing about consultants, and one huge motive for clients to bring them in, is that they are outside help: they lack any attachment to an organization's way of doing things and they lack any allegiances to internal politics. They are often oblivious to certain things that would otherwise get in the way of one's neutrality, and for this reason, users might perceive a consultant as more objective than an internal resource. Whether or not it is accurate, this can give a consultant an advantage for collecting objective end-user feedback. This might also help you articulate another value proposition for your services.

You can be quite systematic in your process and approach for collecting and analyzing user feedback. Thinking about this reminds me of the auditing process an accounting firm can conduct for their clients. The firm would approach auditing their client's business processes and the different aspects of their business in a systematic fashion. They would observe and trace business processes, analyze any paper or electronic forms, examine inventory management, assess internal controls, as well as investigate any financial aspects. Accountants would shadow workers in the course of performing their jobs, look for bottlenecks in the business process, consider supply-chain processes, and on and on.

If you have ever been involved in one of these thorough auditing processes, then you were probably as fascinated by it as I always am. In university, I took a few accounting courses, so I guess I know just enough to be fascinated. If I ever continued with accounting, I might have specialized in internal controls and a few other areas of management accounting. (Of course, financial accounting has its own internal controls built in to the nature of ledgers and double-entry journal entries, where I find the mathematics of it fascinating as well). My point is, this approach works for large accounting firms and is systematic to make the process efficient and to avoid missing anything. You can make your process for collecting and analyzing user feedback just as systematic and then you can use this process to communicate the value in your services.

I would start by looking at the system generated data you can gather to collect the initial feedback. This data can come from those traffic logs and usage reports that reveal how users interact with the system. You can manually look at actual sites to see how users interact with the system. You can review service requests to read what users struggle with using. All of the system-generated techniques in this chapter will help you to make this first pass and build some initial insights into where potential problem areas may exist, and what you want to learn more about, such as what survey or interview questions you will want to ask. From there, you can build a survey to test some of your theories of potential challenges and fine-tune your insights into any usage patterns or usage struggles. Next, you might shadow users in the course of performing their jobs to observe their processes and identify areas where they struggle or face some level of obstruction. Finally, you can use this data to help you design your user interviews and the areas where you need greater insights or feedback.

Once you gather all this information, then your job is to go away and analyze the problem. I mentioned it earlier in the chapter, but it is important, so I will mention it again: for any issues or opportunities that users raise, you need to avoid thinking about how the issue would translate into a SharePoint solution. I am always shocked at how quickly an analyst jumps to a SharePoint feature when they spot a usage problem, or when they let their mind wander and think about SharePoint implementation details while users are describing the business problem. If you do this with too much regularity, then you have not yet learned the ways of an effective business analyst. Luckily the techniques I have given you in this chapter will put you on the right track.

I refer to this process as *solutioning* and it is probably my greatest source of frustration on a project if I have a team of novice or inept analysts who constantly jump into solutions before they truly understand the problem. If you are an analyst and you are working on a project with me, your job is to analyze the problem – to truly understand the intimate details about how users work and where they face challenges. Once you have the problem defined, then it is time to work with me or another solution architect to further analyze what you discovered and to start envisioning potential solutions together.

The time to design a solution is not when you are listening to your users telling you about their challenges or business needs. I do not mean to rant here, but I am stressing the point because I frequently observe business analysts who are interviewing end-users and they immediately jump into a solution. They hear a familiar phrase from the end-user, such as one describing a coordinated process for gathering information. Then, as if it has activated a switch with the analyst, they begin to ask leading questions that are SharePoint specific, such as whether a workflow and an InfoPath form would solve the problem. It might, but the user probably does not even know what that means unless they have subject matter expertise. There could have been a different solution to solve the problem and provide greater value, but the analyst missed the opportunity by focusing on a solution too soon. For example, you might discover an automated process that works with e-discovery to coordinate and combine information, but you will miss this if you pigeonhole yourself into a workflow solution too quickly.

If you narrow in on a potential solution too quickly, you will miss a deeper understanding of the problem and the potential for uncovering other opportunities. Worse still, once you prematurely mention a potential solution to your end-users, then they start to form expectations. Understand the problem first, and then go away to envision the solution. As an outside consulting services provider, you can articulate this as a value proposition included in your systematic process for collecting user feedback, analyzing business problems, and envisioning optimum SharePoint solutions for your clients.

Inside Story: Notes from the Field

Years ago, I was working as a SharePoint administrator managing a few farms. One of the challenges I faced was that people could use whatever system they wanted, whether that was SharePoint or some other server product an IT group offered or a cloud service provided. On the surface, this might not sound so bad as I can focus on providing better service to those who chose SharePoint. However, this was during tough economic times and the company seemed to go through waves of layoffs, and so I certainly wanted to maximize demand for SharePoint, and thus demand for my position.

I needed to attract users to the SharePoint service, and often I had to compete against collaboration and wiki products users were already satisfied with and used to using. Now I was not just pushing technology for technology sake, instead I focused on standardizing a platform and consolidating our infrastructure. Ultimately, the business case was to enable a greater permeation of collaboration. With a consistent platform across departments, franchises, and business units, my users could reach greater cross-team cohesion.

The vision and business case sounded great. Nevertheless, its value depended on everyone adopting a common platform, and so I could not directly link any immediate benefits to motivate adoption. The greater trouble was that no one was going to mandate it either. My only option was to build a great and compelling service, and then to evangelize it across the organization. I needed to offer compelling value that directly aligned with the type of work that users needed to do in their job function.

Early on, I discovered that users across the enterprise lacked confidence in IT systems in general. It seems the organization experienced data loss at times, and systems were not always reliable. This was true, it seemed, with every system in production operations, at least from the perspective of most end-users in the business. Their perception was that IT did not understand the business or their job function; IT just did not engage itself as a business partner as far as they were concerned. They almost thought of IT as an adversary: a group slowing them down and inundating them with needless policies and procedures rather than seamlessly working behind the scenes to support them.

Here sat my challenge: how could I attract and connect with users to deploy an effective SharePoint service when they did not even think that IT had their best interests in mind? If they doubted I wanted their needs to drive the solution, then why would users ever make time for me? My users were very busy, so it is hard to schedule time on their calendars anyway, and especially if they perceive it is for another IT-focused project that my department is forcing on them.

Engaging users is difficult if they do not think of IT as a business partner. This is where some of the other feedback techniques I looked at in this chapter can come in handy. In a way, I can sleuth together some of their biggest pain points by analyzing how they interact with systems and what areas generate the most complaints. If I can uncover a few key problem areas for strategic influencers in the business, then I also uncover my path to engage with them. When they see me being proactive and solving issues for them, then they will also warm up to the idea that I am engaging to build a partnership with them and add value to their business.

A proactive path to engage a reluctant business user is one that removes a headache for them first. It builds goodwill and demonstrates my commitment to providing a service that aligns with their needs. For example, I had users who wanted to view design diagrams embedded within a web page. Currently, the team was using a wiki page with JPEG images, but I sensed that I could offer a richer experience in SharePoint. Now, this was before the Visio viewer functionality available in modern versions of SharePoint, but I still knew that Visio was a rich diagramming tool for processes and layouts. Knowing that Visio worked well with SharePoint, I developed a web part that wrapped a Visio viewer component in HTML to display on a SharePoint page. Anticipating this value, I was able to make this rich diagramming experience available in SharePoint with all of its collaboration functionality, and I addressed their desired web experience as well.

Sometimes addressing the problems and desired experience can be as simple as my embedded Visio example. Sometimes they will be more involved. Whatever the case, the process is the same: gather feedback from your users and come up with a proactive initiative that will solve problems for them or add business value. Accomplishing the initiative itself is good, but it reaches beyond whatever endeavor you are addressing and it nourishes relationships between your IT service team and your business users. It is an approach that bridges a connection and contributes to a healthy service that your users adopt.

This approach resonates with your users, and it has a ripple effect that builds momentum across the business. Similar to the adage, actions speak louder than words, proactive actions that anticipate your users' business needs will speak loudest of all. They will be the most authentic and in turn, they will encourage a rich feedback process. When your users see you take such initiatives that make them and their needs your priority, they will feel encouraged to make the effort and share their valuable feedback on how to improve the service. Surveys and analytics can help, but when you build a relationship between IT and the business into a close and strategic partnership, then you will unlock the most valuable feedback.

GUEST Q&A: ANNIE KALFAYAN, IMASON

As I discussed governance with Annie Kalfayan, an experienced senior SharePoint business analyst, she stressed how important it is to start your governance process and practices. Preferably, she notes, you can start early in your SharePoint evolution, but her message is that the important thing is to get started no matter how far along you are.

Annie mentioned she often sees organizations struggle with kick-starting governance – they wonder if they should address it at the beginning of a project, or if they should address it anytime there is a convenient lull. She pointed out how it can be tempting to think governance is a straightforward task that you can put off and address later, but she noted that this attitude almost guarantees shortcomings.

She emphasized that governance is a process that you should implement throughout a SharePoint initiative, from the very beginning of the project through to its ongoing operations and support. In her experience, she found it is better to adopt governance practices as you go rather than to try to add governance solutions later; or worse, to leave it out entirely.

In describing her approach to governance, she listed what she found to be three core components of governance: whom do we involve and affect (the people), what do we govern (the practices, behaviors, and standards), and how do we govern (the tools and actions). She explained that these are the pillars to help you get started with any governance initiative.

Her advice is that "you can and should start with governance very early" in your SharePoint initiative, but you should also refine it over time as you establish and understand the scope of your SharePoint service and who gets involved with it. She finds that starting with a basic groundwork and growing it over time is the best and most successful approach to governance. She warns, "An all-in, one day governance plan is over-ambitious and almost never works."

Annie Kalfayan is based in London, UK and works as a Senior Business Analyst for Avanade. In her role, Annie engages with clients to help them establish a SharePoint roadmap, define and adopt a SharePoint governance model, and assist in adoption planning and business user training.

Wrapping Up

In this chapter, I discussed different techniques to capture user feedback on your SharePoint service, including feedback on new opportunities where the service can expand to add additional value and feedback on what problems interfere with their ability to perform certain tasks. I discussed how to capture feedback by using surveys and analyzing system generated usage patterns. From there, I looked at how to interview and shadow users to gain insights into their business processes, and I considered how to use feedback to detect potential adoption issues and to build internal evangelists.

Not all your user feedback will relate to your users' experiences on the existing service. You may also experience a different type of user feedback where user enthusiasm for new features can place demands on what your SharePoint service offers. In the next chapter, I look at how to manage and prioritize these demands for enhancing and expanding the SharePoint service. I pay particular attention to how you can manage and funnel these improvement requests while setting user expectations and avoiding being pulled off course.

■ ■ ■

CHAPTER 9

Managing Your SharePoint Demand Funnel

Instant gratification takes too long.

—Carrie Fisher

In this chapter, I focus on approaches to setting up a demand funnel for enhancements and expansions of your SharePoint service. This will help you have an ordered process to ensure that you do not miss or lose enhancement opportunities, but it will also help you to ensure requests do not pull you off course and leave you chasing every little feature. I offer considerations to establish a triage process where you can prioritize requests and opportunities, some of which you can then add to your roadmap while you capture others in a parking lot of deferred future items.

One key point I stress in this chapter is how to use a roadmap to set expectations, to prioritize feature and enhancement requests, and to facilitate the parking of requests for the future. I first discussed roadmaps in Chapter 7 as a planning tool, but I look at them again in parts of this chapter as an expectation management tool.

After reading this chapter, you will know how to:

- Set expectations with your internal customers and stakeholders

- Define boundaries

- Create a request triage

- Build a parking lot list of deferred feature requests

- Map enhancement demand back to your roadmap

- Forecast upcoming upgrades and new versions

- Evaluate third-party products

- Conduct cost-benefit and business value estimates

Funneling Demand

My suspicions are that if you have deployed SharePoint already, then you have probably felt the tsunami of demand from all the feature requests surging in from all over your organization. If you have not experienced this yourself, then you likely know someone who has or you might have heard tales of this happening. It relates to one of main reasons I have stayed so busy with SharePoint for so long, because SharePoint offers a vast sea of features. There constantly seems to be additional opportunities to expand a deployment and unleash new business value. This only becomes problematic when you find the demand pulling you in every direction all at once, and as a result, you find yourself swimming against a tsunami current that is sweeping you away.

A surging tsunami is certainly a vivid visual for demands for SharePoint enhancements and feature requests. Each individual request probably does not feel like a tsunami; after all, so far in this book I have showed you the ease and flexibility that SharePoint can enable new features and functionality. However, these little demand waves are not isolated, because they participate with other demand waves that all come together into a larger swell. Tsunamis come washing in from every direction, and without protection or controls in place, they can engulf you and pull you under. Some places prone to tsunamis or other surging storm waves will build controls such as dykes and storm barriers to help control where waves flow.

Your demand funnel will serve a similar purpose where it will help you to control the flow of requests and prevent them from flooding your team. This demand funnel will provide a means to process enhancement requests both for developing complex new functionality and for enabling seemingly simple features. In fact, I find requests for seemingly simple features tend to be what most often ends up consuming my time and pulling me off course. Larger development projects typically also come with a project plan and some rigor. Enabling a small feature does not need that level of overhead, but they do need an ordered way to process new requests.

You might get these requests from the end-user feedback you collect using the approaches I discussed in the previous chapter. Some internal customers might be too busy to come to you with requests, or they might just be relatively satisfied with the status quo that enhancement opportunities do not yet motivate them enough to make requests. For these customers, you can go to them and prime the demand by collecting feedback. For other customers, they might be eager to submit enhancement requests to help support their job functions. It is important to consider potential demand from both of these types of customers, because otherwise you run the risk of only responding to the needs of your extrovert customers and ignoring your introvert customers.

Demand funnels process all incoming requests, whether your customers submit them or you uncover them while collecting feedback, whether they are relatively small features to enable or they are large-scale development projects. The demand funnel processes them all and then, funny enough, it funnels the demand for you or your team to address and deliver. A few necessary characteristics required by your demand funnel include: a means to accept new demand items, a process to prioritize and triage these items, and then a way to either schedule the work or to park the item in a parking lot list. Figure 9-1 illustrates a conceptual demand funnel. I discuss details of these characteristics throughout this chapter, but first I consider how you can capture the demand and divide it into distinct items.

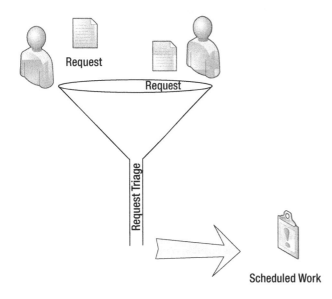

Figure 9-1. A conceptual demand funnel

One option to capture the demand is to use a SharePoint list. You could configure a list such as the issue tracker list and use this to capture and track individual demand items. I like the issues list because it already has some prioritization and detail columns built in to it. You can add other columns to capture information on the risk associated with a particular request, such as the risk to the overall system stability or other types of risks. You can also add columns associated with the rough implementation costs and the estimated business value, as well as columns associated with the required effort and any dependencies involved with a particular feature. All this information can help you prioritize and schedule any work effort. I like to use columns to indicate the status of the item in the triage process, as well as what phase or sprint I want to address the item in or whether I am parking it for some unknown future date.

You will only have so much capacity to deliver features and capabilities, so you need your demand funnel to balance the demand with your capacity to deliver. This is the first objective of the demand funnel. The second is to ensure that you are delivering the highest priority items or those that will deliver the most business value relative to their cost. This exercise is largely an extension of the roadmap planning I discussed in Chapter 7, but I will shift my focus in this chapter to consider how to manage this within the demand itself. One important aspect of managing the demand funnel involves managing expectations, and I discuss this aspect in the next section.

Setting Boundaries and User Expectations

When I read the heading for this section, it almost has the feeling of a parent who is setting a child's boundaries. This is not what I mean by it at all; instead, I am referring to boundaries for you and your team with your processes and operational procedures. They are the things that keep people from turning things on and adjusting configurations at random in response to user requests. Your boundaries define what those things are that requires a formal process and what types of requests your team members can go ahead and resolve right away.

I have discussed this idea of establishing a boundary for your service a few times now. In Chapter 2, I looked closely at how you can define boundaries of the service itself and what capabilities you offer. Then, in Chapter 4, I looked closely at how to set responsibility boundaries for each role involved with providing your SharePoint service. Your SharePoint roadmap that I covered in Chapter 7 provides another boundary, one that sets the course for what areas you have planned to accomplish. This is one place where you can bring these together, at least conceptually.

In hockey, when the pressure is on during a game and the team faces adversity, the fundamentals are what will help them push through it and bounce back. Their fundamentals are things such as making passes, completing checks, and covering an opponent or playing a particular zone. When the pressure is on and the team is slumping, focusing on the basic plays that the team has practiced over and over will help carry them through, and their fundamental systems will give them something to fall back on when fancy plays just are not connecting.

Your SharePoint team obviously faces different types of pressure situations, but having systems in place to fall back on will help everyone handle service demands and feature requests. This is why I stressed putting those fundamentals in place, because with roles defined, the service defined, and a roadmap setting the course, you will have the fundamentals you need to fall back on. This gives you the tools to effectively funnel your demand as it highlights your team's available capacity and the necessary tradeoffs or sacrifices required for a particular feature request. The only things you need to add to this are an intake process for requests and a triage process to prioritize those requests. I return to these topics a little later in this chapter, but first I consider how this system will help you to set expectations with your end-users and other stakeholders.

End-users and stakeholders are both generally reasonable creatures. They may seem unreasonable at times, and this is because someone forced them to act with limited knowledge or a limited perspective. All they may be aware of are their own needs, and to them these may feel as if they should be the highest priority and will deliver the most value to the business. From their limited vantage point, they may even feel as if you and your team are being the unreasonable ones. After all, they might not otherwise know why they face a delay with their request or what else might be in your queue.

Granted, some people may operate at a more selfish level than others do. People have their own objectives and their own priorities, and these can easily conflict with other people's priorities. Perhaps their objectives all link to a reward such as a bonus or promotion, in which case they may have a valid reason to want to push their own agenda for feature requests that will support their objectives. I do not find anything particularly bad about this, because you have a demand funnel with a request triage process to help you prioritize enhancement requests and balance this demand.

The goal is to provide your internal customers with a place to request enhancements or new functionality rather than leave them on their own to search for solutions. Ideally, this will establish a formal intake process that they will use and that can satisfy their needs. An important aspect of a formal intake process is it will provide you with the opportunity to take a holistic view of all the demands for your SharePoint service. It will also provide your internal customers with a holistic view of competing demands that require trade-offs and prioritization to determine what value to deliver.

Having a transparent process helps reinforce expectations because end-users and stakeholders will no longer be operating from a limited perspective. They will have insights into why you prioritized things the way that you did, and they will (hopefully) see how a particular approach will meet the needs of the greater good for the organization. Now, they might not be happy if you delay or park their enhancement requests, but understanding why should help you avoid having them resist or protest the approach. Unfortunately, you cannot satisfy every need, at least not all right away, and so you will need to make trade-offs with the needs you do fill. The essence of considering and making these trade-offs is the request triage process.

Creating a Request Triage

A triage simply means a process of determining the most important item or the degree of urgency for an item, from a large number of request items that require attention or offer an opportunity to expand the service. I have already spent some time at different points in this book discussing how SharePoint creates an environment with plenty of opportunities. SharePoint is overflowing with the potential opportunities and business value that it offers an organization and this can lead to an overwhelmingly large number of requests to come in. Your request triage provides a way to process and prioritize these requests in a systematic manner.

In a medical use, a triage provides a process where medical professionals assess the degree of urgency in a patient's wounds or with their illness. From this assessment, they then determine the order of treatment for a large number of patients or causalities. If you went to your local hospital's Emergency Room (ER), you would no doubt notice that they do not process patients in a first come, first served manner. Instead, they go through an ongoing triage process where they assess the severity and the urgency of incoming patients and prioritize them for treatment based on their priority relative to all the other waiting patients. They also continuously reassess patients waiting in the queue to determine if their illness is escalating.

An ER operates with a formal and systematic intake process. If a major incident occurs and causes a spike of patients to arrive in the ER for treatment, the staff might use a color-coding system to organize the priorities. An expert or specialist might do an initial assessment to determine a patient's severity and urgency for treatment. They cannot process everyone all at once, especially if there is a large spike in their patient intake. The staff also cannot process everyone in a first come, first serve manner because someone with a more urgent need for care could die waiting while someone with an insignificant symptom receives treatment first.

You might design your intake process in a similar manner. Similar to an ER, you can establish a rolling prioritization and request triage process to ensure that you are focusing on the most valuable items for the organization. A request triage resembles a bug triage, a process such as having your team meet regularly to review the list of bugs and decide what you will address first. Figure 9-2 illustrates where a request triage can fit in an overall sample business process to handle requests. In the case of a request triage, you will schedule a regularly recurring meeting where team members and stakeholders can meet to review the list of requests and determine what the team will focus on delivering first.

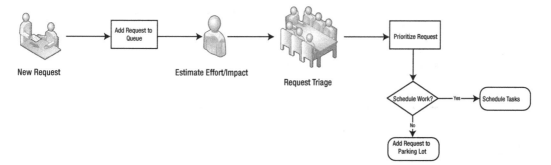

Figure 9-2. *A sample request triage process*

When you are deciding who should attend these ongoing request triage meetings, include sponsors or key stakeholders who will represent the needs and priorities of the business. You want to include enough representation from the delivery team and the business to help validate priorities, identify dependencies, and estimate efforts. By bringing a diverse group together for these request triages, it can help build support and buy-in as they face each other and understand each other's needs and objectives. This can also help everyone understand the constraints you are working within, and this will involve everyone in the process of making trade-off decisions as you come to agreement on what requests to address first and which ones to park for a later undetermined date.

You do not have to fix or obligate the membership for the triage meetings. Stakeholders can attend if they are interested or if there are requests that will impact their area of the service. Someone needs to chair the meeting, typically the SharePoint service manager or team lead. Everyone else is optional, although you should have a minimum representation to form a quorum before making crucial decisions on priorities. I find that by keeping membership and attendance in this group as optional, you will help to keep it productive and avoid having it morph into a chore that nobody wants to attend.

If you schedule a recurring meeting on everyone's calendar, you can mark the majority of people as optional so they can leave a tentative placeholder on their calendar. Then, before each request triage meeting, you can send out a meeting update with an agenda that provides a concise summary of the major requests you plan to triage. This can help attendees decide whether it will be productive or relevant for them to attend the triage. You might also set up a meeting workspace or a community site in SharePoint where you post all the details about the requests you plan to triage, and you can even use this to store the meeting minutes to capture and publish triage decisions. This helps keep everyone informed even if they are unable to attend the triage.

This triage process is a crucial governance action you can take to ensure discipline on your team's service delivery. Most notably, it keeps your team on track by avoiding informal or unplanned projects, and it prevents the chaos that comes from users pulling your team in any direction. With a request triage, you can enforce the types of checks and balances that keep your team focused on delivering the right things and delivering the right value.

THE DANGERS OF THE INFORMAL "PROJECT"

I refer to this as an informal "project" because it resembles a project, yet at the same time, it does not. All the pieces of a formal and disciplined project are what I consider the essence of any good project, and these informal projects bypass those. Omitting steps such as prioritizing, estimating, scheduling, resourcing, and other such planning steps will add risk. I find allowing requests and delivering work in this manner adds risk to the work itself and to the other projects that your team is delivering.

Your risks in this undisciplined approach stem from over utilization of resources, uncoordinated work, cost overruns, and a lack of scope control and a completion plan. This is because you have not captured and planned for these informal projects in your resource plan and budget. Your risk is that without formality, likely there will not be the same discipline and rigor for the project.

In Chapter 2, I discussed how to define the scope of a delivery. As I mentioned then, if you have not defined what you are going to deliver, then how will you know when you are done? A formal request process and triage ultimately lead to defining and scheduling the work, and this avoids having your team pulled in every direction for ad hoc and uncoordinated requests.

Capturing Requests

To triage and process requests, you first need to capture them somewhere. Any tool that provides your internal customers with a means to submit a request will do just fine. I find the best solution for capturing requests will be one that has triage workflow capabilities built in, allowing you to automate the process and track any history of decisions and dependencies. E-mail offers minimum functionality to capture requests and set priority categories, where users can send an e-mail with their problem or need. However, it does not offer an easy way to track the work history or to link it with any dependencies. Instead, I prefer to use other types of lists to manage requests.

SharePoint offers a built-in list that provides a rich set of functionality you can use for your request intake and triage. I use the Issues list type to provide this sort of list, and then I customize it to fit my needs by adding columns and creating a workflow. With the right combination of permissions and workflow, you can make this list fit a good portion of whatever you need. You might even tie it in to whatever feedback process you set up based on my discussion on feedback processes in Chapter 8.

A SharePoint list works well for many of your needs to capture and triage requests. However, it might not fit with your change management processes or any of your existing request ticketing systems. You may already have a requirements management tool or you may want to incorporate requests into your service desk's request management system. You might also consider using any of your existing bug and work item tracking software, such as Microsoft Team Foundation Server (TFS).

TFS is already set up to track work items, to associate them with other work items or tests, and even link them to source code that your developers check in. It has built-in process templates to manage the workflow process of an item, or you can customize your own to fit your request and triage processes. It also has built-in fields to categorize an area of the system that the request relates with and you can specify an iteration that you want to schedule any work. Another thing that I like about using TFS to manage requests and work items is that it already has built-in reports for reporting on progress, such as your burn-down rates.

Using TFS, you can capture your requests, risks, issues, scheduled work, and test cases from within the same tool. This can give you a view of the work your team is preparing and it gives your internal customers a single place to submit bugs or enhancement requests. You can manage the backlog of items through the iteration field, which is initially blank when a user creates the item. You can later set the iteration value during the request triage. One option is to set it for a scheduled iteration if you want to complete it during a known cycle of work.

I also like to add an iteration that I call "Someday Maybe" or "Parking Lot" to designate the iteration for items I am not yet scheduling for work. This captures the item and its details, allows me to assign a priority and work estimates, and it assigns the request to an unspecified backlog iteration. This way you can process the request triage by selecting any item that does not yet have an iteration set. Later in this chapter, I return to discuss the idea of a parking lot to park requests for a future undetermined date.

Whatever solution you use to capture the requests in a list, you need to ensure that you also capture relevant details that you can refer back to in the future. You can attach extra files to supplement the details of the request and help your team as they prioritize and estimate the request. This information will also help you later to design the solution. The following lists several of the types of attachments you might want to attach to the request item, depending on its complexity and size.

- Use cases

- Wireframes and mockups

- UML diagrams

- Entity-relationship (ER) diagrams

- Process and swim-lane diagrams

As you can no doubt tell, capturing requests involves capturing different amounts and different types of data at different times throughout the funneling and triage process. You might triage an item and decide it needs more information, and so you can assign it to a team member to investigate further. You might assign it to a business analyst to gather more requirements or to a solution architect to add some preliminary designs. I find it is valuable to capture this extra information while the request is fresh in everyone's mind. Often this process might be a feasibility study and an initial assessment that can later feed back into the triage process.

If team members pass a request between them while they analyze the requirements or they contribute preliminary solution designs, they need a place to add comments. This offers people a generic field for text where they can ask or answer unstructured questions. They can also add other notes if ideas or assumptions come to them, thereby capturing this information in the tool so it is not lost later. In TFS, this can be the history field, and in SharePoint, this can be an append-only comment field.

Once you collect all the information, you have a package consisting of solution designs, estimates, and the like, all of which you can use for prioritizing and planning your team's delivery. It also helps to define what success looks like and where you are going. If you do not know what success looks like, then how will you know when you have achieved it? And even more critically, how will you determine what direction success is in if you have no concept of it?

If you built a SharePoint roadmap, as I discussed in Chapter 7, then you have a direction and the roadmap will provide waypoints to guide you through your triage process. In the next section, I discuss how to map requests back to your roadmap.

Mapping Requests Back to Your Roadmap

Setting priorities, estimating effort, and identifying potential value in a request are all important for analysis, but you cannot schedule work based on that information on its own. You also need to consider your roadmap with what else you have scheduled, including any other related work. Your roadmap will also identify whether fulfilling the request will take you in the correct direction or leave you delivering one-off solutions. As I discussed in Chapter 7, your roadmap sets your overall course for how your SharePoint service will evolve. For this reason, it is critical to include it as you triage and schedule work for enhancement requests.

First, you need to identify whether you already have an item scheduled in the future. If you do, do you need to adjust that schedule and reprioritize the roadmap? Ideally not, but sometimes this becomes necessary as you learn more about a requirement or as business conditions change. If you do not already have it scheduled, then you need to determine whether it depends on other work in your roadmap. Your roadmap gives you a good at-a-glance view of the feasibility of a particular request and any of its potential ripple effects throughout your system and your team's resourcing.

Your roadmap sets your baseline for where you want your team to focus their efforts based on multiple factors, such as resource availability, underlying system maintenance or upgrade plans, and dependencies between capabilities. This guides the triage process and helps you to make quick decisions about whether to schedule or park a request. Therefore, as you consider an item, consider whether it fits with your strategy and the overall direction that you want to take your SharePoint service. Sometimes you just need to accept that an opportunity is not right for your strategy, or at least the timing is not right for it. I discuss the idea of parking an item in the next section, so for now, let's assume that the item is work you want to schedule.

Once you have prioritized an item and determined that you need to schedule it to enhance your SharePoint service, the next step is to determine when. As I mentioned previously, identifying any dependencies can help give you a general sense for where in the roadmap you can slot in the work. This helps you to avoid over-utilizing your resources and it allows you to consider whether your team is working on any related items that would complement a particular feature. It can reveal these types of synergies as well as any dependencies that you are planning to deliver.

This approach helps you to avoid chasing features. Chasing features in your project delivery might make your internal customers happy at first, but chasing them might eventually sink you in a pit of quicksand. I do not know if you have experienced this yet, but I sure have. This occurs when people get excited about a seemingly simple feature that someone wants to add to your project's scope. Without doing any analysis, the team then goes ahead with the assumption that the feature is as simple as it appears, but they begin to discover that there are dependencies they need to address. One after another, these unanticipated dependencies begin to add up and they form the quicksand that sinks the team.

Earlier in the book, I also referred to a related risk as I discussed the idea of a similar scenario where you find yourself caught in a death by a thousand paper cuts. This is similar to the quicksand example, but rather than having a stream of dependent work activities engulf you into a pit, it is a practice where you continuously add independent features. Each additional, nice-to-have feature by itself does not seem to add excessive scope, and the added value it would deliver is too tempting. Eventually, just as the quicksand will consume a team, these paper cuts will add up and wear you down.

A roadmap helps alert you when your team is trending toward sinking in quicksand or you are experiencing a slow death by a thousand paper cuts. When work items and the demand you are chasing does not align with your roadmap, you should take a step back and ask yourself if you are trending off course in one of these two danger areas. Your roadmap serves as more than a planning tool, because it also helps to reveal the health of a project and it guides how you prioritize your service delivery.

I touched on it briefly in Chapter 7, but just to reiterate, this is where your roadmap supports your efforts to maintain a certain course in your service delivery. It helps you set your overall direction and plan your resourcing as you consider the upcoming projects you have planned. Beyond this though, it gives you a support tool to refer back to and rely on to keep you and your team grounded. It really is easy to find yourself carried away with all the wonderful features SharePoint can offer your organization, especially without a plan or focus. Your roadmap gives you that plan and it generates the focus you need.

Your roadmap opens up a path that allows you to build momentum to deliver on. You can use this as part of your demand funnel to identify where you can leverage related efforts and follow a wave of momentum with a particular feature. So, if you have not read Chapter 7 and built a roadmap, I strongly encourage you to work on this. In my experience, this will be one of the best gifts you can give yourself and your SharePoint service. It gives you a tool to guide you, and it helps you to avoid being blinded with the excitement of new features that you do not have the capacity to deliver or that would pull you too far off course.

As you map your new requests back to your roadmap, you will consider where an item can fit within your roadmap. You will base this consideration on the dependencies you identify between other items, the item's priority, and your available resourcing to deliver a feature, as I discussed in this section. But what if you have a request and it simply does not fit with your roadmap? Either its priority is too low or it has too many dependencies that your roadmap does not accommodate. You will likely face times when people want things that you just do not have the capacity to deliver right away. In those cases, you will find it is still worth capturing their ideas and the details about the opportunity, yet not plan to deliver the solution. One place you can capture these types of requests is in a backlog or a parking lot list.

Building a Parking Lot List for Future Enhancements

You cannot be everything to everyone, at least not all at once. You will face the need to make tradeoffs and prioritize what you can deliver and when. This trade-off decision and prioritization is the main output from the request triage. This is also what keeps your team focused on delivering the right value to best meet the needs of the business. Some items are what you will want to get to right away, while others are ones you will schedule for some later date. Many are items you will defer until some undetermined date, and these are what you will capture in your parking lot.

■ **Note**   The term "parking lot" list comes out of the toolbox for running effective meetings, where when questions or issues come up during a meeting that could possibly derail the meeting, you record it on the parking lot list to later revisit. These are issues people raise during the meeting that are not on the agenda but that could be important to revisit and address another time.

On development teams, I have always sensed a sort of anxiety among stakeholders whenever I needed to cut features. It is almost as if these features make their way off into some black hole, never to be seen again, and these stakeholders are mourning their loss. In their defense, this was often the case as I cut features and promptly forgot about them while moving on to what I would deliver. Without a place to capture those items that I needed to cut, they would be lost. I often refer to it as a parking lot where I can park requirements I am not currently addressing. You might call it your backlog, or any other name you find meaningful. The important point is that without this net in place catching these requirements, they will likely be lost.

A parking lot helps to capture the details about requirements and it saves them for some unknown future day when you want to address them. You might want to reference the information you collected as part of the requirement to help you answer questions about another requirement. Or better yet, you might clear your queue of work items and want to deliver on those lower priority requirements that you deferred to your parking lot. Whatever the reason, capturing this information provides you with the option to recall it at a later date. It also provides direction and knowledge transfer to anyone else who may take over and look to deliver some of these requirements or look to understand the reasons why you deferred them.

Building an informative repository of deferred requirement details is one reason you will find a parking lot list of requirements useful. Another is that it will assure your team and your stakeholders that their input is not simply lost, or worse, ignored. Capturing the details can help validate their input, even if you are not going to act on their requirements today. This can help reduce the urge for stakeholders to resist having their requirement cut, because if you capture it in a parking lot then you have not cut and lost it, you captured and deferred it to a later time that is to be determined.

Your parking lot may exist in the same list as the items your team is planning to deliver, where you update the status of a field to indicate whether the item is current or parked. As I mentioned earlier, this might be the iteration field for your Team Foundation Server work item where you designate a special parking lot iteration. This allows you to maintain a single list that you can filter into multiple views based on field values, such as a parking lot list or by feature area. The benefits of maintaining a single list are that you can maintain your items and their history in the same place. It also allows you to easily re-categorize a work item that you need to defer or your team was unable to complete in a given iteration.

You also might consider opening up your parking lot list for your internal customers to view. This can help them to understand the trade-offs that your team faced and why you made the decisions that you did in selecting a particular scope. They might not read through the list and all the details you collect, but in scrolling through, they can see the vast number of requests you had to balance. I have found this level of transparency can help build support for the demand funnel and the request triage process, especially if you include representative stakeholders in the process. This all reinforces the notion that you and your team are working with your internal customers to provide the right service that meets their needs, rather than simply forcing some IT initiative on them.

As you work through delivering a phase or iteration, continue to collect new ideas and new requirements as they come up. You cannot control when great ideas will come to people or when they will discover some new opportunities. All you can do is have a system in place to capture them when people think of them. Once people can capture their ideas, then their creativity is not lost and your team can continue with your current delivery. This allows you to capture the creative process, yet not have it pull you off course.

Once you complete your phase or iteration, then this should align with another request triage meeting. In the meeting, you can triage the new requests and revisit the parking lot items to determine what to prioritize for the next phase or iteration. This allows you to continuously cycle through your parking lot as you evolve your SharePoint service. As I mentioned, it ensures that ideas and deferred requirements are not lost, and it helps you to manage scope.

UTILIZING A PARKING LOT FOR SCOPE MANAGEMENT

I have found that teams who do not use a parking lot to capture deferred requirements seem to struggle more with managing their scope. I think this relates to the idea of having a requirement end up lost when the team cuts it from the current scope if there is nowhere else to capture it. Therefore, those people who come up with a valuable requirement are motivated to expand scope to include it, and so they might push for its inclusion. Conversely, when they see their valuable contributions are captured and stored for some future date, I find they are more accepting and supportive of maintaining the current scope.

You can turn this experience into a routine that reinforces your scope management just through the very nature of cycling through the process of selecting items to deliver. As you select some items and park others, you set your team's scope and begin to deliver. Then, as new items come up, you can park those as well until your team has completed delivering the current phase. At that point, you can revisit the parking lot and select the new items your team will deliver. This cycle reinforces the idea that a requirement is not lost when you park it, and this builds confidence in the parking lot list and your team's scope management.

Forecasting Upgrades and New Versions

In Chapter 7, I discussed the idea of the software support lifecycle and the eventual need to plan for software upgrades. In Chapter 11, I come back to this topic to look at planning considerations for upgrades as I discuss this topic in more depth. For now, I want to consider upgrades from the perspective of feature requests and your demand funnel. Your support lifecycle helps you determine those dates you might want to upgrade before in order to remain within mainstream support, but this might not necessarily align with the demand you are funneling for new features found in those newer versions.

An upgrade project can be a significant piece of work and it is something you should represent on your roadmap if you are considering one. You will face several dependencies and things you can do to prepare for an upgrade, as I discuss in Chapter 11, but the process to funnel demand remains the same. You still need to break down a request into the dependencies and start to estimate all the work efforts involved. This is similar to how you would expand your roadmap if you were considering expanding your service with a major SharePoint capability such as business intelligence or enterprise content management. The details in the actual work activities vary, but the demand funnel process remains consistent.

If and when Microsoft announces a new version of SharePoint and your users get excited about a new feature in that version, then that new feature is the request and all the steps in the upgrade make up the dependency. Similar to rolling out a major new capability, you will have a variety of planning, analyzing, and testing activities to prepare for the upgrade. These are all the dependency work items you can include in your roadmap to help you schedule when your team can reasonably accomplish the upgrade.

I find it is best to begin considering when you can approach an upgrade as soon as you know a general timeline for when Microsoft will release the next version of SharePoint. I have had several customers who prefer to wait until they have demand from the business – they sort of delay the inevitable. Many enterprise products seem to work well with this approach, but I find SharePoint is slightly unique with how quickly excitement and demand from your internal customers can build. I always prefer to be proactive when considering upgrades to prepare myself for when that demand does come.

When you forecast and prepare in a proactive way, you will have the answer when your demand funnel begins to process requests for features that the next version offers. You will know all the dependencies and the related work activities that your team will need to perform before you can approach an upgrade. This gives you the insight you need during the request triage to assess whether your team can take on the work and when, or whether you need to park the request in the parking lot list until you have more capacity.

Another benefit from looking ahead to the next version is that you will be aware of the features and capabilities it will offer. This will help you avoid developing or purchasing those capabilities if you can avoid doing so by delaying until you upgrade to the next version. When users request features that you know Microsoft has developed into the next version of SharePoint, you will have a good explanation for why you would rather delay and leave that request in the parking lot.

One good trick to stay ahead of the curve is if you can get on some sort of early adopter program with Microsoft. It has gone by catchy names such as Technology Adoption Program (TAP) and Rapid Deployment Program (RDP), and essentially, it involves you deploying early alpha and beta versions of the next version of SharePoint into your organization's *production* environment. This also gives you a chance to provide feedback directly to the product team. A warning though: this is not for the faint of heart. You read that right a couple of lines ago, I did say deploy to production.

■ **Note** Vendors usually limit early adopter programs to a select group of customers that their account teams select based on the customer's deployment scenario and how well this matches the type of feedback that the product team hopes to learn.

You can also plan to deploy a pilot farm of the next version once it ships. This will allow you to learn about the features and to start getting a sense about the impacts and dependencies you will require. You might even go through a trial upgrade, and this will give you a good indication about what an actual upgrade will require. Again, this will all help you understand what it will take to perform an upgrade and where you can fit it on your roadmap, so that if your demand funnel begins to process requests for an upgrade then you will be prepared to triage them.

Evaluating Third-Party Products

Another area in which your demand funnel may collect requests is for third-party products. Your internal customers may find a third-party product that extends SharePoint to provide additional functionality, and this functionality may fulfill a business need or add value to some business process. This is not a lot different from your approach to evaluate and plan for an upgrade of SharePoint itself. However, a typical third-party product does not usually require as many dependencies that require your attention as a SharePoint upgrade would.

Third-party products can range in size and complexity, from a simple SharePoint App or web part, to a complex server application. They contain some level of new functionality that they add to a SharePoint farm. These products may affect the entire farm or just a single site. Even though their size and scope varies, the process I use to evaluate third-party products remains consistent. I treat them all as new components that pose a potential risk to the SharePoint farm and the overall stability of the SharePoint service.

There are many third-party products available in the market that vendors sell as an install package for your SharePoint farm. In addition, you can find many open source projects that you can download and install in your farm. I treat both commercial and open source solutions in a similar fashion and consider them both as third-party products. They both offer new functionality and enhancements to extend the SharePoint service, and they both require a similar evaluation process to ensure the product is a suitable match for your environment.

■ **Note** Apps for SharePoint can include third-party controls that you can allow your users to purchase and enable on their sites. You may or may not evaluate these in the same manner as other third-party products. Since they execute custom code on vendor hosted or cloud servers and not on servers in your SharePoint farm, then you may not require the same level of rigor for testing these, if you even get involved in the decision.

Third-party products do involve some complexity, and this is why it is important for you to give them extra consideration through your demand funnel and request triage. The challenge can be that users have a perception that a packaged solution should be easy and straightforward. After all, all you have to do is install it, or so they assume. Unfortunately, there is more to it than that, and this is where a little extra rigor can help you. I like to focus my attention on a few key areas to evaluate a third-party product. The following lists my considerations when I am selecting a vendor and a third-party product solution.

- Evaluate the product's functionality

- Test the product's stability and compatibility

- Assess the vendor's support policy

- Project the product's upgradability

Of course, price is an important consideration as well, but for now I will assume you have an internal customer offering to fund the cost and you are deciding whether to install the solution in your farm. Notice that the functionality makes up only a part of my overall considerations. I am much more interested in how stable a product is and what level of support I can expect for it. I care the most about what types of implications it will have on my eventual upgrade efforts, whenever they may come, and how well I can sustain the product.

Assuming you want this product, you might also want to pilot it on a pilot or staging server farm. Eventually, you will be ready to actually deploy the software components on your production server farm. Once installed, you will need to configure the solution and finalize the deployment. Some third-party solutions may also have integration, migration, and training requirements. All these evaluating, testing, deploying, and configuring activities have dependencies you need to consider and factor in to the overall decision. If you have decided to move forward with the third-party solution and you have thought through all these details, then you are ready to update your roadmap with the work activities.

Before you begin to select third-party solutions, you may face the question of whether to develop the solution internally, or purchase a product. I refer to this as the build versus buy decision. This decision is not always as straightforward as it may seem. However, you can go through a similar process as I discussed previously and consider the different products with their support and long-term sustainability. If a vendor offers the solution that you need, it meets your evaluation criteria, and it is cheaper to buy or license than to develop yourself, then you likely want to buy the solution.

If you cannot find the right solution or something about developing it yourself makes it cheaper or more attractive for you, then you likely want to build the solution. One reason this would be true is if you want to license or sell the solution in the future to recover some of the development costs. Another might be for competitive reasons, where you create a competitive advantage and a point of differentiation by developing your own custom solution. I discuss development considerations in more detail throughout the chapters in Part IV of this book.

A BUILD VERSUS BUY DEBATE

I appreciate both sides of this debate. Coming from a developer background, there was a time when I often preferred to build as much as I could. Being a young software engineer, I enjoyed developing software and creating new functionality, and I found this allowed me to get exactly the functionality I wanted. As I later moved into operations and service management, I discovered this could become very expensive. Sometimes this expense was my opportunity cost, or the value I was not delivering because I was spending my time developing something else.

This debate does not have a right or wrong answer. Both sides are valid, and which one you choose depends on your situation and your business need. I like to consider the trade-off of what else I can spend my time and money on and other aspects such as product support. I also like to weigh this decision by considering the expertise and service I am buying against a tailored solution I build myself to fit a unique business problem.

On the one hand, you are purchasing a certain level of expertise in a domain. Software companies that sell third-party products build expertise as they work with a variety of customers and potentially a number of industries. They usually absorb the research and development costs, and they can offer guidance on your rollout.

On the other hand, a product has to be generic enough to fit enough different customer scenarios to appeal to and sell to a large enough market. Adopting this product may mean you have to compromise some of your unique requirements, whereas when you build the solution you can tailor it to fit your specific business needs.

Of course, the solution may be a hybrid of the two. This is often the case, because SharePoint provides a module architecture that enables you to extend the platform by combining third-party products with those custom components you develop.

Piloting Enhancements

I have mentioned deploying pilots a few times in this chapter and in other places in this book. I truly believe in using pilots and proof-of-concepts as tools to vet requirements, designs, dependencies, and estimates. Everything is simply theory until you deploy actual working software and have users begin to try to use it. Theories are useful because they help us to understand problems, to build hypotheses, and to think in abstract terms to solve complex problems. However, much remains unanswered while you consider theories. You can glean information about the feasibility of an approach or a solution quickly by running a pilot or a quick proof-of-concept. This gives you a chance to test your theory and some of your early hypotheses. Pilots give you and your team a great chance to validate your ideas and confirm a particular solution.

Pilots also give you a chance to learn from your users. Because you are putting working software in the hands of users, you can observe to see how users interact with the software and whether it meets their needs. You can validate user requirements and you can refine your understanding of user requirements as they use the software and explain why it does or does not meet their needs. This helps you confirm that you are working on the correct solution and that it delivers the intended business value.

Through a pilot, you can also learn about what types of support requirements it will require and what user training you will need to accommodate. It gives you a chance to learn about how much effort it will take to deploy as well as a detailed list of the steps involved. It will also help you uncover any hidden issues or challenges you otherwise might not be able to predict. This helps you learn about the solution's implementation details and it enables you to fine-tune any designs early in the process.

Ultimately, piloting reduces the risk by proving the feasibility of a solution and validating that it meets the business needs. It aligns well with the gradual approach of incremental and continuous improvement by introducing a small change. Once you have piloted it, you can then plan to deploy it into production. Not only do I like to take small incremental steps as I deploy new features and enhancements, but I also like to take small incremental steps with how I deploy them. By piloting, I can restrict how much I affect to a limited number of users in a controlled and non-production environment.

To set up a pilot, you can deploy an isolated farm. This helps you to keep your pilot separate and avoid affecting your production environment. I find an isolate farm works best and it offers the most flexibility because you do not have to worry about affecting normal operations if you need to perform maintenance tasks such as restarting a server or deploying an update. It also offers you the option to deploy different product versions. Most importantly though, an isolated environment ensures that you do not leave any artifacts and the like on the production servers or in the production database after the pilot concludes.

■ **Note**   There are licensing implications with running pilot servers. As business users use them in their operations and the servers process production data, they typically require a server license. You should check your licensing agreement to confirm your usage rights and licensing requirements. You might also investigate whether beta or trial software meets your needs.

One approach I usually take to manage pilot environments is to use virtual servers. I find this makes it easy to rollback changes, which allows me to test ideas without worrying about causing a lot of extra work for myself. Using virtual servers gets a pilot environment up and running very quickly. On a project, I am constantly in a state of wanting to pilot things and prove concepts, something I can practice when I make the process of provisioning a new pilot environment as quick and easy as possible.

To achieve this ease, I prefer to set up a virtual server with the SharePoint software and all its patches installed, but not configured. I use a PowerShell script to quickly provision a farm after I clone the virtual server. I provision the farm using a shared SQL Server database server, often a cluster in a lab designated for test and pilot farms. Figure 9-3 illustrates an example of a pilot farm consisting of a single server sharing the same SQL Server database server as a production farm with load-balanced SharePoint web servers.

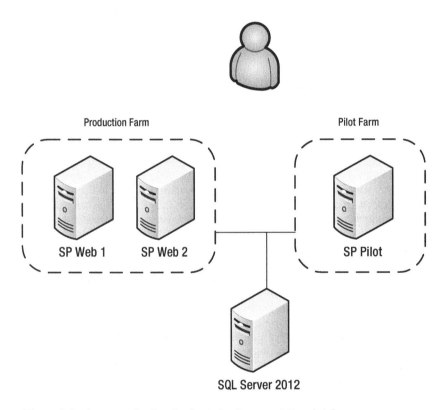

Figure 9-3. *An example of a pilot farm sharing an existing database server*

I try to avoid sharing the production SQL Server instance whenever I am provisioning farms where I want to perform load or stress testing. Whenever I expect a pilot farm to consume excessive database resources, I also avoid sharing the production SQL Server. Typically, this would be for applications that consume heavy processing or memory resources on the database tier, such as business intelligence or analytics applications. I would separate these more resource-heavy applications so as not to negatively affect the production farm during the pilot.

Estimating Cost-Benefits and Business Value

At some point, you probably need to calculate a rough estimate on the cost of the solution and its projected benefits. You can use this information to help you prioritize the work required to enable the solution, and this can help you determine where to schedule it on your roadmap. You might already have a good idea about what the expected costs are from considerations such as your build versus buy decision, your effort estimates, and the licensing costs. This gives you a great starting point and it provides a reasonable rough order of magnitude on the costs involved.

In Chapter 3, I discussed some considerations you can use to map SharePoint features to business value. I also looked at some approaches for how to calculate a dollar value for any efficiencies or savings that a solution introduces. Those are still certainly useful and they provide you with the most accurate business value information, but they can be time consuming to calculate. To work around this and get a reasonable indication of the potential business value, I like to assign a category for a rough order of magnitude during the request triage. This gives me a sense about the scale of potential business value and I can use this to get a sense of its priority.

Table 9-1 lists several sample cost-benefit categories you can use as an indicator and an estimate of potential business value. This can help you make an initial assessment based on limited knowledge as you process a request in your demand funnel. In your request triage, you can use this information to help prioritize the item or to schedule additional analysis of the potential business impact and business value.

Table 9-1. *Sample List of Cost-Benefit Categories for Estimating Business Value*

Cost-Benefit Category	Description
Reduces med-low frustrating process	Indicates potential to decrease an acceptable level of frustration in a process
Reduces highly frustrating process	Indicates potential to decrease an unnecessary frustration to complete in a process
Removes med-low frustrating process	Indicates opportunity to replace an acceptable level of frustration in a process
Removes highly frustrating process	Indicates opportunity to replace an unnecessary frustration to complete in a process
Replaces partial redundancy	Indicates a mildly redundant process
Replaces significant redundancy	Indicates an overly redundant process
Increases cross-team awareness	Indicates an opportunity to increase awareness
Increases corporate communications	Indicates an opportunity to increase communication
Increases legal compliance	Indicates an increase in legal compliance
Automates a routine process	Indicates a simple or routine process
Automates a complex process	Indicates a complex workflow or business process

These categories help give you a rough sense about the type and degree of business value a potential solution can provide. You can reword them, add or subtract, or adapt the list to fit with how you and your team can visualize categories of potential business value. The point is to use something that gives you a sense of the business value and that supports your decision-making during your request triage. This helps you increase your effectiveness and your efficiency as you process your demand funnel, and that helps you to avoid an overwhelming sense of demand. It also helps you avoid having low-priority requests pull you off track.

Meeting Demand and Fulfilling User Needs

The one thing your demand funnel is not is a means of resistance to change. I mention this because too often, at least for me, an IT group may come across to its users as resistant. Often this seems to stem from IT facing their own constraints: resource constraints, budget constraints, and even regulatory constraints. These constraints are important and they are a legitimate reason why you cannot meet a user's request. However, when you become overly fixated on your constraints, then you often come across to your internal customers as resisting their needs. I have sometimes heard jokes related to these perceptions where stakeholders refer to IT as "the department of 'No'" – a particularly negative perception.

How can you avoid these negative perceptions when constraints are a reality of any operation? I already discussed how you cannot be everything to everybody. How can you avoid becoming the department of *No* even when you have to say no at times? The answer is the reasoning behind my entire demand funnel process. When you encourage stakeholders to participate in the decisions and you offer transparency behind the trade-offs and decisions, you show you want to work with your internal customers. You validate their needs and work to collaborate with them to fulfill those needs where possible.

The outcome can often be the same in both approaches: you might be too constrained and unable to deliver on a particular request. However, I have found the perception in the collaborative approach of managing and processing a demand funnel generates a perception of teamwork and service, not resistance. This creates a department of "Let's see what we can do together!"

■ **Note** One book with advice I found especially helpful for working through trade-offs and compromises with stakeholders is *Getting to Yes* by Roger Fisher and William Ury. They offer a wealth of advice for focusing on interests rather than problems and on working together to find options that will satisfy everyone. You may find their advice particularly useful during your request triage.

As you build this collaborative cycle, remember that you are the expert there to analyze their business problems and envision solutions for them. You are not there to simply take an order and then go off to start fulfilling the list of requirements they gave you. Your internal customers are domain experts in their business process and they can provide you with details about the problems they face or the opportunities they perceive. Your job is to analyze this information and design a graceful solution. Therefore, your demand funnel is not simply a list of wants in the form of a checklist of items that your users submit. Instead, it is a list of solutions, each of which you can trace back to specific business problems or other needs.

Consultant Comrade

One thing I like to do when I engage with a new client is to start with an envisioning engagement. In this, I can deploy a pilot SharePoint instance with a default install and basic functionality for whatever the client wants to utilize. I like to keep this part very quick and very basic – no bells and whistles or fancy features, just out-of-the-box functionality. I like to start here because I have found that clients can easily start dreaming about all the magical things that they think SharePoint can do for them. When they have a basic pilot deployed that they can try out, then this resets some expectations.

This pilot SharePoint deployment gets my clients using SharePoint and in the process, it sets their expectations. In setting their expectations, I am also managing my own demand funnel because when they see it working, they keep their requests from drifting too far from the general area of what we want to accomplish. When SharePoint remains only in their imagination, it seems to be harder to see the relation between it and their feature requests, and thus it gets easy for them to wander off course into unrelated areas.

I mentioned in Chapter 8 that I like to use this pilot SharePoint deployment to set up a survey and begin to collect requirements and feedback from my potential users. Here is another opportunity to begin to guide your client's SharePoint usage and adoption. When I worked for Microsoft, we called this *dogfooding* our products – this is where Microsoft IT deploys a product internally and the company uses it to support the business functions to ensure the product is ready to release to Microsoft's customers. If your customer does not have TFS or some other work item tracking system, then setting up a pilot SharePoint deployment and SharePoint lists to track risks and requirements is another great way for you to get your customer dogfooding SharePoint early.

As a consultant, you can add a lot of value to your client by helping them to establish this process. If it is a new deployment, then you can get them started with a pilot deployment. Moreover, if they have an existing deployment that you are helping them enhance or stabilize, then you can still help them get started with this process by having them list and prioritize your tasks in a SharePoint list. Once they build out a list, you can work with them to work through the request triage.

I find that sometimes when I help to prime the process in this way, it helps give clients confidence on how they can continue the process after my engagement with them ends. Another effect that this has is we start building a parking lot list together. Usually by starting the parking lot list with them, I help them work through any anxieties or resistance to parking an item for some undetermined date. This usually helps my client to see that it is okay to save some items for another time and focus on the truly high-priority items.

This has two effects: your client internalizes the process under your guidance, while you also get them started with prioritizing and organizing your work. Through this pilot and envisioning engagement, you can guide them toward disciplined practices that will help manage scope during your project delivery, but it will also lead them to continue with the good habits after you roll off your project. They will ideally adopt the triage and parking lot habits that you teach them, and this will help them plan future enhancements in a sustainable, disciplined manner.

Other benefits you realize from getting your client started with a triage process are scope control and expectation management. As new requirements or enhancement requests come up, you can give your client practice with a triage meeting. This is great because it helps build their skills and confidence with conducting a triage, but it is also great because it forces them to face the trade-offs in your project scope as well. If you are engaged to deliver a portal and all of a sudden they want a full enterprise content management solution as well, then you can help them work through the triage for this chunk of work.

Rather than dismissing the item by declaring it as out of scope or too large of a piece of work for your resources to achieve, you can walk them through the process to where they come to that conclusion on their own. In my experience, this helps them internalize and understand why something is too large and complex to simply tack on to an existing project scope. Whenever I have tried to just declare it as out of scope or too large, frequently people on my client's team resisted and maybe even resented that I was excluding something from scope.

I have found this resistance is because they are usually interested in a capability within SharePoint that they perceive as valuable, but that they do not know much about, particularly with the ramifications of tacking it on to our current scope. However, when I work through the triage with them and I start to discuss the rough order of magnitude I would require in effort and the trade-offs for the current initiative, they get a better sense of what it would involve and they are more likely to accept that it is not feasible within my present project.

For me, when a client seems emotionally invested in a capability that I am not there to deliver, I like to pay particular attention to any dependencies involved during a triage session. Once they start getting a sense of the dependencies, I reframe what may appear to them as a simple capability and I start breaking it down into all the pieces of work that need to occur. For example, if they suddenly become interested in records management, I walk them through all the activities such as content classification, enterprise taxonomies, retention policies, and the like. Once they begin to understand the scale of business analysis that this capability would require, they get a sense for how quickly this would take us off course from whatever else I am there to deliver. Only then are they more likely to accept the approach and the project's scope.

This may seem as if it is a time consuming effort, but it gets your client into good habits and it helps you manage scope. Best of all, it can help you help them build a roadmap of future opportunities that you can help them deliver. This keeps everyone focused on the current priorities and it ensures that everyone understands what tradeoffs any changes to scope would require. In my experience, this has been the only consistently effective way to negotiate an acceptance of scope with all the project stakeholders.

Inside Story: Notes from the Field

Years ago, I worked for Electronic Arts (EA), a video game software development and publishing company. I worked in the worldwide IT department and I was based in Vancouver, Canada while most of my team operated from Redwood City, California. Despite any of the benefits that I may have realized if I was in the same location as my team, having the team spread out helped provide access to different internal customers. I am a firm believer that nothing beats face-to-face. I love how far technology has come with video conferencing and the like, but it still does not beat face-to-face interaction with users and stakeholders.

EA had a couple of large studios in the Vancouver in those days, but they have since consolidated those into a single studio in the area. Each studio runs in a semi-autonomous fashion with their own leadership and they focus on the game titles that the studio develops and needs to ship. Game titles roll into franchises, which loosely map to studios. EA also has a large publishing division responsible for marketing and distributing the games to retail outlets. Some of these publishing units share locations with studios, and some have their own locations. Each location has their own needs and priorities to support their teams (some game teams can have 200 or more people, while others have just 10 or 20, depending on the franchise and the title).

These quasi-independent studios and publishers exist all over the world. Some are small and can adapt to whatever service is already in use by the larger locations, while other locations such as Vancouver are large and demanding. My job was to provide a global SharePoint service consisting of multiple farms on multiple continents, serving a diverse set of needs. The challenge was to prioritize my resources across my internal customers. This, of course, was not just a challenge for the SharePoint service, but held consistent across all of what my team referred to as service lines – the different platform services we offered the business.

One way IT approached this was to collect and funnel the demand from each of our internal customers. For our larger customers, such as the Vancouver area studios, some team members acted as account managers. These internal account managers engaged with the business, working to understand their needs and priorities. They then funneled this demand back to the worldwide IT group to triage and prioritize. For major projects, IT maintained a plan of record. This was a prioritized list of approved and funded projects for the upcoming period.

For me as the SharePoint lead, I coordinated between two lists of projects. For major projects, the IT executive level funded and scheduled these. They would triage and prioritize the work for me, coordinating resource availability and change management across the different service lines and other organizational constraints. I would contribute some items to the demand funnel and offer recommendations for the triage process, and then I would work through the process with the rest of the IT organization. Once the plan of record is set, then I could adapt my roadmap and service delivery plan based on the projects approved and planned for the next couple of quarters.

For smaller or more routine projects, I managed the backlog and triage process within the SharePoint team. There were constantly quick wins or value-add opportunities rising. The prime candidates for me to deliver were those that did not require significant funding or resourcing. I like to think of these sorts of opportunities as low hanging fruit – the bounty I can easily reach and quickly deliver value to the business. These types of activities add incremental value, and I prefer to evolve a SharePoint service by adding incremental value rather than through large projects. This lowers the risk and delivers value quickly.

To give an example, when I wanted to deploy an enterprise search platform, I included this in the plan of record because it would involve resources to analyze the different content sources I wanted to index and the different user experiences I wanted to provide. At the same time, some of our internal customers wanted access to add an RSS feed to their team sites. This was before the RSS feed web part came as part of SharePoint, so I looked at developing my own. Because I could build a basic RSS feed web part with little risk and use it to satisfy several internal customers, I prioritized this against my team's capacity and delivered it as incremental value.

Other activities I included in my request triage process were consolidation and migration efforts. I had a bloating of SharePoint farms across the organization. There are many reasons for this: some came through company acquisitions, some I inherited from other teams, and some were simply discovered as a covert service deployed under someone's desk. If you have ever been involved with a large-scale migration effort involving hundreds of sites and thousands of users, then you share my pain and know what is involved. I needed to schedule downtime, URLs had to change and caused broken links, and in some cases I wanted to promote sub-sites to their own site collection.

I could not migrate everyone all at once, because teams were on different schedules. I did not want to simply move an entire web application to consolidate farms and retire servers. Instead, I wanted to reorganize and correct some of the issues I inherited, and part of this involved this migration effort. Even though this is more a maintenance task, I still processed it through my request triage because it involved effort and required prioritizing. By using the triage process, I was able to coordinate my migration efforts with other initiatives. This allowed me to regularly work away at the backlog of sites I wanted to migrate or reorganize.

This example shows how you can coordinate between different types of initiatives when prioritizing resource activities. Your demand funnel can funnel requests from the business and requests from the service delivery team. I consider these latter activities more as investment requests – those requests users might not care for and probably did not ask for, but that the team knows will improve or make the service more manageable in some way. It also shows how you can use your roadmap to coordinate activities with an organization-wide list of IT projects with your team's list of smaller initiatives.

Wrapping Up

In this chapter, I discussed approaches to setting up a demand funnel for enhancing and expanding the SharePoint service, including considerations for establishing a triage process. I looked at ways to set expectations, build a parking lot list of enhancement requests, and how to map requests back to your roadmap. I also considered the need to forecast future upgrades to plan for their eventual impact, and I looked at when and why you might want to pilot enhancements to learn more about their impacts and to validate their underlying requirements.

As you funnel the enhancement requests through your demand funnel, it will lead you toward growing and expanding your SharePoint service to offer these new features and capabilities. Some of these enhancements will consume additional resources on your servers, requiring you to grow and scale your SharePoint farm. In the next chapter, I look at how to plan for growing your SharePoint farm. I consider the scalability and expansion capabilities architected into SharePoint and how this allows you to avoid over architecting the farm up front.

CHAPTER 10

■ ■ ■

Growing Your SharePoint Service

You never know what is enough until you know what is more than enough.

—William Blake

In this chapter, I provide guidance on how to plan for growing your SharePoint service. I define general infrastructure components and server roles related to SharePoint. From there, I introduce considerations to scale for availability by adding redundancy and planning for growth. I also discuss how to add servers to expand a farm's infrastructure capabilities, as well as how to allocate and distribute services on different servers. Finally, I discuss some considerations for planning subordinate farms and how they can work alongside an enterprise farm.

One key point I stress in this chapter is that you can evolve and grow SharePoint over time as the usage pattern changes, eliminating the need to feel constrained or to have to over-architect your farm upfront.

After reading this chapter, you will know how to:

- Understand and plan for scalability

- Explain the scaling options

- Plan and prepare to grow in the future

- Understand the infrastructure components

- Allocate services to servers

- Plan for subordinate farms

Continuously Evolving and Growing SharePoint

Throughout this book, I have suggested the idea of managing your SharePoint deployment as a service that you continuously evolve over time. Some enterprise products have a requirement that you deploy it all at once; whereas the beauty with SharePoint is you do not have this constraint. Often times you may have to take big steps, but you do not have to, and frequently you will do well to take a series of smaller steps with the deployment. In Chapter 7, I discussed this idea using the metaphor of eating a SharePoint elephant, and I want to return to this discussion now to revisit SharePoint as a progression you evolve rather than as a switch you turn on.

You might grow your SharePoint service to expand its capabilities and the functionality it offers. I first discussed this idea back in Chapter 3, when I looked at the different capabilities that SharePoint offers. As you want to provide more business value and meet more business needs, you can grow your SharePoint service to start delivering new capabilities. For example, you might grow your service in a related area, such as growing an intranet deployment to begin offering social networking MySite capabilities. Alternatively, you might grow your service into less related areas, such as growing an intranet deployment to also offer business intelligence reporting capabilities.

Another driver to grow your service comes from increased adoption. As users grow more comfortable using SharePoint, they also find more uses for their sites and portals. They might store more content on their sites and they could access the service more frequently. They might get excited about the social computing capabilities and begin to store more information in their profile and more data in their MySite. This compounding adoption consumes additional resources as the overall load increases on your servers. In turn, you will need to scale your servers to handle the increased load.

As your SharePoint service evolves, it needs you to be proactive and adapt it to the changing needs and increasing load. SharePoint 2013 is great at load-balancing and routing requests, but it does not dynamically reallocate background services to run on servers based on resource characteristics. Instead, you have to start and stop services yourself. It also does not automatically repartition databases or migrate site collection data to optimize the storage. Again, you have to plan for and perform these tasks.

■ **Important**   Your SharePoint farm will evolve in a variety of ways, but it needs you to shape and steer its evolution. SharePoint does not have artificial intelligence capabilities to do this work for you.

I often find myself stressing this important need for ongoing and proactive involvement in a SharePoint deployment. This is most common when I am on a team to deploy capabilities such as enterprise search, where I stress how it will require planning and tuning the search service as users use it, not just up front during the initial deployment. With people generally used to public search engines seemingly figuring out relevancy automatically and the search experience just working, they often project that expectation on SharePoint. Yet, what they forget about are the thousands and thousands of employees working for a public search engine's company, working to continuously tune and adjust their search engine. They also tend to forget about the mass industry of search engine optimization (SEO) organizations and specialists who help tune public websites to improve search relevancy. SharePoint, just as for public search engines, requires ongoing proactive tuning.

The same is true for other capabilities that SharePoint offers. They require ongoing maintenance and tuning to evolve your SharePoint service, and at times, they will require additional resources as your SharePoint service grows. For instance, as more content finds its way into a SharePoint repository, you will require additional disk space. You might purchase much of these anticipated needs up front, but you do not have to. Instead, you can look at your service's growth path and plan to add additional capacity closer to when your service will need the added resources.

Ideally, your service's growth path reflects a plan that you layout in your roadmap. This helps you stay focused on expanding and growing in an intended direction that provides value to the business. As you approach items on your roadmap, this offers you a good time to take a step back and revisit your reasoning behind the item. Is it still valid? Have you thought through and questioned all of its related assumptions? After revisiting your assumptions, you will be in a good position to continue growing your SharePoint service.

QUESTIONING ASSUMPTIONS

There is a danger in simply accepting ideas and running with them without stopping to question whether there is a better way. This issue can sometimes show up in a team brainstorming session when an idea comes up that sounds good on the surface, it gets everyone excited. You may have heard this termed as *groupthink*, where the desire for harmony and a resolution drives a team to become overly excited on the prospects of an idea, and in the process, they do not question its validity or consider alternatives.

Another danger is in making decisions by basing them on the way your organization has always done things. For example, why are railway tracks the width that they are? They are 56 and a half inches, which came from the wheel spacing on horse-drawn wagons. The wheel spacing on these wagons in turn came from the width of

Roman chariots, a width they designed based on the width of two horses. Although a wider train track may have been more stable, no one ever questioned the assumptions that they based on the width that carriages have always been.

To avoid these dangers, play the devil's advocate and question whether another way is possible. Question whether you have made assumptions and if those assumptions are valid for the problem you are trying to solve.

Understanding Scalability

Scalability relates to how you can adjust your farm to handle an increasing load or to provide additional capabilities. You achieve scalability when you maintain service performance levels as you increase the load on your SharePoint service. Your system is scalable when you can add resources to it to maintain or improve on the performance levels under an increased load.

One common reason to grow a SharePoint service stems from scaling to meet growing adoption rates and increased demand on the service. You might face the need to scale from increased usage or expanded services, or a combination of the two. As you scale to handle the increased load, you will add resources to the service that provide additional capacity for handling requests. You can scale your service by selecting either or both of the following scaling options:

- Scaling Up

- Scaling Out

Scaling up refers to adding capacity to existing components that the service runs on. When you scale up, you improve performance by replacing a resource in the existing design. For example, if you want to scale up a given SharePoint farm, you can replace the RAM with a larger amount of memory or the CPU with a faster processer. As Figure 10-1 illustrates, you can also scale up by adding additional hard drive storage space. If you had two SharePoint servers and one SQL Server, after scaling up you will still have a farm consisting of those three servers, but they will have the increased power or additional capacity from the resources you added. Scaling up is an effective way to remove bottlenecks based on over utilized resource components.

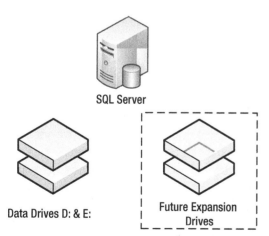

SQL Server

Data Drives D: & E:

Future Expansion Drives

Figure 10-1. *An example of scaling up by adding additional hard drive capacity*

Scaling out refers to adding components to add capacity. When you scale out, you typically improve performance by adding more servers or farms to grow the existing design. For example, if you want to scale out a given SharePoint farm, you can add more SharePoint web front-end servers and a network load-balancer (NLB) to spread the load across additional servers. Figure 10-2 illustrates an example of scaling out the web front-end servers in a farm. Scaling out is an effective way to remove bottlenecks by allowing for more processing of requests in parallel across additional servers or farms.

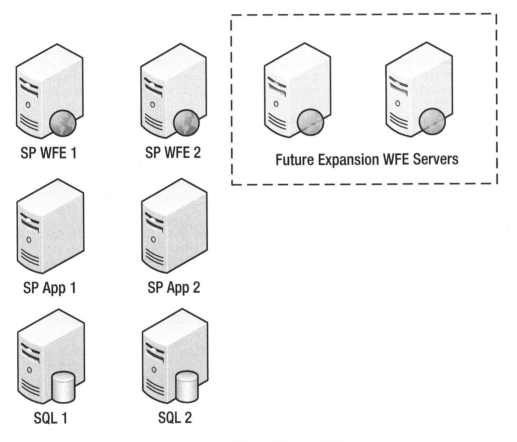

Figure 10-2. *An example of scaling out by adding additional web front-end servers*

■ **Important**   You can grow and scale your SharePoint service later by adding resources, additional servers, or even peripheral subordinate farms. You do not have to feel constrained or intimidated ahead of time when you deploy your initial farm, because you can adapt your SharePoint service as your needs change rather than trying to over architect it up front.

Another way you can scale out your SharePoint service is by adding peripheral subordinate farms. You might add a subordinate farm for several reasons, including providing a farm to meet the needs for customizations that you do not want to implement in a shared environment. You might also deploy subordinate farms to meet geographic needs by providing a farm in a remote region for quicker network access. Subordinate farms might help you segregate and organize different services or provide different service levels, although they will also add to the administrative overhead to manage and support your overall SharePoint service.

You might scale out to subordinate farms hosted in the cloud, such as with Office 365, or you might scale out to a subordinate farm hosted on-premises. Although the implementation details differ, I still group these scaling options together and I refer to them both simply as a subordinate farm. Later in this chapter, I return to discuss considerations to help you plan for subordinate farms. For now, I just want to point out that this is one approach to scaling out a service.

In short, I use scalability to relate to your ability to add resources and components to your SharePoint service to increase its capacity. As your user base grows, so can your SharePoint service. As the characteristics of usage evolve, so too can you evolve your SharePoint service. This does not mean that you should start aimlessly throwing servers and additional resources at your SharePoint farms because something feels slow or you suspect you might need something. Instead, base your decisions on performance measurements either from actual production usage or from load testing. You can then use this data to help you make scaling decisions and to help you plan for scalability.

■ **Note**   For more information on the types of performance measurements you can use to determine where and when to scale your SharePoint service, please see Chapter 6.

Planning for Growth and Scalability

Microsoft has already done a lot of the scalability planning for you. They designed SharePoint so that you can add components to it in the future without causing a major interruption or rework of the existing service. They also expose many of the product's capabilities through a service-oriented architecture (SOA), the SharePoint 2013 service applications. This architecture allows you to target how you allocate your server resources for specific services, while SharePoint abstracts away the complexities of balancing the load.

Many of the low-level details to support scalability are already in place for you. However, you can still plan some aspects of the service to prepare for future growth and scalability. The following lists a few of the main areas you may consider as you plan for future growth.

- **Budget:** As you grow and scale your SharePoint service, you will encounter additional expenses to expand resources to scale up or scale out. When you look at your projected trajectory of growth, consider what that means in cost and how that aligns with your budget. You may need to delay or piecemeal growth until you have available budget to accommodate it, particularly for growth involving capital expenses such as servers and other infrastructure components. You can anticipate this piecemeal approach in your roadmap, as I discussed in Chapter 7.

- **Infrastructure Components:** With an increasing demand and an expanding range of capabilities, you will eventually require additional hardware to process the load and maintain performance levels. You can plan for hardware acquisitions in your budget, as I mentioned in the previous bullet point. You can also plan for this by setting up the hardware in a manner where you can add additional components at a later date. For example, you can plan for future growth and scale by installing a SQL Server Cluster even if you are only using a single SQL Server node to start. This allows you to add additional database server nodes without much reconfiguration. You can take a similar approach with the web front-end servers by including load balancing hardware or software proxies in your initial architecture design.

■ **Note**   Although it is not difficult to update a database server's name in SharePoint to point to a new SQL Server instance, you can also use the SQL Client Configuration Utility to create a server alias on each SharePoint server in your farm to make the SQL Server instance details more abstracted. You will find using a SQL alias especially helpful if you need to move the configuration database, because that database stores the server name and makes it more difficult to move to another SQL Server instance if you do not use an alias. For more information on how to create a server alias, please see this MSDN article: `http://msdn.microsoft.com/ms190445`

- **Isolation:** Growing and scaling might require you to process an increasing load on the same hardware. To achieve this, you might have to isolate applications that consume heavy amounts of resources and that could degrade the overall service availability. You can achieve this isolation by allocating the application's services to run on dedicated servers in the farm or you can dedicate subordinate farms specifically to run and isolate these applications. You can plan future growth and scale by planning how you can isolate and constrain certain applications to prevent them from consuming all the available server resources and affecting overall service availability.

- **Request Routing:** As a quasi mixture of load balancing and isolation, request routing provides another option you may consider to help maximize your resource utilization and prevent one application from negatively affecting the availability of the entire service. SharePoint 2013 contains a Request Management capability that allows you to apply logic to distribute requests based on additional criteria, rather than simply balancing the load across a group of servers. For example, you can throttle requests from certain user agents or to certain applications. You can direct certain requests to specific servers based on static rules you configure or based on dynamic health scores that SharePoint maintains for each server. You can use SharePoint 2013 Request Management to throttle and balance loads across your farm using sophisticated logic, and this can help you plan how you want to grow and scale your service. Figure 10-3 illustrates how the SharePoint 2013 Request Manager handles user requests and then routes them to available SharePoint web front-end servers.

■ **Note**   For more information on the Request Management capability in SharePoint 2013, please see the following Microsoft TechNet article: `http://technet.microsoft.com/jj712708`

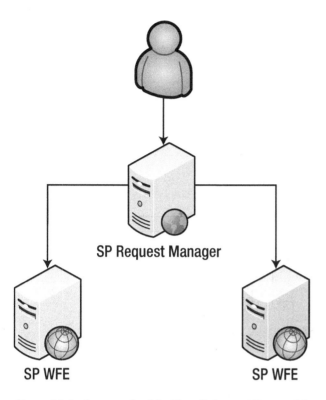

Figure 10-3. *An example of the SharePoint 2013 Request Manager routing requests between two SharePoint servers*

In planning for growth and scalability, you will also need to consider how you will implement customizations and application development so that it does not limit your ability to grow or scale your service. You also want to avoid having the implementation choices you make today cause extensive rework in the future. These are topics I address in Part IV of this book, where I return to discuss planning considerations, actions, and behaviors to guide you for different aspects of customizing your SharePoint service. For this chapter, I focus on the SharePoint platform itself – particularly on the components and services that make up the SharePoint platform. In the next section, I describe the infrastructure components that form a SharePoint farm.

Understanding the Infrastructure Components

You might hear people refer to SharePoint web front-end servers and SharePoint application servers when they describe a SharePoint farm. These are all SharePoint servers with SharePoint software installed and running. Conceptually, the differences between a web tier and an application tier are the services running on the server. A web server runs the "Microsoft SharePoint Foundation Web Application" service, and it responds to HTTP requests for sites and content that the farm provides. You can grow and scale your service on the web tier by adding servers and configuring network load-balancing or SharePoint Request Manager to spread the web requests across these servers. Figure 10-4 provides an architecture diagram to illustrate the different servers in a SharePoint farm as well as other servers the farm may depend on.

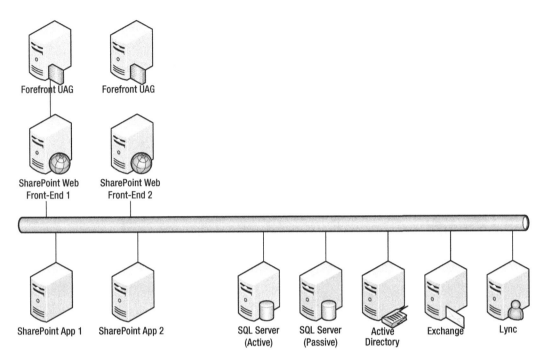

Figure 10-4. *An architecture diagram of a SharePoint 2013 farm and other servers it may depend on*

Application servers run other services, typically providing the functionality behind an application or a background job. Your farm can include a variety of application servers, ranging from running all the services on the same server (including the web server) to dedicating a server for a particular service. For example, you can dedicate servers to run different components of the search service such as indexing and query components. This architecture allows you to allocate your services in a granular fashion to optimize your server resources. You can grow and scale your service by adding new servers to the farm and then allocating services across your application tier. I return in later sections in this chapter to walk you through how to add servers to a SharePoint farm and how to allocate services on different servers.

The next group of servers in a SharePoint farm involves your SQL Server database servers. The data tier consists of one or more SQL Server nodes running the databases where the SharePoint farm stores its content. Typically, you mirror or cluster these databases to provide redundancy and reduce the risk for outages. As a SharePoint service is data-driven, it relies heavily on the database servers to serve content and for the overall farm's performance. You can grow and scale your data tier by adding SQL Server nodes to host databases and process requests.

■ **Note** For more information on SQL Server 2012 clustering and how to install a failover cluster, please see the following MSDN article: http://msdn.microsoft.com/hh231721

Another important infrastructure component you may include in your SharePoint farm is the Office Web Apps Server 2013. This server product provides functionality to render Microsoft Office documents as a web page within SharePoint libraries and as preview thumbnails in search results. Formerly, SharePoint 2010 included this functionality as a service application, but beginning with SharePoint 2013, Office Web Apps is now its own stand-alone server product. The reason Microsoft separated these products is to make Office Web Apps available for other products such as Exchange 2013 and Lync 2013, which also now use its Office document rendering capabilities, and these other products can use Office Web Apps without also introducing a SharePoint dependency.

■ **Important** You cannot install Office Web Apps Server 2013 on a server where you have installed SharePoint 2013. Office Web Apps requires its own server.

You will also consider other infrastructure components as you plan to grow your service and farms. One notable component may include any virtualization server components that you use to host any virtual servers in your farm. Some network components you may require include the load-balancing servers or other hardware devices, as well as any firewalls and intrusion detection components you require to protect your farms. Other components may include any enterprise backup products you use to capture backups of server states and databases.

Part of growing your SharePoint service may involve scaling out individual farms. Often, scaling out a SharePoint farm involves adding servers to it – either SharePoint servers or database servers. You can scale out your database servers by adding additional SQL Server nodes to a cluster and distributing your databases across the active nodes. You can scale out your SharePoint servers by adding additional servers to the farm. In the next section, I walk you through how to add an additional SharePoint server to the farm.

Adding Servers to a SharePoint Farm

You might recall the SharePoint Configuration Wizard from your initial install of SharePoint. If you only installed SharePoint on a single farm, then you ran this wizard to provision the farm and it configured that server to join the farm. If you installed SharePoint on additional servers, then you ran this wizard on those additional servers and configured them to join the farm. You can add additional servers to the SharePoint farm at a later time by running that same wizard and following those same steps.

The SharePoint team designed SharePoint with this flexibility to add and remove servers from a SharePoint farm with relatively few complications and little complexity. To ease this process of joining a new server to a new farm, I like to go through the following steps:

1. Install the Windows Server 2012 or later operating system.

2. Install any server service packs and Microsoft updates.

3. Install the SharePoint 2013 Prerequisites on the server.

4. Install the SharePoint 2013 software on the server.

5. Install any required language packs, if applicable.

6. Install any SharePoint service packs, if available.

7. Install any other SharePoint updates, if available.

8. Install any add-ons or third-party components, if applicable.

9. Run the SharePoint Products and Technologies Configuration Wizard, selecting the option to join an existing farm.

This approach will help you to avoid any incompatibility issues between the new server and the farm. This is important because once you run configuration wizard, SharePoint will join the server to the farm and it will begin to process requests. Inconsistent version numbers may cause unexpected results in processing a request on the inconsistent server. You can verify the SharePoint versions and patch levels for each server and each content database in the farm on the Manage Patch Status page in SharePoint Central Administration, as shown in Figure 10-5. You can navigate to this page by clicking the "Check product and patch installation status" link under the Upgrade and Migration section on the SharePoint Central Administration homepage.

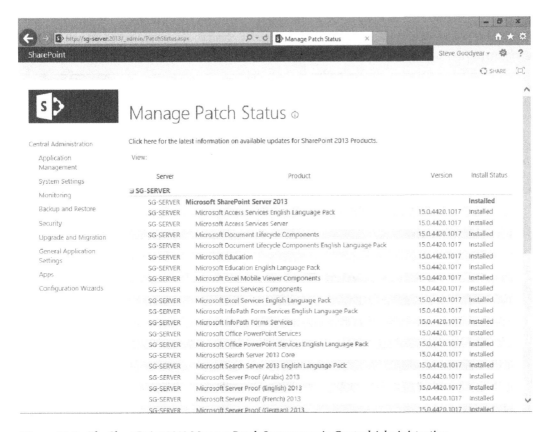

Figure 10-5. *The SharePoint 2013 Manage Patch Status page in Central Administration*

As you add new servers to the SharePoint farm, you can grow and scale your service. You may have additional steps to configure the server for your farm, depending on your environment and individual situation. Some other tasks you might have to perform on the new server include adding any necessary certificates to the server, configuring system monitoring, and configuring any routing or load-balancing components.

■ **Note**   Although this is not a how-to book, I wanted to include this general discussion on how to add servers to stress the flexibility of adding servers to a SharePoint farm. This should help reinforce the notion that you do not need to over-architect your SharePoint farm upfront, and instead you can adapt it later as its usage grows.

By default, the configuration wizard starts the Microsoft SharePoint Foundation Web Application service on the newly configured server. After you join a server to a farm, you can start and stop the desired services you want on that server. In the next section, I walk through the steps for allocating the desired services on a server.

Allocating Services and Servers

SharePoint exposes management of what services run on what servers through the Services on Server page in the SharePoint Central Administration, as shown in Figure 10-6. On this page, you can select the server and then click to start or stop each of the desired services. This allows a SharePoint administrator the ability to manage background services on a server without having to grant them any administrative access to the server itself.

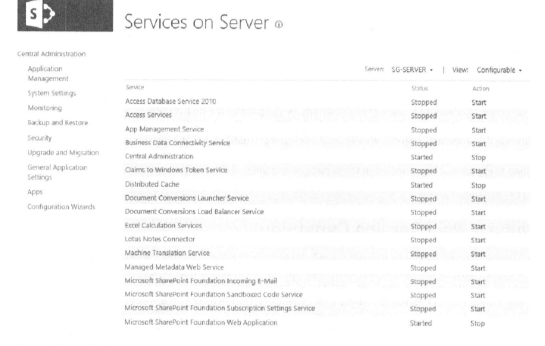

Services on Server ⓘ

| | Server: SG-SERVER ▾ | View: Configurable ▾ | |
Service		Status	Action
Access Database Service 2010		Stopped	Start
Access Services		Stopped	Start
App Management Service		Stopped	Start
Business Data Connectivity Service		Stopped	Start
Central Administration		Started	Stop
Claims to Windows Token Service		Stopped	Start
Distributed Cache		Started	Stop
Document Conversions Launcher Service		Stopped	Start
Document Conversions Load Balancer Service		Stopped	Start
Excel Calculation Services		Stopped	Start
Lotus Notes Connector		Stopped	Start
Machine Translation Service		Stopped	Start
Managed Metadata Web Service		Stopped	Start
Microsoft SharePoint Foundation Incoming E-Mail		Stopped	Start
Microsoft SharePoint Foundation Sandboxed Code Service		Stopped	Start
Microsoft SharePoint Foundation Subscription Settings Service		Stopped	Start
Microsoft SharePoint Foundation Web Application		Started	Stop

Central Administration

Application Management
System Settings
Monitoring
Backup and Restore
Security
Upgrade and Migration
General Application Settings
Apps
Configuration Wizards

Figure 10-6. *The Services on Server page*

You can access this page by clicking the "Services on Server" link under the System Settings section on the SharePoint Central Administration homepage. Notice the server name in the top-right table header area of this page. Clicking the link of the server name opens a drop-down menu with the Change Server menu option, as highlighted in Figure 10-7.

Services on Server ⓘ

| | Server: SG-SERVER ▾ | View: Configurable ▾ |
Service	Change Server	Action
Access Database Service 2010	Stopped	Start
Access Services	Stopped	Start
App Management Service	Stopped	Start

Figure 10-7. *The Change Server menu option on the Services on Server page*

If you click this menu option, you will open the Select Server modal window, listing all the SharePoint servers that are available in the farm. Inside this window, you can click the server name to select the server and dismiss the modal window. Notice that the server name in the top-right area of the Services on Server page reflects the newly chosen server. With the desired server selected, you can now allocate which services run on that server, effectively assigning the server's role.

■ **Note**   Some services may have dependencies that you will have to address before you can start them, such as the User Profile Service that depends on you first creating a User Profile service application. For some other services, you have to manage them and which server they run on through their service application, such as components of the Search service application.

You can allocate and reallocate services to balance and redistribute the load on the servers in the farm, and you would do this either after adding a new server to the farm or to optimize the distribution of services on existing servers. Through this approach, you can grow your SharePoint service to handle an increasing load on your existing services. By following this approach, you can also expand the service capabilities that your SharePoint service offers. When you expand your service, you start the new services on the desired servers, and you will often create a respective service application to expose the functionality in the expanded capability. In the next section, I discuss some considerations to be mindful of as you approach expanding your SharePoint service with a new capability.

Approaching a New Service Capability

As you approach enabling a new capability for your SharePoint service, the first and most important step is to determine the resource characteristics of the capability. You can start by asking whether the capability consumes resources from the SharePoint servers in the farm, or if it runs elsewhere. For example, a Business Connectivity Services (BCS) application might consume the majority of its required resources on a SQL Server database server where SharePoint queries the data from, and it might require only minimal resources on the SharePoint servers. In contrast, an Excel Calculation Services application might consume the majority of its required processing resources on the SharePoint servers.

Once you know what types of servers that the new capability will affect, you can continue to analyze the resource characteristics by identifying how it will affect the servers. This will help give you an idea about what kind of load the application will put on the server or servers. To get a general sense of how the application will affect server resources, I ask the following questions.

- Is the application heavy on processer (CPU) usage?

- Is the application heavy on memory (RAM) usage?

- Is the application heavy on disk reads or disk writes? Are the disk reads or writes local to the SharePoint server(s) or do they occur on the SQL server(s)?

- Is the application heavy on network communications?

At this point, you can consider whether your existing servers can handle the expected load, given the expected resource characteristics. In Chapter 6, I discussed different performance metrics that you can measure to determine the health and resource availability on your servers. You can use those same measures now to get a sense about whether your servers are nearing an over-utilized state or whether they have capacity to handle the additional load of the new application. After deploying the new application, you can use these same measures to monitor the new application along side the rest of the SharePoint service.

This is another case where you will want to plan for adequate server resources in a capacity plan. However, similar to your initial deployment of the farm itself, your capacity plan is an estimate. As you estimate the amount of capacity that you need to handle the load of the new application, you will make some assumptions on usage and estimate your initial capacity plan. Once you have your estimates, you can run load tests to increase the level of accuracy in your capacity plan. You can return to validate your estimates as the application runs in production by monitoring the performance metrics, as I mentioned above. This allows you to revisit your assumptions and make any adjustments as needed.

■ **Note**   For more information on capacity planning for SharePoint 2013, please see the following Microsoft TechNet article: `http://technet.microsoft.com/ff758645`

You may need to add additional servers to a farm to support the load of the new application, and you can allocate the services to run on designated servers. I discussed both of these topics earlier. You might dedicate one or more servers on which to run an application's service, such as potentially dedicating servers on which to run the PerformancePoint services to support a heavily used business intelligence application. Alternatively, you might dedicate an entire farm on which to run an application, such as potentially dedicating a farm to run an enterprise search application that you want to share across many farms. In the next section, I discuss when you might want a subordinate SharePoint farm and how you can plan for one.

Planning for Subordinate Farms

Subordinate farms can help you segregate and address differing needs from your internal customers. They allow you the flexibility to isolate applications or to create a centralized application service that you share with other farms. Deploying multiple farms enables many uses that may be of interest to you, but I do not take this decision lightly because additional farms will have additional operations costs and add support complexity. I generally default to a single enterprise farm, and then analyze and debate why any additional farms would benefit the service.

The benefits of operating a single farm relate to a simplified administrative burden. With a single farm, there is only one farm to maintain. Whereas, multiple farms add a level of complexity, most notably with keeping each farm's patch levels synchronized and consistent. A single farm also provides a single environment to troubleshoot and maintain. Consolidating in a single farm also reduces the number of required servers for test and staging environments, which you might want to mirror with your production environment for testing and pre-production purposes.

Running one centralized enterprise farm simplifies your ongoing operations and support. For these reasons, I prefer architectures with one centralized farm until there are compelling reasons to add subordinate farms. Through this approach, I find it helps to avoid a potential sprawl of unnecessary farms deployed throughout an organization. I am not opposed to deployments with multiple farms; I just prefer to avoid the added complexity if it does not add sufficient value.

There are many reasons why you might want to have multiple farms. In some cases, trying to fit everything in a single farm would add more complexity than segregating the design into multiple farms. For example, it may add more complexity to work around isolating certain customizations or third-party software products, particularly if they involve installing components or services directly on the server. The following list includes the most common reasons to consider when to add a subordinate farm:

- You want to provide different levels of service, including dedicated farms

- You want to isolate an unstable or risky application

- You want to segregate customers to reduce the potential of one affecting another

- You want to isolate for security reasons, such as internal versus external farms

- You want to run different versions as part of a gradual upgrade and migration

- You want to provide regional farms to minimize network latency for remote locations

- You want to segregate administration between different groups

- You want to simplify the scope of coordination for maintenance activities

Another reason you might want a separate farm relates to reducing the impact and degree of those affected in the event of a failure or a loss of service. For example, separating applications and groups of customers into multiple farms reduces the surface of potentially affected users during a single farm outage. This can help you reduce the overall risk of lost productivity and the overall severity if a major incident does occur. Figure 10-8 provides an example of a multi-farm architecture.

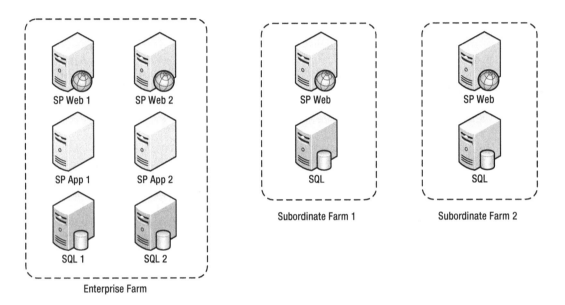

Figure 10-8. *A multi-farm architecture diagram*

After you determine that you do need multiple farms in your environment, you can begin to design which farms will be responsible for which applications. You might also identify which farms will serve which regions or which segments of customers. As you identify your farms and their scope, you can begin to identify what services each will need – both the local services they will require and the remote services they can connect to and consume. You do not need to duplicate every service on every farm, and by going through this process, you can minimize and avoid running any unnecessary services. This also helps you to identify what farm trusts you will need to establish.

■ **Note** Farm trusts involve one SharePoint 2013 farm to publish services that another SharePoint 2013 farm consumes. An administrator establishes the trust by exporting a certificate from the host farm and then using the certificate to create a trust on the consuming farm. For more information on trusts and how to configure them, please see the following Microsoft TechNet site: http://technet.microsoft.com/ff621100

As I describe these additional farms, I refer to them as subordinate farms because I generally designate one farm as the enterprise farm. Typically, this farm hosts enterprise applications such as the enterprise search, the managed metadata service, MySite profiles, and the main intranet portal. Any additional SharePoint farms can then consume services from the enterprise farm such as consuming the Managed Metadata Service application or redirecting search queries to the enterprise search portal. This allows one farm to provide central services that are global across the enterprise while other farms are conceptually subordinate to the enterprise farm as they consume those global services. Figure 10-9 illustrates an example of an enterprise farm that provides service applications for a subordinate farm to consume.

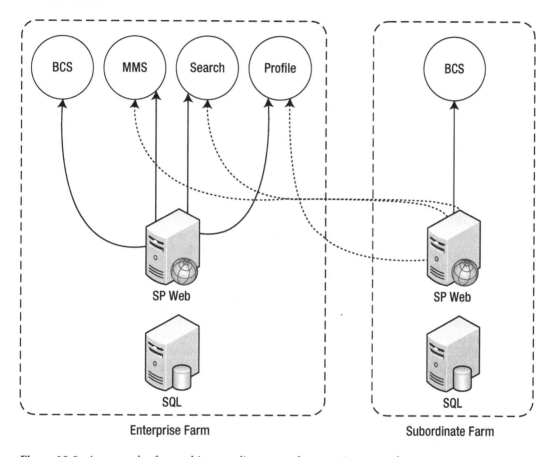

Figure 10-9. *An example of an architecture diagram to share services across farms*

The following lists the default SharePoint 2013 service applications available to publish for remote farms. For those applicable services, I have made a note where they are best to share with farms on a local LAN rather than geographically distributed farms over a WAN.

- Access Service

- Access Services 2010

- App Management Service

- Business Data Connectivity Service – Microsoft recommends considering the access to the underlying data source in the BCS models, and then use this to determine whether a farm's availability access across the WAN will have a negative impact on performance.

- Excel Calculation Service

- Lotus Notes Connector

- Managed Metadata Service

- PerformancePoint Service

- Search Service

- Secure Store Service – Microsoft recommends only sharing this service within the same data center or LAN, as sharing the service across a WAN has a negative impact on the service.

- SharePoint Machine Translation Service

- User Profile Service – Microsoft recommends only sharing this service within the same data center or LAN, as this service utilizes direct database access rather than the service application proxy in order to optimize performance.

- Visio Graphics Service

- Work Management Service

Sharing these services can help you to establish a centralized and consistent service for those enterprise applications where consistency adds value. For example, you help optimize your information management policy as you maintain a consistent enterprise taxonomy. With an enterprise taxonomy, your entire organization categorizes their content and information processes using a common controlled vocabulary. I return to discuss the enterprise taxonomy and your information architecture in more detail in Chapter 15.

As you plan a subordinate farm, you also need to decide where to host the databases. SharePoint does not require a one-to-one relationship with a SQL Server database server. Instead, you can host databases from several SharePoint farms on a single database server or a database cluster. Alternatively, you can also spread the databases of a single farm across multiple database servers. The choice you make for the new subordinate farm you are planning depends on the available resources on the database server and whether it can handle the load of the additional farm. Other factors in your decision include whether the database cluster is in the same data center and whether you want a complete segregation between your farms.

Subordinate farms can help you scale out your service, allowing you to improve system performance by segregating and running different applications in parallel. You can also improve performance when you deploy a subordinate farm to a remote region with poor network connectivity back to the enterprise farm. Whatever your reasons are, you need to define the service level of the new farm in the same fashion as you have for any other farm. You can then include this farm's scope in your service description, as I discussed in Chapter 2.

I mentioned earlier that the primary factor why I might want to avoid multiple production farms is the complexity they add to operations. However, you can plan for this and mitigate the complexity. I approach this by considering how consistent I can make the farms, and especially how consistent I can keep the SharePoint version and any add-ons that I deploy in the organization. The following questions will help you consider how consistent the farms will be.

- Do you need to keep the patch levels synchronized with the enterprise farm?

- Are there custom or other third-party components you want to keep consistent across the farms?

- Are the other operational tools, such as any backup or administrative software, consistent across the farms?

- Can you configure the farms with the same configuration settings?

- Can you build the farms using the same server image or virtual server template?

Generally, you will want to keep the farms as consistent as you can. By consistent, I am referring to consistent patches and service packs, consistent components, and consistent configurations. The more your farms are alike, the less you risk operational issues from developing in the future. For example, when the patch levels are the same and each farm has the same add-ons installed, you can migrate sites from one farm to another with more ease and compatibility. When the configuration settings are similar, administrators can switch between administering environments more smoothly and they will be less likely to introduce an error due to differing configuration settings. Finally, the more alike the environments are, the more you can script and automate the operational tasks. In the long run, consistency reduces operational costs and overhead.

Consultant Comrade

Planning to accommodate future growth is one roadblock I often face with clients on an engagement to plan a new SharePoint deployment. This type of roadblock can stall progress, and this can be especially true when it comes to accepting an infrastructure architecture plan that I will move forward with deploying. Clients might be nervous about painting themselves into a corner, and the nervousness might come from a fear of the unknown of what the actual adoption and load will be like.

This nervousness seems to almost paralyze some with a worry that they might limit the infrastructure in the farm and they cannot handle the load. Alternatively, they may worry about whether they are limiting their options in the future, such as if the requirements change. As far as I have been able to tell, this type of worry that stalls commitment to moving forward with a plan typically stems from a lack of knowledge about SharePoint and the implications of any decisions. The product might feel like a black box to them, and the unknown can cause anxiety.

The best way that I have found to work through this issue involves holding a SharePoint architecture overview session. I usually make this a general overview of the main components in SharePoint and how they come together. Typically for me, this session lasts about 45 minutes or more, depending on how many questions that they may have and how large the group is. I have a basic PowerPoint slide deck that I use to walk through the following topics during the architecture overview session:

- A high-level product overview and how to set an initial scope (see Chapter 2)

- An overview of each of the core capability areas (see Chapter 3)

- The typical roles and responsibilities involved in the service (see Chapter 4)

- An overview of the types of performance metrics and reporting available (see Chapter 6)

- The concept of a roadmap to break down deployments into small phases (see Chapter 7)

- An overview of the infrastructure components in a SharePoint farm (see this chapter)

- An overview on how to allocate services to servers

- A discussion on how to install and join new servers to a farm

With the understanding from this SharePoint architecture overview session, clients usually feel more at ease. By the end of the session, they should have a sense about the level of flexibility that SharePoint offers so that they can make adjustments in the future as their needs change. They should also have an idea about how SharePoint works and what are the main components involved in a SharePoint farm. This session also helps give their team a sense of the scale of SharePoint and all the capabilities involved. I find this helps with expectation management, as it tables all these issues during this session rather than having team members run with private worries that affect their decisions or their commitment to scope.

My ideal engagement starts with a meeting where the entire team comes together to kick-off the project. During this meeting, I like to present the scope and success criteria to ensure the entire team shares a common vision for what I am there to do and what I am saving for later. I then like to collect a list of risks from the team members and other stakeholders, and I can use this to start a risk registry right away. From there, I move into a SharePoint architecture overview session to provide the entire team with a good understanding of what SharePoint is, its capabilities, and how they can build a roadmap to grow it over time as it evolves.

As a consultant, you can build yourself a PowerPoint slide deck and schedule this type of session to help set your client's expectations early in your next engagement. I bet you will find, as I have found, that this helps get everyone on the same page and it removes some of the mystery about SharePoint that can cause anxiety for team members. You might build on to this session as well by deploying a pilot – another expectation management tool that is a favorite of mine on almost any project. You could even provide team members with a quick reference guide similar to what I discussed in Chapter 5, and they can use this to explore the pilot environment on their own.

The combination of these techniques can help set your client's expectations early. And the closer the expectations of the team members and other stakeholders align with your expectations, the greater the likelihood is that your project can be successful.

Inside Story: Notes from the Field

A few years ago, I engaged with a major construction company to help them build a vision and strategy for where they wanted to take SharePoint. They rank as one of my favorite clients for several reasons, starting with how great they are to work with through to their passion for technology. They have technology at the forefront of their operations, delivering business value, anticipating new opportunities, and aligning it with how their users need technology to support their jobs. What I love the most about them is how the business drives technology, and so they always align technology decisions with business value.

They also did a great job growing their SharePoint service to provide functionality to the business. Their challenge in deciding where to grow and extend SharePoint arises from the diversity of their business. They range from major industrial construction projects such as arenas and oil refineries to residential construction projects such as houses. On the surface, it may not seem as if technology would play a large role beyond managing blueprint files and tracking tasks, but it does, and their technology decisions largely focus on helping them achieve competitive advantages.

I, of course, do not want to reveal details about their competitive advantage, but I do want to tell the story about how I helped them progressively expand and grow their SharePoint service to provide additional capabilities that could work to their advantage. For starters, I had to stabilize the platform – they were a couple service packs behind, due mostly to some of the customizations they made that broke when they tested applying the patches. They were using SharePoint as a large document repository and document collaboration workspace, and they customized many aspects of SharePoint to address custom security requirements or to implement custom document control processes.

My next order of business was to get different development groups communicating with each other, sharing ideas and best practices. I could not have one group developing components that would prevent operations from patching or upgrading the farm or that would interrupt the performance levels for other groups. Some of their developers suggested that we segregate the farms to make their job easier, but I resisted because I knew through experience that this would only provide short-term gains at the expense of long-term sustainability and maintenance. Instead, I worked on developer processes and involving architecture reviews of custom applications early in their design and development stages.

■ **Note**　I return to discuss development and testing processes in more depth throughout Part IV of this book. You will find lots of advice in those chapters to address and govern team development in ways that will help maintain your farm's overall stability and sustainability.

With a stable platform and several groups working on different yet compatible custom applications, they were trending well toward growing and expanding the service beyond document management and collaboration. One of the projects was to replace the intranet by deploying the web content management (WCM) capability within SharePoint. The business driver for this initiative was to take advantage of modern web technologies to enhance the communication experience, while also aligning the intranet and document collaboration on a common platform. This allowed for rolling up content across the intranet and it simplified the mobile browsing experience.

Mobile was the next area of expansion. They already had a mobile experience, but they were working on expanding it to expose additional functionality beyond accessing content, such as interacting with a workflow to support business processes on different job sites. This required infrastructure to provide external access and handle the extra load from the mobile requests. It also required resources to process things such as InfoPath forms and workflow logic. They had to plan for this growth, both for the budget and for the operational capacity to physically do the work.

From there, they also had a work stream focusing on SharePoint MySites. They wanted to expand into this area, not based on some social computing platitude, but based on actual business requirements to provide everyone with a personal portal. The business needed a single gateway for managing business processes such as vacation requests and training bookings, and the SharePoint MySite capability provided the base portal functionality that they could use to develop and host the rest of the application.

I like this construction company example of how they grew their SharePoint service because it illustrates a steady progression of growing and expanding a SharePoint service into many areas. However, what I like the most is that a business need or opportunity drove every decision to grow the service. They did not simply enable capabilities just to make a popular feature available; they planned their growth based on business drivers. The operations team started with a basic SharePoint deployment consisting of a small farm that hosted collaboration sites. They did not need to over-architect that farm to plan for anything and everything; instead, they continuously added on and expanded that farm as additional needs arose.

GUEST Q&A: MICHAL PISAREK, DYNAMIC OWL

As I discussed governance with Michal Pisarek, an experienced SharePoint consultant and business analyst, he stressed how important it is to consider the outcomes you want to achieve with SharePoint and relate them to underlying business issues and opportunities. He cautions against letting generic and abstract SharePoint platitudes such as "improved collaboration," "increased find-ability," and "employee engagement" substitute for real business outcomes or specific and measurable business value.

Michal described governance as a means to help you get to where you want to go. He explained that the word *governance* comes from the Latin word for "to steer" – something for him that emphasizes how important it is to know where you want to go. He mentioned that if you do not know where you are going, then you may not feel lost because you do not have a direction; but you also run the risk of having every direction feeling like the right way, and this can leave you feeling lost, baffled, or running aimless.

He boiled down SharePoint governance to four simple things: the what (what are we trying to achieve by implementing SharePoint?), the why (why are we tackling these issues or opportunities and not others?), the how (how are we going to do this?), and the who (who will do what?). For him, focusing on these simple things will help you understand the business value that drives where you want to go, and from there, governance can help you steer to stay on course.

His advice is to "focus first on defining what you want to achieve with the platform" rather than getting caught up with chasing features or diving headfirst into implementation. For him, when you know where you are going and what outcomes you want to achieve, then "everything else with SharePoint will be a lot easier."

Michal Pisarek is the founder and a principal consultant with Dynamic Owl Consulting, a SharePoint consulting firm based in Vancouver, Canada. In his role, Michal engages with clients to help them drive SharePoint projects while maintaining a focus on business value. To learn more about Michal, please see his company website: www.dynamicowl.com

Wrapping Up

In this chapter, I discussed how to plan for growing your SharePoint service, including considerations to scale for availability, general infrastructure components, and the server roles in a SharePoint farm. I looked at how you can evolve and grow your SharePoint service over time as the usage pattern changes, and how this eliminates the need to feel constrained or to over-architect your farm upfront.

Enhancement requests can involve more than growing your existing SharePoint service, as some might include deploying service and feature packs or even upgrading to a newer version. In the next chapter, I discuss how to plan and prepare for upgrades and patches. I pay extra attention to techniques to take advantage of structures within SharePoint that you can use to lower your risk against interfering with cumulative updates, service packs, or version upgrades.

CHAPTER 11

Preparing for SharePoint Upgrades and Patches

All's well that ends well.

—William Shakespeare

In this chapter, I provide guidance on how to build policies and standards that maintain the supportability of the farm and maximize its compatibility with upgrade processes. I offer considerations for designing solutions in a manner that takes advantage of structures within SharePoint, and implementation strategies that offer the lowest risk against interfering with cumulative updates, service packs, or version upgrades. I also introduce approaches for rollback planning.

After reading this chapter, you will know how to:

- Address any anxiety or fear of painting yourself into a corner
- Maintain product supportability
- Plan for cumulative updates and service packs
- Build a rollback plan
- Plan for major product upgrades

Inevitability of Patches and Upgrades

Whether it is sooner or later, eventually most SharePoint environments will face patches and upgrades. At the very least, yours should be facing patches and service packs – updates for Windows Server, updates for SQL Server, as well as updates for SharePoint. Microsoft regularly releases updates to address issues such as bugs, defects, or security vulnerabilities, and by applying these regularly you will help to ensure that your environment runs with the latest codebase, making it the most compatible with any future upgrade path.

The only time when this is not inevitable might be because the environment is so fragile that patching or upgrading it will cause a toppling of dominos where all the shortcuts or hacks from the past unleash their wrath. It is fine for me to say that in a perfect world none of us will need to face these issues or deal with these constraints. However, I know it is an imperfect world and sometimes you will need to take shortcuts or hack a solution together to get things working, even if it comes back to haunt you later. I have done it, my peers have done it, and perhaps you can think of a time when you took a shortcut rather than following some best practice.

I like to relate this type of scenario to the types of bank accounts available. The bank account might be a high-interest savings account, where the account holder deposits money and remains disciplined with their spending. The bank then pays monthly interest to the account and rewards the account holder for their savings. The account holder's risk is low and they do not have to feel the pain of over spending, because they follow a disciplined approach to savings. Another account holder might open an overdraft account to take advantage of some of the spending that they can do today. This might offer them some short-term benefits, and those benefits might outweigh the risks and interest expenses, but it will cost them more than the savings account. SharePoint environments that resemble the overdraft account are not necessarily bad, but eventually you might want to transition it to resemble the more disciplined and stable savings account.

Back in Chapter 6, I shared some of the ways that you can measure and assess your SharePoint environments to identify where any limiting shortcuts exist. I also talked about how you can then build a plan to mitigate these shortcuts and improve the stability and sustainability of your SharePoint service. If you do find yourself in the type of situation where your environment feels too fragile to apply any patches or upgrades, then you might want to look at where you can add stability, as Figure 11-1 illustrates with some examples. Whatever condition your SharePoint service is in, and whatever trade-offs you had to make with some short-term hacks that you needed at the time, the good news is that you can make improvements. Every little bit that you do will help, and eventually you will have built enough momentum that your environment is stable and healthy.

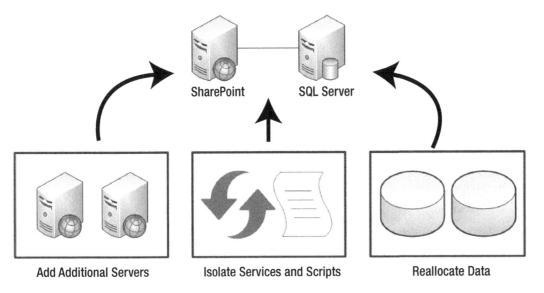

Figure 11-1. *Examples of adding stability to a fragile SharePoint environment*

■ **Note**   Please review some of the strategies in Chapter 6 that you can use to assess your SharePoint environment and build a plan to address any issues that affect your ability to apply patches or to upgrade. Identifying the issues and then building a plan to address them will put you back on the right track.

There are many reasons you will probably want to patch your SharePoint environments regularly. They relate in some way to a general desire to keep your SharePoint environments healthy. A regular patching process can contribute to a healthy SharePoint service in several ways. The following lists a few of the primary motives for me to regularly apply the latest patches and service packs to any SharePoint environment that I am managing:

- Correct any known security vulnerabilities

- Correct any other known defects in the product's codebase

- Apply any performance improvements Microsoft identifies

- Maintain a current version

Maintaining a current version is important for several reasons. First, if you encounter an issue and have to escalate to open a support ticket with Microsoft, you will save troubleshooting steps and money by ensuring your issue is not one they have already released a patch to resolve. Second, Microsoft typically releases patches and service packs with features to prepare for an eventual upgrade as the product team moves closer in their release cycle to the next version of SharePoint. Therefore, being current will ease some of the tasks you will need to perform during your upgrade process, and this will help to reduce your upgrade risk. Finally, the product team will typically test the upgrade process the most frequently and the most thoroughly with the most recent fully patched version. This too will help to reduce your upgrade risk.

■ **Note** In Chapter 10, I mentioned how you can identify your patch level on the Manage Patch Status page. You can access this page by clicking the "Check product and patch installation status" link under the "Upgrade and Migration" section on the SharePoint Central Administration homepage.

My point is that you ideally already want to apply the latest patches, and in all likelihood, you will eventually want to upgrade to a newer SharePoint version. And as I show throughout this chapter, the more current you maintain your SharePoint environment, the healthier you will keep it. I find this is because the more current an environment is with patches, the more compatible it also is with applying the latest patches. I also find the more current a SharePoint farm is with the latest patches, then the more compatible it is for the upgrade process to the next major version as well.

Throughout this chapter, I come back to this idea of avoiding things that will cause you grief with patching and upgrades. In short, an environment with only a default install and no customizations will be the most streamlined to patch and upgrade. However, sticking with a generic install also limits the amount of value you will garner from the product and it will limit your users' overall experience using your SharePoint service. Even still, it can be tempting for an operations group to force these limiting experiences to optimize how well they can patch and upgrade in the future. In later sections, I share some ways to balance the desire for a customized user experience with the ease to patch and upgrade an environment.

Another reason I see people who want to avoid venturing too far from a default SharePoint install relates to anxieties that they will inadvertently limit themselves or cause excessive rework in the future. I think this stems from stories of grief someone experienced that they relate back to making what they consider was a bad decision. People then seem to perpetuate these anxieties in blog posts, user group meetings, and conference sessions. It is good to try to stay forward-compatible, but do not let that paralyze you from moving forward with decisions today. In the next section, I look at this anxiety I have seen where people avoid committing to decisions today out of fear of painting themselves into a corner in the future.

Painting Away from the Corner

I have seen people corner themselves with decisions that limit future options or cause future headaches, and these decisions usually revolve around customizations and custom development. The SharePoint infrastructure itself is flexible and can adapt to changing needs. Microsoft architected SharePoint in this way on purpose because needs change as more information and new opportunities arise. I discussed this in more detail back in Chapter 10, but I wanted to stress it again here because the flexibility of the infrastructure in a SharePoint farm can liberate you from the worry about constraining yourself.

The product team also designed a means to customize the SharePoint experience and to develop applications on top of the platform. They designed the product's extensibility in ways that minimize how limiting or constraining those custom changes will be for you in the future. I return to look at how you can take advantage of these design decisions in Part IV of this book, where I provide guidance on how to make optimum design decisions for your own custom development.

Having said that, even if you do find yourself in a situation where your team has hacked system files and they somehow managed to limit the infrastructure design, not all is lost. SharePoint can be very forgiving. You just might require a few extra steps on your way to patching or upgrading your environment. Even in the worse case scenario, you can always migrate the content to a fresh environment. The market even has a few tools to help automate and ease the burden of a mass migration. No matter how constrained you feel, you can always move forward with a content migration.

If you do feel this anxiety that you might be painting yourself into a corner, let me reassure you that the platform will adapt and allow you to make changes in the future. You will not lock yourself into any decisions, but for some choices, you may face some pain with having to rework any decisions that prove to be limiting. I will try to help you avoid this scenario with the guidance in this book. However, even if you do later discover that the assumptions you have today took you in the wrong direction, please take comfort in knowing that you can always change your mind.

My formula to avoid painting yourself into a corner is not magical, and it is not even groundbreaking. In fact, I have already shared it with you. The best approach I have found to avoid limiting or constraining decisions is to take smaller steps. Figure 11-2 provides an illustration of taking a gradual approach to a solution through many smaller steps. I find that even when I make an assumption that I later discover is taking me in the wrong direction, the investment in that direction is small because the step is small. As such, backing out or correcting the course is also small and manageable.

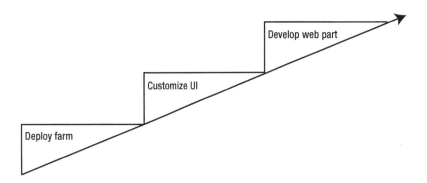

Figure 11-2. *Take smaller and more frequent steps to gradually deploy a solution*

I do not have an algorithm to calculate and factor every possible outcome. You cannot always forecast the second and third-round effects of an action. Instead, your experience and knowledge about the world helps you to make assumptions, and you can use those to make decisions. You can make a hypothesis and you can then test your hypothesis. Economists have the same challenge, and since there are so many factors they cannot predict, this may be why economies do not always perform as an economist intended.

Unlike world economists though, you do have a lot of control over your environment and how quickly you can respond to changes. When you apply small, frequent adjustments and then reassess, you mitigate your risk of later finding yourself painted into a corner. Therefore, you can increase your chances to work toward a successful outcome with a SharePoint deployment, despite the fact that you cannot possibly tell the future and the domino effect of any decision you make (assuming that like me, you do not possess adequate psychic abilities).

In summary, I hope to assure you that I have never faced a situation with SharePoint where I felt painted into a corner. The product is just too flexible. Even with any perceived pain of rework or content migrations, one never seems to be far from a healthy, supportable state. Once you get yourself into a healthy supportable state, then your next task is to maintain supportability.

Maintaining Product Supportability

You can probably find several best practices from a variety of site references that list many "thou shall" and "thou shall not" rules you can follow. This can be a great source of insight to help get you started by drawing on the collective intelligence of the community. Some topics may be obvious (or obvious to you), while other topics may help steer you away from potentially causing a support nightmare for yourself down the road.

The good news is that SharePoint will usually try to guide your environment in a supportable direction. You will have to make a special effort to put yourself in an unsupported state, or you will have to neglect your environment altogether. The product team has added validation to different configuration steps in an attempt to validate the configuration settings you choose. Sometimes you can circumvent this validation by applying settings through PowerShell or through the SharePoint API, so you should take extra care when you make configuration changes in this way.

Even when you make changes programmatically, SharePoint will still maintain data consistency and integrity, though it will not always validate the settings you chose. However, if you were to make a change directly in the database to data there, then you may cause a data inconsistency. Do not do this. Microsoft did not design SharePoint and its underlying databases for you to update the database directly. Instead, they provided you with the user interface, PowerShell, and the SharePoint API to use to make any and all changes.

For people who have a database background, this may feel as if it is strange advice. I remember when I first started working with SharePoint, and I wondered why people warned against working with the databases directly. After all, I felt quite comfortable with my SQL Server expertise, and perhaps this advice was for those who were not as familiar with working with databases as I. This is not the case; the advice is for everyone, including me and anyone else with database skills.

There are a couple of key reasons for the advice against modifying SharePoint databases directly. First, the product team used discipline in the order that their code accesses tables in a database to avoid any deadlocks. If someone directly accesses a table, they may cause a deadlock. Another reason is that SharePoint enforces the referential integrity through the API rather than have SQL Server enforce it at the database level. This is necessary because SharePoint spans databases and potentially database servers with related data for a site, such as a content database and the configuration database. SharePoint abstracts away the database implementation details through its API, so whether or not you have the database administration skills, you should make all data changes through SharePoint and not through SQL Server.

■ **Important**   You should never make any data changes directly to the database. You should only apply configuration setting through the user interface, PowerShell, or the SharePoint API.

SharePoint provides an abstraction over a database and an ASP.NET application. Figure 11-3 provides a logical architecture to illustrate how SharePoint conceptually layers on top of SQL Server and ASP.NET. SharePoint adds its own functionality and logic on top of what a developer's previous experience and understanding is in a typical data-driven web application. The platform simply provides a lot of functionality as a product. Yet, it also provides a hook for developers to customize and tailor the platform to fulfill a business opportunity or to provide some enhanced user experience. Since the developer is not starting from scratch, they may feel disoriented with how to align their development approach with SharePoint.

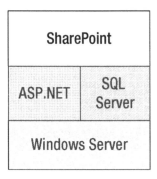

Figure 11-3. A logical architecture conceptually illustrating SharePoint layered on top of SQL Server and ASP.NET

■ **Note**   Please see Chapter 14 for a deeper discussion on how to approach custom development in a sustainable and supportable manner on top of the SharePoint platform.

One significant way to maintain supportability is to avoid changing any of the SharePoint system files. This typically relates to development and other customization tasks, and I cover this advice in more depth throughout Part IV of this book when I address those topics. However, I wanted to mention it explicitly here because you might not be a developer, and therefore you might not read that part of the book. I qualify this advice against modifying files in Chapter 14, but for now I just want to point it out in a more general sense. I sometimes come across SharePoint administrators who wanted to change some element in their farm, and through their investigations, they found a file somewhere in the SharePoint root directory (also known as the "15" directory) that they directly edited the file with Notepad. For example, perhaps they directly edited a site definition file, a feature file, or some other application file. You should avoid making changes on your SharePoint servers in this way to help maintain a healthy and supportable environment.

Another way you can maintain product supportability is by staying current with cumulative updates, security updates, and service packs that Microsoft releases. In my experience, Microsoft Premier Support Services frequently suggests applying the latest updates whenever you escalate a support ticket to them. I have found that this is especially true for any service packs that Microsoft released a year or more ago. Although a support resource wants to help you, they also want to avoid troubleshooting an issue that Microsoft has already addressed in a service pack. Therefore, by maintaining the latest patches, you are helping to maintain the overall supportability of your environment. In the next section, I discuss how you can plan for these updates.

Planning for Cumulative Updates and Service Packs

I still remember the first time that I applied a service pack to a SharePoint farm in production. It was a while back with a service pack for SharePoint 2003. Now, I have always been the type of technology geek where I enjoy applying patches and keeping my software up to date. In fact, I sometimes feel a little disappointed if no updates are available when I check for updates on Windows Update. With Microsoft releasing a service pack, and me being both inexperienced as a server administrator and yet compulsive with applying updates, I clicked to apply it without any thought for testing or anything else.

This service pack applied itself and then maybe it rebooted the server. All appeared successful on the update front and I promptly forgot about it. I forgot about it until support tickets started to come in with mysterious symptoms. At this time, I was in a meeting, and because I also did not tell any of my teammates about me applying the service pack, they were scratching their heads wondering what could cause the weird behavior that some users were reporting. Once they figured out that I had installed the service pack, they continued troubleshooting. First, they discovered that they were unable to uninstall the service pack to undo the issue. Then, they tried to address the symptoms without success. Finally, I discovered that Microsoft designed this and future SharePoint service packs to require an administrator to run the SharePoint Products and Technologies Configuration Wizard to finalize the service pack installation.

My first service pack experience is an example of what not to do. It represents a potentially worse case scenario, particularly because I had not tested the service pack and I had no rollback plan. I come back to look at how to build a rollback plan in the next section, but for now, this is basically a preplanned procedure you can take to back out of any change. By not testing, I clearly had no plan and I was blindly making changes to an enterprise application. My unplanned changes lead to support issues, stress for my users and for my support team, and to my own personal embarrassment (embarrassment I get to relive here, too).

The good news is that since then I have applied many service packs in a variety of environments across all the SharePoint versions. I never had another problem with a service pack, in part because my experience taught me how important planning and testing are for any change, especially with service packs. Perhaps the experience left me traumatized, which might be why I tend to be extra vigilant with planning and testing service packs. For the most part, my process is routine for applying a service pack or cumulative update to a SharePoint farm. Typically, I go through the following list:

- Apply the latest service pack for SharePoint

- Apply the latest service pack for any additional products installed, such as Project Server

- Apply the latest service pack for each language pack installed in your farm

- Repeat all the preceding steps on each SharePoint server in the farm before proceeding

- Run the SharePoint Products and Technologies Configuration Wizard on each server in the farm, one server at a time

---

■ **Note** You can learn more about SharePoint language packs and how to install a language pack in this Microsoft TechNet article: http://technet.microsoft.com/cc262108

The reason I follow this approach boils down to how the product team designs updates. They want to release patches that can update a multi-server farm without requiring that the SharePoint administrator take the entire farm offline. This can create challenges because an administrator will not be updating every server simultaneously, so some changes can break functionality or cause inconsistencies until the administrator has updated all the servers in the farm. For example, a service pack can include schema changes to the database. If the service pack applies those changes right away, then it will break functionality on other servers that do not yet have the service pack installed. The result would require an administrator to take the entire farm offline before installing a service pack.

To work around this challenge and maintain consistency in a farm during service pack installations, the team designed the service pack installation as a two-part process. First, you install the bits on all the servers in the farm, and then you run the wizard to finalize the installation and apply any changes to the databases. Figure 11-4 illustrates the staged approach to install and apply a service pack in a SharePoint farm. This allows you to install the binary files from the service pack to stage the changes on each of the servers in the farm before committing the updates and applying any changes to the database.

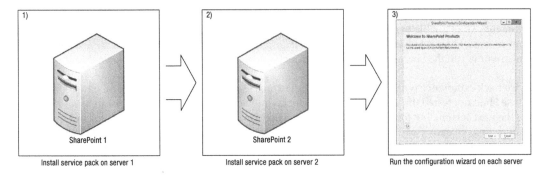

Figure 11-4. *A staged approach to install and apply a service pack in a SharePoint farm*

Within SharePoint Central Administration, you can verify the patch level applied to each component on each server within the farm. You can find this information on the Manage Patch Status page by clicking the "Check product and patch installation status" link under the "Upgrade and Migration" section on the SharePoint Central Administration homepage. Figure 11-5 provides a screenshot of the Manage Patch Status page where you can see the patch version and install status for the different SharePoint components on the server. I first mentioned the Manage Patch Status page back in Chapter 10, but I find it is important to mention it again here as a tool you can use to validate the success of any patches or service packs that you install.

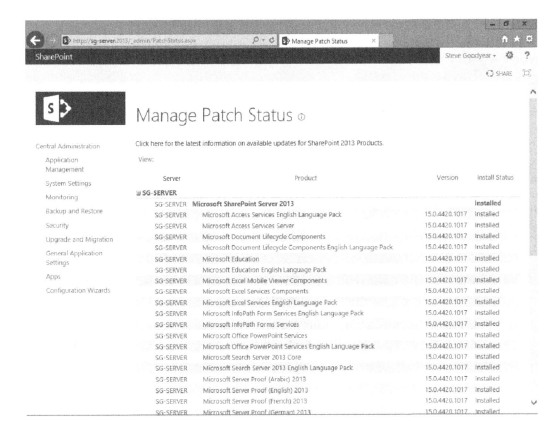

Figure 11-5. *The Manage Patch Status page*

If a patch fails to install correctly, the Manage Patch Status page will show you what components it failed to patch. You can also check the SharePoint log files to track down more details about what went wrong. I also typically check the Windows Event log to check if anything else occurred. Between these sources, I can often quickly identify the culprit behind why the patch is failing to install. Sometimes the failure can be a customization in the farm that interferes with the patch, but sometimes it can be as simple as having the patch time out during the installation. When I have a patch fail to install, I sometimes respond by restarting IIS or even running the configuration wizard to cycle all the processes, and then I attempt to install the patch again. Once in a while, I get lucky and correcting a failed installation turns out to be this simple, even though it is not very scientific and I should probably be investigating the issue deeper.

As much as you hope that every patch and service pack will install smoothly, you can sometimes run into unforeseen issues. Even with plenty of planning and testing, an update can sometimes fail during its installation. Whether caused by a timeout or some other unexpected incompatibility, an update causing a breaking change can sometimes catch you by surprise. You might have a vigorous change-management process that includes planning and testing, and every patch might have gone smoothly for you in the past. However, at some point you may face an issue and you need to back out of your changes. Having to rollback changes *should not* be routine; however, having a rollback plan *should* be routine. In the next section, I discuss how to build a rollback plan.

Building a Rollback Plan

Rollback plans are similar to an insurance policy: you only truly realize their value when something comes up and you need to utilize them, and you must put them in place *before* an incident occurs. You could go through every Microsoft "Patch Tuesday" and successfully apply updates without experiencing any issues or any need to rollback. Yet, when something does come up after you install an update and it causes a disaster in your production environment, you will be grateful for your rollback plan, if you have invested the time ahead of time to create one.

Figure 11-6 shows a flowchart example of a potential process you might use for applying updates to your SharePoint farm. Essentially, I would begin with a test environment that mirrors production and I would first apply the update there. With a test environment, I can test whether the patch is compatible with the customizations and custom components in the production farm before installing the update there. If the update appears compatible, I then would install it in production. If I discover an issue during any stage, I would rollback the update by following my rollback plan.

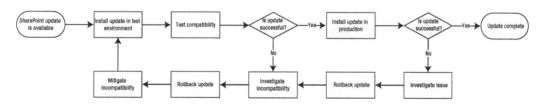

Figure 11-6. *A flowchart example of a potential process for applying updates to your SharePoint farm*

The first step in any rollback plan is to capture a database backup immediately *before* you make any changes. Patches can update or add binary files on the server, but they can also change the database by changing the configuration data stored or the actual schema of database tables. By capturing a database backup or a database snapshot before you apply the patch, you give yourself the option to rollback to the earlier state.

■ **Note**   You should also use PowerShell to backup any service applications that do not have a database. To learn more about backing up service applications, please see this TechNet article: http://technet.microsoft.com/ee428318

For the same reason, you should also capture the state of the servers. If you are using virtual servers, then you can take a snapshot of the servers. Server states change much less frequently during regular operations than databases change, so you have a larger window for capturing the server's state than you do for capturing a database snapshot. As such, my rollback plans generally start with capturing a current snapshot of all the servers in the farm. Then my next step is to take a snapshot of the farm's databases. At this point, I am ready to apply the patch, security update, or service pack to the farm.

If something does go wrong with applying an update, then I rollback to the pre-update state by restoring the snapshots or backups that I captured before attempting the update. I want to know that my rollback plan works before I get to this stage, because this is the point when I will need it the most. To ensure that my rollback plan works and it is effective, I test it in the test environment by running through any restores or any other step I have as part of my rollback plan. Testing and validating any rollback plan ahead of time will give you the confidence and assurances that you need in case something does go wrong.

You have probably noticed my emphasis on preparing ahead of time. You will want to design a rollback plan ahead of time so that you can simply follow it without having to think about what to do if something does go wrong. You want a rollback plan in place before you begin any patching, updates, or even major version upgrades because it gives you the option to back out of a change if an approach does not work out or if something unexpected happens. Having a rollback plan will also help to relieve stress and avoid a panic if things start to go wrong, because all you have to do is follow your rollback plan and back out of any disaster. You can back out and avert a code red situation and then head back to your test environment to troubleshoot without any pressure to restore service.

As good as they are, a rollback plan is only useful if you rollback right away, before people start to use the system again. Otherwise, you could cause data loss if you restore a database and overwrite any changes users have made since you captured the backup. Once you have applied a patch and allowed users to interact with their sites and data again, you have pretty much committed to the patch or update. If you discover an issue with the update a couple of days later, then you have to troubleshoot the issue rather than rollback. At that point, you could only use a rollback as a last resort, and probably in combination with efforts to identify what data users have changed that a database restore will overwrite.

ROLLING BACK IS ALWAYS AN OPTION

From time-to-time I find myself on a project were I fall into a dangerous routine of simply moving forward, no matter what. At those times, forward seems to translate into progress, and progress feels good. This is similar to how I handle traffic: I might take the long way where I can keep moving even if it takes a little longer just so I can feel like I am getting somewhere. It is an illusion, and I know it, but it still feels better when I am moving than when I am stuck in traffic.

One can easily slip into this state on a project. People want to feel successful, and when they feel like they are moving then they can feel the illusion of success. But halting and rolling back does not mean failure. In fact, you can avert a failure by suspending and taking a step back.

When a surgery is not going right, a doctor will stop and back out without hesitation. When an airplane is approaching a runway at too steep of a decent, the pilot will abort the approach and circle around again without any concern. IT projects are usually not life or death, and perhaps not having such an extreme consequence tricks me into thinking I should continue to push forward, even when all signs point to shutting down a project.

Rolling back is always an option. It can give you an opportunity to learn more details about a problem, and it can help you avoid making things worse. I try to have at least a vague sense about what my shutdown and rollback point will be before I engage in any project.

Planning and Preparing for Major Version Upgrades

In time, Microsoft will release a new version of SharePoint. I feel reasonably confident making this claim, because they have historically done so and they would be silly not to do so again. As great as SharePoint 2013 is, I feel they still have room to improve and fine-tune the product. I also feel there is more that they could add to the product – adding to areas such as expanding the social computing capabilities or adding to the compliance capabilities. Whatever it is, a new version is sure to come, and you can start planning for it now.

Every time I have installed a default SharePoint environment and then turned around to run the upgrade process to upgrade to the next version, it almost always works seamlessly. When I try that with a copy of a SharePoint environment in the wild, it often proves to be much less seamless. This is because once you start using a SharePoint environment, you probably start customizing it and adding data – all the things that might get in the way or slow down an upgrade. Of course, I do not want you to avoid using your SharePoint deployment, because then there would probably be no real point to deploy SharePoint in the first place if you did not use it, and probably less of a point to upgrading it then. Instead, I want to encourage you to do some things that can help make your upgrade process a little easier.

Now, one of the biggest challenges with planning for major version upgrades is that most of the time you do not know what is coming or when to expect it. In my experience, I have noticed that Microsoft seems to hold their cards close to their chest when it comes to future SharePoint versions. It seems to follow a cycle of going a while without hearing anything to hearing some rumors about a new version, and then all of a sudden it seems as if a new version is coming at you in the blink of an eye. As you take a look at the new version and try to get a grasp for what the team changed in that release, you realize that they depreciated some part of the API or they dramatically changed how some underlying structure works. Surprise! These things are difficult to plan for, but the good news is that Microsoft usually offers a migration path to help you address these changes.

Even with so much left as unknown about the next version, you can still plan for this and prepare yourself for the eventual upgrade. One strategy that will usually benefit you is to avoid drifting too far from the product team's guidance. Try to avoid situations that they recommend you avoid. This can be things such as avoiding any direct database access; instead, use the API they provided for you. Try to avoid editing system files; instead, use the feature infrastructure to add components or custom pages of your own. These are two prime examples of things that you can do to help yourself out later when it comes time to upgrade. If you make edits through the SharePoint API and you follow other supported practices, you can rest assured knowing that the SharePoint product team will be working hard to try to take care of you during your next upgrade.

As the team makes progress with their development on the next version, they will start to get a sense about what changes will be necessary and how this will affect current deployments. When these changes come up, Microsoft will begin to communicate recommendations on how to prepare for the next upgrade. Sometimes, these insights may come out informally, such as through team blog posts, and other times they may be a part of a service pack. Eventually, Microsoft will set up a TechNet resource center saturated with content meant to help you plan and prepare for your upgrade.

■ **Note**   Please see the SharePoint 2013 Upgrade Resource Center for more details about upgrade planning and troubleshooting: http://technet.microsoft.com/fp142375

As the product grows more mature and the product team settles in with some of their fundamental architectures, you can expect to see less dramatic architecture changes from version to version. The upgrade from SharePoint 2003 to 2007 was dramatic, as the team introduced major platform changes such as the feature and solution package infrastructure. The upgrade from 2007 to 2010 was also fairly dramatic, as the team made a significant shift from the shared service provider to service applications. I found the upgrade from 2010 to 2013 was less dramatic from an underlying platform architecture perspective. This maturity in turn helps with upgrade planning as well, because it provides you with confidence if you want to invest in development around particular structures without having to worry as much about introducing potential incompatibilities with upgrading to the next version.

You also have a few specific things that you can do to prepare for an upgrade. One of my personal favorites is to allocate your site collections across many content databases rather than storing them all in just a few databases. The database attach upgrade method has long been my preferred upgrade method, and smaller databases upgrade much quicker. You can also open multiple PowerShell windows and perform multiple database attach upgrades simultaneously on different SharePoint servers. Having a greater number of smaller content databases can help you improve the performance of the actual upgrade process and this can reduce how long it takes an upgrade to complete.

Smaller content databases also mean that you can focus your scope of things to upgrade more granularly to smaller groups of site collections. This benefits you in two ways. The first is that you have a smaller range of content to focus on as you troubleshoot the upgrade issue. The second is that the upgrade issue only affects a smaller scope of sites, as you can continue with the upgrade for those other content databases with unaffected sites. Having a greater number of smaller content databases can help you keep an upgrade moving forward and allow you to upgrade the majority of an environment even when a couple of sites have issues you will need to address before you can upgrade them.

■ **Tip** I like maintaining smaller content databases for many reasons, including easing the overall effort and complexity during an upgrade process. I also like smaller content databases because they are quicker to restore and reinstate availability in the event of a disaster. For archival or repository types of sites, I usually design for much larger content databases, possibly as large as several hundred gigabytes in size. For collaboration sites, I generally prefer to stay in the range of 25–50GB.

You can plan for your eventual upgrade today by reallocating your site collections across many content databases. The product team has streamlined the process of moving a site collection to a new content database by implementing a PowerShell command specific to this purpose. After you create one or more additional content databases for a web application, you can then run the following PowerShell command to move the data for the site collection to use the new content database.

```
Move-SPSite <Site Collection URL> -DestinationDatabase <Content Database>
```

With your site collections distributed across multiple content databases, you are getting yourself in good shape for your next SharePoint upgrade. The next database-related task is to ensure your content databases do not have any corruptions in them. A corruption can occur after a failed operation such as a failed site restore. The corruption then results from the operation inserting some content into the database before failing, but where the operation fails before it commits the content to a particular site. You can execute the following STSADM command in the Windows Command Prompt to test whether a content database contains any corruptions, and if so, to return a list of them.

```
STSADM -o DatabaseRepair -Url <Web Application URL> -DatabaseName <Database Name>
```

If the preceding command returns a list of orphaned objects or database corruptions, you can opt to delete those corruptions and clean your database. An orphaned object is not accessible through any SharePoint interface, because it does not belong to a SharePoint site – hence why the utility considers it orphaned. Unfortunately, this means you cannot navigate to a site to see the actual content. Because the orphaned content is usually the result of a failed operation, such as a failed site restore, then you are likely only deleting a corrupted copy of the data. You can delete the orphaned objects and remove the database corruption by executing the following STSADM command.

```
STSADM -o DatabaseRepair -Url <URL> -DatabaseName <Database Name> -DeleteCorruption
```

Maintaining your content databases in a corruption-free state might just sound like good database administration to you, and I would agree. To clarify, these are SharePoint application corruptions, not SQL Server corruptions. Nonetheless, they are corruptions of the underlying data, and so it is a good practice for you to perform these tasks ahead of an upgrade. You should verify all your content databases on occasion and then repair any corruptions as needed.

Another task you should complete in preparation of a new upgrade is to finish any previous upgrade. If you still have sites in different states or running in different compatibility modes, you will add complications to your next upgrade process if you attempt to upgrade while the sites are in these modes. To check whether you do have sites in an unfinished state from a previous upgrade, you can run a script to query the upgrade status of each site collection and its sites. You can run the following PowerShell command to display a list of site collections still running in an old experience mode.

```
Get-SPSite | ForEach-Object{$_.GetVisualReport()}
```

Once you have a list of sites, you might build a plan for resolving any compatibility issues with each site. Alternatively, you might want to run a batch process to upgrade the experience of all sites. You can run the following PowerShell command to upgrade all those sites to the current experience.

```
Get-SPSite | ForEach-Object{$_.VisualUpgradeWebs()}
```

With your sites upgraded to the current experience and your databases free from any corruptions, you can rest assured knowing you are maintaining a healthy environment that will avoid many upgrade issues. Some other maintenance tasks you might consider include removing content or components that you do not need. The following lists a few particular areas you can consider as you are cleaning up your SharePoint environment.

- Delete unused or underused site collections or sites

- Remove unused or underused web parts and custom components

- Remove unused or underused features and site templates

- Delete unnecessary document versions

Cleaning up and removing unnecessary things from your SharePoint environment will help ease the actual upgrade process. With a healthy environment, you can next move to plan for the underlying infrastructure requirements for the next version. Occasionally, Microsoft has released a version of SharePoint with new hardware requirements, such as an increased amount of required memory. If this is the case for your upgrade, then you can plan and prepare for the upgrade by upgrading the underlying hardware ahead of time in preparation for the SharePoint upgrade.

In summary, you can take several activities to prepare your SharePoint environment for an upgrade, whether or not you have all the details about the next version. All the pre-work you take to clean up your environment will improve the health of your existing deployment and it will help to reduce the number of issues you will face later during the actual upgrade. Figure 11-7 illustrates an example of an approach to upgrading to a newer version based on some of these activities.

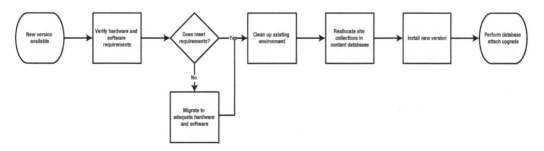

Figure 11-7. *An example flowchart illustration for approaching a SharePoint upgrade*

You can do as much upgrade planning and analysis as you feel comfortable with for your next upgrade. If you follow the maintenance tasks I shared in this section, you can keep your environment healthy and prepared for the eventual upgrade. The planning tasks will help give you a sense for what activities the upgrade will entail and roughly how much effort it will involve. I find there are some things that can come up during an actual upgrade process, and the only way to draw attention to them is in going through an actual upgrade. In the next section, I discuss the idea of performing a test upgrade first to identify and work out all these unexpected issues.

Performing Test Upgrades

Upgrades can be a lengthy process, and I find that I spend the majority of that time analyzing compatibility – compatibility with customizations and configurations. The actual operation of the upgrade itself tends to be quite straightforward. For this reason, I find one of the best approaches to analyze compatibility with a newer version is to run through a test upgrade and analyze the actual results. Actually, I cannot think of an example of when you would *not* want to bother going through and testing the upgrade process beforehand.

My upgrade preference is the database-attach method. I find it a useful approach for performing test upgrades as well, because it allows me to upgrade a content database in isolation and test how compatible it will be with the upgrade. Often, I can perform this isolated test using a single server rather than a mirror of the production environment. This provides me with insights into functional compatibilities between versions and it helps me to discover any functional issues that may interfere with the upgrade process.

Depending on the server I use though, this type of isolated upgrade test may not give me any insights into the overall performance I can expect during the production farm's upgrade or how long of a time window that upgrade will need. For that, I will need to test the upgrade using hardware that resembles the production servers that I will use during the actual upgrade. I always find that comparable hardware will give me the best indication about how long something will take and how the servers will perform during the operation. Therefore, if testing performance and duration are important to you, then you should test the upgrade on comparable servers. If testing functionality and compatibility are more important to you, then the type of servers you test on is less relevant.

I approach test upgrades by copying a backup of the content database, and then I restore it to a database server in a test environment. You can consider taking a database snapshot of these databases in the test environment before you start the upgrade, and this allows you to perform subsequent test upgrades with ease. This also enables you to analyze the SharePoint logs in isolation, which helps to ease the troubleshooting process because you have less activity for SharePoint to log in the test environment. Figure 11-8 illustrates the conceptual architecture of the production and upgrade test environments.

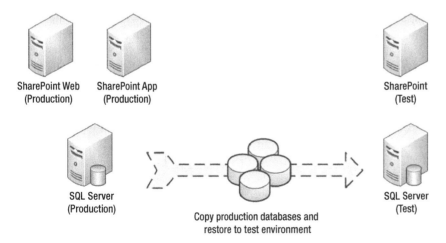

SharePoint Web (Production)   SharePoint App (Production)   SharePoint (Test)

SQL Server (Production)   Copy production databases and restore to test environment   SQL Server (Test)

Figure 11-8. *Copy databases from the production environment and restore them in a test environment to test the upgrade procedure*

Once you copy a database to your test environment, the first step is to test whether the components it depends on are compatible with the new farm. This lets you identify whether the web parts, solution packages, and any other customizations that the content database references are present in the new farm. You can run the following PowerShell command to test a content database against a web application in the new farm and confirm that you have all the custom components installed.

```
Test-SPContentDatabase -Name <Content Database> -WebApplication <Web Application URL>
```

If the test farm is compatible with the database and you do not need to install any missing components, then you are ready to attach the database and begin the upgrade. The database attach upgrade method is straightforward and it only requires one line of PowerShell where you mount the content database to a web application. You can run the following PowerShell command to mount a content database and perform a database-attach upgrade.

```
Mount-SPContentDatabase <Database Name> -DatabaseServer <Database Server> -WebApplication <Web Application>
```

After you have successfully mounted the content database to the new farm, you can navigate to its sites and confirm that they are running in compatibility mode and are rendering the site in the old SharePoint version's experience. You can then click the link to upgrade the individual site to begin using the current experience. Alternatively, you can use the PowerShell I mentioned in the previous section to perform a bulk site upgrade operation. Once you have the sites upgraded to the new SharePoint version's experience, then you can click through and visually verify the upgrade.

Working with a content database through a test upgrade will help you understand all the steps an upgrade process will require to successfully move to the next SharePoint version. As you review sites to assess their compatibility with the upgrade, you can also use this as a good chance to identify any unused content that you can delete. You can also use this review as a chance to identify coaching opportunities where you can help your users utilize their SharePoint sites in ways that are more effective. Of course, if you have thousands of sites, then this probably is not practical. In those cases, I generally focus my time on a percentage of the largest or the most used sites.

If you cannot physically review each site because of the site volume in your environment, then another option you might consider is to e-mail site administrators with a link to a copy of their site in the test environment. I frequently use this option, and to make it more efficient, I script the process as much as possible. You can use PowerShell to batch upgrade every site, and in the process, you can identify the site collection administrator's e-mail address. With this information, you might write a PowerShell script to set the site in a read-only state and then e-mail the administrator to invite them to review their upgraded site. In the e-mail, you might encourage them to let you know if they notice any issues. This way, someone can give the majority of your sites a visual review, but you can spread that burden out across many site administrators rather than attempting it yourself.

As you mount and upgrade your content databases, you can see that SharePoint maintains the database name. You can rename it at this point, but that might add complexity and lead to confusion about which previous database maps to which upgraded database. Maintaining consistent names can help you to stay organized, but sometimes those names are less desirable and you will want to rename them. Alternatively, you can plan your database naming convention ahead of time so that a database name will still fit well with the next version of SharePoint after you upgrade the database. In the next section, I share my typical database naming convention and how I avoid naming databases with a relation to a particular version.

Naming Your Databases for the Future

One of my pet peeves is naming conventions for SharePoint databases. I cannot believe how many SharePoint environments I come across where the person who set up the farm initially has named the databases with some reference to the SharePoint version number. I have seen database names from "SPS2003_Config" to "MOSS2007_Config" and "SP2010_Config". It is my pet peeve because I am fussy when it comes to naming conventions; I do not know why. I realize the person who chooses these names is just not thinking ahead to the occasion where they will want to upgrade this farm to the next version.

It is not horrible if you have a farm where someone has chosen names that will look silly after you upgrade to the next version. You will just have to plan to rename your databases at some point or live with having them look a little silly. Seriously though, having a database named "MOSS2007_WSS_Content" in a SharePoint 2010 or a SharePoint 2013 farm would look silly. Somewhere along the way, that type of naming convention became popular, at least with the clients I have visited, and so I wanted to use this space to make you aware of the effects and to steer you in a better direction while you are planning your upgrade.

The other database naming that I am not too fond of are those automatically generated databases with a GUID in their name. Again, these are not horrible, but they do not look pleasant, at least not to me. I think you can do better, and in the process, you can come up with a name that is human-readable and one that is also meaningful. The aesthetics of a good naming convention are valid in my books (or at least this book), but a clean database name is also easier to use whenever you write scripts for maintenance jobs or any other time you need to type it somewhere.

I hope at this point that I have succeeded in convincing you to adopt a good database naming convention. My naming convention involves utilizing consistent prefixes to the database name. This groups the databases in the Microsoft SQL Server Management Studio, which makes it easy to find databases I need to work with as well as to find related databases. Even more importantly than that though, consistent prefixes allow me to use wildcards in any of my database scripts to automatically perform any maintenance tasks on related databases or database groups.

For example, I prefix all my SharePoint databases with "SP" to identify them with SharePoint. Following that, I might add a farm identifier if I have multiple farms sharing a database cluster, such as including "ENT" to identify the enterprise farm. Next, I often add an environment identifier such as "PROD" or "TEST" to identify them with production or test environments, respectively. Finally, I add the service application name and database identifier. For content databases, I first add the "Content" identifier to specify it is a content database, and then append the name of the web application. Applying this convention, I might use "SP_PROD_Content_CentralAdmin" to name the resulting content database for the SharePoint Central Administration web application in a production farm.

Figure 11-9 provides a screenshot with an example of a SharePoint database naming convention that I use. In this example, I have omitted the farm and environment identifiers because I limited this SQL Server database instance to host only the one SharePoint farm. Therefore, I have used only "SP" as a simplified prefix to the databases. Otherwise, I have followed the remainder of the database naming conventions that I described here to group the content databases and the databases for service application types.

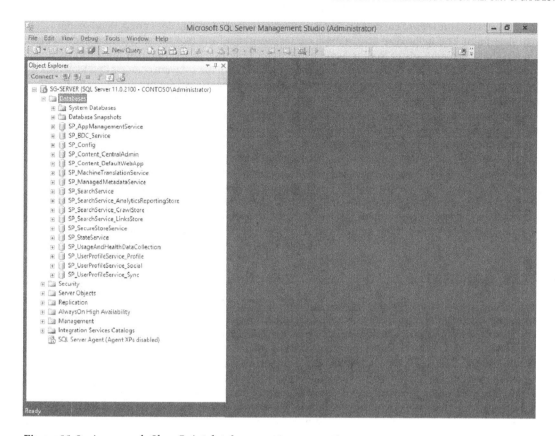

Figure 11-9. *An example SharePoint database naming convention*

One challenge you may face for maintaining a consistent database naming convention is that SharePoint does not always let you choose the database name before it provisions it. In particular, for some reason the team who developed the SharePoint Products and Technologies Configuration Wizard did not provide an input method in the wizard interface for you to specify the Central Administration content database's name. Whenever you provision a new farm with this wizard, they programmed the process so that SharePoint will choose a database name for you. If you want to specify a database name, you have to provision the farm using PowerShell. I find this unfortunate, because it means a lot of SharePoint farms will have a Central Administration content database that does not follow a naming convention while it also has an ugly GUID in its name.

■ **Note**　You can rename a content database by detaching, renaming, and reattaching the database. This also works for the Central Administration content database. Please see this TechNet article for the steps on how to detach and attach content databases: http://technet.microsoft.com/ff628582

Please see this TechNet article for the steps on how to rename select service applications:
http://technet.microsoft.com/ff851878

In this section, I discussed the idea of choosing a database naming convention that does not depend on the specific version of SharePoint. This helps keep the database names meaningful and relevant after you upgrade to the next version. You can apply this same advice to your server naming conventions. I try to avoid naming servers with anything that indicates the actual version of the software on the server, because the software changes and I upgrade it frequently. I also try to avoid naming a server specific to any function or role, because that too can change frequently. For example, I would prefer not to name a set of SharePoint servers with a "Web" and "App" identifier to specify web front-end and application server roles, respectively. Instead, I prefer to name the servers by omitting any role indicator and thus preparing for the possibility that performance measures may move me to redistribute the services running on the servers and effectively change their roles.

Good naming conventions are version independent, because I presume you will upgrade to a later version at some point. Therefore, good upgrade planning will involve choosing good naming conventions for your farm, and then applying those conventions as part of the upgrade if your existing databases and servers are tied too closely to specific version numbers. It is a small detail and it is something that does not have any significant or direct impact on the upgrade, but it does keep your environment looking professional and well organized. It also makes it easy for whoever takes over managing the environment in the future to make sense of how you have organized it.

Consultant Comrade

First, I have to confess that performing upgrades of any sort is one of my least favorite activities. It is not that I do not want to upgrade; in fact, whenever Microsoft releases a new SharePoint version, I am always eager to take advantage of all that it offers. I just do not enjoy having to go through the pain of going through the upgrade process, especially with the inevitable migration tasks that upgrade projects often seem to entail.

I do not think I am alone in my impassivity toward upgrade projects. From what I can tell, upgrade projects seem to be very common engagement types for professional services firms to offer clients. Given this popularity in outsourcing upgrade projects to outside consultants, I would dare to say that many clients also have more favorite types of project than the SharePoint upgrade project. Assuming this is true, I do not blame them. However, it also provides a great opportunity for a consultant – even if you are similar to me where an upgrade might not be as exciting as another type of project.

Upgrade projects may not sound exciting, but they can be very satisfying. Through an upgrade project, you can help your client correct the sins of their SharePoint past. In the process, you will likely remove issues and other things that have been bugging your client or causing them grief. An upgrade offers an opportune time to make corrections and take care of all those loose ends that have been building up as their SharePoint environment evolved to its current state. It provides you with a chance to work with your client to review what has worked well and where things may have become problematic. This process will then enable you to help your client make resolutions for the new environment – the pristine upgraded environment that you will leave them with after you complete the upgrade project.

Think about how the end of a calendar year marks a common time to reflect on the past and make resolutions for the new year. The date itself does not have any specific meaning beyond the meaning we (humans) associated to it, yet it serves as a date when many people reflect and resolve. There is nothing stopping them from reflecting on another day about the previous period, and perhaps they do as part of their continuous improvement process, but for many, New Year's Eve provides an especially convenient time to take stock and prepare mentally for the year ahead.

Similar to New Year's Eve, an upgrade provides a convenient time to take stock of the existing SharePoint environment and look at ways you want to improve it. It is also a convenient time to build a project around. Upgrades are a time when your clients can often bring in outside help to work through the upgrade with them. It is also a time when outside consultants can help resolve and rework other issues – issues that might not warrant a project or engaging a consultant over, but which they might appreciate addressing during the upgrade.

In addition to cleaning up things, an upgrade also helps enable new SharePoint functionality for your client. Often Microsoft will add new or enhanced functionality just in the default team site, as well as the rest of the added capability in the newer version. Therefore, an upgrade allows you to wow your client twice by getting things back on track and then catapulting them into the future. Even though you may feel similar to me that upgrade projects might not seem as if they are the most exciting project, at least initially, they certainly offer potential excitement. Moreover,

I find consultants are the ideal resources to drive these projects, not only because others might not want to, but also because a consultant is more likely to have more experience with the upgrade process.

Although a SharePoint administrator in an organization might go through the upgrade process several times in a test environment, their experience will still be limited. They may even have several production environments to upgrade. However, a consultant can often bring more experience simply because they do upgrade projects repeatedly for different clients. They bring a wider perspective from going through upgrades in different environments on different projects. You should not undervalue this experience and the amount of risk it reduces for your clients. You should also try to help your potential clients understand this value.

The point I am hoping to make is that SharePoint upgrades offer a big opportunity for consultants. They might not be the most exciting on their own, and I hope you do not complicate them by adding on a bunch of other work streams, but they can lead to exciting outcomes and to you delivering significant outcomes for your client. They can also lead to much more work, especially if you end your upgrade engagement with a checklist of next steps, such as a follow-up engagement to deploy a new capability available in the latest version. For example, if I was delivering a SharePoint 2010 to SharePoint 2013 upgrade engagement, I might encourage a follow-up engagement to help them establish an enterprise Apps catalog for their SharePoint 2013 environment to host a catalog of their internally developed applications.

Inside Story: Notes from the Field

Years ago, I worked for Electronic Arts, where I was responsible for a multi-farm global SharePoint deployment. I had several farms spread around the world, and none of the farms were standardized – some had SharePoint Portal Server 2003, and a few ran Windows SharePoint Services 2.0. Some had a dedicated SQL Server, while others shared a SQL instance or they had SQL installed on the same server as SharePoint. Most of the farms existed in a data center somewhere, while a couple farms ran under someone's desk.

Almost all the farms contained some level of customization or custom developed components, yet the customizations were rarely shared or consistent between farms. Some farms had customizations built by internal developers, while other farms had customizations by one or more outside consulting firms. Almost all the had involved modifying the site definitions and other system files on the servers. As if that was all not enough, some of the content databases had large amounts of orphaned objects left over from failed site restore operations. Welcome to what felt like the nightmare I inherited.

People say that any journey begins with a single step, and that was true for me in this case as well. I began working on consolidating environments and retiring any unnecessary farms. With less, more centralized farms I could concentrate my efforts and make changes that were more effective and more efficient. By doing a content migration as part of this farm consolidation, I was also able to restructure some of the sites so that I would have a greater number of smaller site collections, rather than a few very large site collections. This also allowed me to spread the content across a greater number of content databases, which would later make a database-attach upgrade process easier.

Next, I started planning to upgrade the underlying infrastructure, starting with the database servers. I had SQL Server 2000 deployed for every farm, and most had Microsoft Software Assurance with upgrade rights to SQL Server 2005 (the latest version at the time). At the time, the general buzz in the market was that upgrading to 2005 would help improve overall performance, and so this was one motivating factor I wanted to explore. I also wanted to stay current with the latest software versions and begin to move my database servers to 64-bit hardware.

All this work helped to pave the way toward an eventual SharePoint upgrade, while also providing some immediate benefits with improved performance and a more supportable global deployment. At this point, I was beginning to feel the effects from taking several small steps in the right direction toward a healthier SharePoint deployment. As I continued to make progress, I also looked at what was coming in SharePoint 2007 and I knew that demand would begin to build for an upgrade. Upgrading to SharePoint 2007 presented an opportunity to continue taking steps toward a healthier state.

I participated in the Technology Adoption Program (TAP) with Microsoft to help them test alpha and beta builds of SharePoint 2007 with production data and usage. This helped spark me on the road to upgrading my environments from SharePoint 2003 to 2007. It also helped me recognize that there were just too many things wrong in some environments and I needed to find ways to begin to get back to operating a healthy service. One major task was to bring in a consultant to develop the XML files to map site definitions to the new and pristine SharePoint 2007 site definitions. This allowed me to return to a healthy state by reversing the hacks on the SharePoint system files that previous groups and consultants had done.

Moving away from edited site definitions helped build my confidence about the stability and the supportability of my SharePoint farms. As a part of this move, I had to redo how I implemented user interface elements, and in particular, I began to take advantage of the newly introduce master page capability in SharePoint 2007. I also began to take advantage of the new SharePoint feature infrastructure that Microsoft also introduced in this version. To utilize these new capabilities, I had to wrap many of the existing custom developed components in features and package them in SharePoint solution packages (WSP). All this work helped to reassure me that an upgrade to SharePoint 2007 would no longer be a monumental task. In fact, I put most of the pieces in place and could move forward with an upgrade once I had a business need.

What seemed like an impossible state was quickly stabilizing. An upgrade provided an ideal opportunity to repair the damage from teams taking shortcuts or making less optimum architecture decisions in the past. What felt as if it would be a nightmare quickly began to accumulate successes. I could do the majority of the work before I even approached the upgrade itself. Although I moved on to join Microsoft before I completed upgrading every farm, my team was set up to continue with the momentum I started.

My point is that even in an organization where SharePoint grew organically without any central plan as ad hoc farms found their way on the network, I still brought it back to a more sustainable state. Even with farms deployed with heavy adoption and without experienced SharePoint resources, I made minor adjustments and laid the groundwork for an eventual SharePoint upgrade. Best of all, all these activities occurred over just a few months. By making continuous improvements, I made a dramatic change in a short period, and these efforts opened up the possibility for a lower risk and a more straightforward SharePoint upgrade process.

Wrapping Up

In this chapter, I discussed how to build policies and standards that maintain the supportability of the farm and maximize its compatibility with upgrade processes. I looked at considerations for designing solutions in a manner that takes advantage of structures within SharePoint, and implementation strategies that offer the lowest risk against interfering with patches, security updates, cumulative updates, service packs, or version upgrades.

Expanding your SharePoint service involves adding new capabilities, handling demand for new features, and upgrading to new versions. This third part of the book covered broad topics such as building a SharePoint roadmap, adding new capabilities, handling demand for new features, and upgrading to new versions. With this information, you can handle evolving requirements and expand your SharePoint service to adapt to meet new business needs. However, eventually needs arise that require customized functionality that SharePoint does not offer.

In the next part, chapters focus on topics related to customizing your SharePoint service for things such as facilitating end-user customizations, designing development standards, and managing a release process. I start in the next chapter with how to structure sponsorship for your SharePoint service, and in particular, how to establish sponsorship for customizations. This can structure funding, expedite decisions, and establish accountability.

PART IV

Customizing the SharePoint Service

Those who customize their SharePoint deployment tend to also have the highest satisfaction with it. Although that also assumes that they have customized it in a way that is manageable and maintainable, and does not simply paint them in a corner and cause them grief. One might not be as satisfied if they implement their customizations in a way that causes a major limiting constraint or is unnecessarily costly to maintain. One might find customizations that are unstable or cause support headaches are just as unsatisfying. Yet you can increase your satisfaction with SharePoint by customizing it, and you can do this in a way that does not constrain you or add unnecessary support costs.

The chapters in this part focus on factors specific to custom design and development as they relate to governing a SharePoint service. These chapters highlight key strategies and considerations for all the different types of customizations, and they include approaches on how you can design development and testing processes. As I have done in other parts of this book, I will leave the degree of formality or informality of this documentation up to your own discretion to fit with how your organization operates.

■ ■ ■

CHAPTER 12

Committing Sponsorship and Ownership of Customizations

Not everything that is faced can be changed. But nothing can be changed until it is faced.

—James Arthur Baldwin

In this chapter, I focus on the idea of sponsorship for your SharePoint service. I start by looking at sponsorship in a general SharePoint sense, and then I look at sponsorship specifically as it relates to customizations such as custom developed components and even end-user site customizations. As I review sponsorship of customizations, I walk through an approach to establish a policy that links sponsorship to any server customization. I also offer guidance on requiring a chain of custody for any enhancements and considerations for global customizations. Finally, I discuss how to isolate and delegate ownership of customizations to site administrators using Apps for SharePoint and other delegation capabilities.

One key point I stress in this chapter is to ensure that someone owns or is accountable for different aspects of your SharePoint service, and in particular, those political aspects and those areas that relate to customizing your service.

After reading this chapter, you will know how to:

- Describe the purpose for sponsorship and its importance

- Link sponsorship to a RACI chart

- Set sponsorship conditions for any customization

- Establish a chain of custody for service customizations

- Identify sponsors to fund customizations and development

- Explain sponsorship considerations for global customizations

- Plan for and utilize Apps for SharePoint for customizations

- Delegate ownership of customizations to site administrators

Sponsoring Governance

Sponsoring different aspects of governance must be important, for it seems to play such a pinnacle role in almost any governance presentation or governance "plan" I come across. I am not necessarily referring to sponsorship in the sense that may be common in these other governance discussions. I think I share the intrinsic theme of sponsorship as any other SharePoint governance approach, but I do seem to differ in its application. As you read through this chapter, I share these differences, and I ultimately answer the question about how to establish effective sponsorship.

Before I jump into my practice of sponsorship within a SharePoint service, I want to quickly explain what I think sponsorship is not. As I looked at governance references and guidance, sponsorship appeared to play a pretty significant role. To paraphrase and over-simplify some of this governance guidance, it said that I needed to document some governance "plan" based on a template, and then identify a sponsor. From there, it recommended that I set up a governance committee to meet regularly with the sponsor, who would presumably be the ultimate decision maker. Just to be clear, sponsorship is *not* simply the chair of some recurring governance committee meeting.

Unfortunately, the typical governance guidance seems to end there – fill out a template and then have a committee meet regularly, and everything else should just fall into place. This type of advice falls short of answering what a sponsor actually does or what they are accountable for. I find the advice also does not provide much direction on the governance committee meetings it recommends, nor does it identify any outcomes or goals for these regular meetings. You may find these meetings valuable, but for now, I will just assume that we all have enough wasteful or aimless meetings on our calendar. Later in this chapter, I come back to explore the idea of a governance committee and some different ways that you can structure it to make it effective.

If sponsorship is not simply someone who signs off on governance documentation and policies, and it is not simply someone who chairs a governance committee meeting, what is sponsorship? To answer this, I want to return to the very beginning where I quoted the definition of governance as the actions one takes in order to govern. I unpacked this idea to think of SharePoint governance as the actions, behaviors, and commitments that contribute to running a healthy and intentional SharePoint service. Essentially, I want to focus on the things you need to do to offer a stable and valuable SharePoint service.

■ **Important**   Sponsorship in governance is about who you need to involve so that you can do what you need to do to offer a stable and valuable SharePoint service.

So, what does a sponsor do then? To answer that, first let me return to my trusted *Oxford English Dictionary* and consider the definition of a sponsor. A sponsor is a person who provides funds for a project or who holds official accountability for its actions and outcomes. Based on this dictionary definition, I can paraphrase sponsorship into the following:

- A sponsor is someone who funds and owns the budget for a SharePoint project or an aspect of a SharePoint service

- A sponsor is someone who owns the ultimate accountability for a SharePoint project or an aspect of a SharePoint service

Therefore, a sponsor is someone who is accountable for a budget or accountable for an outcome. A sponsor can wear one or both of these hats. You can have multiple sponsors for different aspects of a SharePoint service or a SharePoint project, but you need to ensure that you do not have any overlap of accountabilities. If you look back to Chapter 6 where I discussed roles and responsibilities, I stated that only one person can be accountable for a particular area or aspect of the SharePoint service. As you develop and enhance a RACI chart for your SharePoint service, your sponsor roles will hold the accountability for certain tasks and activities that the service depends on.

A sponsor can set the commitment aspect of your SharePoint governance. They can commit to a particular approach or a particular behavior, and they can provide their commitment and support to the resources that the RACI chart identifies in the different roles. They can manifest their commitment and support through providing adequate funding to do things in a preferred way, as well as by reinforcing the notion of following a disciplined process and avoiding shortcuts or hacks. They hold ultimate accountability for an area, and as such, they typically are the ultimate authority and decision maker for that area.

You might wonder why I delayed the topic of sponsorship until now, in this last part of this book. I had a couple of reasons for this. First, I wanted to signal that establishing sponsorship is not necessarily a prerequisite to deploying a SharePoint service and establishing SharePoint governance. I find that when sponsorship gets too much emphasis too early in the process, the rest of the governance initiative begins to fizzle and wait on a sponsor to wave their magic wand and solve all the issues. However, there are actions that you can take to govern your SharePoint service in the absence of sponsorship, as this book shows. You can drive these behaviors long before you establish a sponsor or a governance committee, if they even fit with your SharePoint governance needs. I delayed this discussion until now to highlight that the need for a sponsor should not stall any other progress you can make.

The other reason I wanted to discuss sponsorship in this part of the book relates to the nature of customizations and development. SharePoint as a product is quite resilient. Even when things feel as if they evolved in some ugly way, SharePoint still manages to work and provide value. Its site structure may be a hodgepodge from some random hierarchy generator. Its servers and databases may feel clunky. It may not be as optimal as you would prefer, but in most cases it still works. However, once you throw in a bunch of custom development, this resilience can quickly degrade. Therefore, I find sponsorship in a default environment is something that leans more toward a nice-to-have aspect in an action-focused habit of governance. Whereas I find sponsorship plays a crucial role whenever you are customizing your SharePoint service.

The bottom line is that someone needs to own a SharePoint project and someone needs to own each aspect of a SharePoint service once it is implemented. They may not do the work, but they own the accountability if the work is not done correctly. They may not involve themselves in the day-to-day details, but they own any decisions that a team is unable to resolve and needs to escalate to them. A sponsor completes your RACI chart by giving you the person you hold accountable and establish ownership with.

Importance of Ownership

In economics, there is a theory referred to as *the tragedy of the commons*. This occurs where a group of people who are sharing a common resource each act rationally and in their own self-interest as they deplete the common resource. The tragedy occurs because even though they are aware that over-depletion of the common resource is not in any of their best long-term interests, in their self-interests they will continue to deplete the common resource. This is because they all share ownership and their self-interests end up outweighing their collective long-term interests. Generally, in the absence of private ownership, it is the government's job to protect the long-term interests of a common resource.

My point is that without ownership you will have to act as that government and balance all the interests and motives for the different ideologies. Even with an executive sponsor owning the entire service, you still have to do some balancing. Presumably, your SharePoint service is a common resource, shared by different groups within your organization. Your job is to balance the service so that one group does not over-consume and deplete the service. One strategy I looked at is to define the service and its boundaries. Another strategy you can use is to delegate ownership of different aspects of the service.

By establishing ownership, you can delegate some of the balancing, and preferably to someone with authority to push compromises for the greater balance and everyone's long-term interests. The challenge though, is that their self-interests will typically drive them because they do not own the entire service. However, they will balance the interests within the area they own within the boundaries you define. The onus is still on you to act as the government body that protects the entire service, to govern, to define the service and balance the interests of each group with the long-term interests of the service.

If you return to my RACI chart discussion from Chapter 4, then you will hold the responsibility in the RACI chart for balancing and protecting the long-term interests of the service. If you establish an executive sponsor for the entire service, then they will hold the ultimate accountability while you retain the responsibility. Delegating ownership then is essentially delegating accountability for particular areas. It may not solve the tragedy of the commons problem, but it will help you deal with it. To refresh your memory on the difference between accountability and responsibility in a RACI chart, I will briefly describe the two roles again.

- A role you list as accountable holds the ultimate accountability for the work or the decisions.

- A role you list as responsible identifies the role that actually performs the work. If you do not list another role as accountable for this work, then the role you identify as responsible is both responsible and accountable for the work.

The most important aspect of defining ownership is that it establishes accountability. To quote a phrase that former U.S. President Harry S. Truman made popular during his presidency by displaying it on a sign on his desk, "The Buck Stops Here!" The phrase referred to Truman's belief that the President is accountable to make decisions, and the President must accept the ultimate responsibility for those decisions. You want ownership where you can establish accountability for a particular area or a specific customization so that the buck will stop with someone.

An owner with authority can drive decisions, and using the owner as a decision maker can resolve political situations or disagreements on an approach. Even in the most politically charged situation, you can have them make the authoritative decision and mandate the direction or approach when you need to move things along. Although I always prefer negotiating and building support for an initiative, sometimes you may find yourself facing polar opposite stakeholder opinions with those stakeholders unwilling to change or compromise. On top of that, sometimes you may find yourself facing stakeholders who simply enjoy bureaucracy and dragging processes out to avoid doing any work. In those cases, you may just need an authority to own a decision and move an initiative forward.

When you establish ownership, you will also generate order and a certain amount of organization. By establishing an authority that you hold accountable for a particular area, you begin to form a hierarchy of accountabilities and responsibilities. Better yet, you delegate the forming of much of an area's hierarchy to the owner of the area by specifying their accountability. This structure of ownership also helps to create an effective escalation path when something does go wrong or when someone has a suggestion.

In short, sponsors add structure and they provide accountability for a particular area, and this adds stability to your SharePoint service. It organizes and adds stability either to an operational area, a project delivery, or to customizations and enhancements. You can use this stability to plan around, such as when you create service-level agreements similar to those that I discussed back in Chapter 2. You can also use this stability to plan your roadmap that I discussed back in Chapter 7. Your ultimate goal for identifying sponsors and the underlying importance for delegating them ownership then is to build stability in your SharePoint service through the accountabilities that you associate with sponsors.

Although these principles apply to sponsorship for any aspect of your SharePoint service, I want to focus on how sponsors can help stabilize customizations and any other custom development. As I mentioned earlier, SharePoint as a product already coordinates its different features and capability areas. When the product team discovers an issue, they work on developing a patch. Therefore, in this sense, Microsoft plays the role of a sponsor for the product's code-base. When you develop your own features, you do not automatically inherit sponsorship from a vendor for the code and any enhancements it requires. Nevertheless, you still can set up accountability for any code or customization by requiring a sponsor for any customization, and I discuss an approach for you to consider in the next section.

Requiring Sponsors for Any Customizations

You may find a common role for a sponsor on a project delivery team. They may fund the project or approve the resources and each resource's time to deliver on a project team. You may copy them on status update emails, and they may even come to the odd status meeting. However, they probably are not hands-on with the project, and instead they delegated that responsibility to a project manager or a team lead. Once the project completes, they might check it off their list, hand it off to operations, and in the process, they might also hand off their accountabilities that they held as a project sponsor.

Here comes the danger: where does the ownership lay and whom do you hold accountable for a customization? This void does not end there, as the lack of ownership directly adds risk and instability to your SharePoint service. When a project sponsor simply hands off a project delivery to an operations team and they absolve themselves of ownership, they leave the team with a number of questions, many of which go unanswered and will place a burden of risk on the operations team. The following lists some significantly important questions that you might consider before accepting any project hand-over.

- What happens if you later discover a bug and you require more development effort to fix the issue?

- Who owns the source code and who will have access to it?

- What happens if you find this customization is no longer compatible with future versions of SharePoint? Will someone rebuild it or migrate the code? Can you simply remove it?

- Who will respond to support tickets that relate to the customization?

- What happens if another group begins to also use the customization and they want to enhance it to better fit their needs? With whom can they coordinate with and will they even have access to the source code?

- Who will perform an architectural review of the design and how sustainable the solution will be in the future with a wide adoption rate?

Too often, I find these questions seem to go unanswered, and the result ends up putting the onus on the operations team to fill in the gaps when things go wrong – and chances are, things will go wrong if you are accepting customizations without considering fundamental questions such as these. You can address these issues ahead of time by putting these questions front and center before you ever agree to move forward with deploying any customizations. This adds a level of discipline to your process that helps prevent short-term hacks from becoming the norm. If you make your process known, including the requirement to identify the ownership who will hold accountability for these questions, then the checkpoint should come as no surprise and your internal customers should anticipate and come prepared to meet the sponsorship requirement.

People may find it easy to simply throw their name in as the owner for any customizations, or they may try to bully their way through. You need to prequalify that they hold the necessary authority to take on the required ownership, and on top of that, you need to capture their commitment for you to hold them accountable for the those areas I identified previously. You definitely do not want a situation where you felt as if you did your due diligence by identifying an owner, but later discover they were just going through the motions to get a component deployed that they need.

It is an imperfect world and this is an imperfect system. Occasionally, you may have someone who commits to own the ultimate accountability for a customization, only to later have them evade their commitment and shift the responsibility. You did what you could: you ensured that they held enough authority to make the commitment, you explained what they were committing to, and you walked them through what that commitment meant and how you would later rely on them. At the time, they agreed profusely and maybe acted a little offended that you would spend so much time explaining their commitment to them. Yet, when the time came, they welched on their commitment.

Usually, when you identify an owner with the appropriate level of authority and list the details about what you will hold them accountable for (such as answers to those questions listed earlier), then they will honor the agreement. Most people are reputable, or at least I like to believe so. Even if they turn out not to be, then you can rest assured knowing that you did what you could. The reality is that any number of reasons could prevent them from following through with their sign-off on their commitment to ownership, including some of the following:

- Their budget is now frozen or significantly reduced

- People on their team have since resigned and moved on

- They moved on to a new role and no longer have the authority

- Enough time has passed that they no longer feel accountable

- They were overly optimistic on how few defects they expected

I would not ask an executive to sign their name in blood, unless I was looking at a reasonably significant project and I faced serious risk. However, I would still recommend that you have some formality to the sign-off on a sponsor's commitment so that you can explain your increasing support costs to your own manager later if the sponsor does not follow through on their commitment. It would not be an ideal situation, but on the other hand, it would not be very different than if you did not have the process to identify owners for customizations in the first place. Therefore, even if it is not perfect in practice, you will still be better off than if you did not identify owners at all.

In most cases, I find that establishing ownership with their commitment to address any issues is a practice that works quite well. For one reason, it incentivizes them to have their developers follow a disciplined approach so that the customization will not come back to cause them too much grief down the road. This process encourages good habits early on, particularly as they involve you to work through these preconditions on the ownership of customizations. With you involved in their development process, you will have the opportunity to offer architecture guidance if this is in your skillset, as well as the chance to coach them on adopting disciplined development standards and testing processes.

■ **Note**   Please see Chapter 14 for a deeper discussion on development standards and testing processes that you can encourage teams to adopt if they want to deploy global customizations to your SharePoint service.

My approach for establishing ownership typically involves some form of a service-level agreement. For example, if an internal customer came with a request to deploy a web part that they developed so they could make it available to the entire organization, then I would work through a service-level agreement with them to answer all of the questions I noted earlier. Within the agreement, I would identify the owner who will hold the accountability to uphold the agreement. I would also identify the support plan if any issues arise, and what their patching or updating policy will be. Finally, I usually then include a clause that states something to the effect that if support issues come up and they are unresponsive, then operations will uninstall the component and discontinue its availability.

When you identify owners, it is important that you base the owner on a position (job title) rather than on a named individual. People change jobs – they receive promotions, they retire, they quit, and they face layoffs. Someone may hold the authority today to commit to the accountabilities you both agree to in a service-level agreement, but if they switch jobs, they may not hold the authority to act when an issue comes up. Or worse, if they leave the company, then they definitely will not hold any authority. However, if you associate the ownership with their position, then whoever holds that position can fulfill the obligations of the support commitments.

You may face times when a sponsor will not be available. I shudder to think about these situations, but they do occur. This may stem from an internal customer who needs custom features, but who is unable to take on accountability for those features. For these situations, I usually try to find a compromise somewhere and I would look for funding to compensate for taking on the added support maintenance for the customization. Typically, most plans are a hybrid that mixes existing support and operations with what the requestor of the application contributes. This makes good sense in many cases as well, because for instance, you probably do not want to start introducing several different frontline support groups, as this adds complexity to your service desk processes. Figure 12-1 illustrates a sample flowchart of a support transition from the project team to the service desk during a warranty period.

Figure 12-1. *A sample flowchart for a support service request during a transition period from the project team*

Table 12-1 provides an example of how you might structure ownership of accountabilities for a custom developed web part for a corporate communications group. The project sponsor holds accountabilities during the actual project and the warranty period – the period of transition from the project development and delivery team to the operations team. This model offers a compromise where the business sponsor holds a high degree of accountability during the warranty period, but eventually he or she transitions all accountability except funding for bug fixes to another owner as the enhancement moves into operations.

Table 12-1. An Example of Transitioning Ownership in a Service-Level Agreement for a Custom Web Part

Accountability	Warranty Period Owner	Regular Operations Owner
End-user support	Business sponsor	Service desk
Funding development for bug fixes	Business sponsor	Business sponsor
Funding development for upgrade compatibility	Business sponsor	SharePoint service team
Architecture review and sign-off	SharePoint service team	SharePoint service team
Funding for enhancement requests	Business sponsor	Requires a new sponsor

THE SURPRISE CUSTOM APPLICATION

A while back, I was working in an IT department, and my team discovered that one of our customers, a group within the organization, had hired an intern to develop an application for them. My team tried to get involved to help influence the architecture and ensure they thought about the supportability of the application, but they refused. They claimed that their intern was going to do a fine job developing it and that they were going to own and support the application anyways, so there was no need for IT to get involved.

If you have been in IT long enough, then you know things never work out that way, no matter how insistent the business might be. My team knew it was only a matter of time. Low and behold, eventually the intern student went back to school and they released the Ruby on Rails application into the wild. It was, as any senior developer would expect, largely a student development project and definitely not an enterprise-grade application. The application had scale issues, which was a problem because its user base was growing rapidly.

Seeing things not follow the happy path that they had hoped and with their intern student now back in school, the group was ready to wash their hands of this application and hand it off to IT. Now it was my department's problem (though thankfully it was not my problem directly as it went on another team's plate). I imagine the only thing worse than trying to stabilize an intern student's code in production might be the pain of having to live with many of his or her architecture decisions because no one will fund a redevelopment effort.

These are the custom applications that you want to avoid popping up in your SharePoint service with an unexpected support challenge. By establishing checkpoints that require ownership sponsors and other standards that I look at in the chapters still to come, you can help to reduce your risks for the surprise custom application.

Establishing Ownership and a Chain of Custody

When I am managing a SharePoint service, the first and paramount precondition I seek is access to any source code before I deploy customizations and custom development. In the rush of things, developers may move on from the company and forget the source code on their desktop; vendors can disengage after project sign-off and forget to hand-over any source code. I have been stuck in this position before, and it has come back to haunt me when I needed to fix a defect or redevelop a component for compatibility with an upgrade. Therefore, now I am extra vigilant about getting a copy of the source code and I check that into my own source repository as a precondition to any deployment – including any deployment update.

In the case of a third-party product, then I understand that the vendor probably does not provide any source code, but they will provide a warranty and an ongoing support policy. My precondition in this case shifts to where

I verify their support policy in lieu of access to the source code. Including this step ensures that you capture the vendor support information before any deployment, and thus before anyone rolls off a project and disappears with the details. I usually set up a SharePoint site where I can store vendor details and support information about any products that I have deployed.

I find that capturing the source code or the vendor support details is valuable, as the operations team may require it someday, and this precondition ensures that you have captured it somewhere. However, it does not mean that the operations team has taken ownership of the customization. You still need to answer the questions I pointed out in the previous section when I looked at why it is important to require sponsors. Capturing the code and support policies is merely a step to check in the process to ensure you have what you need stored in a known location before you need it. It also gives you access to the things you need to test and to validate customizations before you accept them.

■ **Note** I discuss testing processes for customizations in more detail in Chapter 14.

For me, putting the right checkpoints and change management processes in place helps to enforce discipline, and this helps you keep a healthy SharePoint environment. Part of this approach would include having teams identify valid ownership to sponsor a change, and part would include preparing a change package that includes any source code, installers, and support or other documentation references. If these things are "coming" then you freeze the deployment. The checkpoint enforces that you have all the required pieces in place before deploying any customizations or third-party products. It is not that I do not trust these teams; I just have the checkpoint to enforce the rule for everybody so that I do not have to track follow-up items.

I may come across as a little militant when it comes to controlling my SharePoint environment, and the truth is that I can be. Rather than thinking of myself as being overly controlling and militant with the environment, I prefer to think of myself as safeguarding it. When I am responsible for a SharePoint environment, then I am the last line of the defense and my job is to ensure everyone meets standards and that I am not hacking together a future nightmare. I also need to make sure that someone is not trying to play hot potato with the added support and maintenance costs down the road because they cut some corner today.

If you know who Chef Gordon Ramsay is, then the idea of having someone maintain standards might sound familiar. One of my favorite television shows is *Hell's Kitchen*. It is one of the only reality shows that I watch regularly, but I enjoy it on many levels. (It even inspired me to learn how to cook a risotto recently because it is one of the dishes I watched the contestants mess up.) Chef Ramsay is relentless with upholding standards. He would rather have the kitchen recook a dish and send it late rather than send anything out that is less than perfect. He constantly stresses standards and doing things right. I do not think of myself so much as a gatekeeper for a SharePoint environment; I prefer to think of myself more akin to an expeditor in Chef Ramsay's kitchen: someone with an eye for detail and a drive to uphold standards.

Just as not every chef holds the same standards as Chef Ramsay, your standards will be unique to you as well. I looked at some of the ways you can set performance standards for the servers in your SharePoint environment back in Chapter 6. Setting standards for the core infrastructure is part of the puzzle. However, at some point you may need to go beyond out-of-the-box functionality for all sorts of reasons, such as to add business value to a process, to meet additional user needs, or even to integrate with another system to reduce data redundancy. In those cases, you should maintain your high standards and expand them to include checks that relate to customizations.

The effort to uphold standards pays itself off with a healthy SharePoint environment and a stable SharePoint service for your internal customers. It creates a habit of excellence, which takes your ongoing efforts to stay disciplined; otherwise, it would just be a habit of average. Whenever you find yourself wondering how incessant you need to be with your standards, just watch an episode with Chef Ramsay and note how many things he lets slide in his quest for excellence. This often helps me put my own discipline to maintain standards into perspective, particularly when it comes to the checkpoints in my release process.

■ **Note** I look at how to formalize a release process in Chapter 16, where I also work through how to build a code promotion process to facilitate an ordered and disciplined deployment.

Earlier in this chapter, I mentioned the two areas for sponsorship: funding and ownership. I have predominately focused on sponsors who will take on the ownership for a customization. However, what happens for those internal customers who do not want to outsource the development of a customization and who are unable to do the development themselves? Does your team prefer to manage any vendors and take on the ownership for any outsourced customizations? Perhaps your team offers development services to internal customers. In these cases, you or your team will take on the ownership aspect of sponsorship, while your internal customer takes on the funding aspect. In the next section, I discuss considerations for managing sponsorship for short-term customization and development funding.

Charging Customization and Development Funding

If you operate a SharePoint service and your team has the skills and availability to offer development services, perhaps you will want to take on the ownership of any customizations in the environment. Typically, these would only entail the global customizations, unless you have enough resources to provide such a hands-on service to individual sites. Even in this case where your team takes on the ownership of customizations, you will still need a sponsor to fund any development efforts.

Some teams may not operate with a chargeback funding model, and so this section may seem less relevant. Nonetheless, somewhere along the way, someone has to approve funds for a development project. If departments in your organization do not pay for each individual service that they consume and each project that they request, then they pay at the organization level. For example, finance may allocate a certain amount of budget for IT operations, and these funds come from the organization's same general ledger account that each department contributes to or operates under. A Chief Information Officer (CIO) can then allocate that budget across projects within his or her department.

This top-down approach to funding projects can help to ensure IT delivers on a global view of the organization and its needs, rather than simply favoring departments with the most funding. With this funding approach, an IT department can operate strategically by balancing different departmental needs and long-term goals. In these cases, the sponsor directly funding a development project may be the CIO, who is also the sponsor who will own the ultimate support and maintenance accountability for the customization. Even still, I would prefer to include the CIO as a stakeholder in the project and find someone else from the business to be the sponsor.

It is easier to identify a project sponsor from the business when there is someone who owns the budget and funds the projects, otherwise it may require some discussions and negotiations to identify a sponsor when the funds come from a general organization-wide pot. Nevertheless, a sponsor from the business will help to keep a focus on contributing value to the business rather than on IT efficiencies, and so I find it worth having one regardless of where the funding comes from. This approach will also give you someone to signoff on the delivery, which is important because it will give you a way to track whether you are delivering the right solution or you are simply managing scope and checking off work items in a list.

You might not provide internal development services or you might not always have the available capacity to take on development requests. However, you might still want to take on the ownership of any development activity by managing the vendor and their delivery rather than have each department engage their own SharePoint consulting firm. Even if your team is not doing the development, you probably still possess a certain level of expertise on the product – or at least probably more so than a typical internal customer from the business does. This can put you in a position to guide the process and enforce standards with the vendor throughout the entire project.

Another benefit of taking on the ownership of a project delivery even when you are outsourcing to an outside vendor is that you build relationships with a group of regular vendors. These SharePoint consulting firms get to know your standards and expectations, which helps them to plan their project delivery process. They can also work closer with you and your team to understand the wider organization goals and direction with your SharePoint service, rather than having them operate and design a solution within a single silo view of the organization based on the needs of a single group or department.

Ultimately, taking ownership of customizations can give you the control to promote and enforce standards throughout the entire development process. You can manage accountability for the support and maintenance of the customization while your internal customer can sponsor the funding to ensure that what your team develops aligns with their needs. Whether you are set up for chargebacks to change a group directly or your funding comes from a general organization pot, I find it is useful to identify a sponsor and discuss the project in terms of cost. This helps the team and the customer think in terms of the project as a cost to the organization, which helps guide any cost-benefit discussions that may come up.

As you are calculating your costs for a customization, I recommend you also factor in future costs that a customization will involve. This will help you understand your true costs. Will a customization require extensive training for the operations team or for end-users? Will your team have to absorb bug-fixing costs or upgrade costs? You should consider these costs ahead of time and factor them into the cost of deployment. These costs can be true whether you are developing a solution in-house, outsourcing development to a vendor, or are purchasing a third-party product.

FACTORING TOMORROW'S SUPPORT COSTS TODAY

Whether or not you provide development services, you will still need to factor future support and maintenance costs as you determine the cost of customizations. This is true even if you defer billing for any support or maintenance cost until the actual expense occurs. This approach may work well if you have a reliable internal customer for whom you are confident that they will pay any of these costs when they come up. Alternatively, you may charge for any of these anticipated costs upfront to ensure a type of insurance and avoid any need to chase down support funding later.

I can find an example of this type of upfront charging within the mining industry. Some local governments may allow a mining company to set up operations to mine minerals or other resources from a local site, but the government may also worry about whether the mining company will live up to its obligations to clean up the mining site and offset any environmental impacts from their operations. The worry is that a mining company can set up a temporary corporation to absorb all of the parent company's liabilities, and then they will simply bankrupt the temporary corporation and abandon any of their responsibilities.

To prevent this, a government can charge the site environmental cleanup and restoration costs upfront. This security deposit can ensure that the funds are committed and that the mining company will not leave the local taxpayers with the burden to regenerate the land and reverse any impacts from the operation. A security deposit can hold a mining company accountable upfront before any operations begin, and then it passes on the ownership of that accountability to the government who holds the deposit.

In a similar fashion, you and your team can take ownership of the accountability for future support and maintenance. You might apply this idea of collecting a security deposit in a number of ways. For example, you can charge funding to pre-purchase vendor support and maintenance hours. Alternatively, you might charge a recurring maintenance chargeback as part of a service-level agreement, such as those I mentioned back in Chapter 2.

Considerations for Global Customizations

The idea of making a global change usually gets my attention right away. It is similar to when you are lying in bed, about to drift off into a nice sleep. The surroundings are fading away and you can feel yourself approach dreamland. Then all of a sudden, you jolt up remembering that you forgot to purchase the tickets for your holiday – tickets that are only on sale tonight! That is the kind of attention-grabbing jolt a request to deploy a customization with a global change to a SharePoint farm that I am managing.

Global customizations are probably inevitable in a busy farm where you want to tailor it to meet user needs and provide value to their processes. They are good things because they can help standardize processes and they can help multiple groups leverage the same investment. Global customizations add efficiencies to a SharePoint farm. They do not grab my attention because of anything bad; they grab my attention because they warrant attention and they can require special care and planning. The wider the scope of a change, the greater the number of users a change will typically affect. The greater the number of users affected, the more planning and attention a change requires; otherwise you are looking at a recipe for an overwhelming flood of user support calls and complaints.

First and foremost, you need to assess the compatibility of a customization. If you have a wide deployment and your user sites have an array of customizations already, this can be a significant task. This is the first step in your release management process, but it can also be the most critical. Before I can deploy a global change, I need to be confident that it will not break existing functionality that sites depend on.

■ **Note** Please see Chapter 16 where I discuss release management in more detail.

One example of a breaking change would be a delegate control that overrides any existing delegate control that shares the same delegate placeholder. What if the placeholder only accepts a single delegate control (a web control you can add to a placeholder by deploying and activating a SharePoint feature)? It sounds as if it is a simple example, but when you have different teams developing solutions independent of each other, it is not far fetched. Long before you get to the deployment phase, you can coordinate these development teams and influence their approach to maximize compatibility.

Along with compatibility, a global customization needs to be scalable. If you deploy something globally, it needs to be able to scale to handle a potential load of the global user base. In order to scale, it has to properly and efficiently manage resources such as sessions, caching, site objects, and database connections. Basically, I need to ensure a global customization does not consume significantly more server resources within the SharePoint farm as the user load increases.

After compatibility and scalability, my next biggest concern is usually how reusable a team designs a global solution to be. If they are developing something that I have to deploy globally because of how they have to develop it, then it has to be at least somewhat usable for everyone. Not everyone will use every feature, so I would not expect every global customization to be so generic that it can appeal to everyone. Instead, I just want the team to design it to be generic enough that multiple groups can find a use for it.

On top of all of that, you need someone to sponsor the change. Your sponsor will need enough authority to sponsor a global customization that can potentially affect everyone. If you do not establish a sponsor who holds enough authority and has funding to fix any bugs, then you are potentially putting your team at risk for having to take ownership of these issues. As users adopt the new features, they will grow to depend on them. If things only go wrong under load, then that means issues will only develop once you have a critical mass of users adopting and depending on the customization – a critical mass of users who will contact you and your team if any problems arise.

Hence, this is why requests to deploy global customizations get my attention. There are a few crucial aspects to consider and plan for to ensure that such a change goes smoothly. Mostly, I just want to make sure it does not create some ripple effect that has me chasing problems – I do not want to introduce weird dependencies or to create a fragile environment that can crumble and fall apart at any moment. Sadly, I never have the luxury of having excess capacity on my team to risk anything like this. As a result, I handle global customizations with care.

They add some extra due diligence to my process, but the end result is that global customizations provide a sweeping opportunity to deliver value to all my users. One group has a need and develops a solution to meet their needs, and now every site can take advantage of that group's investment. This creates a Dr. Jekyll and Mr. Hyde situation for me: I want every customization generalized enough so that I can make it available and useful enough for everyone, but I also want to minimize any risks associated with a global change that will affect a large user base.

Not every global customization has to be a global change that can instantly affect everyone. You can make a global customization available to everyone yet not automatically affect everyone. This approach can help reduce the risk of deploying a global customization. You can make a global customization available to everyone in a disabled state by deploying it using the SharePoint feature infrastructure. By default, you can have the feature deactivated, and then whenever a site administrator wants to utilize your customization, they can activate the necessary feature. Alternatively, in SharePoint 2013 you can deploy the global customization as a SharePoint App and make it available in the SharePoint App Catalog, which I look at next.

Utilizing the Apps for SharePoint Catalog

One approach to organize global customizations with the customization owners who will manage and support them is to deploy them in the Apps for SharePoint Catalog. Developers can develop Apps that contain functionality for an application, functionality that runs on another server outside your SharePoint farm. Their Apps also provide functionality to any site owner who wants to add the App to their site, and they can discover it by browsing the App catalog.

Your team's role can then become something of an internal marketplace provider, as you manage the catalog and provide the platform for the Apps. You can require that any Apps to first have a support policy and an owner before you add it to the catalog. Similar to any other customization, you can require this sponsorship so that when your users adopt any Apps, you can be reasonably confident that the users can find a support structure and a point of contact for different Apps.

You can set up a SharePoint site to host and manage your internal App Catalog. In addition, you can share the same App Catalog across farms, which allows you to centralize the hosting and management on your main enterprise farm while other subordinate farms can consume the catalog and the Apps it lists. Figure 12-2 provides a screenshot of the Manage App Catalog page located in SharePoint Central Administration. You can navigate to this page by clicking the Apps link in the left navigation area, and then clicking the Manage App Catalog option. From this page, you can crate a new App Catalog site or enter the URL for an existing one.

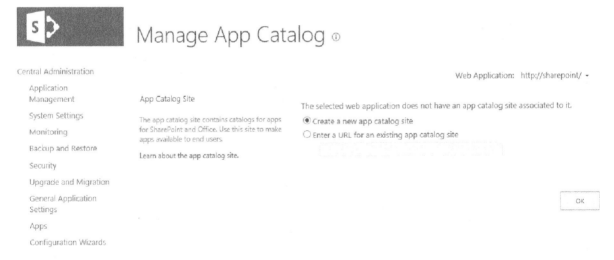

Figure 12-2. *A screenshot of the Manage App Catalog page in SharePoint Central Administration*

Once you configure the catalog and enable Apps, site administrators and page designers can then add the additional Apps to their site. Figure 12-3 provides a screenshot of the Your Apps page, where end-users can select the available Apps that they want to add to their site. From here, they can add internally published Apps as well as those that come with SharePoint. In addition, notice the SharePoint Store link in the left navigation area where site administrators can go to purchase additional Apps available from vendors who publish their Apps in the Microsoft marketplace.

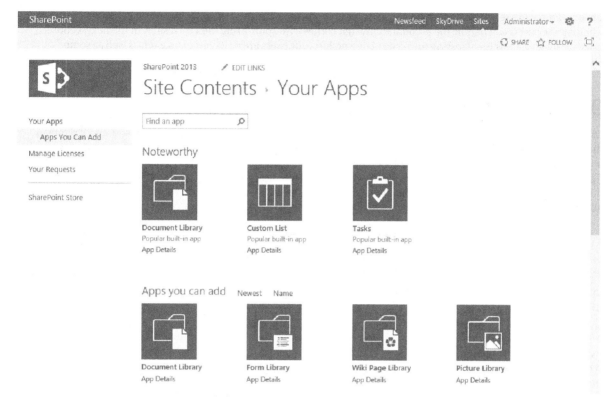

Figure 12-3. *A screenshot of the Your Apps page available in a SharePoint site*

Enabling the SharePoint Store and allowing site owners to purchase their own Apps directly will provide you with an effective way to allow users to procure the functionality they need without having to request a global change on the SharePoint environment. As such, Apps can provide an alternative to global customizations, whether you purchase Apps from the Microsoft marketplace or you make Apps available in your internal catalog, or both.

You may not want your users to purchase Apps directly for a variety of reasons, but I imagine the most common reason will be to mitigate risks for any potential support and training issues. Another reason might be to centralize the purchasing and procurement of Apps through a formal IT process. Instead of allowing direct purchases from site administrators, you can configure Apps in your SharePoint farm to receive requests. Your internal Apps catalog will capture user requests for different Apps, allowing you to process and make the App available if you want to allow them on your SharePoint farm.

Apps provide a nice alternative to traditional server customizations, and especially for minimizing the number of global customizations where possible. They can also provide a venue to provide customizations from an internal development team to the organization. You can use the Microsoft marketplace to help remove some of the bottlenecks on a SharePoint team by purchasing Apps that meet one of your needs from SharePoint vendors through the SharePoint Store.

Ultimately, Apps offer a platform with a nice fusion of all the customization approaches I discussed in this chapter, and you can maintain supportability by requiring an owner to sponsor each App before you add it to catalog. You can also delegate App decisions to site administrators. Whether you are simply delegating the decision to add an available App to their site or you are empowering them to purchase the Apps they need directly from the Microsoft marketplace, you can decide how much freedom you want to grant and how much you want to involve your team in the process.

Apps are not the only aspect of SharePoint that you can delegate to site administrators, but they do provide one powerful option for putting site administrators in charge of their own destiny. However, delegating ownership of site operations to site administrators comes with some special considerations – most notably, you have to consider whether your users can handle the accountability that comes with sponsoring their own sites. In the next section, I share considerations for assessing the types of ownership your users are prepared to take on, as well as some approaches to identify potential sponsors for a site.

Delegating Ownership to Site Administrators

One of the reasons that SharePoint is so successful is its ability to distribute and delegate administration. It removes the burden (and bottleneck) of IT to respond to every little user request. You can delegate a significant amount of ownership to site administrators to control their own destiny. Of course, as in the Marvel Spiderman comic where Peter Parker's Uncle Ben quotes Voltaire, "with great power comes great responsibility," your site administrators might not be ready for that responsibility or even interested in it. Nonetheless, it does provide a wonderful option to simply allow your site administrators to make their own choices and live with any consequences.

■ **Note**   In Chapter 13, I look at strategies and approaches to enabling end-users with functionality to customize site features and user experiences. Throughout that chapter, I provide more of a discussion on the tradeoffs and considerations for how much you delegate to your end-users.

Some tasks are excellent candidates to empower users with, especially if the product team has simplified the user experience in SharePoint for working through that task. Quickly changing the look and feel of a site is one example of a regular business user-friendly process in SharePoint 2013. Figure 12-4 provides a screenshot of the "Change the look" page in a SharePoint site, where a site administrator can click the sample that they like, and then easily update the look of their site without knowing HTML and without possessing any web design skills.

Figure 12-4. *A screenshot of the Change the look page for a SharePoint site*

It is easier said in theory than actually carried out in practice, but one option I have used in the past was a support policy where I would reset the site to the site definition and deactivate any custom features if a site had any support issues. You might consider a policy such as this if you have a community of users who want to be in charge of managing their own customizations and fulfill their own business requirements. If they mess things up badly and cannot seem to back out of whatever issue that they created, then you can hit the reset button for them. However, you do not want to be the one to make this decision and you certainly do not want to be the one who has to break the news to each site user. Instead, you will want a site sponsor who will own the decision and any user fallout.

A good site sponsor candidate might be the site collection administrator. They basically own the site and control its destiny (and they can also hold enough privilege to hit the reset button themselves without any IT involvement). The trouble is that there can be more than one site collection administrator, so this complicates the process in determining who the site sponsor is. Another complicating factor I have found is the site collection administrator can often be the sponsor's executive assistant rather than the sponsor themselves. For example, the sponsor might be a director or some other department head who holds ultimate authority and accountability for a site, but they do not get involved with the actual administration of it – they delegate this to their assistant or someone else on the team.

Therefore, part of your planning and preparing for delegating to site owners will require that you capture who the site sponsor is. Perhaps you can customize the self-service site creation form to collect this information as users provision the site in the first place, if you allow your users to self-provision. Alternatively, if you use a site request form or if you require users to submit a ticket to the service desk to request a new site, then you can require the requestor identify a site sponsor as part of the request. I would probably create this process as a workflow that first validates the site sponsor holds enough authority to be a sponsor (such as requiring a director level or above to sponsor a site), and then request their approval to sponsor the site.

With an identified sponsor and support policy in place, you will be set up well to delegate many of the decisions and implementation details to your internal customers. I am of two minds on this approach: on the one side, you are getting out of their way to enable them to implement their priorities as they see fit; but on the other side, their expertise may not be in technology and so they may not know how to map the right technology to their business needs. They probably are not IT professionals and therefore do not have the expertise to make decisions as they relate to information technology.

Things you may find simple within IT may not seem so obvious to a regular user, and so they may struggle with decisions on what to do with their site. For example, many technical people in IT are familiar with the concept of account permissions and security groups, but for a regular user, their experience with managing permissions may be fairly basic or non-existent. These users may have an even more difficult time making sense of how to manage User Solutions and their site resource quota, as shown in Figure 12-5. This knowledge and experience gap can be problematic when you delegate ownership of these types of things to a regular business user.

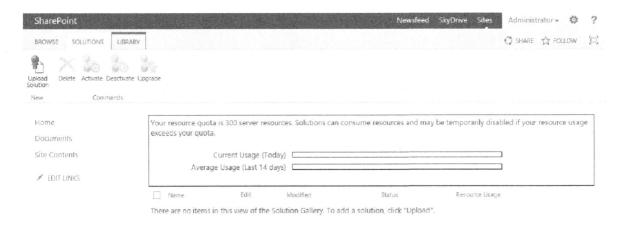

Figure 12-5. *A screenshot of the site User Solutions page and its resource quota*

You might fill some of these gaps by offering end-user training where they can learn about the different features available in their SharePoint site, as well as how to effectively use them. Within the training material, you can include guidance on when to use a particular feature and how it aligns with a business need. This type of direction can help your site users to make an informed decision on which core features they will need in their site to function in a way that will support their processes and needs. It will also help to make them aware of the different ways to use the tool as the training resources steers them toward different use cases.

■ **Note**   Please see Chapter 5 for more guidance on planning and designing end-user training resources.

Alternatively, you might offer support services for your users to help them work through specific functional tasks. You can empower your more technologically adept users to go ahead and customize parts of their site to suit their needs. For your other internal customers, you can do the site setup for them. When the site sponsor or their delegate has a particular need, they can submit a service request and someone on the SharePoint team can configure what they need. For example, they may submit a ticket to add new users to a site or to help them create a new document library. What end-user services your team offers depends on your users' level of confidence and experience using the technology. Of course, what services you offer will also depend on resource availability on your team to fulfill these requests.

Ideally, I recommend that you try to find a hybrid of all the options and seek the right balance between enabling your users and supporting them. The world really is not so black and white, as there are many shades of gray and different hues of colors in between. I find choices and tradeoffs are never so binary with a single correct answer. Similarly, I do not have an easy formula that you can use to calculate what the balance should be for your internal customers. Instead, I suggest that you experiment with different mixes of empowering your users until you find an effective tolerance.

I discuss this idea of how to effectively empower end-users and their sites in more depth in Chapter 13, where I look at the range of tradeoffs and options available for you to set at the end-user site level. Part of finding this tolerance and making this decision involves input from your internal customers. When you identify a site sponsor, you also name a point of contact who can provide input into this decision. Or better yet, a site sponsor can own the decision with you serving as their advisor.

Consultant Comrade

When I get involved as a consultant to advise a client on sponsorship, I try to help them focus on the concepts of a sponsor who funds a project and one who will hold accountability for the decisions and work that will come out of a project. From there, I walk them through the idea of a transition period and the potential of handing off sponsorship to another owner for ongoing operations. By clarifying the idea of sponsorship, you can focus on who the sponsor or sponsors are, and then you can work on getting their commitment. Otherwise, this exercise can quickly grow problematic and disrupt or stall the project.

As a consultant, I try my best to remove any dependencies that block or stall a project from moving forward. I do this because I am engaged with a mandate to deliver consulting services for a piece of work that I agreed to in a work order or a statement of work. As such, I need the project to move forward to meet my deliverables, and one area I occasionally need to work around is the notion of identifying an executive sponsor when no executives are available or interested. From my sense, this vague idea of sponsorship requirements seems to stem from a misguided notion that you need to establish an executive sponsor before a project can go well.

Indeed, a sponsor will help a project go well, and you should have your clients identify one on every project. However, the sponsor you require does not necessarily need to be an executive. That might be overkill for what the project needs. Instead, you should guide your client to consider what you need from a sponsor and what role they will play in the project. By working through and answering the following questions with your client, you can help your client understand what they need in a sponsor.

- What is the relative scope of the project in relation to the organization?

- How much resistance or political opposition to the project is there?

- Who funds and approves the budget for the project?

- What level of authority does the project need to resolve any roadblocks?

- How much risk and organizational change will the project entail?

- What degree of sponsorship involvement does the project require?

Without understanding what you need from a sponsor, you will have a hard time articulating the commitment you need. Quite frankly, sponsors do not usually like to take on the accountability for open-ended and ambiguous commitments. For me imagining myself as a potential sponsor, this would be a non-starter, because the ambiguity would mean that neither of us would be set up for success. After putting myself in the potential sponsor's shoes, I can see that I need to clarify the role of the sponsor first, and then use this information to identify the appropriate level on the organization chart I need a sponsor from rather than simply defaulting to the executive level.

I also prefer to explore and define sponsorship with my clients to steer them away from any preconceived notions of sponsorship. One in particular that I try to help them avoid is a generic notion of an executive sponsor. Executives do not usually have time to sponsor every little initiative – and probably even less time for those ambiguous requests for sponsorship. This can affect a project if the team ends up in a holding pattern waiting for the elusive executive sponsor before they feel they can move forward. Worse still would be the team that pushes ahead without any sponsorship – essentially delivering a project without any authority or accountability.

I am downplaying the need for executive sponsors on purpose only because you will not always need one at that level. However, I am not downplaying the need for sponsors in general. Ownership on a project team and in operations is a critical role because it defines the authority and accountability structure. Without it, you risk finding yourself stuck in situations of indecisions or the wrong decisions. At its extreme, a lack of ownership risks developing a culture where team members neglect responsibilities by passing the buck or shifting the blame. The buck has to stop with someone if the project is to have any chance, and I identify who the sponsor is on day one of the project before I conclude the kick-off meeting and move forward with the project.

Another reason I work with my clients at the very beginning of a project to help them identify a sponsor is to establish an escalation point. In my experience, it is always easier to identify who the escalation point will be and to get their commitment to hold that role before something goes wrong. When things are on fire and a project is falling apart, people avoid it as if it were a sneezing passenger on a public transit bus during the swine flu outbreak. I always want to plan for these worse cases, and then put the right pieces in place so that I have what I need to work through any issues as they arise, all planned for and decided *before* issues arise.

In short, although I might not require an executive sponsor, I do require a sponsor – someone who holds enough authority to take on the ownership and accountability of the project or the ongoing operations. I have found that a team can quickly become dysfunctional without a sponsor in place. Even if they are not active on the project or daily operations, they hold the accountably and are available to get involved if I need to escalate any issues to them. As such, I find that identifying the sponsor or at least the acting sponsor is a good checkpoint before a consulting project can move forward.

Inside Story: Notes from the Field

Several years ago, I was engaged on a project with a client to deploy a SharePoint farm. They wanted help to install and configure the infrastructure to setup a basic team site environment to enable online document collaboration. This project comes to mind as I discuss sponsorship because I had a great project sponsor from my client who knew how to move things forward and unblock any roadblocks. He was their chief architect and formerly their CIO. Although he was not an active member on the project team, he was always available to immediately resolve any escalations I raised.

At the start of the project, he stressed how important it was to move the project forward and deliver a victory for the IT department. He then made a joke about how whenever a roadblock came up, I should let him know and he would provide me with a tank to smash through it. What a sponsor! This sponsorship approach and support was effective for my project for three main reasons:

- He held enough authority to influence and move things forward

- He knew how to navigate their internal politics and bureaucracy

- He was committed to the project's successful delivery

I took him up on his offer and stuck with the tank metaphor. Whenever things seemed to lose momentum, he would ask how the project was going and I would tell him that I needed the tank. He would then reply, "The keys are right here," and then he would ask what I needed. True to form, he quickly smashed any roadblock and continued to move the project forward. He meant it when he offered his commitment to remove anything that stood in the project's delivery path.

It did not matter what came up; if I escalated an issue to him, he would either resolve it directly or send the support I needed to work through the issue. He never once came to a status meeting, and instead he preferred to receive a synopsis of the project's status in a couple of words informally as we passed in the hall. If things were going well, then he left it to us; and if things were struggling then I just had to mention what was causing grief. There were no long discussions and almost no meetings, yet I could depend on him to be responsive and to get results – sometimes immediately, and sometimes within a day or two. Roadblocks would simply disappear without a word or warning, and things would start moving along again.

This experience, naturally, left me with a taste of what effective sponsorship can be like and what it can add to a project's delivery. I had to reflect and wonder how I could establish similar sponsorship on every project, with every client. Sadly, other clients' sense of ownership and overall commitment to a successful delivery are things that are beyond my control and influence. I can suggest and describe the kind of sponsorship that I found to be the most effective, but if they do not buy in to the vision or they simply just do not possess a tank, then this type of power sponsorship will be unavailable.

Nevertheless, when I describe this sponsor and the tank metaphor, clients seem to understand what I need and the impact a strong sponsor can have on the project. I may not be able to smash through any roadblocks, but I will ideally identify a sponsor who can help navigate any political or bureaucratic situations. This can work very well and help to ensure the project can work through any issues that arise. Besides, sometimes just blasting through any objections or obstructions will be less effective than negotiating and soliciting buy-in on the approach. Although the styles differ, the sponsorship outcome of mitigating or resolving issues is the same. This outcome is what matters the most.

You might be wondering what I do if I find myself on a project where my client has not identified a sponsor or they have an inappropriate one filling in the role. As I mentioned earlier, I try to address this during the project kick-off meeting, or better yet, during the project scope and work order planning session. Sponsorship is something I require to deliver the right aspects of the project. Without it, I have no one to check-in with regularly and get sign-off on my progress, or at least no one who I will feel confident as having the necessary authority that I can depend on. Once I describe the risk and talk through what I need in place, I can usually get the right sponsor to commit to sponsoring the project.

Some months later, I found myself back engaged with the original client who started the tank metaphor for sponsorship. I was kicking off another project with a different group, but I still had access to the tank if I needed it. Before I even kicked-off the project, I had confidence that I could deliver and be successful. Having such strong and committed sponsorship is a treat and it can generate confidence for the entire team, which helps to build momentum and move a project forward.

Wrapping Up

In this chapter, I discussed the benefits of establishing sponsorship for customizations to commit ownership or funding for sustainable customizations. I looked at capturing a chain of custody that leads back to commitments to fix defects and mitigate upgrade issues. I also considered topics that relate to support policies for global customizations, utilizing Apps for SharePoint, and delegating ownership of customizations to site administrators.

Not all customizations will involve the SharePoint service team. End-users may customize their site and maintain their customizations on their own. SharePoint provides capabilities that you can enable to allow end-users to build their own solutions without affecting other sites and users that the SharePoint service supports. In the next chapter, I discuss how to facilitate these end-user customizations in a safe and isolated manner so they do not negatively affect the performance of the overall service.

CHAPTER 13

Facilitating and Isolating End-User Customizations

No snowflake in an avalanche ever feels responsible.

—Voltaire

In this chapter, I provide an approach to determine which customization abilities are available, and to what degree you can decide to empower your end-users to make those customizations on their sites. I also provide considerations for planning safe isolated user containers that limit the fallout or global impact from suboptimal user site customizations. Throughout the chapter, I point out some of the different customization-related features available to you within SharePoint 2013.

After reading this chapter, you will know how to:

- Empower your users

- Enable end-users to apply custom site designs through Design Manager

- Plan an optimum default site experience

- Delegate access control and site management

- Plan for safe isolated user containers

- Limit the support demands with customizations

- Detect problems with site customizations

- Describe Apps for SharePoint and the role they play for site customizations

Predicting Doom

I am always silently amused when I start a new project and hear about how I need to lock things down to protect the users from some vaguely imagined disaster (well, not so silently any more I guess, thanks to this paragraph). The client seems to have a type of panic based on their speculation and imagined fears of all the things that could go wrong unless they work hard to prevent them. Their rash decisions lead to requirements to lock the environment down as they hope to protect the users from themselves. They try to rationalize this approach by assuring me that their users are different and they need to take this extra step.

"Our users just are not that technical" is a common thing I hear. "They need a lot of hand-holding." You have no idea how often I hear this. Almost as often as I hear how unique a particular organization is. You are in your own unique place, I have no doubt, and with your own unique culture of users. This is what makes governance difficult, because otherwise you could simply carbon copy a solution. However, you are probably not as unique as you think. To start, I can honestly tell you that I almost never find that the users turn out to be as helpless as IT believes. They also do not usually go out of their way to break things on their sites or on your servers. They usually just want to do their jobs.

Sometimes in doing their jobs, users need to find creative ways to work around IT constraints that they feel make a process inefficient. In my experience, this is the reason behind why they change things and develop workarounds. They are trying to find creative solutions to the problems they face. They are probably not trying to be defiant toward IT (or at least not initially, but after a lot of us-versus-them cycles, their motives might degrade to this). Setting your users loose in a SharePoint collaboration site is not like setting a herd of cats loose in a yarn store.

I am trying to convince you that you do not need to spend your time predicting all the doom that can come if you empower your users. Your users can most likely handle it, and they might even appreciate some flexibility and freedom. Most users will probably not care and will not bother with doing much to their site, but some will. Those who do will unleash value and a positive impact with their SharePoint use. This can also benefit your SharePoint service through positive side effects, such as:

- Increased overall adoption as users can tailor their experiences to meet their needs

- Reduced burdens and bottlenecks on IT for changes and customizations

- Less demand for global applications as users can develop isolated solutions

- Improved user sense of empowerment and support from IT

Your fears may be well grounded, but do they outweigh the potential benefits to the value your SharePoint service can deliver with empowered users? They may do things that require a support ticket to help them back out of whatever they did; but do not let this potential support ticket cause a moral panic on your team. Without the ability to do things, different types of support tickets still come up, so locking down your users would not be saving much. This would only be an illusion in one's support ticket moral panic, one that can lead everyone to convince themselves that if they do not lock things down then there will be an overwhelming tsunami of support requests. I hope I have succeeded in making you aware of some blinders that people can put on, and so you can now avoid making rash decisions based on moral panics, such as fears of support tickets.

I try to avoid predicting doom and thinking about how bad we expect users to mess up their sites. Instead, I try to focus on how I can empower the users in a safe and sustainable way. If you set up things well, you can steer users in the right direction and help facilitate how they manage their site with a minimal support impact. This chapter can give you some tips on how to balance the amount of control you put in the hands of your users with the ease of how supportable you can keep their sites. It all starts with deciding to what degree you will empower your users.

Empowering End-Users

SharePoint provides a rich tool that you can empower users with taking charge of their own sites. Microsoft designed SharePoint with this ideal of empowerment in mind. This means that if you follow the philosophical design of SharePoint, then your users can manage their own needs, and in their own time. Now, as much as I like to put the control of things into the hands of empowered users, I also recognize that this is not as easy as it sounds. Not only that, but I appreciate that this approach might not fit everyone's situation. If it does not fit your situation, you might want to skip this section and jump right to the sidebar where I describe how to lock down your site.

Empowering your users can range from simple activities, such as creating new lists and libraries to manage their content in, all the way up to more complex aspects of managing a site, and everything in between. It is not a binary on or off, yes or no option. It does not have to be all or nothing; you can empower your users to whatever degree you feel comfortable with and to what you find appropriate for your organization. The following lists some of the different areas you may empower your users with, either in some of these areas or in a combination of them.

- Manage site membership and permission levels

- Create content containers such as new lists and libraries

- Purchase Apps from the SharePoint Store

- Add Apps to the site homepage

- Close or delete the site

- Build custom workflows

- Construct custom design packages

- Deploy user solution packages

- Activate and deactivate site features

- Change the site theme, title, and logo

If you think of empowering users in a site as a continuum of options and combinations that you can make available, then you can also think of those options on a continuum as well. One example of this continuum is the site design and user interface look and feel. For the more advanced users who possess the relevant skills, they may want to thoroughly customize site pages using a tool such as SharePoint Designer or Adobe Dreamweaver to match a particular brand for their group. Meanwhile, for other more basic users, branding and HTML may not be within their skillset and it may be over their head. Some of those basic users probably would still enjoy the feeling of changing the look of their site. Figure 13-1 shows one option for changing the look of a site, which provides a simple interface where users can click on one of the visual previews to apply that design to their site.

Figure 13-1. *The SharePoint Change the look page*

Providing your users with these capabilities enables users to make their site feel as if it is their own. Whether this is as simple as selecting site themes from a finite list of branding options, or if you want to allow them to use the site Design Manager to create their own composed looks, empowering them with options can go a long way toward user adoption and overall satisfaction.

You have several choices about what you want to enable to empower your users. Again, this can be along a continuum, rather than simply on or off. For instance, you might allow them to add Apps to their site, but not allow them to purchase Apps from the SharePoint Store. You may allow them to purchase Apps from the SharePoint Store or add any from your internal catalog, but you may not allow them to upload and deploy user solution packages. On the other hand, you may allow them to do all of the above. There is no single correct answer.

How do you determine the right tolerance and balance for how much to empower your users? Let me first say that I generally default to wanting to empower my users with more freedom rather than restrict them. I then work my way back from this open and empowered default to add more restrictive settings based on a few considerations. I usually work through the following decision considerations when I am determining how much functionality to enable to empower the users:

- Is there a security or privacy requirement for a more restricted site?

- Does any other compliance or regulatory requirement depend on a more restricted site?

- Is there a lack of experience with SharePoint in the organization and a general desire to start with more restrictions until the SharePoint team feels more comfortable?

- Does the infrastructure have enough capacity to handle any additional load for customizations?

- Is the type of site one that does not lend itself well for ad hoc changes or customizations?

- Does the IT department have available resources to provide site management services?

You do not have to empower your users with all the capabilities available to a typical site collection administrator. However, you do have to decide and then take the actions to implement and govern your decision. I encourage you to consider it rather than simply dismiss the idea, but once you have thought it through then you are ready to put a box around what aspects of the site you will enable, and which ones you want to lock down and restrict.

KEEPING SITES LOCKED DOWN

The opposite of empowering your end-users, according to the *Oxford English Dictionary*, is to forbid them. If you do not want users to have the authority and power to manage their own sites, then they will rely on IT to administer it for them. The implications are that someone from IT has to be the site collection administrator, rather than delegate this to a site owner. One option in this case is to have the service desk create document libraries, perform restores, administer permissions, and the like.

It is possible to lock down a site and continue to have IT manage it for them. However, this implies a burden on IT to respond to needs and perform site administration services. I have had customers who wanted to implement SharePoint in this manner, and so I assigned the service account as the site collection administrator for each site rather than an individual. I then added users either as content contributor site members or as read-only site visitors. This approach adds overhead to IT, but if you want to maintain control, it may provide a solution.

Enabling Design Manager for Custom Site Designs

SharePoint 2013 simplifies the process of implementing your own user interface design through the Design Manager. In the past, a user interface designer needed to know about all the SharePoint elements on a page if they were going to create custom page designs. They needed specialized knowledge and skills that go beyond coding the markup and styles to implement their design. Instead, they had to know about the SharePoint and other ASP.NET controls that would be on a page, particularly content placeholder controls. They had to understand things such as the relationship between master pages, regular SharePoint site pages, and page layouts. As if all that was not already enough, user interface designers also had to figure out the complex nesting of SharePoint CSS styles and style sheets.

For a long time now, SharePoint has had less than ideal ways to customize the user interface, and this has led to governance challenges in many deployments. The challenge comes from the complex relationship between all the elements that make up a page and the specialized knowledge that customizing these elements requires. Frankly, it can be tempting to do things in less optimal or less sustainable ways, such as directly hacking system files or modifying site templates. The other problem is the toolset's barrier to entry: a designer cannot pick the design tool he or she is used to using; instead, they would have to use SharePoint Designer. It was also difficult to package and replicate designs across sites.

I do not mind SharePoint Designer as a tool, but I also know there are more world-class HTML design tools available that a web designer is probably more familiar with and used to using. I can tell you that people have found SharePoint Designer to cause enough governance-related grief that the SharePoint product team eventually added the ability for administrators to disable it completely. It can be a handy tool for creating workflows and making changes to your site design, but if you are used to using a tool such as Adobe Dreamweaver, then you might find SharePoint Designer constraining and frustrating.

Design Manager in SharePoint 2013 enhances how you govern a SharePoint site because it will fit with how site designers are used to working. Best of all, it does not require any specialized SharePoint skills. User interface designers can focus on what they do best, and Design Manager will translate what they produce into how SharePoint structures a site design. By simplifying the process and allowing designers to work in a way that is intuitive to them, Design Manager removes the barriers to entry and helps to minimize the support issues you may have previously experienced when designers unknowingly made a change that broke something on the site.

You enable the Design Manager capability with the publishing site feature. Once enabled, you can upload an HTML page and have Design Manager convert it into a SharePoint master page. At that point, you can add snippets to the page, which are HTML representations of a SharePoint component that Design Manager will use to add the component to the master page. This feature enables interface designers to focus on their strengths designing a visually appealing site without having to figure out the details and intricacies of all the SharePoint components.

■ **Note** To learn more about the SharePoint 2013 Design Manager and how to use it, please see this MSDN article: `http://msdn.microsoft.com/jj822363`

As you design the user interface for your SharePoint site, you will want to design an intuitive site that users will know how to use and where to find what they need. Although you might design individual sites with their own design to give them their own brand and specialized experience, I find it is best to start with a simplified design as the default for all sites to help make it easy for other users to get started with their sites. In the next section, I share some considerations to help you plan these default site designs and experiences.

Planning Default Site Experiences

Teams within Microsoft, and I am sure countless other software development companies, work hard to plan the optimum default experience for users – the out-of-the-box settings and layouts that will provide the starting point for users. These defaults translate into how the majority of users will use a product, and this is especially true for those users who are new to the product. As such, you need to set the default so it helps to make those users productive with the software by ensuring the core of the features are accessible and discoverable.

A default provides everyone with a consistent base, a common place to start from and a common way to meet the majority of your users' needs. It also simplifies the process for creating the training materials that you need, because you can use processes and include screenshots based on the default experience. This offers the newer or less technical users detailed direction on how to accomplish tasks, while the more advanced users can translate the training to fit whatever customizations they have introduced to their sites. Notice that this is the same process that technical reference books take. For example, in this book, I have used screenshots from a default SharePoint 2013 team site. Even though I suspect that your site might not look the same as the default anymore, I know you at least started with the default and so I can be confident this will be familiar to you.

I find the trouble comes when teams blur these two different types of users when they try to make a policy about how much they will empower users with at the site level. Sometimes I see clients merge the two needs and go with a more restrictive policy where they lock down the site and enforce a basic experience. My approach is quite different from this, as I prefer to separate the two types of users and consider their needs independently. For the basic users, I focus on planning a default experience that will address the majority of their needs. If you get the default right, most users will not have any need to go beyond that, and so you will not need to worry about all the ways that you need to lock down things in the site. Hence, this why the default is so important and why it demands so much planning and thought.

For those advanced users, I like to leave the ability available for them to manage and adjust their sites as they see fit. I hold a general philosophy that IT operates best when it is in the business of providing value and acting as a strategic partner to the organization, rather than having IT get in the business of policing or restricting the organization. Your situation might be different, so I am not offering this as a golden rule, but I am stressing it because I find this philosophy works well and I want you to make an informed decision.

By default experience, I do not mean that you should create a template and add a bunch of web parts to the homepage. I also am not saying that you should create a document library with a bunch of empty folders that you want users to organize their content. Users do not need that much handholding, and this design strategy almost never works out. From my experience, a hierarchy of empty folders confuses users and makes a site difficult to use. A better solution is to focus on a metadata strategy rather than a folder structure, because this allows users to organize the content in whatever way that makes sense to them while also maintaining consistency through the content's metadata.

■ **Note**   Please see Chapter 15 where I look closer at information architecture and using metadata to organize content rather than a hierarchy of nested folders.

In a similar fashion, I find that adding a bunch of web parts or Apps to the site template will only crowd a site and it can be equally as confusing for users. It can be too much for new users to take in all at once, and this can confuse them or leave them lost with how to use the site. Not only that, but it almost always leads to bloating the site with a lot of unused features that someone added to the template. I see people add features to a template because they think they will be helpful or add some level of consistency across the organization, which sounds nice in theory, but in practice, it rarely ends up being the case.

Forcing a bunch of Apps and features on every site template does not save time nor does it benefit your users. This way of thinking about site and template design is antiquated and limiting. I prefer to focus on providing the simplest experience with easy ways to activate different functional aspects that a user might need. I make these experiences available for the user to provision or activate on-demand, which means my users do not have a lot of empty folders or crowded pages with unused Apps. Instead, the result is simple, clean interfaces that users can build out and tailor to fit their needs.

SharePoint 2013 provides a wonderful example of this approach. If you look at the screenshot in Figure 13-2 of a default team site's homepage, you can see how simple and clean the interface is. The product team did not over crowd it with different things as the SharePoint team site templates have in the past. The team site template used to include a Task list, a Shared Documents library, an Announcements list, and the like. This resulted in a majority of the sites containing an empty Task list, for example. As you can see in the SharePoint 2013 default team site, they made this option available as a sort of wizard or easy button in the Getting Started App, and as a result, all the sites do not end up polluted with unused containers, while users who do need a task list can easily add it to their site by clicking the "Working on a deadline?" tile.

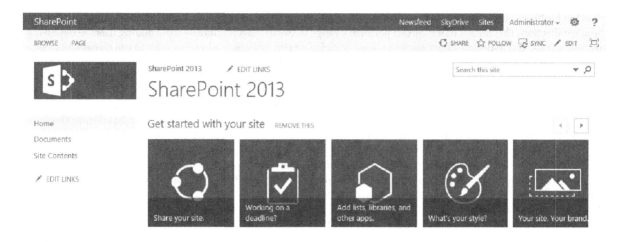

Figure 13-2. The default SharePoint 2013 team site homepage

I think the SharePoint 2013 team site template provides a great example to model for the default experience you design. Rather than bloating a site with a bunch of unused and useless things, keep it simple and expose an easy way for users to add or activate what they need. This keeps sites relevant and it offers a way to guide users into the available features of the site a little bit at a time, as they are ready to expand and add more capabilities. A SharePoint 2013 team site implements this strategy through the Getting Started App, which includes several tiles for different actions that site owners might be interested in to customize their sites. You can use the Promoted Links App to implement a similar concept with your own tiles, and you can link each to a different action to activate or enable an aspect of the site for your users.

With the right default site experience and a clear path of least resistance, you can balance the needs of both your basic users and your more advanced users. The basic users can use sites without being overwhelmed with functionality that they do not understand, while at the same time, you do not constrain and limit the advanced users from customizing the site to fit their specific needs. For both sets of users, you can provide a functional site that fits their needs. Part of how you provide a site to meet the needs of both types of users involves how you delegate management and control of the site.

Delegating Access Control and Site Management

SharePoint has always provided a site model where you can delegate the site management and access control to site administrators. When you create a new site, SharePoint requires that you identify one or two site collection administrators, and they become the ultimate authority for the site and any sub-sites they create within the site collection. SharePoint grants site collection administrators to have full control of every site in the site collection, including the ability to delegate site administration or other site management privileges to other users. This enables you to effectively delegate the security administration to site collection administrators, who can then also delegate security and management at a more granular level.

Just because you can, this does not always mean that you should. Delegating security management to ordinary business users can be both a blessing and a curse. It certainly puts the control within a click of their mouse and allows them to grant permissions to provide access when they need it. However, it also puts the control within a click of their mouse – within a click of a non-IT administrator who probably does not have much experience managing security groups and permissions in an enterprise setting. Now, all of a sudden, you are throwing a site at them and expecting them to manage the security in a way that experienced IT folks have been doing for years. SharePoint 2013 simplifies the process of managing site groups by using more common terms for regular users, such as *sharing* the site rather than managing permissions.

One problem with assigning a user as a site collection administrator is that they then have full control throughout the site collection. This means that they can perform a range of site management tasks from adding users to deploying customizations. You may have times when you want to delegate site collection administration to site owners, but you might not want to grant quite as much privilege as what a default site collection administrator role includes. In those cases, you can create a custom permission policy level at the web application level to deny the privileges you want to restrict, and then you can assign that policy to the site collection administrators.

For example, if you want to deny the ability to perform custom design tasks on a site for your site collection administrators, then you can create a custom permission policy level on the web application that denies these permissions. You can create this policy level by navigating to the page where you manage web applications in SharePoint Central Administration. On this page, select the web application for which you want to create the policy level, and click the Permission Policy button in the ribbon. This button pops up the Manage Permission Policy Levels modal window, which looks similar to the one shown in Figure 13-3. If you click the Add Permission Policy Level link at the top of this window, you can specify the details of the custom permission policy level. In this case, I named the permission level "Deny Design" and checked the Deny checkboxes next to the design-related permissions.

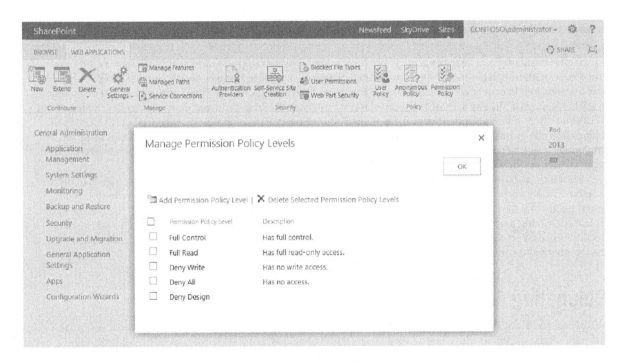

Figure 13-3. *The Manage Permission Policy Levels modal window in Central Administration*

Once you have created the desired permission policy levels, you can then click on the User Policy button in the ribbon to assign the policy to users or groups. Deny policies will override anything else for a permission, which will effectively enable you to fine-tune how much access and the degree of site management that you want to delegate to your site owners and site collection administrators. You can experiment with some combination of the different permission levels at the site level and through the web application's user policies to find the best mix for your particular needs.

■ **Note** I often grant web application-wide permissions for the service desk's administrative accounts through a user policy to ensure the support resources automatically have the access they need to work with users and handle support requests.

After the site collection administrator, a SharePoint site contains groups to organize users within to grant them the group's permission level. By default, SharePoint provisions three groups for a site: the site owners, site members, and site visitors. These groups provide full control, contribute, and read-only permission levels, respectively. Site groups can provide an intuitive way for regular users to manage security without having to get involved with setting individual permissions. This simplifies the security administration while it also organizes users into different groups in the site, depending on their role.

By default, any child site you create in a site collection inherits the permission settings and site groups from its parent site. This default provides a clean and simplified way to manage security across a site collection. However, you may have times where you do not want to have a child site share the permissions of its parent site. For instance, if you create a team site to share information and collaborate across an entire team, you might then create a child site for a specific working group within the team. You might break permission inheritance for that site to grant contribute permissions only to that working group rather than the entire team. You might also want to create a child site only for the managers on the team, in which case you would break the security inheritance and grant permission only to a SharePoint site group for the managers.

Breaking site security inheritance can quickly become a mess and difficult to manage if your site hierarchy grows to any complexity within the site collection. I try to avoid these types of deep layers of sites within a site collection, but if you do need them, then I try to ensure that they will be manageable through a careful design of the SharePoint site groups you will need to manage the different sites. This can help keep the site permissions centralized and orderly throughout the site collection, but the site owners may need your help to think the group design through and to implement it in their site collection.

You do not have to use SharePoint site groups strictly to manage site permissions. You can use group membership to target content to a particular audience, such as if you only want to show an App on the homepage to a particular group of users. With these types of groups, you can configure them to allow users to self-join by adding a link to the homepage or some other way to allow users to easily manage the content they want to subscribe to or unsubscribe from being targeted to them. Delegating group membership to the individual group members themselves is another way that you can ease the administrative burden for managing a site's membership, but this will not be appropriate for all sites.

One example of a site where you might want to delegate the administration of the site's group members is a community site. For a community of practice, the site provides a collaboration environment for members interested in participating in the topic. A SharePoint 2013 community site provides community-based discussions for community members, but you might want to expose a self-forming and self-managing community site on a wiki or a team site instead. To enable users to join and leave the site, you can configure a site group with the option to automatically allow members to join and leave the group. Figure 13-4 provides an example of a group configured with these options.

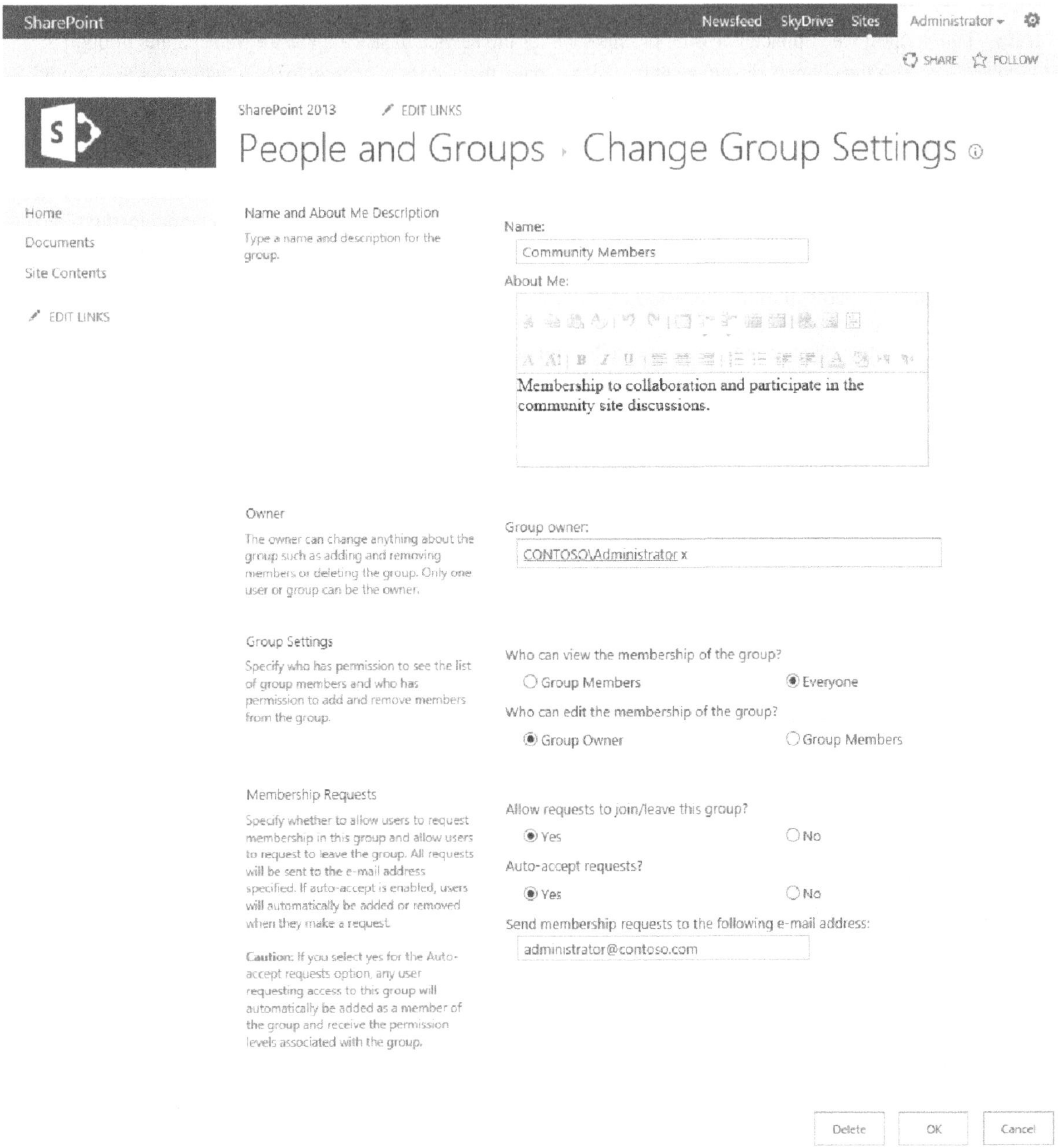

Figure 13-4. *The Change Group Settings for a SharePoint team site*

SharePoint provides many options for delegating site management and it offers different levels of permissions that you can delegate. Because a site collection provides the main container for sites and their management that you then delegate to users, the security model also revolves around site collections. This allows you to delegate a range of administration duties at the site collection level for site collection administrators. These administrators can then further delegate management of individual sites within their site collection, but those sites will share common site collection resources that the site collection administrator will have to manage. Since site collections are isolating containers, they provide an effective way to delegate administration, but they also provide you with a way to isolate anything contained within those sites. In the next section, I look at how you can use site collections as a container to isolate any customizations from affecting the rest of your SharePoint service.

Planning Safe and Isolated End-User Containers

If you decide to empower your users by giving them the option to customize their sites, then you are going to want to ensure that you give them a safe and isolated area for their customizations. For instance, you do not want them to interrupt service for the entire farm by over consuming resources, and you certainly do not want them to make changes that conflict with other users. The answer to isolation is a site collection.

I prefer a site design that distributes users and content across many site collections rather than structuring a deep hierarchy of sites and child sites within just a few site collections. I like the design with many site collections for several reasons, and using a site collection as a container to isolate users and their customizations is one of those reasons. SharePoint uses site collections as the main boundary for content and security, so they serve as a natural container to use in planning your site designs for isolation and delegation.

A site collection provides an area to allow users to manage their site experience as they see fit. It allows them to do this without having to worry about overlapping with other users or experiences. This segregation of site customizations can take the form of site visual designs or custom applications such as workflows. It can also simply provide a space for how they organize Apps for content and how they want to display web parts on the welcome page. As I mentioned earlier, most users will be happy with whatever the default is, so for them the site collection is simply a container to help them organize their content. It will also help keep them safe from users in other site collections who want to customize their sites.

You do not have to set limitless boundaries and allow the site to go in whatever direction the users want to take it. A quota can help set boundaries for overall resource usage – from the amount of disk space the site consumes for its content to the amount of server resources a user solution can consume each day with its processing. Quotas transfer any enforcement of the site's boundary for SharePoint to manage and monitor. When a site reaches a quota limit, SharePoint can lock the site and alert a site owner that their site has reached its quota threshold.

Using quotas allows a SharePoint administrator to provide space in a site collection container without having to consume him or herself with the details of the site's implementation or to consume him or herself with micromanaging how users use their site. I do not consider quotas as a tool to limit or restrict users; instead, I prefer to think of them as a tool to manage growth. Rather than letting a site grow aimlessly unbound, a quota offers a system-enforced point to review the site and decide whether to apply a new quota or not.

Quotas can offer you a checkpoint when you or your team can review a site and its usage. During this review, you can confirm the users are using the site appropriately and offer any coaching for areas that you find the users could be more efficient. I try to set a quota threshold so it is big enough to give users some freedom to do things with their site without having to constantly burden IT with requests to increase their quota through insignificant quota levels. I want a threshold where I do not have to care how efficient users are being with their sites—they may not set things up as perfect as I might prefer, but below a certain level I am not concerned about their overall efficiency.

For lower usage and smaller sites, they will consume little total resources, even though they may not be efficient with the marginal resources that the sites do consume. As their overall resource impact is minimal, I generally find they are just not worth my time until they grow to a certain size – usually the same size that I set the default quotas to. I usually adopt the philosophy that I cannot scale if I get caught up in the details of every little site and that I will be most effective as a SharePoint administrator if I focus my efforts on the largest or most heavily used sites. By using quotas, SharePoint can let me know once a site reaches a size that interests me (if a site ever does actually grow to a size of interest, since most sites probably will not).

You can set quotas directly on an individual site collection, but this approach will prove unmanageable once the number of site collections grows to any significant number. A more manageable approach is to create quota templates and assign those to site collections. With a quota template, you can adjust the quota size and it will automatically change for all the site collections. As you increase the size of a quota for an individual site collection, you can assign a different quota template with a larger quota size to continue linking all site collections to a quota template. Figure 13-5 shows a screenshot of the Quota Templates page that you can find in the Application Management area within SharePoint Central Administration.

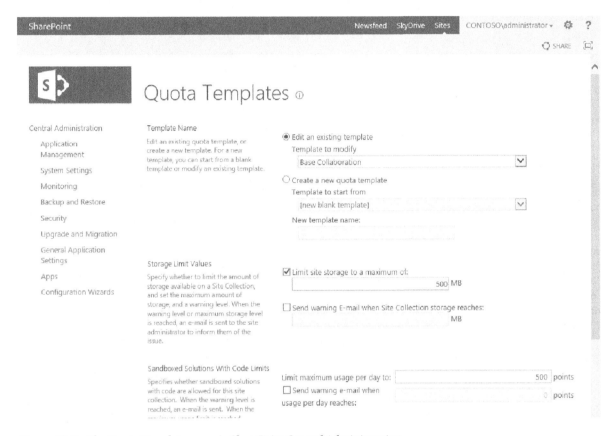

Figure 13-5. *The Quota Templates page in SharePoint Central Administration*

Site collections can also exist in their own content database, which helps you isolate it even further. For example, when you allocate a site collection in a dedicated content database, you can set a schedule of frequent database backups for just that site. This dedicated database option might offer a handy solution for a site that end-users are prone to breaking, because then you can offer a range of point-in-time options to restore their database and rollback their site. It will also give you the option to implement any other unique database configuration or schedule requirements for a particular site.

In short, site collections provide a level of isolation between groups of users and their customizations. Quotas provide boundaries for those site collections so that they do not grow excessively and over consume significant amounts of system resources without you noticing them or at least being able to contain them. This can help you to provide a SharePoint service to diverse sets of users without having them conflict with or affect each other. Nevertheless, even after isolating sites and setting quotas, you may still need to take further actions to limit the support demands from user customizations.

Limiting the Support Demands of Customizations

The biggest objection I hear against allowing user customizations relates to a fear of a perceived tsunami of support calls. As a result, I find the first, and probably the default for most SharePoint teams, is to look at how you can restrict your users to protect them from themselves. The logic seems to follow the idea that if they let users customize things, then those users will mess everything up and overwhelm support with requests to repair the damage. These fears may be true, so it is not for me to quash. Even still, I usually find that the support burden does not have to be gigantic, and you can manage this by setting the right expectations about what you will support.

Just because users make a mess of things does not mean you need to help them continue on whatever path that they were heading before things became so unmanageable. In fact, I suggest the opposite, and here's why: if you constrain your users too much, then they will either find a workaround that circumvents your restrictions, or they will take their business elsewhere, such as by using a free cloud solution. Either way, this could end up causing you more grief in the long-run than good. One can quickly go crazy trying to predict all the ways they need to lock down and constrain their users.

Imagine a dam with a reservoir of water behind it that just wants to flow through, water that is even starting to leak through in spots. Rather than look at all the ways you can plug each of the holes in the dam, look at how you can let the water flow in a controlled way to relieve the pressure on the dam. Similarly, I look for ways to enable users and their customization needs to flow through the system in a sustainable way. This approach helps you avoid sweating the small stuff, and it allows you to focus your attention instead on the more important or strategic stuff.

If you are worried about the volume of support that allowing customizations will generate, then perhaps you should revisit your support policies. You can limit the fallout and support burden by limiting what you support. For example, an approach that I prefer is to set a support policy such as a Service Level Agreement that defines the extent and limitations of support your users can expect for any of their customizations. If a user messes up their site, your support policy might be to reset the site to its default state and reapply the default master page. This would return them to a workable and supported state, which is usually a state where users can be productive collaborating on their site.

Users may not like a support policy that simply undoes any changes that broke a site. They may not be satisfied with a site restore to an earlier point-in-time or reverting any customizations to the default site template. Their frustration probably comes from wanting to do something but they lack the skills or knowledge required to accomplish the customization they desire. They may express this frustration to you if you only offer to undo whatever progress they feel they have made. In this case, I find the ideal solution is to offer a chargeback service to troubleshoot and rework their design or developments to help them reach the customization solution they require.

As an alternative to providing the chargeback service from your team directly, then you might consider offering the site owner a list of preferred SharePoint professional services vendors that they could contract and work with to redevelop their customizations. This is an especially useful option if your organization is not set up for chargebacks. I would avoid taking ownership of the problem without a funding sponsor, such as those that I considered in Chapter 12, since this would effectively circumvent your sponsorship requirements and introduce a loophole in your demand funnel for customization projects.

▓ **Note**   Please see Chapter 9 for more information on how to manage your demand funnel for customizations and other changes.

As long as their customizations are contained, the support demands will be relatively contained. A special challenge presents itself with user solution packages, also referred to as sandboxed solutions. These can contain code that executes within the SharePoint farm, and if you enable the option, users can deploy them unchecked and untested to their site collections. The risk can amplify if the users begin to share these solutions to other site collections. It is only an issue for poorly developed solutions and does not mean that you should simply disable the entire option for user solutions. Most solutions will probably work just fine, and so it might be an overreaction to disable the option for everyone just because a few may cause issues.

If a user develops and deploys a poor solution that constantly consumes their available daily quota because they coded their solution with inefficient code, you can choose to block and disallow the solution from executing. This can be a particularly valuable option when one group develops an inefficient solution and then tries to distribute it to several other groups. You can set the solution as blocked, which will prevent sites within the farm from activating and using that specific solution. It may seem like a drastic step, but it can be a necessary one sometimes. You may want to block a poorly built solution to force a group to improve it before they start spreading it around the farm. Figure 13-6 shows a screenshot of the Sandboxed Solution Management page found in the System Settings area of SharePoint Central Administration where you can block a user solution.

Figure 13-6. *The Sandbox Solution Management page in SharePoint Central Administration*

Of course, you can go the route of locking down all these options and steering your users toward creating or purchasing SharePoint Apps instead. Disabling and restricting options can be prove difficult in many cases, because Microsoft designed SharePoint with a distributed and delegated model in mind. They provided several options to disable features on sites, but it is still not perfect, especially at the granular level. I generally find taking an approach of setting restrictions can lead to complications and it will add complexity to your SharePoint service. My best advice is to start slow rather than overreact, and where possible, implement the restrictions through permission policies on web applications or through service application permissions. However, even with the best plans and restrictions, problems may still arise.

Detecting Problems with End-User Customizations

If only your biggest problem is that you do not hear about problems from your end-users. I would guess that whenever a problem arises, your service desk quickly knows about it through one or more support calls shortly after your users discover the problem. Nonetheless, you can still be proactive in detecting and addressing potential problems before they become an issue for users.

I do not expect you to check every site with any sort of regularity. If you have a sizable deployment, then I expect you have many sites that you will never check or even visit. Chances are you will have too many things vying for your time, which means that investigating every site for problems will not be a luxury you can afford. I tend to pick the biggest sites or the busiest sites to focus my attention on how I can help to improve the experience that these select sites provide their users. On the other hand, if you have a sizable SharePoint team and this is a proactive service you want to provide, at least initially while you improve the state of your SharePoint environment, then this proactive work can help you discover areas to make improvements.

Whether your team can scale to investigate every site or you can only focus your attention on select sites, at the site level the process is largely the same. As you investigate the site itself, you can check for potential performance issues, such as the following:

- Very large lists that do not have an indexed column

- Very large document libraries that do not use a folder structure or have an indexed column

Sites that have user solution packages present their own challenges. This is because solutions packages contain custom code that can slow down the rendering of a page or consume excessive resources on servers in your SharePoint farm. You can detect these inefficient solutions packages by checking the solution quota for a site collection. If the site regularly consumes its quota, then you can investigate how efficient the solutions are developed. Figure 13-7 provides a screenshot of the resource quota for user solutions on the Solution Gallery page that you can find a link to on the Site Settings page.

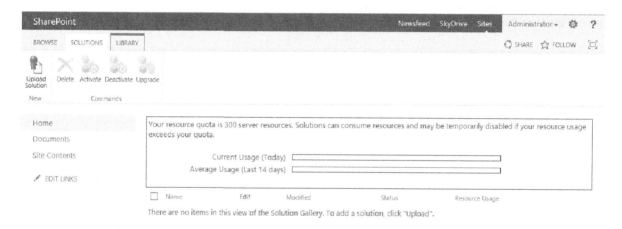

Figure 13-7. *The Solution Gallery page on in a SharePoint site collection*

Performance monitoring is one technique that you can use to help detect when something is changing or a problem is emerging. I discussed performance monitoring and the different metrics you can use back in Chapter 6. As you analyze your performance metric reports, you can look for signs of problems emerging. For example, you might notice that the usage patterns and the number of users remain consistent while the overall usage consumes more system resources. This type of measure can tip you off to things such as inefficient code processing on servers within your farm.

As an alternative to having code process on servers within your farm or having to manage custom solution packages, you might consider using SharePoint Apps. In the next section, I discuss how to enable and take advantage of Apps for SharePoint so that site owners can add desired functionality to their site without having to deal with things such as solution packages or the site Design Manager.

Understanding Apps for SharePoint

An App for SharePoint is a self-contained piece of functionality that end-users can add to their site. Site owners can discover Apps through different catalogs, depending on the type of App and its source. SharePoint sites come with a number of default Apps, such as a document library or survey. In this case, the App provides the list or library definition, and you can see which are available to add to a site by navigating to the Site Contents page and then clicking to add an App. You can also add additional Apps for different types of lists and libraries by activating the appropriate SharePoint site features.

You can find Apps in other areas as well. This is where I find the concept of Apps may seem a little confusing at first. An App can be more than simply a list or library; an App can provide functionality and it can even integrate with another system. You can find these other types of Apps in different catalogs, such as by activating a feature and adding it to the site catalog. The other possible catalogs for Apps include your organizational catalog and the SharePoint Store.

Your organizational catalog enables you to provide a catalog of any custom Apps you make available to the entire SharePoint farm and any other farm that shares the catalog. This offers a central and well-known directory location for users to discover relevant Apps that are available for them to add to their site. Typically, these will include those custom Apps that address needs or fit with processes specific to your organization. This catalog also tracks licenses and requests for Apps that site owners have requested for purchase from the SharePoint Store for their site.

The SharePoint Store is the public marketplace hosted by Microsoft, and it contains Apps from different vendors. This provides a convenient way to purchase add-ins to enhance or extend sites in your SharePoint deployment. It simplifies the entire procurement, development, and deployment process with a low-risk approach to adding new functionality to SharePoint. It also puts a range of different custom Apps in the same directory to make it easy for site owners and SharePoint administrators to discover what custom functionality is available.

■ **Note** To learn more about Apps for SharePoint, including how to plan for and configure an environment for Apps, please see this TechNet article: `http://technet.microsoft.com/fp161230`

Apps allow site owners to add functionality to their site without any IT involvement or intervention (although, you can configure the SharePoint Store so that site owners can only request Apps rather than purchase them directly). These Apps empower the site owner with controlling the life cycle of the App where they can add, remove, or upgrade it on their site. This can provide a convenient way to delegate the decision-making of what functionality a site needs to the site owner, while also isolating the change to just their site and minimizing any compatibility risks.

Consultant Comrade

For me, the most challenging aspect of end-user customizations from a consultant's perspective has been in helping my client get past any mental block against the idea of empowering their end-users. Sometimes this is a non-starter and they do not even want to discuss the idea. Their support staff or their SharePoint team is often too lean and is spread too thin, and so they do not want to risk allowing anything that will end up being a further drain on their scarce IT resources. They may have other reasons, such as wanting to maintain some abstract idea of a consistency across sites, but the end result is the same: they do not even want to discuss the idea of empowering their users.

Unfortunately, locking down their SharePoint implementation just might be the direction things will have to go. I say unfortunately because there is always a danger of lost opportunities or overreacting in making such overarching decisions if they have not thought them through. They could be limiting themselves and their users without even realizing it. Be that as it may, in the end I still support their decision and help them achieve the implementation they want, even if that means constraining their SharePoint service when I think they have a greater opportunity to take a more open approach. In these cases, I tend to note my recommendations to take a different approach, but I accept that they are the ones who have to live with their SharePoint environment.

I must admit that it can be difficult to accept and support a client's decision when I suspect they are heading in the wrong direction. As their consultant and the expert they brought in to guide them, I feel a responsibility to always steer them on the correct path. However, they own the decision and I am merely there to advise. It can be easy for me to embrace the idea of empowering end-users and creating a user experience that allows them to manage their own needs, but I am also an expert with SharePoint. My clients may not have the same confidence-level in their ability to manage an environment such as how comfortable I would feel, and so they may not be able to see the same opportunities that I see.

Sometimes the idea of putting control in the hands of end-users is simply too big of a culture shift; it would lead to what I refer to as a *breakthrough* improvement rather than an *incremental* improvement. A breakthrough improvement occurs where you attempt to make a major change all at once, whereas an incremental improvement seeks to make continuous improvements in smaller yet frequent steps over time. I first mentioned this idea of continuous improvements in Chapter 7 when I looked at creating a roadmap for your SharePoint service. Then, as now, I prefer to make a series of smaller steps that continuously make or introduce an improvement in a system, but I hold the same idea when it comes to changing a culture. Rather than try to make a giant change all at once, I look for ways to introduce a series of smaller changes and continuous improvements that will take the culture in the intended direction.

Accordingly, if you are trying to guide your client toward empowering their users and you find your client is resisting, then perhaps you are trying to introduce too big of a change. Perhaps you are trying to make a breakthrough improvement in their culture and instead you should consider introducing an incremental improvement. The following lists a few areas that I have found can provide a start in a more empowering and delegated direction:

- Allowing users to manage the membership and permissions for their site
- Allowing users to control the layout of their site
- Allowing users to change their site's visual theme and apply composite designs
- Allowing users to provision built in SharePoint Apps, such as lists and libraries
- Allowing users to purchase Apps from the SharePoint Store
- Allowing users to design and build their own workflows

Each of the items in the preceding list might be a big enough step for your client. I may take them all and more for granted as simply being a part of SharePoint. However, for someone new to the SharePoint paradigm, they may need to start smaller and build their comfort-level with the culture-shift this may entail. I try to step away from focusing on wide-reaching implementation constraints that seek to lock down everything and focus instead on individual capabilities that we can provide users. This strategy usually helps move stakeholders away from making blanket decisions based on a fear of the unknown.

The other strategy I use to try to break down some of these barriers and mental blocks is to deploy a pilot environment of SharePoint as soon as possible. I find that the sooner we get working software in the hands of users and stakeholders, the better. For me, this always seems to help them work through their perceptions and fears better than a series of meetings debating the details. It also provides an opportunity for actual end-user feedback on their experience and what they find valuable. We can monitor how they handle any empowerment and their overall ability to manage their own site, and this can help to resolve misconceptions or false perceptions. Ultimately, by putting working software in the hands of users, I find we can consider actual usage and feedback, and this can provide a balance to those more theoretical meetings.

Inside Story: Notes from the Field

Some time ago, I worked for a company where the majority of my users were software engineers – developers who built software for a living and who wanted to have the ability to develop and customize anything in their SharePoint site to fit their needs. You might not face quite the same degree of demand for site customizations, and I have not faced it since. Having so many developers form such a large proportion of the company, and thus my user base, presented an interesting scenario: I wanted to leverage their skills and potential to customize the SharePoint experience to whatever opportunity they imagined, but at the same time, I needed to protect and ensure the long-term stability of the SharePoint service.

Primarily, I did not want to get in their way or limit them. My company included a lot of software engineers, and most of whom had much more expertise and practice in software development than me, especially when it came to certain low-level areas deep within the system. After all, not only was I involved in less development activities, but most of my software development in recent years involved C# and Microsoft .NET, which abstracts away many of those low-level implementation details. I wanted to take advantage of this creativity and expertise so that they could tailor their own experiences to fit with how they wanted to work and not feel constrained by the default.

My objective was to empower developers to build whatever utility they wanted and to try my best to not constrain or limit them. This strategy would help me for two reasons: it could take the pressure off my scarcely resourced team from having to process enhancement requests, and it could drive user adoption. My team simply did not have the available capacity to offer any sort of enhancement, particularly at the individual site level, because we were already spread too thin. I wanted to leverage these developers throughout the company who had availability capacity and who wanted to build enhancements. Through this approach, I had the idea that empowering developers would help drive the overall adoption in a similar fashion to how Microsoft leverages developers in the community to enhance and drive adoption for their products.

Historically, Microsoft has had success in overall market adoption with many of their products because they empower independent software developers to build on and enhance a product. Of course, much of Microsoft's success for a particular product comes from providing a great product, but by allowing and even encouraging developers to build solutions on top of those products, then these solutions made Microsoft's products even more compelling. Microsoft is not able to efficiently scale to tailor each of their products to fit every customer's way of working; instead, they provide a generic product and Microsoft partners can specialize and build solutions to meet individual needs. By following this model, I wanted to focus my team on providing the core SharePoint service, and allow other developers and groups to customize discrete sites to meet needs that are more individualized.

The key was to enable customizations at the site collection level, and to do so without causing an impact on the rest of the service. I needed to use the site collection as a container—one that I could delegate to a group to manage and customize as they saw fit. The challenge was that we were using an earlier version of SharePoint, one which did not have the capabilities of SharePoint 2013 that I mentioned in this chapter. User solutions, also referred to as sandboxed solutions, were not yet invented and available. User solutions later formed the essence of how I achieved this goal, and they continue to provide an excellent solution to empower developers to customize individual site experiences with rich features and functionality.

In those early days on SharePoint, before user solutions became available, an easy option was to encourage developers to find ways to use the Content Editor web part to wrap another HTML page in a frame they could embed on the page. I had to encourage these types of workarounds to limit the number of customizations and components I had to deploy globally on a farm. When embedding the functionality in a frame on their site page would not achieve what they needed, then I would work with them to design a solution we could deploy in the Windows IIS directory rather than to the Global Assembly Cache (GAC), and this would allow me to apply a restrictive .NET Code Access Security Policy (CASPOL). Essentially, with this approach, I could restrict and contain a customization to some degree, but user solutions later superseded this implementation complexity.

The reason I am so fond of user solution packages is that they encompass all the complexity of isolating and restricting code execution. As I mentioned earlier, they also have a quota system that you can use to set boundaries around the amount of server resources that you will allow a given site's user solutions to consume. This is all great stuff, but my personal favorite feature is the ability to select the servers on which to execute the code within user solution packages. You can dedicate one or more servers for this role by starting the "Microsoft SharePoint Foundation Sandboxed Code Service" on the Services on Server page in SharePoint Central Administration. You can then stop this service on other servers and effectively isolate where this code executes and you can contain the available server resources for code in user solution packages to consume on specific servers.

SharePoint Apps are wonderful; and I think with SharePoint 2013 introducing them, they will augment and provide additional ways for users to customize their sites. User solution packages (and farm solution packages for that matter) will still play a vital role in adding and extending functionality in a SharePoint farm. As long as the SharePoint team maintains user solution packages in the product, I will continue to enable them when I need to empower my end-users with abilities to develop their own solutions for their site.

Wrapping Up

In this chapter, I discussed how you can facilitate end-user customizations and how you can isolate those customizations so they do not have a negative impact on the performance of your SharePoint service for other users. I looked at how to empower your users in a safe and contained environment so that they can adapt and tailor the service to meet their needs without introducing an unnecessary burden on support.

Although you can enable your users to customize much of their experiences and capabilities in their SharePoint sites, at times they will require a more extensive solution that will extend beyond the safe containers of their SharePoint site. This may include developing and deploying custom components that you need to make available across the entire SharePoint farm. In the next chapter, I discuss how you can design development standards and testing processes to help reduce the risk involved with deploying custom components.

CHAPTER 14

Designing Your Development Standards and Testing Processes

Quality means doing it right when no one is looking.

—Henry Ford

In this chapter, I provide guidance on establishing development standards for customizations and testing processes that enforce those standards. I offer considerations for different development standards and processes that will minimize risk to the SharePoint service's availability.

A key point I stress in this chapter is to define benchmarks to test against and an approach to develop an automated testing process against those benchmarks.

After reading this chapter, you will know how to:

- Explain the role of an architect

- Consider global availability

- Decide between SharePoint solutions and Apps

- Set developer boundaries

- Define testing benchmarks

- Design testing processes

- Incorporate test-driven development

- Automate code quality checks

Involving an Architect

As a software developer myself, I know there is a balance between developing and delivering functionality today, and analyzing longer-term impacts and sustainable design considerations. Architecture plays a critical role in a development project, because an architect's job encompasses both designing a solution that can meet the current needs, while also considering the future for the solution. The architect can consider all the moving pieces and they visualize how different aspects will come together. They think about the whole lifecycle of a solution, not just the immediate functionality to develop.

When I discuss architecture and the need for an architect to bridge different solutions and different development teams, I often relate the need with an analogy of the Winchester mansion built in San Jose, California. After the death of her husband, Sarah Winchester moved west from New Haven, Connecticut, to San Jose, where she purchased land and hired carpenters to begin building her mansion in 1884. She decided to just hire a bunch of builders and she would tell them what to build each day – sometimes she wanted them to build new rooms, and other times she wanted existing rooms remodeled. Consequently, the house was continuously under construction for 38 years until her death in 1922. There were never any known architectural blueprints, and instead Winchester herself drew some rough sketches of what she wanted. This resulted in a house with stairs that climb into a ceiling and doors that open to brick walls.

■ **Note** To learn more about the Winchester mansion and its fascinating history, please see this website: `www.winchestermysteryhouse.com`

Building software without an architect leads to similar results as the Winchester mansion: parts that do not go together, extraneous parts, and a perpetual feeling of *chasing* the development. An architect can help you coordinate different development efforts and they can help you avoid the cycle of developing around issues. They take a global view of the system and all its parts, and they think through wider reaching implications such as future support and maintenance needs. Ultimately, they can help you avoid building stairs that merely climb into a ceiling.

When it comes to SharePoint development, I find that SharePoint is no different as it relates to needing architects to plan and design your solution. You will need infrastructure architects to design the physical farm, and you will need other types of SharePoint solution architects to plan and design how development activities and custom solutions fit within the farm. With an architect taking a global view and coordinating the development efforts, you can avoid the chaos of different development teams heading in whatever direction they decided to drive their solution toward.

It is not enough for each development team to have their own solution architects, although they should each involve an architect. You also need an architect for the entire SharePoint service – someone who can oversee and coordinate how the different work streams fit within the system. You also need your architect or your committee of architects to serve as a gatekeeper for any development on the system. I generally structure any gatekeeping of this manner by requiring architecture reviews throughout the entire development lifecycle.

You can use an architecture review to stay aware of the different development activities occurring that will eventually want to deploy a solution to the SharePoint service. If you get involved early and you stay involved regularly throughout the development lifecycle, then you can influence and steer a development team's design decisions to make them more sustainable or compatible for your SharePoint service. And of course, you can prevent ending up with stairs that climb into ceilings.

One key area an architect can contribute to your team is by adding a wider perspective that encompasses the entire service and its lifecycle. Architects think about how current decisions and designs will impact the service in the future, which will help you understand any dependencies that otherwise might not have been as apparent. They also consider the sustainability and availability for your SharePoint service from a global service perspective rather than from individual point solutions. In the next section, I share some considerations you can use to think from a global service availability perspective.

Starting with Global Availability in Mind

Before I get into the details about development practices and testing approaches, I want to start with a mindset: global service availability. In Chapter 13, I discussed different ways you can isolate end-user customizations, particularly by containing them within a site collection. Now, I am shifting my focus in this chapter to those customizations that span site collections and can impact your entire web application or SharePoint farm. These are customizations that a SharePoint farm administrator enables or deploys on the farm. Customizations of this global nature require forethought and consideration for any impacts on the global availability and sustainability of the SharePoint service.

The main issue with global customizations is the scope of potential impact if something goes wrong. By their nature, they are global, and so they can potentially affect every user of your SharePoint service. Because of this, my first requirement is to have maintaining the global availability of the service as the paramount focus of any architecture and design decisions. I also want to make developers aware of the inherent dangers and possible fallout if they implement a component without maximizing global availability.

I am emphasizing that global customizations come with added risk to the availability of your SharePoint server because I find having this mindset will help you frame and enforce the rest of your development standards and testing processes. Without considering the dangers, you might be more nonchalant about your development standards and testing processes. The reason global customizations need your attention and a level of seriousness comes from the scope of how much they can affect. As the scope of reach increases and the range of potentially affected users grows, so too does your inherent risk of how much can go wrong.

When you contain a customization to a site collection and something goes wrong, then it will affect only those users in the site collection – a limited range of users. This would not be great, but it would be manageable because it would be contained. Now, when you have a global customization and something goes wrong, then it can affect everyone. You might not even know who or how many people that an issue affects. This situation is much less manageable because it is uncontained.

There are many areas that a global customization can cause you grief if you do not carefully plan and coordinate these global changes. The main functional areas that I pay attention to include the following:

- Accessing shared data or any other shared resources

- Executing with elevated privileges

- Managing any session state or caching

- Aggregating data from multiple disposable objects

- Integrating with external systems directly

This is by no means a definitive list of areas where things can go wrong with global customizations, but they are where I uncover the most serious problems. Whenever a component handles resources such as those I listed, then it risks mishandling those resources. I am not saying these areas are bad or wrong, only that they are areas I like to pay extra attention to as I review a component for global availability.

For example, pretend I am developing a stock quote web part. I want to set the symbol in the web part properties, and then as the page loads it will display a quote using the latest data it queries from a web service. This sounds simple enough. In this example, I would pay attention to the fifth point in my list: the direct integration with the web service. I might also pay attention to how it manages caching or what opportunities it has for caching. My preference would be for a solution such as this one to make use of the Business Connectivity Services (BCS) to manage the data integration and web service connection. BCS could also manage the caching in a consistent way for all accesses from within the SharePoint service to this data source.

Subtle design changes can make a customization more manageable and they can improve global availability, such as in my example of using BCS rather than directly accessing the web service. By thinking about maintaining global availability alongside a potential global adoption of the custom component, you shape your thinking into what will be in the best interests of your entire SharePoint service and all your users.

Some of your decisions may be reasonably straightforward, such as disallowing any direct database access for SharePoint data; meanwhile other decisions may be much less cut-and-dried. Many options may present themselves, and each might be viable. Nonetheless, you will have an easier time navigating any grey areas when you are looking for the options that maximize global availability, because this may rule out some options.

In some cases, there still might not be a leaning factor to a clear choice, such as when you need to decide between SharePoint solutions and Apps for a solution. For these implementation options, either can work and they each have their benefits and drawbacks. In the next section, I share some considerations to help you decide between the two approaches.

Deciding Between SharePoint Solutions and Apps

What I love about Apps is how simplified and intuitive the team made the user experience for adding a new piece of functionality to a site. To contrast this experience, I consider the steps involved with adding new functionality from a sandbox solution: upload and activate the solution package, activate the feature, and finally add a web part to the page. To add an App, a site owner simply needs to click the Add a New App link and then select an App from the appropriate catalog.

From an end-user's perspective, Apps are very compelling with how they simplify the process of adding new functionality to a SharePoint site. Apps also provide a simplified and centralized way to purchase add-in components from third-party vendors in the SharePoint Store. You can replicate this experience with your internally developed Apps by hosting them in your organization catalog and your users can discover them from a centralized location for internal Apps as well.

■ **Note**   Please see Chapter 13 where I discuss Apps as they relate to end-user customizations.

Apps provide you with the safest option for extending your SharePoint farm with new functionality and they help to maximize your flexibility when developing future upgrades. They also reduce the barrier to entry to SharePoint for programmers who lack SharePoint development experience but who have other web development expertise.

I trust that this all sounds wonderful and that you are probably wondering why anyone would use anything besides Apps. The answer is that Apps do a great job for what they do, and what they do is provide functionality for end-users. That means that Apps are limited to things you can develop with the client object model and contain within a site collection. For all other customizations, you need to develop them as SharePoint features and package them within solution packages (WSP).

■ **Note**   For more information on how to build Apps for SharePoint, please see this MSDN site:
http://msdn.microsoft.com/jj163230

One constraint with Apps is that you cannot execute custom code on the SharePoint servers in the farm. Instead, the code needs to execute on the client such as by using JavaScript, or it needs to execute on a hosted server or through a cloud solution such as Azure. If your solution needs to execute code on the SharePoint servers, then you need to use a SharePoint solution package. You will also have to use solution packages to develop certain other components for your SharePoint farm. In particular, you need to deploy the following through a SharePoint solution rather than as an App:

- Custom site definitions
- Delegate controls
- Custom themes
- Custom actions
- User controls

As you can see, there are still plenty of valid reasons to develop your customizations and your application extensions for your SharePoint service using the SharePoint feature infrastructure and solution packages. You will need to use farm solutions for any global customization you want to develop or any farm administration component you want to build. You will also use farm solutions to package any scheduled tasks or custom health check rules that you develop.

■ **Note**   For more information on building farm solutions, please see this MSDN article:
http://msdn.microsoft.com/jj163902

To summarize, developers have the option to choose between SharePoint solutions and Apps as their means to package and deploy their customization to a SharePoint farm. Apps have compelling benefits and you should choose to develop an App by default if the customization you are developing will fit with what Apps offer. Otherwise, you should develop the customization for a SharePoint solution package. I find this decision process makes it easy to choose between Apps and solutions.

Apps provide a new option, and they are great for what they offer, but they are merely an option. You can still continue with the process you are used to or with the components you have already developed for solution packages. You do not need to rework any previous investment right now just because Apps are available, unless you want to take advantage of something Apps offer such as the convenient organizational catalog for easy discovery by end-users.

Whether you choose Apps or solution packages, or more likely, a combination of the two, you will need to set some boundaries for what your developers can do on your SharePoint farm. This will be more applicable to developers of solution packages, because developers of Apps are already quite limited with what they can do in your farm – mainly, they cannot execute any code on servers in the farm. Nevertheless, it is still good to think through what direction that you want to steer all your developers toward as they develop customizations for your SharePoint service. In the next section, I provide guidance on how to set boundaries, standards, and general guidelines for developers.

Setting Developer Boundaries and Standards

For me, when I am wearing my developer hat building a solution, I just want to solve the particular problem I am working on. Anything available that appears to offer a potential solution is an option for me. The downside of this is that I do not evaluate any and every possible solution, because once I find a solution I start to develop it. I find my budgets and deadlines often do not accommodate exploring multiple solutions. This is only dangerous when I develop a less efficient or fragile solution by developing in the wrong areas of the SharePoint application or with inappropriate parts of the SharePoint API. Even worse is if I develop a solution and build functionality that the API would have provided, had I known it existed.

Of course, my developer perspective has widened over the past few years as I spend more time thinking about sustainable architectures. With a wider system view, I usually cannot help but think beyond a single problem area. Whenever I develop custom solutions now, my perspective goes beyond any individual component to consider its entire lifecycle and how it will affect the SharePoint service.

Not all your developers will have this perspective, and this is not a deficiency or anything bad, it just means they have not had experiences that expose them to the wider SharePoint application. Or, they might not have extensive experience going through the entire lifecycle of a custom developed application or component. This limited view means that without developer direction and architecture guidance, they will focus predominately on the solution itself. You can help to steer your developers in the preferred direction by establishing boundaries for custom development.

Boundaries do not have to come with a lot of overhead and tight restrictions. They can take the form of general guidelines or specific areas to avoid certain things that you want to restrict. For everything else, you can decide whether or not to let them work with an architect and use their own creativity to design a solution, or if you want to define your developer boundaries at a granular level. The following lists the chief boundaries I establish to avoid these specific things:

- All customizations must package any deployment files and manifests in either a SharePoint solution package or an App for SharePoint package for deployment to the SharePoint farm. The deployment package must include all deployment and configuration instructions for SharePoint to automatically apply, including any `Web.config` settings or changes.

- No customization may modify or overwrite the core SharePoint product and system files directly, including all ASPX, XML, JavaScript, CSS, and image files.

- All customizations store any data they require by persisting it to a SharePoint database through the SharePoint API or by providing its own dedicated data store.

- No customizations may query the SharePoint databases directly.

- All customizations must only access the file system in a read-only fashion, except for copying a customization's files and assemblies during its initial deployment.

- No customization may implement its own caching solution and instead must use the SharePoint AppFabric or another persistence strategy available through the SharePoint API.

- All customizations must handle all exceptions gracefully and provide a friendly error message while recording any error details to the log when an error or exception condition exists.

I used strong language with these boundaries, giving the impression that these are absolute rules without any exceptions. Actually, I do make exceptions to these boundaries when absolutely warranted, and only after careful consideration that no other workaround exists and that the developers have a design to implement the solution without affecting the sustainability and supportability of the SharePoint farm. These are areas where I see customizations cause the most problems unless you handle them with due care, and only when truly necessary.

Sometimes it is necessary to go against one of these boundaries, such as when you need to modify an XML file and SharePoint does not provide any other way to modify the file. For example, if you want to add an icon for a particular file type, then you will need to modify the DocIcon.xml file and add a new mapping definition for a file type. In this case, you would need to modify one of the SharePoint system files, which means you would need to make an exception for my second boundary listed previously.

■ **Note** To learn more about adding icons for file types, please see this MSDN article:
http://msdn.microsoft.com/aa979708

All the boundaries I listed address specific things, and you can validate any customization to confirm whether or not it fits within those boundaries. You can even write an automated test to validate compliance, and because the boundaries are explicitly defined, the tests can be pass or fail without any grey areas. Unfortunately, all developer standards cannot be this cut-and-dried, as other aspects of a solution will depend on several factors. You may want some standards to apply in most cases, but it will not require as much rigor when the standard does not apply in contrast to the rigor an exception to one of your boundaries would require. For those cases, I use developer guidelines to encourage a preferred way to design a solution. The following lists several of my developer guidelines:

- Customizations ought to avoid exhausting any SharePoint resources from servers in the SharePoint farm, and instead they should consume a web service to do their "heavy lifting" on another server dedicated to handle the customization's load.

- Customizations ought to verify a requesting client has any necessary privileges for a particular resource or operation prior to attempting access, and where possible, suppress displaying a feature when a requestor lacks those privileges.

- Customizations ought to impersonate the requesting clients' credentials for any privileged request and avoid using the SPSecurity.CodeToRunElevated method to minimize any elevated privileges and circumvented security risks.

- Customizations ought to access data in external systems through the Business Connectivity Services by providing definitions for any web services and databases the component needs to integrate with, rather than connecting to a system directly.

- Customizations ought to write tracing and error information to the SharePoint log file and allow a SharePoint administrator to set the verboseness of tracing information it writes.

- Customizations ought to make any user interface elements compatible with SharePoint themes and CSS classes.

- Customizations ought to explicitly specify and assert the minimum .NET Code Access Security permissions an assembly requires to minimize the scope of any potential security vulnerabilities.

- Customizations ought to create and consume dedicated Service Applications, where appropriate, to offload and isolate custom tasks and workflows associated with custom code.

I am sharing the guidelines I use to help get you started. This is by no means a definitive list; you can add or modify this list as you see fit. The goal is to establish standards that steer your developers to build solutions in an optimum way for the sustainability and supportability of your SharePoint service. The goal is also to promote standards to increase the maintainability of any customization.

In addition to these SharePoint specific guidelines, I also like to consider custom code and component design guidelines. I like to establish consistent coding standards and naming conventions. I find this generally leads to more maintainable and more stable code. You can use the .NET framework and API design guidelines to aid your own developer guidelines. I find this is a good source for general developer guidelines and it aligns well with any SharePoint naming conventions and coding guidelines.

▪ **Note** For more on .NET design guidelines, please see this MSDN article: `http://msdn.microsoft.com/ms229042`

You may have noticed that one of the guidelines I listed previously relates to capturing tracing information. This is one of the best gifts a developer can give their future self because it makes troubleshooting and debugging an issue much easier. It captures code execution, state, and processing information during runtime, which provides you with a real-time view into what is happening with your code and what might be causing a bug. In the next section, I share some tips on how to incorporate this technique into your own coding practices.

Instrumenting and Tracing Code

If you want to make your troubleshooting life easier in the future, you need to plan for the types of things that will help you. For example, if you include trace instrumentation in your code and make a lot of verbose information available for the developer dashboard or SharePoint logs, then your future troubleshooting self will thank you. However, this is not the type of activity you can efficiently do just-in-time or as you need it. You need to invest the time into capturing tracing information *before* you or anyone else needs to troubleshoot an issue.

Think of instrumenting code as a development and debugging technique similar to attaching the debugger to a process and stepping through code. It allows you to instrument different parts of your code to provide information while it runs. The idea is to provide you with the same insights into how the code is executing in a production environment where you should not attach a debugger to step through the process (because it will negatively affect performance and could cause availability issues). If you instrument your code well, then you can get all the same information through tracing and avoid the headache of trying to reproduce an issue in your development environment just so you can attach a debugger and step through the code.

The characteristics of a tracing solution revolve around its primary advantage: tracing through the execution path of code while it executes in production. It does not have to be in production, as I find tracing information useful to help debug issues as I develop, but this availability in production is what makes it great. This allows you to capture tracing information to assist developers to identify the cause of bugs, especially for those peculiar bugs they are unable to reproduce or that only happen under certain conditions in the production environment. It also allows your administrators to troubleshoot configuration issues by reviewing these trace and error logs.

Imagine if you will, that you have a requirement to be able to retrace the execution path of code and check certain state variables, and you want to be able to do this after you deploy to production. However, you only want to capture this tracing data when you need to troubleshoot an issue; otherwise, you want to suppress it. Now, you do not want to recompile or redeploy anything to begin capturing this tracing information; you simply want to flip a switch and enable it, often just for a particular area that you want to troubleshoot. When you instrument your code to capture tracing information, you can meet all of these requirements.

Writing tracing information to the trace log is very easy to include in your code. At its simplest, you can write basic information by making a call to the `SPDiagnosticsService.Local.WriteTrace` method and set the relevant category and severity. For example, you could include the following code in an exception's catch block to write the exception message to the trace log. You can find these diagnostics classes in the `Microsoft.SharePoint.Administration` namespace.

```
SPDiagnosticsCategory diagnosticsCategory =
  diagnosticsService.Areas["SharePoint Foundation"].Categories["General"];
SPDiagnosticsService.Local.WriteTrace(
  0,
  diagnosticsCategory,
  TraceSeverity.Unexpected,
  ex.Message
);
```

This can provide useful information to detect and track down the source of an error while the code executes in the production environment. You can also write this information to the Windows Event log by calling the WriteEvent method instead, as I show in the following code example.

```
SPDiagnosticsCategory diagnosticsCategory =
  diagnosticsService.Areas["SharePoint Foundation"].Categories["General"];
SPDiagnosticsService.Local.WriteEvent(
  0,
  diagnosticsCategory,
  EventSeverity.Error,
  ex.Message
);
```

You do not want to fill up the Windows Event log with excessive tracing information, but for serious errors such as when certain exceptions occur, you can write the error information to the Windows Event log to make it easier for administrators to discover the issue. Unless they are troubleshooting a specific issue, server administrators will likely notice errors in the Windows Event log before they notice them in a SharePoint ULS log file.

In the preceding examples, I chose to use an existing diagnostics category, and you are free to use any of the existing categories that relate to the custom component you are developing. I prefer to use the existing categories where possible, because an administrator knows to toggle the severity levels for these when they wish to trace them. However, you may want to specify your own diagnostics category to make it easier to locate your component's tracing information in the SharePoint ULS log files. The following code example shows how to create your own diagnostics category that you can use to write information to the trace or event logs.

```
SPDiagnosticsCategory diagnosticsCategory = new SPDiagnosticsCategory(
  "Custom Example", // Set the category name you desire here
  TraceSeverity.Unexpected,
  EventSeverity.Error);
```

Between the trace and event logs, you have useful options for writing information about error conditions for your custom component, such as the exception messages in the previous examples. You can also write other types of information at different severity levels. Your tracing severity levels can range from serious issues at the Unexpected level to low-level details at the Verbose level. Your event severity levels can range from serious issues at the ErrorCritical level to noncritical information at the Information or Verbose level.

■ **Note** For more on logging in SharePoint for developers, please see this MSDN site: http://msdn.microsoft.com/ee535537

Instrumenting your code with tracing information will prove useful if anyone ever needs to troubleshoot an issue with your component. I hope you can see how developing this capability into your custom component as you develop its main functionality will help you to track down bugs or other issues much quicker than if you do not have any tracing information. This is why I include it as a guideline for developers to instrument their code with tracing information when they develop custom components for a SharePoint environment.

In addition to tracing information, you may want to view usage statistics in the SharePoint ULS log or on the SharePoint Developer Dashboard. The SharePoint API includes the SPMonitoredScope class to capture usage statistics that you can use to identify where code is failing or where it is experiencing a performance bottleneck. You can use this class to see the resource usage for different parts of your code, which will help you identify the specific areas that are performing less optimally.

To monitor usage statistics for specific code, you wrap the code in a using code block that instantiates a new SPMonitoredScope object. As code executes within the using block, the monitored scope measures the code's statistics and writes them to the SharePoint ULS log and Developer Dashboard. The Microsoft.SharePoint.Utilities namespace contains the SPMonitoredScope class. The following code example shows how to monitor a scope of code to and have usage statistics recorded in both the SharePoint ULS logs and the Developer Dashboard.

```
using (new SPMonitoredScope("Scope Name"))
{
    // Code to monitor
}
```

■ **Note**   For more information on SPMonitoredScope, please see this MSDN article: http://msdn.microsoft.com/ff512758

Instrumenting your code with tracing information is one of the most valuable development practices a developer can adopt. I encourage you to try out the examples I shared in this section and explore how these techniques can help you with your code. Trust me, having tracing capabilities throughout your code that you can later enable by toggling the appropriate severity level will reward you over and over throughout the lifecycle of your custom component. It will also reward your SharePoint administrators when they have to troubleshoot an issue on their servers. You can use the usage statistics to get started identifying your benchmarks for the custom component.

Identifying and Defining Benchmarks

Back in Chapter 6 I shared several performance metrics that you can use to measure and monitor different performance levels in the SharePoint service. These measures can be useful to monitor the performance of a custom application as well, particularly if you monitor the performance trends before and after you deploy a customization. These metrics and trends can give you a general sense for the performance impact on the server and across the farm, while tools such as the monitored scope that I described in the previous section provides detailed usage statistics of a component on an individual page.

Rather than basing a general sense of the customization's performance impact on the server's performance trends, you may want performance metrics that are more specific to your customization. In this case, you can create your own performance counters and use those within your code where you want to capture performance or usage metrics. Use the following code to create your own performance counters on each SharePoint server in the farm. I usually add this code to the FeatureInstalled event receiver.

```
if (!PerformanceCounterCategory.Exists("Custom Application"))
{
    PerformanceCounterCategory.Create (
        "Custom Application", // Counter Category
        "Custom Category Description",
        PerformanceCounterCategoryType.SingleInstance,
        "Application Counter", // This is your counter's name
        "Counter Description");
}
```

Once you create a custom performance counter on your server, you can verify it exists and begin to view its metrics in the Windows Performance Monitor tool. Of course, having a performance monitor category and counter will not be much good to you until you start to record performance data in your custom application. You can use the following code within your application to create an instance of the performance counter and then increment its counter.

```
PerformanceCounter counter = new PerformanceCounter();
counter.CategoryName = "Custom Application";
counter.CounterName = "Application Counter";
counter.ReadOnly = false;

// Increment the performance counter
counter.Increment();
counter.Close();
```

These measures can show you active usage for a particular counter. You can use the `PerformanceCounter.Decrement` method when you want to reduce the counter, such as when users finish interacting with your custom application. This can help you to measure the actual usage metrics for your application. Alternatively, you can use the `PerformanceCounter.IncrementBy` method to increment or decrement by a specific number, such as when you want to capture performance metrics about the specific amount of resource utilization.

You can use Windows Performance Monitor to monitor the performance metrics of your custom performance counters or any other performance counters that interest you. In addition, you can also have SharePoint monitor any of these performance counters on each server in a farm and then record the performance metrics in the SharePoint usage database. You can then query and monitor the performance metrics across the farm and over time. You can use the following PowerShell command to add a performance counter for SharePoint to monitor and record in the usage database.

```
Add-SPDiagnosticsPerformanceCounter -Category "Processor"
  -Counter "% Processor Time" -Instance "_Total" -WebFrontEnd
```

■ **Note**   For more on how to add a performance counter to a SharePoint or database server to record its metrics in the SharePoint usage database, please see this MSDN article: `http://technet.microsoft.com/ff607704`

Designing Testing Processes

Having an effective testing process can serve as your last line of defense to ensure all your standards and guidelines are followed and compliant for a customization. It can also help you avoid issues related to customizations, particularly for those common issues that you test against. A testing process gives you a formal process to ensure that customizations are of quality, and this can give you confidence in the sustainability of your SharePoint server even after you add several custom components to it. Having a formal testing process can also set the expectations of your developers, so they know the quality bar they have to meet as they develop.

You should design your testing process so that it takes the form of a systematic process for reviewing requests, validating standards, and then working through a change management procedure. I have found just from the very nature of establishing and following a disciplined process, you will improve overall stability in your SharePoint farms. This positive outcome for your SharePoint farm comes from making conscious decisions and coordinating between different roles – two activities I find make a significant positive impact, even if your actual tests are not overly sophisticated or thorough.

Figure 14-1 provides an example of a deployment process with the different roles and decision points involved with the deployment. This example shows what role is responsible for what decisions and activities during the deployment process. I discuss the deployment and release management process in more depth in Chapter 16, but I wanted to highlight where testing fits in with the overall deployment process – notice that in this example, the testing occurs in the first step after the customer opens the request ticket.

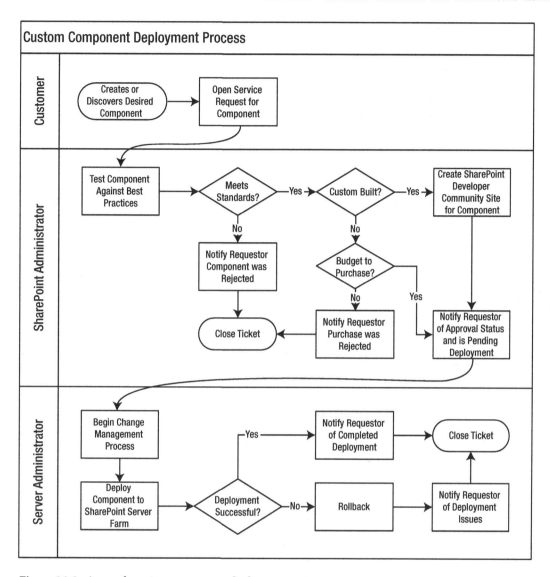

Figure 14-1. *A sample custom component deployment process*

■ **Note**   Please see Chapter 16 where I discuss testing and code promotion as part of your deployment and release management process.

The first and easiest check in your testing process is to test for the standards and guidelines you have defined, and this is especially the easiest if you have automated these tests through a script. For example, you can use .NET reflection to evaluate an assembly to test whether it uses database connections or something else. This can help you build a quick report of areas that you want to highlight and follow-up on with the development team. Your scripted tests could be pass or fail tests for non-negotiable items, or they could be for discussion if you highlight an area you are willing to negotiate and make an exception on.

The following code example uses reflection to test an assembly and loop through all the assemblies it references. You could use this code in a console application that checks for a specific list of assemblies that you want to know about whenever developers reference them directly in their custom SharePoint applications. This can help give you a list of where to focus your attention for additional testing scrutiny.

```
Assembly assembly = Assembly.LoadFile("exampleComponent.dll");
foreach (AssemblyName a in assembly.GetReferencedAssemblies())
{
  // Test whether the assembly name matches assemblies of interest
}
```

You can build on this .NET reflection technique and make it more granular by checking for specific methods or other aspects that interest you. You could also automatically test static files such as XML manifests for specific standards, such as performing a regular expression string comparison of the XML markup with file provisioning patterns that match system files.

Having code automatically test for certain conditions simplifies the testing process and ensures those particular things that you want to test for do not get missed. You can build your library of tests gradually as you discover new things that you want to test for rather than feeling as if you need an extensive library of automated tests to get started. I like automated tests because they make the whole testing and deployment process efficient and consistent. I build these scripted tests on the concept of building automated tests for certain conditions as I code functionality. Typically I build these automated tests as I code functionality in a process known as test-driven development.

Test-Driven Development and SharePoint

Test-driven development (TDD) is an agile development practice where the developer codes a unit test for a piece of functionality before coding the actual functionality. If you are unfamiliar with TDD, then this might sound a little funny. The idea is that if you always build the test first, then you will have a test for every piece of functionality in your custom application when you finish development. You will not have to worry about having to cut an aspect of testing due to budget constraints later on, because you are building automated tests as you go.

I love test-driven development because it generates a suite of tests that will give me instant feedback on whether my code breaks another aspect of the application. This leads to extremely maintainable code. I also find it helps for tracking down bugs or any issues early on, and usually you can then write a new unit test as you fix a bug to ensure it does not reoccur. Having a suite of automated tests builds my confidence as a developer and allows me to stay forward-focused because the tests are automatically monitoring for any regressions from the intended functionality.

The other aspect of TDD that I find particularly beneficial is how much more productive it can make me. This is because I am defining the intended functionality in the test for how I will want a piece of code to function, and then I code the functionality. A unit test simply tests a unit of code for a specific condition, such as an expected method call or field setting. This helps you to explicitly define the intended behavior of a method within the unit test, and then implement that behavior in your code.

Test-driven development generally follows a cycle of adding tests that will initially fail (because the functionality in the application does not exist yet), and then you code just enough functionality and logic to get the test to pass. Finally, you clean up your code by refactoring both the application and the unit test. This process is often summarized as "Red, Green, Refactor." I summarize this process in the following steps:

1. Write a unit test to test for a specific piece of functionality or condition.

2. Run your test to verify the test fails (Red).

3. As quickly as you can, write the minimum amount of code necessary to make your test pass.

4. Run your test to verify the test passes (Green).

5. Refactor your code to remove any duplication, inefficiencies, poor naming conventions, or anything else you refactor and improve (Refactor).

6. Run all your unit tests to ensure every test still passes.

7. Repeat for the next bit of functionality you want to add.

One byproduct with this cycle is productivity you can gain from the separation of writing the functionality and then later refactoring the code you wrote (Steps 3 and 5). This frees you up to focus on adding the functionality you need quickly without self-editing or trying to over think the implementation. You do not have to worry, because you are going to return after you get the functionality working to refactor and improve the code. I find this cycle keeps development moving forward and it makes me more productive.

■ **Note**   One book I enjoyed on this topic is *Test-Driven Development in Microsoft .NET* by James W. Newkirk and Alexei A. Vorontsov published in 2004. I also enjoyed *Test Driven Development: By Example* by Kent Beck published in 2002. Both are excellent sources of additional learning.

SharePoint presents some interesting challenges when it comes to test-driven development. The most notable challenge relates to the complexity in some of the objects in the SharePoint API, such as certain disposable objects that you cannot instantiate directly. You want your unit tests to run quickly and not depend on network or database resources where possible, and so when your application depends on or interacts with these types of SharePoint objects then you risk ending up with complicated and slow running unit tests.

One solution is to build your methods to use interfaces as their parameters where possible rather than the more complex SharePoint object. This will allow you to create a simpler object that implements the interface in your unit tests to test specific functionality in your application. Using these types of stand-in objects in place of the actual object is known as using a mock object. This allows you to test the state and intended behavior of your application without testing around the complexity of the SharePoint objects.

The bad news is that for most objects in the SharePoint API, there is no interface to build a mock object around. Herein lays the problem. The solution I use as a workaround is to create my own interface and then a class to wrap the actual SharePoint object. This leads to a bloating of classes in your project, but it simplifies your unit testing.

To give you a concrete example of how mock objects work and how I wrap SharePoint objects to use mock objects in my tests, I am going to create a simple unit test that verifies that a custom method properly sets the title for a site object, and then it calls the update method. First, I create the interface in the application assembly, and then the mock object in the assembly for unit tests with a reference to the application assembly. The following code provides an example of the interface and the mock object.

```
// Create the interface in the application project
interface IWeb {
  string Title { get; set; }
  void Update;
}

// Create the mock object in the unit testing project
class MockWeb : IWeb {
  public string Title { get; set; }
  public bool HasCalledUpdate { get; set; }

  public void Update()
  {
    HasCalledUpdate = true; // for unit test
  }
}
```

Now, I can create my unit test to test for the intended functionality. Because changing the site title will not be effective without also making a call to the Update method, then I want to test that both occur in my unit test. The following code provides an example of the unit test.

```
[TestMethod()]
public void SiteTitleTest()
{
  string title = "Site Title";
  MockWeb web = new MockWeb();

  SiteConfigurer c = new SiteConfigurer();
  c.UpdateTitle(title, web);

  Assert.AreEqual<string>(title, web.Title);
  Assert.IsTrue(web.HasCalledUpdate);
}
```

At this point, the test would fail because I have not yet implemented the functionality. The following code provides an example implementing the functionality of this hypothetical class. Notice that I used the interface IWeb for the site parameter.

```
public class SiteConfigurer
{
  public void UpdateTitle(string title, IWeb web)
  {
    web.Title = title;
    web.Update();
  }
}
```

Just for completeness sake, the following code provides an example of wrapping the actual SharePoint object in an object that implements the interface. In my application code, this wrapper object would be the object I pass to the method; meanwhile in my unit testing code, I pass the mock object. This works because they both share the same interface.

```
public class Web : IWeb
{
  SPWeb web;
  public Web(SPWeb web)
  {
    this.web = web;
  }
  public Title
  {
    get { return web.Title; }
    set { web.Title = value; }
  }
  public void Update()
  {
    web.Update();
  }
}
```

As you can see, this approach adds a level of complexity to your application with the extra classes you will have to generate to wrap the SharePoint objects. However, if you want the benefits from test-driven development in SharePoint, then I have found this is the best approach. There are other options, including using a mock framework. I encourage you to explore and experiment until you find what will work the best for you. My personal preference is the approach I shared in this section.

If your version of Visual Studio includes the code coverage feature, then you can use this feature to check how well your unit tests cover your application's functionality. Visual Studio will highlight the code your tests cover during execution and the code your tests do not execute. This can help you to identify areas for which you may want to write additional unit tests, particularly if you have an area of complex code without any unit test coverage.

■ **Note**   For more guidance on how to incorporate test-driven development with Visual Studio, please see this MSDN training lab: `http://msdn.microsoft.com/vs2010trainingcourse_testdrivendevelopment.aspx`

Automating Code Quality Checks

Along the lines of creating automated tests as developers develop their components, I like to use some other automated tools to automatically test for code quality. One of my favorite quality checks is to perform a static code analysis to test a custom component against rules for different code conventions and class design guidelines. This can give me a quick sense for how well a developer followed the .NET design guidelines and it will highlight any other issues it detects based on its static rules. I find that when I use static code analysis on my own code as part of my development process, I am more disciplined and write cleaner code, and so I like to project this same technique onto other developers as well.

The original tool I used for static code analysis was Microsoft FxCop. It had a list of rules that it analyzed an assembly against, and then it provided a report with recommendations on what areas of my code I could change. Since then, certain editions of Visual Studio included the same static code analysis capabilities built right into the development environment. This is great because you can include the static code analysis test as part of your build process and Visual Studio will highlight warnings with links to the actual code for any failed rules. Not only that, but if your team is using Team Foundation Server, then you can set code check-in rules to enforce static code analysis every time a developer checks in code.

■ **Note**   To learn more about FxCop, please see this MSDN site: `http://msdn.microsoft.com/bb429476`

Similar to using the static code analysis, certain editions of Visual Studio include a feature to analyze your code's complexity. This is such a wonderful feature in Visual Studio, and I pay extra for the better edition of Visual Studio primarily just for this feature. I use it to identify areas of the code that are more complex according to the analysis – areas of the code that contain a deep nesting of loops or a lot of complex logic such as nested if statements. These things are not bad to have in your code, but I find that when the code complexity analysis reports that an area of the code in yellow or red for complexity, then this is a good area to focus my refactoring efforts. By refactoring and making the code less complex, I make the code more maintainable in the future while also sometimes catching and correcting bugs hidden in the complexity.

In the SharePoint API, there are several disposable objects that a developer needs to remember to dispose of in their code. These disposable objects manage database connections and other resources, and they can hold a lot of data in memory. One common disposable object is the `SPWeb` object. For example, if you open an instance of a site using the `SPSite.OpenWeb` method, then you need to call the `SPWeb.Dispose` method to release any resources when you finish working with the web object. This seems simple enough, but it gets tricky in other cases when you do not call the dispose method. For example, if you open an instance of a site using the `SPContext.Current.Web` property, then you do not call the dispose method because another area of code is responsible for disposing of that object.

This complexity about when to dispose and when not to can lead to accidentally missing places when a developer should have disposed of a disposable object. As such, I like to use the SharePoint Dispose Checker Tool to test any custom assemblies for potential disposable objects that you still need to dispose of. Like the other automated tools, the Dispose Checker offers another way to automatically validate a large amount of custom code and point a developer toward any areas that they can improve.

■ **Note**   To learn more about the SharePoint Dispose Checker Tool, please see this MSDN site:
`http://archive.msdn.microsoft.com/SPDisposeCheck`

This section lists the main tools that I use in my custom development process. There are other venders who make code analysis tools that I might use from time to time, and I encourage you to shop around and experiment with other products as well. My goal is to have an automated way that offers me tips on where I can improve my code quality. I find it especially handy because it offers suggestions on how I can improve code quality as I work in the development process rather than having to rework a large block of code later. This does not replace a manual code review, but it can catch a lot of the common things that can come up in code and free up a code reviewer to focus on bigger picture aspects such as the application's logic.

Consultant Comrade

I always enjoy engaging with a client and helping to revolutionize their development processes to include some of the discipline and quality checks that I discussed in this chapter. If your client is not at a maturity level with their custom application lifecycle management processes, then there is a lot of opportunity for you to help them improve their code's quality and maintainability.

If you adopt many of the development tips I shared in this chapter and they become part of your development process, then it will be easy for you to share them with your client. It will also align their development team with how you develop solutions, and this will help make a smooth hand-over as you deliver the solution to their team. Helping them adopt a new development process offers your client a lot of extra value beyond simply delivering a custom SharePoint solution.

Delivering all this extra value on an engagement is fantastic and it can help to differentiate your consulting firm from other custom solution developers: not only do you have a mature development process, but you can help your client adopt a more mature process. Ultimately, this translates to better code quality, and thus better-developed solutions. Better yet, it results in a solution that is easier to maintain and less risky to introduce any changes to.

In a perfect world, I am sure this sounds great. However, if you have not budgeted to spend time consulting with your client on their development process as part of your scope, then this can quickly put you behind budget. Although I like to help every client adopt healthy and productive development practices, I also have to stay aware of managing my current scope and the actual project I am engaged to deliver. My ideal project would involve a phase where I deploy Team Foundation Server (TFS) for my client and design the development process, and then begin the actual development phases.

My point is that if you adopt the development practices I discussed in this chapter, then you will also be in a position where you can consult your clients on how to improve their development practices and processes as well. Not only does this provide you with new consulting opportunities, but it also aligns you and your client's processes so that future development projects will be more seamless.

Whether or not you offer consulting guidance around these development processes, they can still help you produce high-quality solutions if you adopt them within your own practice. If you are a one-person operation, like I am a one-person operation, then you can focus more on the automated code analysis tools to help point you to areas in your code where you can improve quality. If you are a larger development team, then you might look at how you can incorporate some of these checks into your TFS code check-in policies.

Inside Story: Notes from the Field

Recently, I had a client who brought me in to help them coordinate activities between different internal development teams and developers from vendors they engaged for other projects in process. They had a bunch of projects moving forward with custom developed solutions, all of which they would eventually deploy to a single enterprise SharePoint farm. Each development team seemed to have their own process and set of standards, and they were each working autonomously from each other.

My first goal was to open up communication between these teams and start discussing what common development standards they could share. As I was working to open up communication, I realized what they needed was an enterprise architect to coordinate the different teams and align all the solutions with an enterprise vision. With every team only considering their limited perspective of the enterprise SharePoint service, they would naturally focus on building a point solution that solves a particular problem. This was great at an individual solution level, but at an enterprise service level they were heading toward a support nightmare.

I started the process with them in the same fashion as I have with other clients in this situation and as I opened this chapter: discuss the role of an architect by first looking at pictures and descriptions of the Winchester mansion. This helps to make the point about where unplanned and uncoordinated development eventually leads to without a blueprint. I generally have a receptive audience after considering the Winchester example, and from there I begin to discuss the need for enterprise architecture and common development standards.

It can be a slow process and it can involve a lot of uncomfortable change for developer teams – teams who may be used to having no restrictions with building whatever solution how they see fit. These inaccurate perceptions of introducing restrictions and overhead are what I am trying to counteract with discussions on how bad things can get without enterprise architecture. I want developers to realize that I am not creating policy for policy sake; instead I am working to design a process that can coordinate development across different teams.

I started the process of introducing common standards by working with the development teams to help them understand how common development standards would benefit everyone by facilitating long-term sustainability and maintainability of the SharePoint service. Once everyone understood the benefits and the need, they began to agree on common standards and common development processes. It was a very gradual transition and it involved a lot of discussions and negotiations at times, but eventually it reached a tipping point and began to build momentum toward a more structured and coordinated development process.

Wrapping Up

In this chapter, I discussed how to establish development standards for customizations and what testing processes can help enforce those standards. I looked at how development standards and processes can help lower the risk a custom component poses to your SharePoint service's availability, and how you can automate tests to detect issues early.

Beyond managing the code and testing processes for custom components that provide functionality to the solutions and applications you provide, you might also want to set standards for the application structure and visual design. This helps you to coordinate a coherent user experience, one that you organize in a consistent and reliable way. In the next chapter, I discuss how to start with your information architecture design and where you can set standards for the user interface design, both of which help you organize and introduce consistency across your SharePoint service.

■ ■ ■

CHAPTER 15

Framing Your Information Architecture and UI Standards

Everything should be made as simple as possible, but not simpler.

—Albert Einstein

In this chapter, I share guidance on where to define standards that relate to the information structure and visual layout for your SharePoint sites. I provide considerations for designing your site structure and for planning consistent and intuitive visual designs. I also introduce an approach to building a controlled vocabulary to organize and tag content with metadata.

After reading this chapter, you will know how to:

- Design a user interface for consistency and intuitiveness
- Structure a functional navigation
- Implement a managed navigation
- Create a controlled vocabulary
- Build an enterprise taxonomy
- Standardize templates and metadata
- Organize and utilize people data
- Create a data dictionary

Function over Form

A user interface encompasses a mix of visuals and functionality: its form and its function. SharePoint pages primarily have a function, typically to enable collaboration among users, and you can identify page functions that you want to prioritize by identifying your primary reason to use SharePoint. These functions you identify should be your priority, not a simple user interface (UI) branding exercise. First start with the function and the user experience you want to provide, and then design the branding and visual elements to complement the experience.

There seems to be this drive sometimes to make a fancy design just so a SharePoint site "does not look like SharePoint." I think this motive on its own is silly, and it distracts a project team as they become consumed with visuals on a page rather than focusing on business needs and functional goals that relate to business value. Now, a pretty design and a clean user interface are important things and they can add impact to a SharePoint site, but on its own it is only creating an illusion of delivering business value.

Perhaps it is just me, but I would not choose to work at a company simply because their SharePoint does not look like SharePoint. Now I am a visual person and I love good designs and beautiful art, but I do not let this drive the design decisions unless I am creating an advertisement – an actual advertisement, not simply some vague notion that an organizational brand for an intranet will make people feel better connected to the organization. It may have an effect and people may appreciate it, but if your intranet portal does not serve some purpose beyond that, then it is dead before it even gets started. Its function is more important and therefore that should take precedence in your design process.

I prefer to delay looking at visual design requirements until after I work through the primary business requirements and then I have translated those into the function of a site. Once I have a solution concept of how the site will function and the purpose it will serve, then I begin to consider how to make it pretty. I find that if you get too caught up with the visual aspects of your site too early in the process, then you will begin to introduce constraints into the solution design process with things such as locking down page elements or forcing a particular page banner. These things may end up in the final solution, but you do not need to lock them down before you analyze the function and purpose of a site.

Before you get carried away with how you want your SharePoint service to look, take a step back and identify its function.

- What is the function of an intranet portal? Most likely this will be something related to communicating information or serving as a gateway to other systems or processes.

- What is the function of a MySite? This might be to provide users with a central place to store their content and manage their information for an organization phonebook.

- What is the function of a team site? This is probably to provide team members with a place to collaborate together and share information.

■ **Note** Please see Chapter 3 where I map samples of business value to SharePoint capabilities.

Of course, these are just examples and you will have more functions to list for your solution and with more detail. I abstracted the functions here to highlight some potential primary purposes. When you start with identifying the core purpose of a solution and then continue analyzing its other functions, you will lead yourself toward the optimum solution. Then, later, you can come back and apply the form, the pretty visual design that adds sparkle to your solution. And the good news is that SharePoint decouples visual designs from the site implementation, so you will not add complexity by applying themes or stylizing master pages afterward.

MODIFYING THE TOP BAR FOR ALL SITE PAGES

One page element stands out on a SharePoint 2013 page for stakeholders who do not want the site to look like SharePoint. This is the word itself, *SharePoint*, included in the top bar on all site pages. You can change this text for every site in a web application by executing the following PowerShell script, replacing the URL and branding bar text with your own:

```
$webapp = Get-SPWebApplication $url
$webapp.SuiteBarBrandingElementHtml = $brandingBarText
$webapp.Update()
```

I find that if you change this text early, such as during a pilot deployment, then you can alleviate many distractions and fixations related to making SharePoint not look like SharePoint.

Designing Consistent and Intuitive User Interfaces

A general rule of thumb when it comes to website design is to keep your pages consistent from one page to the next. You do not want to move page elements around and hide them from users as they click through your site, because this will confuse them and it will make their task on your site more difficult. For example, if you have the navigation along the left side of one page, then you should place the navigation along the left side of the next page. If all of a sudden the navigation switches to the lower-right area, then users will struggle to continue to navigate your site as they stumble to find the navigation.

Consistency can go a long way toward making your site easy to use. Consistent layouts and consistent brands can reassure your users that they are still navigating the same web property and that they can expect it to continue to work in the same manner. It orientates them and maintains familiarity. It makes your sites easy to use, and this increases how productive users are with the software while it reduces the amount of support that users will need. Consistent designs ultimately leads to a better user experience with your SharePoint service, and therefore, better overall user adoption as well.

In the context of designing consistent user interfaces, I am mostly referring to the structure of how you lay your pages out across a site. The actual brand and visual identity is another matter. Those things are important, but there are other books written on graphic design that walk you through how to envision a stunning visual presentation for a website. For my purposes in this book, I am only focusing on the benefits of maintaining consistency and what actions you can take to govern a consistent and intuitive user interface. The action I take to create consistent user interface designs is to create rough mockups and wireframes of the main site template pages, such as the master pages and the page layouts.

Creating mockups and wireframes roughly draft the layout of elements on pages and they can show you how the pages relate to each other. The process involves sketching out a page to indicate where you will place different elements. These sketches do not contain much detail and they are not polished diagrams of the site. Instead, they more resemble a quick doodle with just enough information to communicate where to place things on a page. I frequently draft these wireframes on a whiteboard where I can show a series of pages and use arrows to indicate how they link together. I find this process can drive a brainstorming session and produce exceptional site designs for a positive user experience.

Although the whiteboard is probably my most productive tool when it comes to architecting and designing solutions, it produces transitory information – information that I will wipe off right away. I often capture this information and make it less transitory by taking a picture of the whiteboard, but the photo does not offer the best productivity medium for a design team once the whiteboard session is complete. The tool that I use to create mockups to share with team members and other stakeholders is Balsamiq Mockups. This software contains a canvas and different page elements that you can quickly drag onto the canvas to mockup a page wireframe. Figure 15-1 provides an example of a basic page mockup I created in just a few minutes using the software.

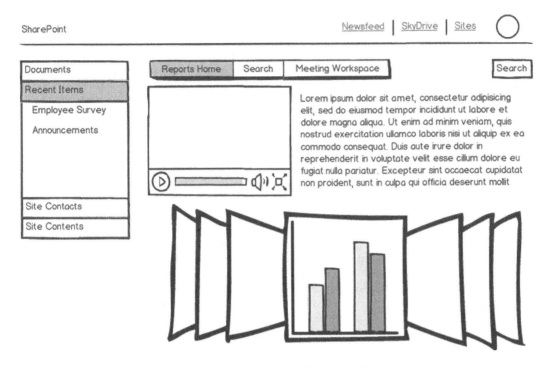

Figure 15-1. An example of a basic page mockup using Balsamiq Mockups

The thing I love about Balsamiq is that it is quick and easy to use. It is also cross-platform, so I can use it when I am working on my Mac and then use the exact same software when I switch back to my Windows PC. You can quickly reproduce any rough mockups and wireframes that you created on a whiteboard and then generate any additional supporting mockups. Within the mockups, you can link between different pages to show the actual click-through process, and then you can export this to a PDF document that will maintain the link references between pages. I usually distribute this PDF to stakeholders to gather feedback on the site's layout and simple page links.

■ **Note** For more on the Balsamiq Mockups software, please see this website: `www.balsamiq.com`

Once I have a set of rough mockups that wireframe the different pages in the site and how they interact with each other, I then work on building a higher fidelity mockup of the site design to incorporate the visual brand and graphic design. By this stage, I have a solution concept architected and I am ready to apply the visual form. I generally build these higher fidelity mockups using Adobe Photoshop and they will more closely represent the actual look and feel of the final solution I deliver. From there, I translate the Photoshop files into SharePoint site assets that I can deploy in a SharePoint feature or in a site design package.

My progression advances from rough mockups on a whiteboard to low-fidelity wireframes using Balsamiq to high-fidelity mockups using Photoshop before finally implementing the design in SharePoint. The most changes will occur at the whiteboard phase, which is also the cheapest place to accommodate and incorporate any changes to the design. As the frequency of changes declines, the cost of making a change increases. This is why I do not start with high-fidelity Photoshop mockups, because they take longer to produce and therefore will cost more to modify or rework. This progression offers you a cost-effective and productive approach to designing a consistent user interface.

Wireframes and mockups can go a long way with leading you toward a consistent site user experience. Maintaining a consistent layout and overall experience in itself can make a site intuitive for users. The main thing for me when it comes to designing an intuitive site is to keep it simple. If you want to design a site that is intuitive to use, then you will want to avoid trying to make an artistic expression with some form of abstract art. Obvious and simple are good when it comes to an intuitive design. Familiar and consistent are other guiding principles you should keep in mind as you design your site experience. The layout of your site contributes a big part toward how intuitive users will find your site, and so does your site's navigation.

Microsoft has done a pretty good job making SharePoint reasonably intuitive to navigate. However, they have left plenty of opportunity for you to improve the experience for your users with a navigation design that helps to guide and orientate them throughout your sites. One area in particular that I find lacking with navigation in SharePoint 2013 is the lack of a prominent breadcrumb. Previous versions of SharePoint included a rudimentary breadcrumb, but that is no longer paramount in the default team site template. You can build or buy a breadcrumb component for your sites to help make them easier and more intuitive for your users to navigate. In the next section, I share other considerations to help you structure a functional navigation.

Structuring a Functional Navigation

A functional navigation provides a dual purpose: it enables your users to ascertain their position within your SharePoint service and it equips your users with a route to follow to move through the different sites and web properties within your SharePoint service. Your navigation structure needs to provide a way for users to navigate to where they are trying to go, and it needs to maintain a way to head back the way they came so that they can always get to the homepage. At its simplest, a site's navigation is a set of links on a navigation menu, and how you organize those links will determine how functional your navigation will be. Beyond the links, how you structure your sites will also impact your navigation.

I prefer to have several web applications for my SharePoint deployments, with each hosting different web properties. I find this approach decouples the applications from each other and it eases the complexity with providing enterprise services across web applications and different SharePoint farms, such as sharing the search service to each of the web applications. For example, when you deploy an enterprise search application in its own web application rather than combined with the intranet, then it is decoupled from the intranet portal. With this separation, you can restructure or redesign (or even re-platform) either the intranet or the search application without causing a major ripple effect throughout the system.

A decoupled design always provides a more sustainable and more adaptable system. It offers a structure to group related functionality, and with these web applications decoupled from each other, you will have the option later if you ever want to scale out the architecture and dedicate a farm for a specific application. For example, with a dedicated web application to host your enterprise search portal, you can migrate the search web application and service application to a new SharePoint farm that you dedicate to host the enterprise search application. This process would be much more complex and would involve more ripple effects throughout your system if your search site is a sub-site within your intranet portal web application.

The following lists several examples of different web properties I often consider. I do not always split up the web applications this granularly, but this should give you some ideas for how you can structure your applications. I usually try to separate the MySites because this will give me the option to enable self-service site creation on the web application for MySites, but I can disable it for other sites such as collaboration sites if I prefer to create these sites for the users.

- Intranet Portal: `https://portal.contoso.com`

- People Profiles and Personal Sites: `https://people.contoso.com`

- Enterprise Search: `https://search.contoso.com`

- Collaboration Sites: `https://sharepoint.contoso.com`

- Records Repository: `https://records.contoso.com`

- Report Center: `https://reports.contoso.com`

As you can see, it is a good design practice to separate these applications into their own web application. These structures also contribute to a useful navigation capability where your users can type a simple URL into the address bar to navigate to key web properties, such as using "http://search" or "http://people" for the enterprise search and MySite applications, respectively. This helps to make a particular web application easy and convenient for users to navigate to by way of typing a simple and friendly URL. However, you also need to provide your users with global links that they can click to navigate between these key web properties.

SharePoint provides some links on the global bar across the top of site pages. These links provide global navigation access to the MySite web application, including the Newsfeed, SkyDrive, and Sites links. The search box is also present on site pages and it allows users to search from whatever page they are on. It would be nice to have a link on the global navigation bar for users to navigate directly to the search portal, and it certainly would be nice to have a "Home" link there for users to navigate back to a homepage such as the intranet portal's default page.

Unfortunately, the product team did not offer a place in SharePoint Central Administration to modify these links. Instead, they have provided a couple of options. First, you can add promoted links by navigating to the User Profile Service settings page, and then clicking the Manage Promoted Sites link in the My Site Settings section. This allows you to add a promoted site link to the Sites page, as shown in Figure 15-2. This option is handy and solves many needs, but it does not quite provide the experience I want on the top global bar.

Figure 15-2. *The Sites page with a "Home" tile as an example of a promoted link*

The second option to modify the links on the top global bar is to develop your own solution in a delegate control. The Newsfeed, SkyDrive, and Sites links are all contained within a delegate control that you can overwrite with your own custom delegate control that uses the SuiteLinksDelegate Control ID. You can also overwrite the "SharePoint" text on the left of the top bar by using your own custom delegate control that uses the SuiteBarBrandingDelegate Control ID. There is one navigation solution I would like to develop one day (and I am sharing it here with you, just in case you have time to get to it first), and it involves this global top bar, also known as the *suite bar*. I would like to see the following functionality on this bar:

- Overwrite the suite bar branding delegate control and display a breadcrumb with active links for sites higher in the hierarchy, possibly using managed navigation or a portal site connector property in the site collection settings.

- Overwrite the suite links delegate control and display those existing links as well as any custom links I can add through a management page within SharePoint Central Administration or through a managed navigation term set, which I discuss next.

I think these missing features are my least-liked gap in SharePoint 2013, but thankfully the product team provided a way to add-in your own solution. You may have to choose different rendering strategies for different devices, depending on the screen size, but the good news is that this is all possible with ASP.NET and the SharePoint API. Sites each have a global navigation that runs across underneath the title area and a quick launch navigation that runs down the left side of a page. You can either configure these navigation menus manually on a site-by-site basis, or you can use the managed navigation feature, which I discuss in the next section.

Designing Structures with Managed Navigation

The bane of a SharePoint administrator's existence has historically been large site collections with a deep nesting of many layers of child sites. The driver behind this design was often because a site collection can automatically maintain a navigation menu that included all sites and pages within the collection. Multiple site collections never used to have the same automatic menu maintenance capabilities. Thus, busy users were motivated to pile all their content and sites in a single site collection to take advantage of its automatic navigation menu feature. Thankfully, in SharePoint 2013 the product team included a solution to this site structure challenge: managed navigation.

Managed navigation is a feature that allows a site administrator to associate their site's navigation menus with a term set in the managed metadata service. Unfortunately by default the managed navigation is bound to a single site collection, but you can use the SharePoint API and implement your own custom navigation component to associate it with the term set and share the navigation structure across site collections. This allows multiple site collections to share the same navigation menu structure that you can update in a central location, and better still, this term set can automatically update itself as site structures change to include any new sites. Managed navigation also makes it easier to change much of the navigation structure without moving sites or breaking links because you can create the navigation menu items without coupling them to actual site structures.

The following JavaScript provides an example of accessing a term set through the SharePoint Client API. You can enumerate through the list of terms in the term set to access each term's properties, such as `term.get_name` and `term.get_localCustomProperties()['_Sys_Nav_SimpleLinkUrl']` for its name and URL properties respectively.

```
var context = SP.ClientContext.get_current();
var taxonomySession = SP.Taxonomy.TaxonomySession.getTaxonomySession(context);
var termStore = taxonomySession.get_termStores().getByName(termStoreName);
var termSet = termStore.getTermSet(termSetId);
var terms = termSet.getAllTerms();
```

You can create a managed navigation by first creating a term set for the navigation menu items. The following steps walk you through how to create a term set for managed navigation.

1. Create a new term set on the Term Store Management Tool page for the Management Metadata Service. You can access this page through the Manage Service Applications page in SharePoint Central Administration.

2. With that term set selected, click the *Intended Use* tab to display the enterprise navigation options.

3. Check the checkbox for the "Use this Term Set for Site Navigation" option to specify the term set for managed navigation, as shown in Figure 15-3.

 Site Settings ᐧ Term Store Management Tool

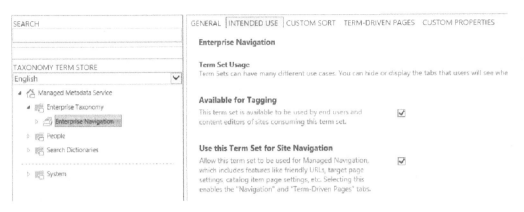

Figure 15-3. The Term Store Management Tool with the site naviagation intended use option

4. Click Save.

With your managed navigation term set created, you can add terms and specify their navigation properties on the *Navigation* and *Term-Driven Pages* tabs for each term. To apply the managed navigation to a site, click the Navigation option in the Look and Feel section on the Site Settings page for each site. On the Navigation Settings page for a site, select the Managed Navigation option and then select the relevant term set in the Managed Navigation Term Set section, as shown in Figure 15-4. Once this is set, the site's navigation menu will draw menu items from the term set.

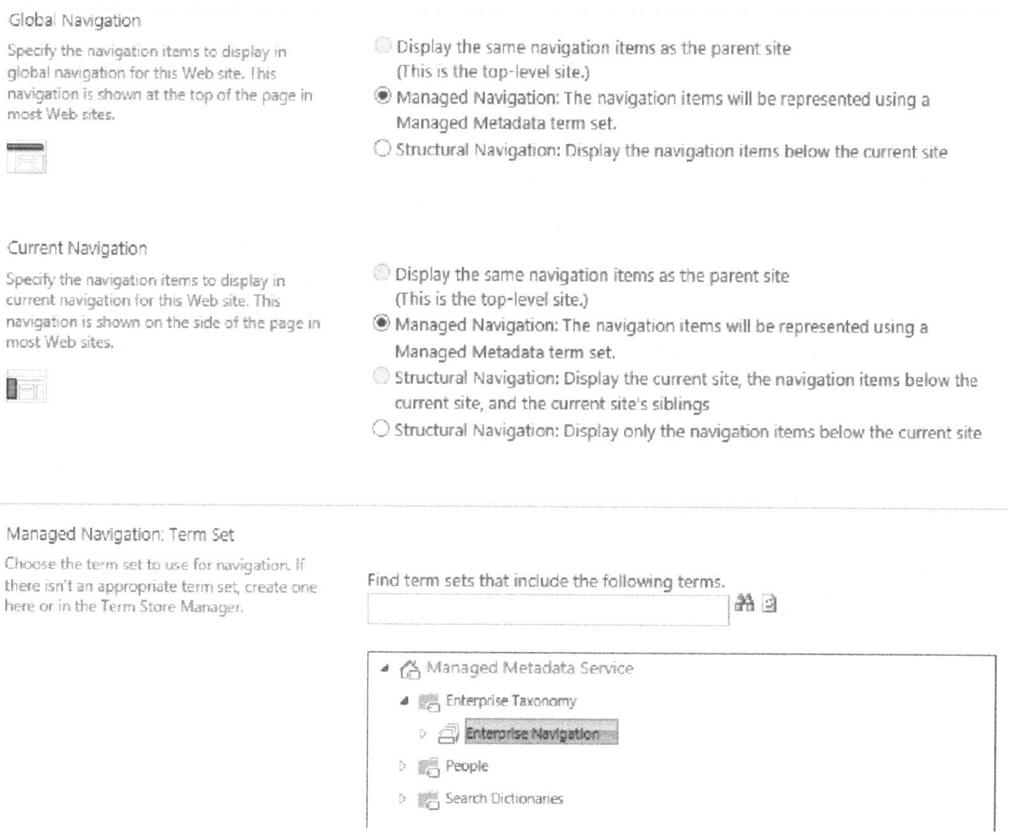

Global Navigation

Specify the navigation items to display in global navigation for this Web site. This navigation is shown at the top of the page in most Web sites.

○ Display the same navigation items as the parent site (This is the top-level site.)

◉ Managed Navigation: The navigation items will be represented using a Managed Metadata term set.

○ Structural Navigation: Display the navigation items below the current site

Current Navigation

Specify the navigation items to display in current navigation for this Web site. This navigation is shown on the side of the page in most Web sites.

○ Display the same navigation items as the parent site (This is the top-level site.)

◉ Managed Navigation: The navigation items will be represented using a Managed Metadata term set.

○ Structural Navigation: Display the current site, the navigation items below the current site, and the current site's siblings

○ Structural Navigation: Display only the navigation items below the current site

Managed Navigation: Term Set

Choose the term set to use for navigation. If there isn't an appropriate term set, create one here or in the Term Store Manager.

Find term sets that include the following terms.

    [   ] 🔍 📄

▲ 🏠 Managed Metadata Service

   ▲ 📇 Enterprise Taxonomy

      ▷ 🗐 Enterprise Navigation

   ▷ 📇 People

   ▷ 📇 Search Dictionaries

Figure 15-4. *A site's Navigation Settings page with the managed navigation options selected*

USING CARD SORTING TO DESIGN YOUR NAVIGATION

Card sorting is a technique where you work with users to identify and organize how to structure your navigation menu. You can also use this technique to organize other structures, such as how you group content in different sites or pages in different portal areas. Essentially, you can use card sorting anytime you need to organize content in an information architecture.

The process involves writing down each of the navigation menu items on an index card, and then you ask users or other subject matter experts to sort and organize these cards in a structure that makes sense to them. You then aggregate and analyze the results by looking for patterns and other commonalities that can help you design a navigation structure or some other taxonomy structure.

Defining Controlled Vocabularies

A controlled vocabulary establishes a list of the proper terms to refer to something. This provides everyone within the organization with a single and common term to refer to a particular subject. A common term then makes it easy to categorize and search for information. These common terms may be industry terms, although they do not necessary have to be. They may just be terms you want to standardize on and make common within your own organization.

I once did a project for an airline, and one of their industry terms is *baggage*, not bags, not luggage, not suitcases. By referring to the checked and carry-on items as baggage, they were able to categorize their policies and procedures with that common term. Within their controlled vocabulary, everyone was supposed to refer to these items as baggage, although not everybody did. In these cases where people use inconsistent terms to refer to an item, you can translate them to the proper term in your controlled vocabulary by using synonyms. Therefore, if someone incorrectly categorizes content as relating to luggage, your controlled vocabulary will be smart enough to categorize the content properly as relating to baggage and use luggage as a synonym.

An information architect designs a controlled vocabulary with a carefully selected list of terms that users can use to tag units of information such as documents or list items. This establishes an efficient system of organizing knowledge for later retrieval. It consists of a predefined list of terms that users can select from when they categorize their content. You can associate a controlled vocabulary list with a column in a document library or a list in a SharePoint site, or you can associate it with an attribute for the people profile data.

You can build controlled vocabularies for many attributes of the information in your organization. These lists can consist of attributes that are specific to your organization, industry, or the information itself. For example, you might build controlled vocabularies for the following:

- Information sensitivity levels

- Security clearance levels

- Privacy levels

- Departments

- Products

- Stages or statuses

- Job titles or roles

A controlled vocabulary is a closed list of predefined terms, which means that users cannot add additional terms and instead have to select from an existing list. The vocabulary designer or information architect can add terms as required, but the lists are carefully planned with relevant terms. For example, the security clearance levels list can include terms such as public, confidential, secret, and top secret. You probably will not change this list frequently, and you certainly do not want regular users to append terms to this list and introduce their own security levels. Instead, they have to select one of the predefined terms to classify their content.

You may not always want a closed and controlled list. For some attributes, you can allow users to add their own terms that they find relevant to tag a unit of information with. You can provide these lists in open vocabularies, where you define the category that users can use to tag information by either selecting from the existing terms in the list or by defining their own. For example, you might build open vocabularies for the following:

- Keywords

- Skills

- Interests

- Projects

- Functional Areas

Your open vocabularies do not have to be completely open and uncontrolled. You can review terms in the Term Store Management Tool for the Managed Metadata Service and make adjustments as necessary. For example, you may merge several related terms by setting some terms as synonyms of others to make information easier for users to discover, or you can correct the spelling or casing of terms to make the list consistent. This can give you the best of both worlds for those lists that you do not need to tightly control but that you want to maintain consistency. You can then use both the controlled and open vocabulary lists to classify a unit of information by using one or more metadata fields.

After building controlled vocabularies with sets of terms or open vocabularies with sets of term containers, you may find that you can organize them into a hierarchy of terms rather than in discrete lists. This allows you to relate terms or to further specify a term with other more specific and granular terms. You can group your vocabulary lists within an enterprise taxonomy, which I discuss next.

Building an Enterprise Taxonomy

Building an enterprise taxonomy is no easy endeavor. The bulk of the effort is the analysis you will need to perform to identify term candidates for the enterprise taxonomy. To build an effective enterprise taxonomy, you have to analyze all the different types of information within your organization and identify all the attributes that can apply to each type of information. These attributes can include open and controlled vocabulary lists or a hierarchy of terms that form a content classification index.

Even if you do not have any formal experience with designing a taxonomy, you probably do have experience with designing a hierarchy of terms to organize content within. For example, you might have created a folder structure to store and organize your files on your computer. This folder structure is a type of taxonomy, with the folder names serving as terms that classify all the content they contain, including other folders. When you want to find a file, you can click through the folder structure from general folder names down the hierarchy to more specific folders until you finally locate the file that interests you. Your folder structures are a taxonomy of terms that you use to classify and organize your content.

Using a physical folder or site structure to implement a taxonomy is limiting because it is only one dimensional, as you have one hierarchy to click through the physical structure to locate content. Implementing the taxonomy in a physical structure also makes it fragile for any change, because if you want to reorganize or rename folders you will also physically relocate content and break links. Physical structures have worked for categorizing content for a long time now, but they are limiting.

Another way to implement a taxonomy is to associate terms to a unit of information using metadata instead of physical structures. Metadata allows you to associate a term with a piece of content without affecting the content's physical location. You can also associate multiple terms for a given attribute when more than one applies, which is useful and it frees you from having to choose a single folder to store the content. Along those lines, you can also associate metadata classifications for multiple attributes to a piece of content rather than having to limit yourself to a single folder naming convention and structure.

Where a folder structure offers you a single dimension taxonomy for organizing information, metadata terms offer you a multiple dimension taxonomy. You can associate term sets from different areas within the taxonomy and associate them each with a column in a list or library. Users can then find content by searching and filtering on multiple categories of terms or by clicking through different hierarchies of terms. This will provide you with the maximum flexibility to classify your content and it will not depend on physical structures that constrain you to a particular implementation.

Folder names and filenames can provide you with a rich source of data to analyze as you design your enterprise taxonomy. This is usually the first place I start because they have worked well for how users are already categorizing and classifying their content. If I have access to a records management office for the organization, then I work with the records managers to analyze the file plan and any other content classification indexes that they work with. I collect lists of terms, such as those I shared in the previous section, and then I organize them into the enterprise taxonomy. There are several sources you can analyze to design your taxonomy, but I find these are the most productive to get you started with a functional taxonomy.

Professional taxonomy design is a specialty within the library sciences, and so if you want to design an optimum enterprise taxonomy for your organization, then I recommend you engage someone trained in library and information science. These specialists are experts in how people interact with a classification system and they can be especially valuable if you want to build a classification index as part of a records management solution. There is a lot of analysis and taxonomy design that you can do on your own, as I have mentioned, but a trained professional can also help you to design an optimal classification system.

■ **Tip** Some industries use standard industry taxonomies that you can consider adopting to stay consistent with your industry's terms and ways of classifying content. Some organizations in the market sell taxonomies designed for specific businesses and industries. Before you embark on an extensive taxonomy design effort, you might want to check to see if someone has already created a relevant taxonomy that you can purchase to get a head start.

As you design or acquire your enterprise taxonomy, your next step is to implement it in your SharePoint environment so that it is available to classify and search for information. You implement the taxonomy in the Managed Metadata service application, which you can provision within SharePoint Central Administration and you can share across farms. This service enables you to maintain a centralized location for your enterprise taxonomy and then use it to classify content across all your SharePoint farms. Ultimately, this leads to consistency for how your users organize and classify their content, which improves their ability to search for and locate relevant content. It also improves their ability to discover relevant information through tag suggestions on their MySite or through tags they follow.

Figure 15-5 shows the Term Store Management Tool with an example of a subset of my sample content classification taxonomy showing the different security levels. You can implement your taxonomy by creating a term group in the term store and then creating term sets within the term group. In my example, the term group is "Content Classification" and the term sets are "Privacy Level" and "Security Level" contained within the term group. You use term groups to contain and organize term sets, and then you use term sets to contain and organize terms. You associate term sets with columns or attributes to use for categorizing content, and then users select or add terms within the term set to tag a particular unit of information with.

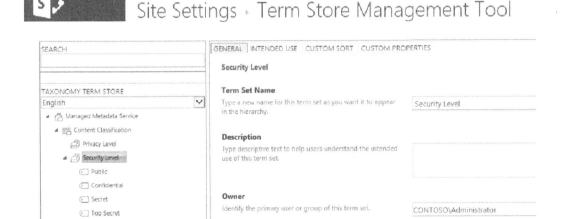

Figure 15-5. *The Term Store Management Tool with a Security Level term set example*

Once you have a taxonomy design and you have implemented it in the Managed Metadata Service term store, your next step is to use it to classify information. You can classify content such as documents and you can classify people information within MySite profiles using the same taxonomy. In the next section, I discuss how to use the terms to classify content, and then in the subsequent section I discuss considerations for classifying profile information.

Standardizing Document Templates and Metadata

As I discussed in the previous section, your taxonomy serves as a central structure of terms that you can associate with units of information. A term becomes a reference pointer to any content that you tag with it, and this allows you to organize your content by using these terms without having to worry about how users structure their content. This is significant, because it provides the flexibility to reference content in many ways by tagging it with multiple terms, and it allows you to reference different types of content by tagging each using the same term. SharePoint provides several options to manage tagging content, from applying a column to every item in a library to applying a column to specific types of content.

You have several options for how you can implement document templates and metadata as part of your information management solution. Because each option uses the same taxonomy of terms, each shares the same content discoverability benefits of those reference pointers. However, they differ in the implementation details and how consistent you can replicate and target the information management details within a site and across sites. If you just need one-off solutions for a document library, then you can add a library column to tag the content; but if you want a consistent solution across libraries and sites, then you can create content types and associate columns and other information management policies in each.

I like SharePoint content types and I find they help implement a sophisticated information management solution that is also quite usable for end-users. For me, the training and documentation material for content types sometimes gets overly focused on content type inheritance, where you can inherit a content type based on another content type (although it is not true inheritance in the object-oriented sense). This is a useful feature and can help with your information management implementation, but I also find it can be distracting and it leads to a bloating of content types as you focus on building out a hierarchy. I find it is more productive to focus on the individual content types themselves, and then come back to the idea of hierarchies later if the information architecture leads you in that direction.

At its core, a content type is really just another piece of metadata to self-describe a unit of information. In addition to identifying the type of content, you can group other relevant metadata you wish to associate with content. It allows you to attach other information management aspects such as policies and workflows to the content type as well. You can associate multiple content types to a single document library, which provides you with a way to apply metadata and other policies to each individual type of content rather than having to share the same for all content in a document library.

This allows you to set and associate information management solutions with the individual content rather than with containers such as libraries. Having it associated with the content and decoupled from specific content containers allows you to manage the solution from a more centralized place, such as the content type gallery in a site collection. You can even implement your information management solution with content types in an even more centralized fashion by creating a content type hub site collection to share the content types consistently across the farm. This allows you to later move content and maintain its content type information management details, such as if you set up a records repository and move content there to declare it as a record.

You can standardize your metadata aspect of your information management solution by associating a site column with a managed term set in your enterprise taxonomy. Then you can use this column in content types to tag content with. Figure 15-6 shows a screenshot of the new site column page where if you specify to use metadata as the column type, you can select a term set to use that users can select terms from to tag content for the column. You can manage site columns by navigating to the Site Columns page found through the Site Settings page for your site collection.

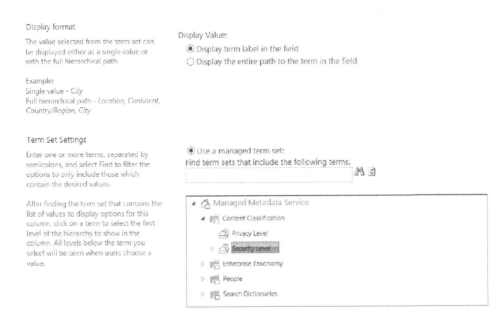

Figure 15-6. *A new site column Term Set Settings option specifying the Security Level term set*

Once you create site columns for the metadata you want to capture, you can associate them with one or more content types. Figure 15-7 shows a screenshot of a custom content type I created with the Security custom site column associated with the content type. You can manage content types by navigating to the Site Content Types page found through the Site Settings pages for your site collection.

Figure 15-7. *The Site Content Type settings page with the custom "Security" site column*

The process I like to go through as I analyze and design a content type solution builds on to the same process for building an enterprise taxonomy: analyze the existing content itself. I gather information about the content and the potential metadata that users have categorized or organized the content with. I ask the following questions to identify potential content types and their metadata:

- What are the different types of content that users create and use in the organization?

- How do they organize the folder structures where they store the content?

- What are the different naming conventions of the files?

- Does the content contain any frontal matter or document properties to categorize it?

Analyzing existing digital content can provide a wealth of information for the content types you need and the metadata structure you can associate with them. You can also analyze physical content such as paper systems as you build your content type and metadata strategy, which will identify opportunities of paper systems that you can replace with digital documents and workflows.

With a list of content types and their respective metadata, you can begin to identify the other policies you need to associate with the content type by analyzing the content's nature and any requirements associated with it. For example, you may have retention requirements with procedures for designating and storing a piece of content as an official record. You may also have auditing requirements to track any access or modifications to the content. As you capture this information, you can build out the rest of your content type design. Finally, you can associate a document template with the content type that users can use to create a document based on the template in exactly the same way that users would create a new document based on a template in a Microsoft Office application.

As you design your information architecture for content, you may face the requirement to store a group of content together and treat the group as a single unit. A Document Set in SharePoint is a special unit of information in which you can package multiple files and store them together in a document library. Essentially it packages a group of documents and other files together as a unit with common metadata and other information management policies. You can implement these policies to document sets in a similar fashion as you would for content types.

Note I find the process of developing and implementing an information architecture and enterprise content management solution can be a lengthy process and will involve a lot of analysis efforts and design activities. Although I gloss over the process in just a few paragraphs, I wanted to call out that this can and probably will be an involved exercise. Nonetheless, you can start small and build out much of your solution in smaller phases, such as by focusing on departments, and then continuously building out and improving the solution from there.

Content types and metadata provide the implementation details of your information architecture and enterprise content management solution for content within your organization. These features enable you to manage and organize the content lifecycle within SharePoint while they also help users to discover relevant content. One way that you can help users to discover content that might interest them is by using the term set that you categorize content metadata with and associating it with profile information for users. This creates a link with relevant content a user might find interesting. In the next section, I discuss other considerations for designing people data solutions as part of your information architecture.

Designing People and Profile Data

I find that people information is one area where people under utilize their taxonomy and the potential attributes they can associate with people profile data. You probably already have a lot of people data in your identity system, such as with their Active Directory account. However, this data is only the start. I think the lack of initiative for building out people profile data stems from not having a vision for what is possible once you have a rich set of people information in the system. For one thing, and probably one of the most common drivers for a MySite implementation, you can search and find people. I often work with clients who have some form of an organizational phone book available, from the Global Address List in Outlook and Exchange to custom solutions and Excel spreadsheets. In all these people directories, I often expose their gaps and limitations by asking one question: how do you find people when you do not know their name?

This question may seem simple, and it is, but it is at the heart of any MySite application. It leads you to think about the types of solutions you can include in the application to facilitate how people find each other, and the primary solutions will relate to the metadata you associate with people profile attributes. That way, you can find people by searching for things about them that they specify in one of the attributes of their profile, or you can discover people by sharing common terms or following common tags. SharePoint MySites provide the platform to connect people with information, either with content or with other people, and metadata in your enterprise taxonomy facilitates these connections.

You can import much of the data for your people profiles from your identity management system. For example, you can import their organizational information and group membership from Active Directory. You can also import additional information from other systems such as your human resources management system by using the SharePoint Business Connectivity Services. This can automatically populate profiles with a lot of valuable information that can make your MySite application useful right away, whether or not every user adopts and maintains their profile. You can extend this value by designating SharePoint as the source system for other attributes that you want to associate with a profile.

SharePoint includes a few default attributes for people profiles to get you started with extending profile information for your users. Figure 15-8 shows an example of the edit details screen for a user profile, which includes some of the default fields SharePoint provides to collect user profile information. The following lists key attributes SharePoint adds to collect user profile information:

- "About me" description text

- "Ask me about" topics

- Office location

- Past projects

- Skills

- Schools

- Birthday

- Interests

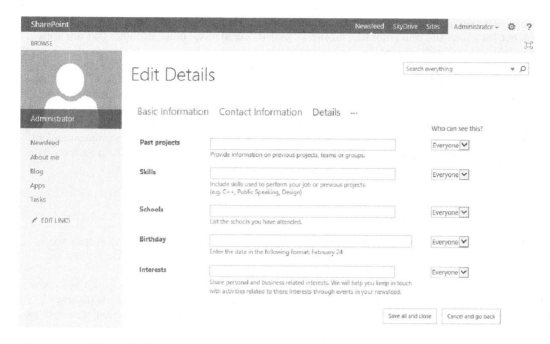

Figure 15-8. *Editing the default MySite profile attributes*

You can add additional attributes to your user profiles by clicking the Manage User Properties link on the Manage Profile Service page for the User Profile service application. When you add additional profile properties, you can import them from your identity management system, import from a Business Connectivity Services application, or designate SharePoint as the source system for the attribute. The following lists some examples of additional profile properties you might add:

- Hobbies
- Committees
- Website URL
- Conferences attended
- Volunteer causes

In addition, you might add profile properties that relate to your organization. For example, I had a retail client who added attributes that relate to merchandising areas and activities. This can help you increase the relevancy of searching for people as your users can filter searches within a particular functional area that they want to find someone. For one of my retail clients, one of their use case scenarios was for an area manager to be able to search and find who the planner, buyer, and merchandiser is for a given product line in a store's department, all from their mobile phone as they walked through a store. This allowed them to connect with relevant people to resolve potential issues before they escalated into problems, all without having to remember who is responsible for what department in each store. They would simply perform a filtered people search based on properties such as the location, department, and product lines. This is their answer to the question about how they find people when they do not know their name.

I usually use business needs that relate to people search as my main driver for a MySite deployment. This can lay the bedrock for a robust and valuable social computing platform for the enterprise, the core of which revolves around the profile data and how that relates to content tagging and other social capabilities in your SharePoint service. Often many of the profile properties that you want to include will exist already in an identity management system such as Active Directory, and your enterprise taxonomy analysis might reveal other attributes that you want SharePoint to host and associate with user profiles.

As you can see, all the data that makes up an individual's profile can come from several enterprise systems. Some may be look-up systems to other data sources and others may be the source system themselves. To add to this complexity, SharePoint may import from a look-up system, a source system, or it can serve as the source system for a particular profile property. This complexity tends to emerge as a challenge once you deploy a SharePoint MySite application because the profiles surface a lot of potentially stale data that may bother users and they may request that you update the data. The challenge can be with knowing which system to update and when the synchronization jobs will run to update any other system, including the SharePoint profile import. One tool that I use to help me trace data fields back to their source system is an enterprise data dictionary, which I discuss in the next section.

Creating a Data Dictionary

For every system interface, I like to know whether I am consuming data or providing data to these other systems. If you are consuming data, are you consuming it from the source system or a look-up system? Conversely, if you are providing data, is SharePoint the source system or relaying it from another system?

Data within an enterprise is complex. Different systems may replicate the data and maintain a cache of it for its own use, while other systems copy the data to provide look-up tables to still another system. One system's use of data may consolidate different sets of data from several systems to present a particular view of the data structures and relationships.

For example, user profile data stores some attributes in SharePoint, making SharePoint the source system for some aspects of a user's profile. SharePoint might import other attributes from Active Directory, where Active Directory is the source system for some attributes such as a user's alias. Active Directory itself might import some of the user attributes from yet another system such as a Human Resources Management System (HRMS). SharePoint might also use the Business Connectivity Services (BCS) to import other user profile attributes from still different systems, such as a customer relationship management (CRM) system or a learning management system (LMS).

Even with a seemingly simple example using user profile data, you can see how complex enterprise data relationships can become among enterprise systems. Add in all the other systems that SharePoint interfaces with, and the complexity of data increases. This can make it difficult to support or manage changes to the underlying data, and it can certainly make it difficult to troubleshoot data reliability issues. One tool I have found to prove invaluable is a data dictionary, and it helps with planning SharePoint data interfaces, as well as troubleshooting and supporting any underlying data issues.

You could create a data flow diagram to illustrate the flow of data between different enterprise systems to complement your data dictionary. A data flow diagram can help you identify the source systems, all the different data interfaces, and how the data replicates throughout the enterprise. This also helps ease your task of creating the data dictionary itself, because it will provide you with a high-level view of how data flows throughout the enterprise.

A data dictionary can take whatever format you like. I like to use a table and I usually make it within an Excel spreadsheet. Within it, I add columns to identify the field, what system contains the field, and if that system is the source system for the field's data. If it is not the source system, I capture details about which system is, along with what the data refresh schedule is and whether the data is read-only. I then include other columns that describe the field, such as the data type, size, and any other validation or requirements related to the data. Finally, I add columns related to the sensitivity and business criticality of the field's data, such as personally identifiable information, confidential information, and trade secrets.

It takes time to build an extensive data dictionary, but you do not need to make it exhaustive of all the data to make it useful. This is true for any dictionary, even in the evolution of the English dictionary. An early English dictionary contained definitions for a portion of the words that we have today. Over 250 years ago, Samuel Johnson created an English dictionary that contained definitions for approximately 40,000 words. Today, the *Oxford English Dictionary* contains definitions for over 600,000 words, or 15 times as many words as what those early dictionaries defined. Even if it is not yet an exhaustive data dictionary, starting to document the data will start to provide benefits.

Consultant Comrade

I combined a few topics in this chapter: interface design standards, site structure and navigation standards, information architecture and enterprise taxonomy design, and even enterprise content management. These topics are loosely related in the sense that they build on or complement each other. However, if your engagement begins to unravel where your client is trying to juggle all of these things at once, it will sink you. Instead, you need to help them address them individually and in smaller, more manageable phases. This is no different than my approach for anything you deliver with SharePoint that I have shared and recommended throughout this book. I am stressing it here again only because things like enterprise content management are big topics and they require a lot of analysis work upfront.

With that said, enterprise content management projects are excellent initiatives for an outside consultant to help drive the analysis. The reason is because you can engage with a fresh perspective to analyze content and how it is used. You can ask the right questions and analyze their content without having prior experience with how the organization uses content blind you from an effective solution. Many clients will not have someone internally with expertise in library or archival sciences, and as such they can rely on consultants to bring these specialized skills. You have many compelling reasons where you can bring expertise and experience to help your clients solve their enterprise content management challenges.

The challenge is that much of the value from an information architecture and enterprise content management solution is not realized until you implement enough of an enterprise-wide solution. You might face a lot of resistance against breaking this into smaller phases, such as clients opposed to the idea of having to go back and retag content later when you build out more of the taxonomy or you add more content types for additional departments. This is tempting yet dangerous thinking because it can halt progress as you try to eat the SharePoint elephant.

Note   Please see Chapter 7 where I discuss the idea of eating the SharePoint elephant and the importance of breaking up your projects into smaller phases.

I like to start small, even for an area as vast as enterprise content management. Rather than jumping in and trying to solve the problem for the entire organization at once, I prefer to focus on a smaller group within the organization. A representative group can lay the groundwork for your information architecture work. You can pilot solutions with them, and then continuously improve and evolve those solutions until you have a solid architecture. If you decouple the information architecture implementation from the physical structure of your content, then changing and adapting your solution as you expand your pilot will be straightforward. For example, you can change your taxonomy by depreciating some terms and merging other terms. This flexibility allows you to continue with your SharePoint deployment in smaller and more focused phases, even for enterprise content management.

Inside Story: Notes from the Field

Knowing the content is half the battle: When you know what the content is, or how sensitive it is, this can make all the difference in keeping it secure. You can then help users to identify a unit of information's sensitivity easily when they interact with it, and this will help to keep them more aware of how to treat the information.

A couple years ago, I had an engagement with a utility company that supplies power for a region. They store a lot of content concerning a wide variety of topics, and with a complex structure of privacy and compliance needs. This company's content security needs ranged from information pamphlets that encouraged people to save power and were available for all to see, across to the other end of the spectrum that included architecture diagrams of power plants that have to be protected and secured.

For example, the company's diagrams had an inherent threat attached to them, for if they fell into the wrong hands, an adversary could use them for something such as a terrorist attack because they may expose vulnerabilities about a power generation facility and the optimum manner to attack it. An adversary could consider the company's power stations as potentially a high-value target for a terrorist attack if they wanted to interrupt the availability of power for a power grid.

Beyond threats of information security breaches leading from potential attacks, the company also had privacy concerns with some of its data. They did not want to leak customer or employee private information, what they classify as personally identifiable information. They had a legislated duty to keep personal privacy information private.

Another legislated obligation they faced relates to the public's right to access certain types of information, classified under the freedom to information legislation. Therefore, they were required to make some information available when requested, and they needed to locate and comply when a member of the public or press submits a request for details about something they have a right for the company to inform them about.

This power utility had concrete information management requirements, all very well defined and documented at a corporation level. With their information types and policies defined at a corporate level, it made the job easier through the SharePoint governance process since they have made all the key decisions. These corporate information policies map to implementation details, and my job was to capture what the policies meant and implement them in the SharePoint environment.

One governance action I took acted on information classification requirements I needed to implement to enforce users to classify required content in a few ways. One way might be by the business impact, risk, and severity, particularly for content that would affect future operations. Another might be the level of privacy sensitivity, such as personally identifiable information. Another might be the degree security or secrecy, such as plans or details that if leaked could support an attack. Finally, another might be whether the information relates to the freedom to information legislation.

Knowing we had to categorize content especially for these areas was clear since executives made the decision at the organization level, well beyond the SharePoint initiative. This knowledge really defined the structure of the SharePoint content types and what metadata each needed. Knowing the relevance of the different information types also led me to decisions about what other policies and workflows to attach to the content types. Without digressing too far into a records management discussion, I was able to identify things such as retention policies and the like, without a lot of analysis.

I skipped the step of taking an inventory and analyzing all their content, because they already had a detailed list of requirements for each type of content. Taking advantage of this existing knowledge, I quickly translated those requirements into SharePoint features and their implementation details. This freed up cycles in the governance process to focus more effort on the end-user's experience and awareness of the type of content they consume.

If a user is aware of the type of content and how sensitive it is, then they will be less likely to pass it on to someone else and unintentionally create a security breach. When users accessed a piece of content, we visibly showed them the explicit sensitivities that classified the content. For extra sensitive or extra secure content, we changed the color in the header. We even changed the background color of an individual list item by using custom XSLT in the list view, and this made it obvious that it was sensitive before the user even opens it.

By making it easy for our users to know about the content they are interacting with, we also made it easy for them to use the content in a proper and intended manner. Our governance plan was successful here because it took static requirements for content classification and translated them into actions we could implement and affect behavior.

GUEST Q&A: STUART MACLEOD, MICROSOFT

As I discussed governance with Stuart Macleod, a Solution Architect at Microsoft, he stressed how important it is to involve the business. A great governance strategy for him includes two aspects: the information architecture with someone such as a librarian from the business, and a vision for the end-user's productivity – particularly when they are off the network.

To address these aspects, he advocates introducing the principles of information architecture early, and to allow those principles to frame any decisions. He also emphasized the need to constantly and consciously involve the business, because a good architect can fake business knowledge, and this leads to a danger of having too much IT and not enough business.

He made an analogy by relating governance to having a horse gallop and buck wildly around a paddock – the horse might be active and move quickly, but it does not get anything useful done. Once one put reins on it and adds a skilled jockey, then it becomes a controlled horse and a productive horse. Stuart notes that reins control direction more than speed, but that a controlled horse also tends to be a faster horse.

His advice is to "think about the end-user's productivity" – because their productivity is ultimately the point for the governance, and you do not want that point to get lost.

Stuart Macleod works for Microsoft Corporation as a Solution Architect in Microsoft Services, where he provides the largest enterprises and government organizations with solution architecture guidance to help them make productive use of Microsoft technologies. He works based in Calgary, Alberta, Canada.

Wrapping Up

In this chapter, I discussed how to define standards related to the information structures, layout organization, and visual design. I looked at how to build a controlled vocabulary and an enterprise taxonomy to tag and organize content, and I considered how to apply this metadata to SharePoint content such as documents and people profiles.

As you build solutions with custom components and user interface templates, you will need a change management process to work through before you deploy these customizations to the production environment. You might need to integrate customization packages from different teams of developers and then stage the solution for user acceptance testing before a final release. In the next chapter, I discuss how to coordinate promoting customizations to different environments as part of your release process to help maximize stability of your SharePoint service and to lower risks involved with deploying custom components.

CHAPTER 16

■ ■ ■

Coordinating Your Code Promotion and Release Processes

It always seems impossible until it's done.

—Nelson Mandela

In this chapter, I provide an approach to establishing a disciplined code promotion and deployment process. I provide considerations for planning for change management and designing a release process that encourages maturity and discipline. I also introduce concepts related to automated integration testing, promoting code through testing and staging environments before deploying to production, and building rollback plans.

A key point I stress in this chapter is determining your tolerance level for deployment risks and consciously designing your release management process around that so it is the right balance and fit for your needs and situation.

After reading this chapter, you will know how to:

- Plan a code promotion process through different environments

- Automate builds and integration testing

- Determine your tolerance for deployment risk

- Build your release management maturity

- Design a user acceptance testing environment

- Implement a change management process

- Plan for rollbacks of customizations

Promoting Code Through Environments

There is a reason why you would not let developers develop and deploy their solutions directly in your production environment, and that is because you do not want them to interrupt service while they are working through issues and trying out ideas. Instead, they can develop and test in isolated environments and then a release manager can deploy their solution to the production environment in a managed and controlled way once the solution is stable and ready. This process of moving code through different environments on its way to the final release is what I call *code promotion*.

I use this metaphor in a similar fashion as you would for job promotions: as a regular worker performs well in their current role, they eventually get promoted to a new role with more responsibility. Similarly, as a developer's solution performs well in a preproduction environment by passing tests and proving its stability, a release manager can promote the solution into the next environment for further testing and preparation until it is finally promoted into the production environment and released for use. This offers you a release process that physically separates development and testing from production use, and this helps you to keep your production environment more stable as a result.

You use different environments through the code promotion process to move the release testing conditions closer and closer to the production conditions. This process reduces the risk that a customization will break the existing production environment because it tests the compatibility before you release the solution. One reason why you need to test the compatibility is because there could be a gap between the environment your developers build their solutions on and the production environment where you will ultimately deploy their solutions.

It would be expensive and it would slow down the development process if you maintained an exact duplication of the production environment and its data for each development environment. Instead, you need to compromise and give your developers an environment that you optimized for the development process. Usually this means that your developers do development on a single isolated server without any or very little data. However, before you release any solutions, you also need to test compatibility with the production environment at some point as well as compatibility with other custom solutions in development.

If you have a team of developers, you have to merge the different solutions your developers are currently working on, since they each are developing on an isolated server in their own development environment. The only way to merge their changes as they go is to have them develop on the same server in a shared development environment, but this would end up having developers interfering with each other. For example, one developer might package and deploy a solution to try out some functionality he or she just built, and this would trigger an application process to restart and cause the system to slow down unexpectedly for the other developers on the server. Hence, most developers do their development on their own isolated development server or virtual server.

To keep all these development environments lightweight and optimized for productive development, most developers also do their development without any content, or at least without a complete copy of the masses of content in the production environment. This helps to keep developers productive and their environment lightweight, but somewhere in the release process you have to bridge the gap between the lightweight development environments and your production environment. As I mentioned, I bridge this gap through a process I call code promotion.

Code promotion takes custom solutions and gradually promotes them through different environments to move the test conditions closer and closer to the production environment. This allows your developers to be productive while it mitigates the risks involved with having development environments that are not identical with your production environment. How many environments that you use to promote your code through will depend on your own processes and how disciplined and thorough your testing procedures are. The following lists some examples of environments you might include in your code promotion process, progressing from an isolated development environment to move closer and closer to conditions that mirror production, and finally into the production environment itself:

- Development environment

- Build or integration environment

- Test and quality assurance environment

- User acceptance testing environment

- Preproduction or staging environment

- Production environment

You can certainly expand or contract this list of environments based on your own needs and your processes, but this should help to get you started with what environments you might include and what your code promotion process can entail. Two environments are obvious and standard for any development team: the development and production environments. For me, the integration environment is the next critical environment, because this is where you can merge all the custom development from each of your developers to ensure the solution continues to build after any changes and that any automated tests continue to pass.

Automating Builds and Integration Testing

This is one of my favorite steps in the entire development process; yet I rarely see teams adopt it and take full advantage of its potential benefits. The more you can automate, the better; and the more feedback you can garner from an automated process and automated tests, the higher quality your end product will be. Integration is the stage to have the system perform any automated work to provide constant feedback on any bugs or inconsistencies it catches early. It is automated, so that means you do not have to think about it unless the process flags an issue for your attention. However, it does require some upfront planning and configuration to set up a highly functional and automated integration stage, and this might be why some people skip over or minimize this step in their release process.

 The integration stage offers you an opportunity to implement an automated build and continuous integration process. This will help you merge all of your developer's code together frequently – at least once per day, but ideally after every check-in. Adopting an automated process will help you catch compatibility issues early, and if it detects an issue, the system can open and assign a bug to the developer automatically.

An effective continuous integration process requires developers to check-in any of their changes frequently during the day. I have been on several development teams where the developers check-in vast changes after long stretches of developing functionality and affecting many files in the solution. Do not do this; check-in small changes and often. The smaller the changes and the more often everyone checks in their code, the easier it is to merge changes together and maintain compatibility. Frequent check-ins also means frequent change sets in your source code repository, and this means that you will have a greater granularity of options to rollback code to a previous state. Similar to how frequent database backups help you to minimize any data loss, frequent check-ins and change sets help you to minimize any loss in the code your developers produce.

It also enables a development team to work with a high degree of concurrency. Rather than a single developer locking a file or series of files with an exclusive check-out lock so they can make a lot of changes without worrying about merging the files later, several developers can check-out and make small changes to the same file concurrently. By checking in their small changes often, they will not face a significant burden to merge their changes. And better yet, everyone's changes are frequently merged and integrated with each other, giving your team constant feedback on their code's compatibility.

I like to perform an automated build every time a developer checks in code to the source code repository, and if something breaks or causes a failed build, the build process can create a bug and assign it to the developer. I usually do my development by creating unit tests, as I code in a test-driven development fashion similar to how I described in Chapter 14, and with these unit tests checked in, I set the automated build process to also run a suite of automated tests. If a test fails, I have the build process create a bug and assign it to the developer checking in the breaking change.

Unit tests can come in many flavors. Most are quick to execute and they do not require any additional resources beyond the processing of a couple methods. These are those lightweight tests that use mock objects to test a specific unit of functionality. This tests the bulk of your solution's functionality and you can execute them frequently and the testing process will only take a few seconds. I group these tests into a suite of fast executing unit tests and these are the tests that I run frequently during my development process. These are also the tests I configure the automated build and integration process to run after each check-in. However, I also want to create automated tests that take longer to run and test other things, such as tests that validate the mock objects by using the actual objects and testing functionality that interacts with the heavier system and network resources.

In addition to unit tests, I also create tests that test a greater scope of functionality than a unit test. The following lists some of the automated tests that you might create and include in your solution:

- Unit tests

- Continuous integration tests

- Web user interface tests

- Load tests

Some of these tests are lightweight and can execute very quickly; others involve additional resources such as database connections or long running processes and they take longer to execute. I generally organize my tests by first dividing them based on how quickly they execute. I might also group and organize them by additional factors based on things such as the test type or feature area, if organizing by granular categories is useful. I organize and group my tests by creating different test suites in Microsoft Test Manager within Visual Studio. This allows me to configure the build process to run those quick tests in a designated test suite as part of every automated build process when a developer checks in code. This keeps the build process running efficiently during the day with frequent code check-ins. I then configure another automated build that I schedule as my team's daily build, and during this build I have the process execute the other longer running test suites as well.

■ **Note** To learn more about how to create different test suites using Visual Studio and Microsoft Test Manager, please see this MSDN article: `http://msdn.microsoft.com/dd286738`.

These different types of automated builds offer a reasonable compromise between thorough testing and a high performing continuous integration process. This compromise is still current and provides constant feedback, as it has a daily build that executes each automated test alongside the build for every check-in that executes a subset of tests for those fast running unit tests. You will catch most of the breaking changes with the unit tests you include in the suite that runs after each check-in. For all the rest, you are never more than a day away from the system identifying a breaking change with a failed test. And if a developer is ever unsure if they just introduced a breaking change and they do not want to wait a day or two, he or she can queue a daily build on demand or execute a suite of tests in their development environment.

If you use Microsoft Team Foundation Server (TFS) as your source code repository and configuration management system, then you have an excellent application lifecycle management tool to automate your build and integration process. You can deploy SharePoint environments with the TFS build agent, and then you can configure build processes to use those build agents and automate a deployment to an environment. You can also configure a build process to take additional actions after a build, such as running a test suite or performing code coverage analysis for your tests.

■ **Note** For more guidance on designing an automated testing process as part of your application lifecycle management process, please see this MSDN *patterns & practices* article: `http://msdn.microsoft.com/jj159345`.

Figure 16-1 illustrates the continuous integration process and the relationship between the development environments, Team Foundation Server, and your integration environment. As a developer checks in code to the source repository, it triggers an automated build in the integration environment. The build process compiles the solution and deploys it to the SharePoint integration farm, and then it executes automated tests to validate the solution. If the build fails or any tests fail, the build process opens a bug and assigns it to the developer who checked in the breaking change.

Figure 16-1. *The continuous integration process with automated builds and tests*

I find a disciplined and automated integration process can make a significant difference on the quality of the overall solution that developers produce. My ideal process includes a continuous integration of code as developers contribute to the solution. It also includes a constant accumulation of automated tests, such as a suite of fast processing unit tests that the system can run after each check-in and suites of longer running tests that the system can run during a daily build cycle. This builds out a great procedure to contribute to your deployment risk mitigation strategy, but whether it is a fit for your team and processes depends on your tolerance for deployment risk. If you have a high tolerance for risk, then you may find building suites of automated tests add too much overhead to your process. Conversely, if you have a low tolerance for deployment risk, then you will find the automated tests catch problems and mitigate risks long before you release code to production. In the next section, I look at tolerance for deployment risk in more detail.

Understanding Your Tolerance for Deployment Risk

So far in this chapter, I have described a formal and disciplined process for deploying any customization into a production environment. You can even get more disciplined and add more rigor to the process. At the same time, you might have less or none at all. You might just want to crank out solutions without any testing and deal with any issues or inconsistencies as your users discover them as they use the solutions in production. Although that is not my approach, I do know a lot of people who conduct their release management processes with more ad hoc and loose (or non-existent) testing procedures. These types of people have a higher tolerance for deployment risk than I do.

I sometimes refer to a high tolerance for deployment risk as running with a *cowboy mentality*. This comes from an image of a cowboy in the old Wild West, riding a horse through prairies and making decisions on the fly. The cowboy rides free, exploring the west without any supervision or formal processes. They explore and they react. Cowboys get the job done, one way or another, often through quick decisions and immediate solutions, and through their own stubborn notions of how to get things done. They do not mind things going wrong, because mistakes happen and they will fix them if they do, but they do not want to waste time worrying about the details when they can implement solutions instead.

Some people have a high tolerance for deployment risk and they would rather deal with issues if and when they come up rather than slow down the process. These people may feel comfortable with developing changes directly in production without performing any testing. Of course, when things go wrong, they will feel stressed just like anyone else, but they fight through the issue until they are finally satisfied with the solution. This is just their process and approach because they either do not know any other way or they are comfortable with their high tolerance for deployment risk.

Other people have a low tolerance for deployment risk and they would rather minimize any change rather than risk introducing an incompatible change and breaking their production environment. They will only feel comfortable with a formal and thorough testing and release management process, and even then they still might not be at ease with a release. If the cowboy is the carefree roamer who deploys changes on the fly, these other folks are the settled and stable rocks who maintain reliability with their low tolerance for deployment risk.

Everyone else will fall somewhere on the spectrum in between the high and low tolerance for deployment risk. Where you and your organization falls will determine how formal your testing and release management process will be. The following lists some questions to help you understand your own tolerance for deployment risk:

- Do you insist on deploying every customization to a preproduction environment before you deploy it into production?

- Do you separate the development and testing duties into different individuals?

- Do you have a formal and predictable testing process for customizations?

- Do you follow a change management process that you use to plan and track every change?

- Do you generally feel confident that a deployment will go as you planned?

- Do you have a rollback plan?

The more of these questions that you find yourself answering no to, the higher I would say your tolerance for deployment risk might be. This is not necessarily bad or uncommon, as I have worked with many clients who could probably answer no to most or all those questions. Some people just work that way and they do not want to get bogged down in process or they cannot afford to delay releases with any extra testing, as in this case the costs of doing so would be higher than the costs of introducing bugs. They are probably aware that things can go wrong and they just accept the risk because they are more interested in deploying new functionality quickly.

If this sounds like you and you are satisfied with it, then I am satisfied and I will leave your processes up to you. For me, I would find this too stressful and chaotic. I would want to add some formality and process to increase my comfort level. Basically, what I would do, and what I have done, is work on increasing my release management maturity. In the next section, I share some tips on how you can build your own release management maturity.

Building Your Release Management Maturity Level

You can build and evolve your level of maturity for release management by refining your processes and adopting disciplined procedures throughout your entire application development lifecycle. A mature release management process relies on your development and testing standards, such as those I discussed in Chapter 14. It also relies on automation and a configuration management tool that facilitates the disciplined and desired behaviors you want.

The configuration management tool I use is Team Foundation Server (TFS), which allows me to define workflows and processes, and it provides a rich set of automation capabilities. TFS is just a tool, so you cannot expect to deploy it and have it magically fix any broken development processes. However, it does integrate work item tracking, test suite management, build automation, and other features with the source code repository. This level of integration between the rich toolset can add a level of maturity to your release management process.

With the right tools in place, you can continue to mature your release management by defining different processes and establishing different automated steps in the process. TFS can enforce or support your standards, and this helps to hold the quality bar high for the team. Furthermore, it helps with onboarding new developers to the team and the team's development standards quickly as code check-in policies and unit test results provide constant feedback and guidance on the new developer's development style.

One key indicator for how mature you are with your release management is how thoroughly you test customizations throughout the development lifecycle. As your developers build components, they can write unit tests to automate the testing of specific functionality. This will make a huge difference for the code quality and for your overall release management, because you will accumulate a test suite that you can configure to run automatically and alert you to any breaking change.

Beyond developers writing unit tests for their code, you can also include dedicated tester roles on your team. People often refer to these roles as quality assurance (QA), because they are on the team to validate and ensure quality before the team considers a component code complete and ready for deployment. Quality assurance resources can act as gatekeepers and as crusaders of quality, as they work to test different aspects of a customization.

Quality assurance extends developer unit tests with additional integration, coded user interface, and load tests. This helps you build out a more complete test suite of automated tests. The more testing and quality validation your quality assurance team automates, the more this investment pays for itself with each daily build. This grows your maturity for release management and it cultivates a high performing continuous integration process.

I like to automate as many test cases as I can, because then these tests can repeatedly run and provide feedback without any involvement or even having to think about them (until a breaking change causes tests to fail). This is a mature state for a team to reach, but you cannot automate all tests, as some will need a person to click through and validate the results. TFS can help you with these test cases as well with the manual tests you can create. Your quality assurance team can then manually conduct those tests and record the results.

Incorporating and enforcing development and testing standards with code check-in policies, automating tests as part of a continuous integration process, and including a quality assurance step to test and validate quality are all things that you can adopt to mature your release management processes. But do not stop there, because there is more that you can do. One thing in particular is to add another gatekeeper to test the quality and validate that the developers are developing the right solution. I refer to this stage as user acceptance testing where actual users test and validate a customization by using it in a test environment.

Designing a User Acceptance Testing Environment

Have you delivered a solution that meets your users' needs, that solves an actual problem for them, or have you simply managed project scope and delivered some vague functional requirement? If you design it right, user acceptance testing (UAT) is your chance to find out. For me, I want to know that I am solving actual user problems and adding real value to their work, and I find the UAT stage of my release management process is the key point to validate and confirm this.

In my experience, it is important to separate the UAT environment from the development and integration environments. Even though the environment is not production, you still need to provide the users with a positive experience for the system's stability and the functionality of the solution. Other preproduction environments may be buggy and tend to offer a less than optimal experience for end-users. You do not want to leave them with a bad impression, no matter how much disclosure you give them about how beta software runs differently than production.

Give your UAT testers stable software that is ready for production. It should be feature complete, at least for the area they are testing. These testers are not your bug testers nor are they your quality assurance department. These are your *customers* and you are using UAT to get their feedback on whether the solution you built meets their needs. If they accept it, then you should be able to deploy the solution into staging and then into production without any rework or changes. That is how complete you need to make your solution before you promote it to the UAT environment.

You have a few options on how you can set up and implement your UAT environment, and which you choose depends on the experience you want to provide to your users for their testing. Specifically, you can choose whether or not you want to replicate their existing site experience. The following lists some options you can choose from:

- For new applications, you can use a basic SharePoint site without any unnecessary data to focus on your solution's functionality.

- For enhancements and extensions to existing applications, you can restore a backup of the users' site to your UAT environment and deploy your solution to this site for testing.

- For new applications that you want to test in context, you can restore a backup of the users' site to your UAT environment.

User acceptance testing is an opportunity for your users to let you know whether or not you built the right solution; it is *not* the time for you to defend yourself or to argue about the requirements. You are conducting UAT to collect user feedback and identify opportunities to make improvements and better meet their needs. I find it is best to prepare myself with these expectations so that I approach a UAT session seeking feedback and suggestions on where I can improve rather than with trying to push a solution or manage scope.

I like to make the UAT environment accessible so that it works the same for users as their experience with production. As part of this, I configure the preproduction Active Directory domain to trust the production domain. This way the users performing the tests can use their regular account and work in much the same way as they are used to. This removes some of the testing complexity and complications for them, which frees them up to focus on the solution and whether it meets their needs.

Regular users might not be familiar with TFS and its process to submit bugs. Again, to avoid complications and distractions during UAT, you might consider having a business analyst capture and submit any issues that come up during UAT for the users. This frees up your users to focus on using the application and on working in their normal way while someone else captures their feedback into the system for the team.

Ultimately, with user acceptance testing, you want users to work in their normal way and report how well or how poorly the solution meets their needs and fits with how they want to work. If you have done a good job with analyzing requirements and engaging stakeholders for constant feedback, then very little should come up during UAT to surprise you. However, this is your last chance to discover and correct any areas in your solution where you might be off the mark.

Using Multiple Environments for Testing and Staging

More preproduction environments can give you more practice with testing functionality and compatibility. They can also give you more practice with testing the deployment process. They allow you to focus on different things and incorporate different gates in your release management process. However, you can eventually go overboard.

There is no single correct number of preproduction environments that will work for everyone. The rule of thumb I use is to have enough environments in your release management process as are necessary for you to feel comfortable and to align with your tolerance for deployment risk. For some people, the number of environments will be much higher; while for others, this number will be minimal.

At the very least, you need a preproduction environment. You need a place to test the deployment process and the solution's compatibility with the existing production environment, and you need to perform these tests before you release the customization in production. You are playing a dangerous and reckless game if you do not have at least one environment for testing before production. If this is the case, I suggest that you are not the only one who does this, but now is the time to do yourself a favor and setup a preproduction environment and start testing before you deploy to production.

As I mentioned earlier, I like to gradually work my preproduction environments closer and closer to match the production environment. This will range from my development environment, which is not much like production at all besides sharing the same components, all the way up to production itself. The number of environments in between depends on the project, the size of the development team, and the complexity and scope of the custom solution.

I noted some of the different preproduction environments earlier, but here I will describe a couple of them in more detail:

- **Staging environment:** A staging environment is the closest representation of the production environment and it is the final stop before you deploy a change into production. I usually setup staging as an exact duplication of production to conduct a final compatibility test with the deployment process and the custom functionality.

- **Testing environment(s):** You can have a range of testing environments, from automated testing in integration to manual user acceptance testing. You might consolidate these into a single environment or across many. I usually setup testing to resemble as much of production as I need to perform the tests.

■ **Tip**   One benefit of setting up a staging environment as an exact duplication of your production environment is that you can use this as a failover environment in the event of a disaster. You might find this option especially useful if you locate your staging environment in a separate data center from your production environment.

These different environments all lay the infrastructure for your change management process. They provide you with testing options to identify issues before you release a change into production and cause stress for users. They also provide the environments where you can define gates as part of your change management process. In the next section, I look at some additional considerations for change management and your change management process.

Considerations for Change Management

Your organization might already have a change management process, and it may or may not be formalized. Change management applies to all of IT as a discipline, not just to SharePoint. IT standardizes a change management process to define all steps and procedures involved with controlling changes to IT infrastructure. Its goal is to minimize the impact to service availability and stability by defining standard steps and procedures to manage every change and mitigate risks of the changes causing a negative impact on the IT infrastructure.

A change management process typically involves IT stakeholders who meet for regular change management committee meetings to review the details of each change and approve or reflect on proposed changes. From there, if approved, the change is scheduled and applied to the IT infrastructure. An effective change management process generally involves the following stages:

- Change details reviewed and assessed by IT stakeholders

- Approval granted for change by IT stakeholders

- Change introduced through process with minimal risk to systems

- Process results of a component or configuration change

- Change provides business value through ongoing system use

Your SharePoint change management process fits within your existing IT service change management process, if one exists. If your IT team does not have anything formal for managing changes, then you can build out and manage your own process with the same formality and standardization as you would if your department had a change management process to follow.

The key benefits you realize from a change management process include your focused planning for the change and the extra perspectives that can help you consider potential risks associated with the change. Change management also ensures communication so that other IT teams are made aware of your proposed change and they can identify if the change will cause any conflict with their service area. It adds an extra check to help protect the stability of your SharePoint service.

You may have noticed me mentioning use cases at different times in this book. I find they are a useful tool for capturing and communicating details about a process, assumptions surrounding the process, and how to handle any exceptions or extensions to the scenario or user story. In the sidebar, I share a sample use case that I use for customization deployments. This can help you get started with designing your customization deployment process, and with building use cases in general.

SAMPLE CUSTOMIZATION DEPLOYMENT USE CASE

Context of Use: A SharePoint internal customer creates or discovers a customization they want deployed to the SharePoint service.

Minimal Guarantees: There is no interruption to the SharePoint service.

Success Guarantees: Customization is deployed.

Trigger: Internal customer requests to deploy a customization to the SharePoint service.

Primary Actors: SharePoint internal customer, SharePoint administrator, server administrator

Stakeholders and Interests

- SharePoint user community: relies on SharePoint being a stable, available, and secure system.

- SharePoint team: interested in balancing the functionality needs against the SharePoint's stability and security.

Main Success Scenario

1. Internal customer requests a customization.

2. The SharePoint administrator validates the requested customization against the best practices and notifies the pending deployment status to the requestor.

3. The SharePoint administrator adds install files to repository and announces their availability to the server administrator.

4. The server administrator goes through a change management process to deploy the customization, and then notifies the requestor of the successful deployment.

Extensions

(The extensions correspond to and extend the matching numbered items in the Main Success Scenario)

2.a The customization does not meet standards: Reject customization.

3.a The customization requires purchasing and SharePoint team has a budget for and purchases the customization.

4.a The deployment fails and the Server administrator rolls back the install. Reject customization.

Considerations for Rollback Planning

In Chapter 11, I discussed rollback planning from the perspective of planning to back out of an upgrade or any patches. The underlying need is no different for deploying customizations, as you should always have a plan to undo any change that did not go as planned, whether the change is a service pack or a custom component. You can use a similar process for custom components as the one I shared for rolling back patches or upgrades. Essentially, that rollback approach included backing up the SharePoint servers and databases and restoring those backups when you need to rollback a change.

However, the challenge with this approach for rolling back a custom component is that you need to schedule downtime with your SharePoint farm. If your rollback plan is to restore a database, then you need to prevent users from making any changes on the farm while you introduce the change so that you can restore any backups and rollback if the change does not go as planned, otherwise you would overwrite and lose their change. Depending on your tolerance for deployment risk, you might find this approach excessive for every little change. On top of that, it just might not be practical in practice even though it is an option.

What this means is that you will need to think through your rollback options on a case-by-case bases for each custom component. The following lists the general options I consider as part of my rollback planning:

- Can I simply deactivate a feature to rollback a change?

- Can I deactivate and remove the solution package to rollback a change?

- Does the customization add any artifacts to the SharePoint server that I need to clean up through a rollback script, such as deleting list items or files?

- Does the customization modify any data or configuration settings that I need to reverse through a rollback script?

- Does the customization change any visuals such as page layouts or web part positions that I need to reverse through a rollback script?

As you can see, my primary rollback plan to back out of any customization changes is to create a rollback script. Typically, this is a PowerShell script that reverses any changes the customization introduces. I have also used the SharePoint API in a console application to reverse these types of changes, particularly before the days of PowerShell, but this approach is still useful. A console application can capture the state before applying a proposed change, so it has the state information to reset and reapply data and settings to when you need to rollback.

Rolling back customizations is slightly more complex and involved than simply restoring server state and database backups, although that approach will also work. Scripting the process will work best, especially if the customization introduces any artifacts such as data or configuration settings. However, your rollback process might be a set of manual steps instead. For example, your rollback process for a component might be to navigate to a site and deactivate its feature and then manually delete any data or reset any configuration changes it made.

You have several options to rollback changes from customizations. The important thing is to think through those options and build a rollback plan before you deploy a customization as part of your release management processes. Once you have a rollback plan, then you need to test and validate it in a preproduction environment to ensure you can back out of any change. With all this in place, you are ready to release your custom component with confidence.

Consultant Comrade

A consultant brings their experience and expertise to help a client solve a particular problem, whether with SharePoint or with processes around SharePoint. The application development lifecycle and code promotion processes are no different, and as a consultant you can help your clients mature their processes. However, a consultant needs to exhibit his or her own mature processes before he or she can transmit the knowledge and practice to a client. You need to lead by example, and then once you fine-tune your own application development lifecycle and code promotion processes, you can champion them with your clients.

A caution though: establishing development practices can quickly unravel a project's scope and consume a budget. It is exciting and important, and it can add a ton of value for your client. However, if it is not in in the project's scope and you have not budgeted time for the activities, this will sink you. The trouble is that consulting activities to establish a mature development practice come early in a project delivery, when you still have a lot of budget and time, but before you get started on the actual project and flush out all the requirements and how much effort they will take. Getting sidetracked with designing development practices up front will leave you chasing from behind for the rest of the project until you finally run out of budget.

This is where it is good to lead by example. If you already have a mature set of processes for development and release management, such as those I described in this chapter, then you can show your client and involve them in the process. And if you do not have these processes already, then you need to work on building them on your own time. A new project that does not have any budget or time allocated for this work is not the place to attempt building processes.

Conversely, if you already have mature development and release management processes, then you are in a great position to consult clients on how to copy and establish similar processes. You need to plan for this and budget for it in the project's scope. I have been on a couple of projects where the client noticed my team's process and they wanted help to adopt it as well. Both times they had a new SharePoint development team and did not have any process. As valuable as this consulting engagement is, I have found that you should always deliver it under its own project and an explicit scope; otherwise it will take you off track and your project delivery will end without as much success.

Typically, I would organize this type of engagement with a Team Foundation System (TFS) deployment followed with configuring all the processes and policies I want to establish as part of the development standards I covered in Chapter 14. Then, I would design the integration environment and configure a TFS build agent to automatically trigger a build and run any unit tests for each developer check-in.

The TFS build process can also work with provisioning new virtual servers and deploying the solution there. A couple of times I have included this option for the daily build and you can even use the templates to provision new development environments when new developers join the team. This takes some effort to setup and configure, so it is probably only useful on large teams with multiple workgroups.

Once the infrastructure is in place, then you are ready to work with and start coaching the developers. This process is really an extension of the development standards I mentioned in Chapter 14, where now you are adding in TFS and a sophisticated set of policies and automated processes such as continuous integration builds and unit tests. This automated aspect is what enforces and reinforces any of your client's standards, and it ultimately leads to a higher quality of code.

I think there is great opportunity for a consultant to help clients establish infrastructure such as TFS to support mature development and release management processes. Your clients might not need everything and all the processes I shared might be overkill for their needs, but every little bit will help. It will also align your clients with your own development standards and release management processes. It will also help to set your client up for success with future application development to extend their SharePoint service.

Inside Story: Notes from the Field

A while back, I was on a development team where we were building an application that integrates with a user's personal MySite portal. My client wanted a custom application to centralize and control communication and approvals. Essentially, if they create a new policy or procedure or they change one, then the application tracks that and notifies each user on their MySite. The user then can review these policies and procedures from their MySite and accept them, and the system will track their acceptance.

It is certainly a nifty application, and one that was also useful for ensuring users receive and acknowledge other types of communications as well. Another team worked on the reporting aspect of the application, so that a manager can review whether his or her direct reports have reviewed and acknowledged a notification. The team built a variety of reports to extend the application for managers and executives. This added complexity and risk because that team was integrating with the components and workflow that my team was still developing.

We designed a continuous integration process to constantly build and deploy the SharePoint solution packages that made up the application. This was our first line of defense because it continuously merged every customization from the very beginning of the development process. This continuous integration process was practical and effective because it automated a lot of steps. This meant that continuous integration would not cause a burden on the team and it would not be tempting to drop or skip parts if the team gets too busy and falls behind, because the process is automated and did not cause any extra overhead.

My suite of unit tests also provided insulation (as did every team's suite of unit tests for their code). When a developer on either team introduced a breaking change that caused a test to fail, the system assigned them a bug. The developer could then look at the failing test and use that information to correct the issue. This process catches compatibility issues early in the process and it provides instant feedback to developers to guide them in correcting any breaking change.

Now, having a continuous integration process such as the one I described in this chapter certainly helps a development team during the initial development for all the reasons I mentioned. But it also helps any future development teams that need to extend or enhance a custom application, because they can start using the automation right away. In particular, they can use the suite of automated tests to help them to avoid introducing any breaking changes to the existing code base that the developers may not be familiar with.

I think every stage of your release management process is important and will benefit you with increased stability and sustainability in your SharePoint service. However, I like continuous integration the best and this is where I place the bulk of my release management design efforts because so much quality control can be automated in this phase. Start with a highly functional and automated continuous integration environment, and build out your release management strategy from there.

Wrapping Up

In this chapter, I discussed considerations for planning a change management process and designing a release management process that encourages maturity and discipline in your deployment practices. I looked at how to automate integration testing and how to promote code through testing and staging environments to ensure stability before you deploy it to production environments.

Customizing your SharePoint service involves facilitating end-user customizations, designing development standards, and managing a release process. This fourth part of the book covered broad topics such as establishing sponsorship, facilitating end-user customizations, designing development standards and testing processes, building an information architecture, and planning your release management processes. With this information, you can handle those enhancements that require customizing and extending SharePoint, and this will help you add rich new functionality while lowering the risks involved with deploying custom components.

As we conclude our journey through these action-focused governance topics, I leave you with one final tool. Next, you will find an appendix where I have summarized rapid concepts from each chapter in this book. I organized the appendix so you can review each chapter at a glance to refresh your memory of the key points I discussed, and then I included a checklist of actions you can take as they relate to each chapter's governance topics.

Rapid Concepts

Never confuse movement with action.

—Ernest Hemingway

In this appendix, I summarize and review the concepts I covered throughout this book to provide you with quick reference material where you can refresh yourself with the highlights from each chapter at a glance. I also provide you with action checklists for each chapter to highlight for you the next steps and actions I suggest you take.

Figure A-1 illustrates the idea I have been stressing throughout this book, the idea of balancing actions with your governance needs and your desired governance outcomes. Governance simply refers to the actions you take to govern your SharePoint service, those things you do to provide a reliable and valuable service. This appendix provides you with a rapid overview and several checklists for some of those actions you can take.

Figure A-1. *Balancing actions with your desired governance needs and outcomes*

Chapter 1 In Brief

In Chapter 1, "Understanding SharePoint Governance," I orientated SharePoint governance and defined it for the purposes of this book. I discussed the approach I take in the book to address governance and the primary audience for this book. The following lists the rapid concepts from Chapter 1:

- Governance goes beyond documentation. Documentation captures and communicates processes to ensure everyone is on the same page, and it can provide a lot of value. Yet, documentation in itself does not affect any change. This book focuses on the actions that do drive change and I leave the documentation options to your discretion.

- Governance encompasses actions, behaviors, and commitments. This involves a way of thinking that matures into values, doing actual things that need doing until they become habits, and staying dedicated to these values and habits.

- This book is for you if you work with SharePoint and you have an interest in learning more about my SharePoint governance experiences with customers in the field. I wrote this book in a manner to enable you to read the chapters that follow in numerical order, or you can skip to particular sections.

- SharePoint 2013 adds exciting new capabilities and it enhances some existing features that aid in achieving different governance objectives. eDiscovery provides the infrastructure for managing and governing content from individual items to entire site collections. SharePoint Apps allow users to purchase and provision their own functionality without modifying or affecting the underlying farm. The site access request process makes permission management and request management more straightforward for ordinary users, and this helps with governing access control as a result. Managed navigation associates a site's navigation with a term set in the Managed Metadata Service.

Action Checklist

- ☐ Determine how formal or informal you want your governance process to be
- ☐ List available resources to involve with governance
- ☐ Identify whom to involve with your governance process
- ☐ List the biggest pain points in your current environment
- ☐ List any governance blocks or obstacles
- ☐ Decide where to start

Chapter 2 In Brief

In Chapter 2, "Defining Your SharePoint Service and Service Tiers," I discussed how to make the scope of your SharePoint service explicit and intentional, how to set up different service levels, and how to design a chargeback-funding model. The following lists the rapid concepts from Chapter 2:

- Consider your SharePoint deployment as a service, and this will go hand-in-hand with treating your users as internal customers. You are providing SharePoint to deliver value that meets the needs of your internal customers. Consider your service's competitive advantage. How will it attract and satisfy your internal customers?

- Look to deliver quickly, deliver frequently, and deliver incrementally. Limit your SharePoint scope and have the confidence that you will continue to add value and expand the capabilities that your SharePoint service provides over time.

- Define your SharePoint service by starting with identifying the scope of what your service offers. A service can grow and expand its scope over time, and it can have different service levels with different scopes to meet different customer needs.

- A functional service request process includes a triage step where a resource assesses, prioritizes, and routes a ticket to the appropriate group. A valid priority level can be determined by using a rubric that defines each level using measurable metrics such as the number of affected users and the cost of potential revenue loss.

- Base your service tiers on multiple dimensions of the factors that define them. Those dimensions can include things such as the number of features, amount of system resources, number of users, size of content storage, range of support services, and the like. Chargebacks can charge a fixed amount for a service tier and then a variable amount for additional options that a customer adds to their service.

- Determine maintenance windows by building out a schedule on a visual timeline for each farm and then layer on each of the activities that occur, such as backups, crawling content, and the like. Coordinate global tasks with those in the local farm and the local peak usage. Finally, highlight core-operating hours for each location.

Action Checklist

- ☐ Identify your internal customers and their needs
- ☐ Analyze existing SharePoint usage to define the as-is service
- ☐ Define an initial SharePoint service with the scope for your phase one delivery
- ☐ Identify the different service levels or service tiers and their scope
- ☐ List your customers and map them to appropriate service tiers
- ☐ Design your service request ticket process with a ticket triage step
- ☐ Create a rubric that defines priority levels for your service request
- ☐ Write out the farm's schedule of activities and layer them on a visual timeline
- ☐ Identify your maintenance windows for each farm

Chapter 3 In Brief

In Chapter 3, "Determining Your SharePoint Features and Functionality," I looked at some of the new features in SharePoint 2013 and what its core capability areas are. I also discussed how to plan for and limit features, and how to map features to business value. The following lists the rapid concepts from Chapter 3:

- SharePoint 2013 provides a wealth of new features and capabilities, yet its underlying architecture is largely consistent with SharePoint 2010, which eases the relearning and training burden when upgrading to SharePoint 2013.

- The key investment and enhancement areas in SharePoint 2013 include eDiscovery and records management, social computing, search, business connectivity services, and request management, among others. SharePoint 2013 core capability areas include collaboration, social computing, portals, search, records management, business intelligence, and composite applications.

- Business value consists of the outcomes that a particular feature, capability, or composite application provides to end-users. You can measure it through dollars such as cost savings or extra revenue produced, amount of time saved in a process, extra contact points in a mass communication campaign, improved goodwill or morale, and the like. There are no shortcuts or cheat sheets that provide a master list mapping SharePoint features to business value, as the perceived value will be unique for each organization. One effective tool is to build use cases for the as-is and to-be states, and then use that to compare the business value gained from the solution.

- You can limit features by restricting permissions to them through web application policies or service application permissions, where available. You can completely disable some features by stopping their service or you can only associate service applications to the web applications you want them to be available within. You can also use custom actions to remove menu items you do not want available to your end-users.

- Evolve your SharePoint service by enabling new features over time. Focus on features that build on existing functionality for frequent and incremental improvements that deliver continuous value, rather than those breakthrough improvements that require a more radical change.

Action Checklist

☐ Determine the measure of business value you will use, such as money or time

☐ Build use cases to capture details of the as-is state of the business process

☐ Analyze the as-is use cases for solutions to solve the business problem

☐ Build use cases to describe the to-be state of the solution

☐ Capture the business value by comparing the as-is with the to-be use cases

☐ List features and services you need to limit and disable

☐ Consider and plan how you will enable features over time

☐ Identify opportunities for continuous and incremental improvements

Chapter 4 In Brief

In Chapter 4, "Establishing Your Team's Roles and Responsibilities," I discussed what resources you require for your SharePoint service and how to identify their responsibilities. I also looked at RACI charts, how to adapt a RACI chart for your organization, and how to use the RACI chart to ensure you have end-to-end support coverage and defined communication protocols. The following lists the rapid concepts from Chapter 4:

- A RACI chart provides the format for a roles and responsibilities matrix, in which you map roles to the tasks they are responsible or accountable for completing. You also map which roles require communication and involvement as part of the tasks by identifying which roles to consult and inform.

- Identify the tasks and roles your SharePoint service depends on by starting with the SharePoint farm and working your way out. Follow the data flow to identify all the systems that interface with your SharePoint environment to identify all the dependencies.

- Ensure end-to-end coverage by verifying that you can account for every task and included it in the RACI chart, that each task has a role specified as responsible for it, and that each role has a resource allocated to it. You can formalize your communication protocols by using a custom workflow within SharePoint that will standardize procedures such as approvals and change management processes.

- You can use your RACI chart to prime and guide your efforts in creating a service level agreement (SLA) because it lists details on all the tasks and roles involved with providing the service, and you can use this to determine what level of service you can provide. An SLA is a formal agreement between the business and IT on what level of service they can depend on.

Action Checklist

☐ Decide whether to create RACI charts for each functional area or one large one

☐ List the tasks involved with your project if you are delivering a project phase

☐ List the tasks for each process directly involved with the SharePoint service

☐ List the tasks involved for each system the SharePoint service depends on

☐ Group the tasks into common roles to identify all the roles for the RACI chart

☐ For each task, identify one and only one role responsible for it

☐ For each task, identify if a role is accountable but not responsible for it

☐ For each task, identify any roles that require consulting or informing

☐ Map each of your resources to one or more roles

☐ Ensure you have end-to-end coverage by validating allocations

☐ Define your communication protocol

Chapter 5 In Brief

In Chapter 5, "Shaping Your SharePoint Readiness and End-User Training," I discussed the need for providing the operations team with readiness opportunities to ensure they have the right skills to support the service, and the need to provide end-users with training to help maximize their productivity using the service. I discussed approaches that utilize classroom and online training, peer mentors, and quick start guides. The following lists the rapid concepts from Chapter 5:

- Training can take many forms, from formal classroom workshops to online self-paced e-learning. Books provide a great return on your training investment and provide a means to reuse them by starting a team reference library. You can also approach learning through blogs and videos, or you can explore and discover functionality on your own.

- People learn best what they try to teach others. For an operations team, you can maximize the learning potential in this concept by dividing the potential topics among team members or pairs of team members to go learn, and later they can teach it to the rest of the team.

- Classroom training and conferences can generate ideas and inspiration for new possibilities and different approaches for solutions. They tend to target a wide audience and can be generic, but they also save time because someone else has already thought about the connection between topics and how to explain them.

- Peer mentoring involves a relationship of peers who can provide alternate perspectives and advice outside a superior-subordinate relationship. You might use peer mentoring to onboard a new team member to the team, or to develop skills in a particular area. The important point is that the relationship is neutral and does not involve any type of reporting or evaluation relationship.

- When you design custom training, design it around the learner and what skills you want the learner to acquire. The formula is to create learning objectives as an action phrase that you can later measure, break each learning objective into the tasks involved with accomplishing it, and then deliver the training to address each task. Measure how well the learner can perform the learning objective to evaluate the effectiveness of the training.

Action Checklist

☐ Identify the gap in required skills on your operations team

☐ List the different types of training you have available

☐ Prioritize a list of training for your operations team

☐ Identify potential classroom training and conferences for team members

☐ Start a book club or peer study group for continuous learning

☐ Establish peer mentors and a process to connect mentees with mentors

☐ Design and create custom training resources based on learning objectives

☐ Create single page quick start guides to walk users through the steps of key tasks

Chapter 6 In Brief

In Chapter 6, "Measuring and Reporting on Your SharePoint Service Performance," I discussed techniques for monitoring and reporting on the health of your SharePoint service. I looked at metrics to measure and thresholds that can warn about potential problems, and how you can use that information to proactively respond and tune the SharePoint service. I discussed how to respond to an incident and how to conduct a root-cause analysis when an incident occurs. The following lists the rapid concepts from Chapter 6:

- You cannot measure and report on everything with the same scrutiny, because there is just too much information drowning out details from each measure. You can manage the amount of information by filtering out the noise and highlighting what is meaningful by setting thresholds and triggering alerts. You can use this process to keep your finger on the pulse of your SharePoint service and to maximize its availability.

- Availability relates to how available the SharePoint service is for use at a desired level of capacity. You can determine your availability needs based on your tolerance for downtime or reduced capacity in normal operations and in extenuating circumstances.

- You can measure and report on operational metrics that support the SharePoint service, such as human input and other indicators of the discipline and effectiveness of your operations team. You can measure on farm and system performance metrics by using tools such as SQL Profiler and Performance Monitor to measure the utilization and availability of resources. You can also use the SharePoint Health Analyzer to evaluate different aspects of your farm's health and notify you when it detects problems.

- Having an incident response plan will help you when things go wrong. Your plan will guide you to a systematic response with a methodical list of activities, such as the information you need to collect, the people you need to notify, and your note taking procedure. An effective incident response plan will help relieve some stress and avoid blame as it guides you to assess the situation and work through the issue.

- A root-cause analysis is an investigative process to examine an incident or situation to look beyond any symptoms and determine the underlying cause. The point of this analysis is to understand what went wrong to prevent the issue from reoccurring.

Action Checklist

- ☐ Determine your required availability level for normal operations
- ☐ Determine your required availability level for extenuating circumstances
- ☐ List your priorities for areas of your SharePoint service to monitor
- ☐ List service metrics you can measure that align with your service priority areas
- ☐ Identify thresholds for reporting on your measures
- ☐ List the information you need to collect as part of your incident response plan
- ☐ List the people you need to notify as part of your incident response plan
- ☐ Establish a root-cause analysis policy to investigate incidents and outages
- ☐ Schedule a team retrospective on a recurring schedule or after incidents

Chapter 7 In Brief

In Chapter 7, "Creating Your SharePoint Roadmap," I discussed techniques for planning and building a roadmap for your SharePoint service. I looked at what makes a roadmap valuable and how you can get started. I examined maturity models and how you can assess your maturity levels for different capabilities, and how this can contribute to your roadmap. The following lists the rapid concepts from Chapter 7:

- SharePoint is a large and complex product with a vast array of features and capabilities. It can quickly overwhelm a project team who tries to deliver too much at once. Focus on delivering smaller portions of value quickly and frequently to increase your success.

- A roadmap lays out a clear picture of where you are going and what you plan to accomplish. You can use it to track your progress and set expectations on what's to come, and it can help you set the pace and scope to support program management. It highlights priorities and reveals impacts from any potential changes. Ultimately, they give you and your team direction, and they can help your vendors and partners share your vision.

- Start your roadmap planning by assessing your maturity levels against an IT maturity model. Use the gaps in the maturity model between where you are and your desired maturity level to identify the opportunities and activities for your roadmap. Prioritize these activities by listing dependencies, expected business value, and estimated costs.

- Apply the maturity model to assess your maturity level: chaotic, where you operate in an unpredictable manner; reactive, where you operate in a fire-fighting manner; proactive, where you operate in a predictive manner; managed, where you operate as an IT service provider; and optimized, where you operate as a strategic business partner.

- Apply the maturity model to assess your maturity levels for each of the seven core capability areas within SharePoint: collaboration, social computing, portals, search, records management, business intelligence, and composite applications.

- A visual summary infographic of your roadmap is the essence of your roadmap and is its primary communication tool. This provides a visual representation of the order of delivery as well as any dependencies. You can create it using diagramming tools such as Microsoft Visio or the SmartArt graphics inside Word.

Action Checklist

- ☐ Determine an IT maturity model to use and define a rubric of the possible maturity levels
- ☐ Assess your organizational maturity level
- ☐ Assess your maturity level for the different SharePoint-related capability areas
- ☐ Determine your desired maturity levels for your operations and capability areas
- ☐ Identify the gaps between your current and desired maturity levels
- ☐ List the expected software and infrastructure upgrade cycle
- ☐ Prioritize your list of roadmap activities
- ☐ Create a visual summary infographic of your roadmap
- ☐ Document any supporting information, such as overarching vision and use cases

Chapter 8 In Brief

In Chapter 8, "Promoting a Feedback Process," I discussed different techniques to gather user feedback about your SharePoint service, including feedback on new opportunities where the service can expand to add additional value and feedback on what problems interfere with their ability to perform certain tasks. I looked at how to gather feedback by using surveys, analyzing usage reports, and interviewing and shadowing users. The following lists the rapid concepts from Chapter 8:

- Feedback can come from upfront requirements gathering and analysis or through ongoing usage. It can reveal the business value that you can deliver to your users, and this can help you understand how to make the SharePoint service more relevant to users.

- You can collect feedback through a variety of approaches, such as surveying users, analyzing usage reports, conducting user interviews, and shadowing users performing their business processes. Surveys and usage reports can scale to collect feedback from a large number of users, whereas interviews and shadow activities do not scale as well.

- Your feedback survey will work best if you balance the amount of time you require for responses with the perceived value in responding. To minimize the amount of time required for a response, you can use predetermined answers such as selection lists or ratings for survey questions. This fixed range of answers will also help you aggregate responses and analyze trends. However, it will also limit some of your ability to discover new findings.

- You can use SharePoint Usage Reports and other types of system-generated metrics to gather user feedback. This information can reveal what is the most popular and what available functionality users might be overlooking. It can help you discover workarounds or areas users have abandoned.

- Interviewing users requires open questions focused on the user and their business processes rather than on technology. Practice active listening to stay focused on the business value and avoid prematurely jumping into a solution design. Avoid leading or solution-focused questions. When shadowing users, focus on passive observing.

Action Checklist

- ☐ List topic areas that you would like to collect user feedback about
- ☐ Identify the number of questions your users will want to answer in a survey
- ☐ Build a list of questions appropriate for a survey and identify response choices
- ☐ Create a SharePoint survey with your questions and analyze user responses
- ☐ Implement a permanent feedback process, such as an ongoing survey
- ☐ Analyze SharePoint Usage Reports and other system-generated usage metrics
- ☐ Identify information you need to interview or shadow users to collect
- ☐ Build a list of user interview questions using open, user-focused questions
- ☐ Select users to interview and users to shadow
- ☐ Analyze the feedback data and begin to envision potential solution concepts

Chapter 9 In Brief

In Chapter 9, "Managing Your SharePoint Demand Funnel," I discussed approaches to setting up a demand funnel for enhancing and expanding the SharePoint service, including considerations for establishing a triage process. I looked at ways to set expectations, build a parking lot list of enhancement requests, and how to map requests back to your roadmap. The following lists the rapid concepts from Chapter 9:

- You can use a demand funnel as a systematic routine to process requests for enhancements or expansions to your SharePoint service. A strong process will help protect you from the chaos of having requests pull you in all directions. It will also help you focus on constantly delivering the highest and optimum business value.

- A request triage assesses requests to determine their relative value, cost, and priority. To assess a request, you should include a representative group of stakeholders and team members who can contribute in the prioritization of an item. You should designate one person to chair the triage and they should facilitate consensus within the group.

- Encourage your team to capture as many details as they can for each request. You can attach design documents such as use cases, wireframes and mockups, UML diagrams, ER diagrams, and process and swim lane diagrams. You can then use this information to build estimates for the cost and effort required to deliver the solution. You can also estimate a rough magnitude of business value.

- A parking lot list or a backlog provides you with a repository of requirements and opportunities your team has captured for an undetermined future solution. This allows you to capture details of ideas as they come to people, while avoiding having the ideas pull your team off course and out of scope.

- For third-party products, you will want to look beyond isolated features as you evaluate its match potential for your SharePoint service. This includes both commercial and open source third-party products. At a minimum, you should evaluate the product's functionality, test its stability and compatibility, assess the vendor's support policy, and project the product's upgradability.

Action Checklist

- ☐ Establish a list to capture requests and request details
- ☐ Establish a parking lot or backlog to capture deferred enhancement requests
- ☐ Configure an identifier for the development phase of items
- ☐ Schedule a recurring request triage meeting
- ☐ List and invite stakeholders and team members as optional triage attendees
- ☐ Map requests back to your roadmap and assess dependencies
- ☐ Forecast the next version of SharePoint and its required upgrade effort
- ☐ Design a process to evaluate third-party products
- ☐ Create a pilot environment where you can quickly provision pilot farms

Chapter 10 In Brief

In Chapter 10, "Growing Your SharePoint Service," I discussed how to plan for growing your SharePoint service, including considerations to scale for availability, general infrastructure components, and the server roles in a SharePoint farm. I looked at the ability for SharePoint to evolve and grow over time as the usage pattern changes, and how this eliminates the need to feel constrained or to over-architect the farm upfront. The following lists the rapid concepts from Chapter 10:

- A SharePoint service will evolve and grow in a variety of ways, such as from expanding the capabilities available and increasing user adoption. However, it needs someone to plan and shape its growth. SharePoint does not have artificial intelligence capabilities built in to it to handle all of this work for you.

- You can scale your SharePoint service by scaling up or scaling out. Scaling up refers to adding or improving the resources in architecture's existing components. Scaling out refers to adding additional components to the architecture. For example, you can scale up by adding additional RAM to servers while maintaining the same number of servers in a farm, and you can scale out by adding additional servers to a farm.

- A SharePoint farm consists of one or more SharePoint servers and one or more SQL Servers. Some farm architectures conceptually divide the SharePoint servers into web server roles and application server roles, and the implementation details then are a matter of starting or stopping the appropriate services on each server. Other servers you may involve in a farm's architecture include Office Web Apps, Exchange, Lync, Active Directory, and Forefront Unified Access Gateway (UAG).

- You can join a new SharePoint server to an existing farm by first installing SharePoint 2013 on a Windows Server. Then you can apply all the latest service packs and patches, language packs, and any third-party components to match the other servers in the desired SharePoint farm. Finally, you will run the SharePoint Products and Technologies Configuration Wizard to join the server to the farm.

Action Checklist

- ☐ Plan a budget for future growth and scalability
- ☐ Design the infrastructure architecture for ease of scaling in the future
- ☐ Consider application or customer isolation as a scaling option
- ☐ Identify the infrastructure components and server roles you require
- ☐ Configure the services you require to run on each server
- ☐ Identify the resource characteristics for new service capabilities
- ☐ List farms you require for regional, service-level, service isolation, etc.
- ☐ Designate an enterprise farm to host enterprise service applications
- ☐ Identify service applications that subordinate farms will share
- ☐ Verify the patch levels for each server on the Manage Patch Status page

Chapter 11 In Brief

In Chapter 11, "Preparing for SharePoint Upgrades and Patches," I discussed how to build policies and standards that maintain the supportability of the farm and maximize its compatibility with upgrade processes. I looked at considerations for designing solutions in a manner that takes advantage of structures within SharePoint, and implementation strategies that offer the lowest risk against interfering with cumulative updates, service packs, or version upgrades. The following lists the rapid concepts from Chapter 11:

- Maintaining your SharePoint environments with the latest patches and service packs can help contribute to a healthy SharePoint service. It will correct any known security vulnerabilities, correct any other known defects, apply any performance improvements Microsoft identifies, and maintain a current version.

- Microsoft designed SharePoint to allow you to adapt it to fit changing needs as more information and new opportunities arise. If you feel particularly constrained by historical decisions that led your SharePoint environment to where it is today, you can migrate the content into a fresh environment. Knowing this option is available can help to relieve any anxiety about potentially painting yourself in a corner.

- Maintain product supportability by not making changes to system files and not directly changing data in any of the SharePoint databases. You can also optimize supportability by applying the latest service packs and by following the guidance in Part IV of this book when implementing customizations or custom development.

- A rollback plan is only valuable if you create one and test it before you need it, because then you will have it to simply undo whatever change caused a problem. Your rollback plan will typically consist of first capturing a snapshot of the server state and the databases before applying any updates or attempting an upgrade. Then if something goes wrong, you simply revert to the previous state.

- You can prepare for upgrades by maintaining your SharePoint environment in a supportable state. Typically, Microsoft will not provide you with many details too far in advance of a new version releasing, so it can be difficult to predict before the actual release. You can set yourself up for a good upgrade experience by spreading your site collections across several smaller content databases rather than a few large ones. You can also prepare by completing any site experience upgrades left over from upgrading the previous release.

Action Checklist

- ☐ Develop a rollback plan to back out of any patch updates or major upgrades
- ☐ Apply the latest service packs to your SharePoint environment
- ☐ Plan for and schedule regular environment patching maintenance
- ☐ Develop a rollback plan to restore an upgrade to the previous version's state
- ☐ Remove any unnecessary sites or custom components
- ☐ Plan for major version upgrades
- ☐ Perform test upgrades in a test environment
- ☐ Analyze upgrade compatibility with a test upgrade using production data

Chapter 12 In Brief

In Chapter 12, "Committing Sponsorship and Ownership of Customizations," I discussed the benefits of establishing sponsorship for customizations to commit ownership or funding for sustainable customizations. I looked at capturing a chain of custody that leads back to commitments to fix defects and mitigate upgrade issues. I also considered topics that relate to support policies for global customizations, utilizing Apps for SharePoint, and delegating ownership of customizations to site administrators. The following lists the rapid concepts from Chapter 12:

- A sponsor can be someone who funds and owns the budget for a SharePoint project or an aspect of the SharePoint service operations. A sponsor can also be someone who owns the ultimate accountability for a SharePoint project or an aspect of the SharePoint service operations.

- Identifying ownership will help to prevent neglecting and shifting of responsibilities. An owner with authority can help to drive decisions and resolve any political disagreements. Ownership can also help organize structure and create an effective escalation path.

- A customization's costs continue long after the actual development and the deployment costs. Customizations may require user support and training, bug fixes, and rework to make them compatible for future upgrades. Sponsors for customizations can commit to own the burden for bug fixes or future upgrade costs, typically for a given duration.

- With global customizations, you first need to assess their compatibility with the existing environment, and then you will need to assess the overall scalability of the customization to ensure it will not consume unnecessary server resources in the farm. You will also need to determine whether your team will own the accountability for customization, either by taking on this accountability from another group or by developing it yourself.

- Apps for SharePoint provide modular functionality users can add to their site. SharePoint 2013 includes built-in Apps readily available for site administrators to use and it provides a connection to the SharePoint Store catalog where vendors sell their Apps through the SharePoint Store. You can also host an Apps catalog for internal Apps.

Action Checklist

☐ Identify a sponsor who funds and owns the budget for the project

☐ Identify a sponsor who owns the ultimate accountability for the project

☐ Build a sponsorship transition plan from the project to regular service operations

☐ Identify a sponsor who owns the budget for the SharePoint service operations

☐ Identify a sponsor who holds ultimate accountability for SharePoint operations

☐ Define sponsorship requirements for customizations

☐ Establish a checkpoint to receive source code or product references before a deployment

☐ Setup an Apps for SharePoint catalog to host your internally developed Apps

☐ Determine what level of customizations you will delegate to site administrators

Chapter 13 In Brief

In Chapter 13, "Facilitating and Isolating End-User Customizations," I discussed how you can facilitate end-user customizations and how you can isolate those customizations so they do not have a negative impact on the performance of your SharePoint service for other users. I looked at how to empower your users in a safe and contained environment so that they can adapt and tailor the service to meet their needs without introducing an unnecessary burden on support. The following lists the rapid concepts from Chapter 13:

- As you are determining how much you want to delegate site management to site owners and empower your end-users, avoid having pessimism consume your thinking. You may hold fears of empowered users leading to potential demand on support, and this can blind you from considering whether the benefits will be worth any added support cost.

- Empowering users can increase adoption rates, and it lets users tailor their site experiences to meet their needs while reducing the IT burden and bottleneck for changes and customizations. Empowering users is not a yes or no option, and instead it involves a range of permission levels and functionality to enable or disable for a user.

- SharePoint Design Manager enables interface designers to use whatever HTML and CSS editing tool that they are comfortable and proficient with to design a custom interface for a SharePoint site. This removes the barrier to entry because they can code their markup and styles without requiring any specialized SharePoint knowledge. Design Manager then translates pages into a SharePoint construct.

- Planning and providing a default site experience will provide all users with a consistent base, a common place to start from and a common way to meet the majority of your users' needs. It should offer the newer or less technical users a simplified and intuitive way to accomplish tasks. Use wizards and promoted links to guide users to add features to their site and avoid bloating a default site with empty folders and Apps.

- You delegate management control of a site to a site owner by granting them the necessary permissions within their site; they in turn can manage the permissions of others.

- A site collection provides an isolated container to separate end-users and their customizations. You can apply a site quota to set boundaries around a site collection.

- Apps for SharePoint are self-contained pieces of functionality that end-users can add to their site. Site owners can discover Apps through different catalogs, such as Apps available in the site, in an organizational catalog, or in the SharePoint Store.

Action Checklist

- ☐ Determine the degree you will empower site owners and end-users
- ☐ Identify permission areas you want to restrict or lock down
- ☐ Decide whether to allow site owners to brand their site using Design Manager
- ☐ Plan a default site experience that balances the basic needs and a simple interface
- ☐ Design your site structure for a safe and isolated site collection container
- ☐ Enable the Apps for SharePoint organization catalog and the SharePoint Store

Chapter 14 In Brief

In Chapter 14, "Designing Your Development Standards and Testing Processes," I discussed how to establish development standards for customizations and what testing processes can help enforce those standards. I looked at how development standards and processes can help lower the risk a custom component poses to the SharePoint service's availability, and how you can automate tests to detect issues early. The following lists the rapid concepts from Chapter 14:

- An architect can help you coordinate different development efforts and they can help you avoid the cycle of developing around issues. They take a global view of the system and all its parts, and they think through wider reaching implications such as future support and maintenance needs.

- Customizations of a global nature require forethought and consideration for any impact on the global availability and sustainability of the SharePoint service. The main issue with global customizations is the scope of potential impact and the number of affected users if something goes wrong.

- SharePoint Apps provide a simplified and centralized way to purchase add-in components from third-party vendors in the SharePoint Store or select from your organization's catalog. Apps provide you with the safest option for extending your SharePoint farm with new functionality and they help to maximize your flexibility when developing future upgrades. However, they are limited to things you can develop with the client object model and contain within a site collection. For all other customizations, you need to develop them as SharePoint features and package them within solution packages (WSP).

- Developer boundaries do not have to come with a lot of overhead and tight restrictions. They can take the form of general guidelines or specific areas to avoid certain things that you want to restrict. Set these boundaries to address specific things so that you can validate any customization to confirm whether or not it meets the boundary criteria.

- Instrumenting and tracing code allows you to instrument different parts of your code to provide information while it runs. This can provide you with verbose information about state information and the control flow of the code as it excutes in production without having to attach a debugger.

Action Checklist

- ☐ Establish an architect to serve as a gatekeeper for any development on the system
- ☐ Conduct architectural reviews throughout the entire application development lifecycle
- ☐ Identify all the customization areas to pay close attention to for a global customization
- ☐ Decide between SharePoint Apps and solution packages for each customization
- ☐ Establish developer boundaries for rigorous implementation criteria and constraints
- ☐ Establish developer guidelines for preferred ways to design and implement solutions
- ☐ Implement tracing in your code to support future debugging
- ☐ Implement instrumentation in your code for performance measurements and bottleneck detection
- ☐ Design automated scripts to test custom components against standards and guidelines
- ☐ Adopt static code analysis and code complexity analysis policies to support code quality validation

Chapter 15 In Brief

In Chapter 15, "Framing Your Information Architecture and UI Standards," I discussed how to define standards related to the information structures, layout organization, and visual design. I looked at how to build a controlled vocabulary and enterprise taxonomy to tag and organize content, and I considered how to apply this metadata to documents and people profiles. The following lists the rapid concepts from Chapter 15:

- Design your pages to keep them consistent from one page to the next so users will find your site easy to use. This also orientates and maintains familiarity for your users. You can create wireframes and mockups to roughly draft the layout of elements on pages and the interaction between pages.

- A functional navigation provides a dual purpose: it enables your users to ascertain their position within your SharePoint service and it equips your users with a route to follow to move through the different sites and web properties within your SharePoint service. Your navigation structure needs to provide a way for users to navigate to where they are trying to go, and it needs to provide a way to head back the way they came so that they can always get to the homepage.

- Managed navigation allows a site administrator to associate their site's navigation menus with a term set in the managed metadata service.

- An enterprise taxonomy is a hierarchal structure of terms your organization uses to categorize and organize information. Users categorize their information by tagging a unit of information with a term from the taxonomy. To build an effective enterprise taxonomy, you have to analyze all the different types of information within your organization and identify all the attributes that can apply to each type of information.

- You can import much of the data for your people profiles from your identity management system or a Business Connectivity Services application using the User Profile Service profile synchronization job. You can also make SharePoint the source repository for people profile properties and allow users to edit them through their profile.

Action Checklist

- ☐ Decide between function and form with your user interface design objectives
- ☐ Design a consistent and intuitive user interface
- ☐ Design a functional navigation that helps your users orientate themselves and find where they want to go
- ☐ Overwrite the top suite bar as needed for branding and navigation
- ☐ Implement a managed navigation structure using metadata
- ☐ Design a controlled vocabulary for domain-specific lists within your organization
- ☐ Evaluate whether a company has designed an enterprise taxonomy for your industry
- ☐ Build a standardized set of enterprise content types and associate relevant metadata and policies with them
- ☐ Analyze the available people data attributes
- ☐ Determine which people profile properties you will import and which SharePoint will be the source system for
- ☐ Create a data dictionary for the different data fields in your organization

Chapter 16 In Brief

In Chapter 16, "Coordinating Your Code Promotion and Release Processes," I discussed considerations for planning a change management process and designing a release management process that encourages maturity and discipline in your deployment practices. I looked at how to automate integration testing and how to promote code through testing and staging environments to ensure stability before you deploy it to production environments. The following lists the rapid concepts from Chapter 16:

- Your release management process involves multiple environments to physically separate development and testing from production use, which helps you to keep your production environment more stable. As you promote code through the preproduction environments, you move the release testing closer and closer to the production conditions.

- Preproduction can include the following environments: development, build or integration, test and quality assurance, user acceptance testing, and staging. You can expand or contract this list of environments based on your own needs and your processes.

- The integration stage offers you an opportunity to implement an automated build and continuous integration process. This will help you merge all your developers' code frequently. Adopting an automated process will help you catch compatibility issues early, and if it detects an issue the system can open and assign a bug automatically.

- One key indicator for how mature you are with your release management is how thoroughly you test customizations throughout the development lifecycle. Have your developers and quality assurance group build a suite of automated and manual tests.

- User acceptance testing (UAT) is an opportunity for your users to let you know whether or not you built the right solution. You are conducting UAT to collect user feedback and identify opportunities to make improvements and better meet their needs.

- A rollback approach for customizations needs a more granular strategy than restoring backups of server state and databases. This is because you will not schedule downtime to deploy most customizations and users can continue to make changes to their sites. The best rollback plan to back out of any customization changes is to create a rollback script. Typically, this is a PowerShell script that reverses any changes the customization introduces.

Action Checklist

- ☐ Determine the preproduction environments to promote code through as part of your release management process

- ☐ Design a code promotion and release management process

- ☐ Configure an automated build and integration testing process

- ☐ Identify your tolerance for deployment risk

- ☐ Identify your current and desired release management maturity level

- ☐ Implement a configuration management system such as Team Foundation Server (TFS)

- ☐ Establish a quality assurance group to test and validate solution quality

- ☐ Design a user acceptance testing (UAT) environment

- ☐ Schedule user acceptance testing to validate the solution before releasing to production

- ☐ Design a change management policy and customization deployment process

- ☐ Build and test a rollback plan for customization deployments

Final Thoughts

We have come a long way, and in the process, I have shared all my practices and approaches to successfully govern a SharePoint service. I tried to especially share those techniques that I found work well, but that I do not hear about often enough in the market. Really, I wanted to fill the gaps and move beyond what appeared to be an overly fixated discourse on simply documenting a governance plan.

Documentation can be very valuable, and it can serve to establish a shared vision and a shared understanding with everyone. In taking a focus on those actions you can do, to actually have a tangible and immediate impact on your SharePoint service without some extensive governance planning exercise, I purposely avoided discussions on documentation. At the same time, I tried to avoid diminishing the value documentation can provide and I encouraged you to find the right level of documentation for your situation.

Your governance documentation should reflect the actions you are taking to govern your SharePoint service, and it should reflect it in a way that is consistent with your organization's culture and standards. When you start with a generic governance planning template and become too fixated on its static aspects, you trend away from building documentation to reflect actions. In my experience, I have found generic governance templates simply do not reflect dynamic actions you do to govern, and this is because those templates tend to be overly prescriptive and policy-driven. Policies are nice and they are certainly essential, but you need actions before you will have any effect.

■ **Important**   Governance documentation ought to reflect the actions you are taking to govern. A generic governance "plan" rarely seems to reflect actions.

Throughout this book, I considered many actions you can take to govern your SharePoint environment. Now that you have a good sense about what actions you want to take, you are ready to go on now and build whatever documentation you feel will reflect those actions. Your documentation can help establish a shared understanding of how your SharePoint service will run and what actions everyone will take to govern it. I encourage you to consider many of the templates and prescriptive guidance on documenting governance artifacts, because many of these might have relevant and valuable parts you can adopt and adapt. As you move forward with your documentation efforts, try to approach it as a reflection of actions.

SharePoint governance can feel tough and certainly a little mysterious. This is because SharePoint can fit so many situations and scenarios – it packs a lot of punch and delivers what can at times feel like an overwhelming amount of potential value. Through all of this, it is able to adapt and fit whatever circumstances it finds itself in, whether that is well planned and highly orchestrated, or it is a more organic and free flowing. SharePoint can find a way to adapt.

A while back, I saw a nature special on TV about raccoons. These little creatures seem to adapt no matter what conditions they face. When development brings urban sprawl all around them, they find new sources of food in urban waste. When roads bring traffic, they learn how to negotiate crossing the road mostly avoiding cars. When developers cut down forests for neighborhoods, they find new places to nest and new ways to navigate the area. Country raccoons hunt while urban raccoons scavenge.

Not that there is a direct parallel between SharePoint and raccoons, but they share the concept of adapting to find a way to fit whatever situation they face in their environments. This might be why SharePoint governance can feel challenging at times, because SharePoint finds a way to adapt and work to some degree. Herbert Spencer coined the term that Charles Darwin later made famous, "survival of the fittest." Both used *fittest* to refer to how well something can adapt to fit a situation, not in the sense of what is the strongest or most physically fit. SharePoint adapts to fit different situations particularly well, but it also packs a lot of punch, so perhaps it fits no matter how you want to read *fittest*.

I hope you have gotten a lot out of this book. I tried to pack a lot of information and experiences from a variety of perspectives that you can apply to a broad range of environments. I tried to wrap all this into a concise book that you could read quickly if you need to, but at the same time to provide you with a book that would have the answers you need and concrete direction on what actions you can take.

I would very much appreciate hearing about what your experience was like reading this book – what you liked and what else you were hoping to learn. Please do send me a tweet @SteveGoodyear and let me know what your reading experience was like, what your favorite tips or features were, or simply what you thought of the book. I look forward to hearing from you and I wish you the best as you take the actions and tips that I shared in this book and put them into practice to govern your own SharePoint service!

Index